AF624414

भर्तृहरिकृत शतकत्रयम्

THE ŚATAKAS

OF

BHARTṚHARI

भर्तृहरिकृत

शतकत्रयम्

THE ŚATAKAS

OF

BHARTṚHARI

with Hindi and English Translation, Copious Critical and Explanatory Notes, Parallel Thoughts from Numerous Authors

PUROHIT GOPI NATH

BHARATIYA KALA PRAKASHAN
DELHI (INDIA)

First Edition : 2010
Second Edition : 2026

© Bharatiya Kala Prakashan

All rights reserved, no part of this Publication may be reproduced in any form or by any means without permission of the publisher.

Published by C.P. Gautam *for*
BHARATIYA KALA PRAKASHAN
2242, Gali No. 175, Ganesh Nagar, Tri Nagar,
Delhi - 110035, Mob.: 9811642997, 8595139625
E-mail : info@bkpbooks.com, sales.bkpbooks@gmail.com
Website: www.bkpbooks.com

ISBN : 978-81-8090-153-9

Laser Type Setting by
A-ONE GRAPHICS
X-4, Street No. 2, Brahmapuri, Delhi-110053

Printed at
Excel Prints, New Delhi-28. Ph. 011-25776555,

CONTENTS

Vairāgyaśatakaṃ (वैराग्यशतकम्)

PREFACE

For clearness sake we shall divide our preface into the following heads :—

I. The Author—his life and writings.

II. Writers on Bhartṛhari :

[A] Commentators, critics etc.

[B] Translators, and

[C] Books about Bhartṛhari.

III. Works and writings wherein we find stanzas from Bhartṛhari's Śatakas either with any particular note or notice about them or without anything of the sort.

IV. Sequel.

V. Places of interest relating to Bhartṛhari.

VI. A plea for the present edition.

Following this order we shall now take them one by one in hand, and dealing separately with each give our opinion upon all of them in turn.

I. THE AUTHOR—HIS LIFE AND WRITINGS

[A] Bhartṛhari's Life

The father of Bhartṛhari is said to have been one Gandharvasena (गंधर्वसेन) who had also got a younger son Vikramāditya. Bhartṛhari and Vikrama were, therefore, sons of the same father by different mothers. The chief of Dharā took great pains and care in educating his two grandsons, who soon acquired mastery in the several Śāstras, Laws, Ethics, Archery, Music, Dancing and all other polite arts and princely accomplishments. Though the old chief liked both his grandsons, yet his love was naturally stronger for Vikrama than Bhartṛhari. Consequently, after finding the former quite well-up in every branch of Literature, Science and Art, he being himself devoid of any male issue, one day thought of giving his Rājya to Vikrama, and summoing him to his presence told him his heart's wish. But Vikrama nobly answered him thus. "It is not proper for me to reign before my elder brother ; please, therefore, let Bhartṛhari rule over the State and I will conduct the administration as his prime minister." The old Rājā was quite pleased with the high-mindedness of young Vikrama and subsequently through Vikrama's earnest entreaties, he made Bhartṛhari the king of his territory. Vikrama thereupon changed the capital of Mālvā from Dhārā to Ujjain, and there gave himself heart and soul to the good government of the country, as the prime minister of his elder, brother. Bhartṛhari, through well-versed in the Śāstras, fell so much in love of women that he passed day after day, and night after night in the seraglio, and left everything pertaining to the State into the hands of his brother. Vikrama, on whose hands the onerous and responsible to run the government did not hang heavy, was however very sorry for the dissolute conduct of Bhartṛhari, and he spared no pains to estrange the king's hearts from women of whom he had a large number as his wives and mistresses, and devote his attendtion to the affairs of the kingdom God had put into his trust. But, as mostly common in such cases, the more he offered his sound and wise counsels, the futher went the heart of Bhartṛhari from Vikrama; so much so that disaffection took its root into the former's mind, and the result was that the once loving brothers soon became inveterate enemies to each other. The fire of hatred was kindled with increased strength by the fuel of Zenānā intrigue and curtain influence which had quite enslaved the man in Bhartṛhari. In the end, Vikrama was cruelly forced to take off his hands from the premiership and go abroad into the country as an exile, leaving Bhartṛhari to himself and his loves.[1] After his leaving Ujjain, Vikrama travelled throughout India Proper, and was once near Dāccā in Eastern Bengal, where he lived for some time and established himself. This place is still known as Vikrampur after him.

Having nothing more to do with Vikrama and his movements, we again return to Ujjain and finde Bhartṛhari to be daily sinking more and more into luxury and licentiousness. As he never cared a straw for the good government of his kingdom, his subjects became totally tired of his recklessness, and becoming disgusted with his vices they were forced to disregard his authority. Anarchy soon came into being, and there was nothing but disorder and confusion throughout Mālvā. In the meantime it so happended that the henpecked husband was one day conviced of the infidelity of his queen[2] through the present of some virtuous fruit by a pious Brāhmaṇa.[3] Her infidelity being clearly discovered, the Rāni rushed away from her husband's presence and dashed herself to pieces by falling down from the heights of the palace. Bhartṛhari then took another wife,

---

1. Colonel Todd Says that Bhartṛhari, the eldest son of Gundrupsen was so devoted to wife that he neglected the affairs of government, which made brother expostulate with him. This coming to his wife's ears, she insisted on the banishments of Vikrama (See Todd's "Annals & Antiquities of Rajasthan" Vol. II p. 369 foot note, popular edition Calcutta, 1884).
2. Opinions differ widely on the name of this particular Rāni. Some say her name to be Anaṅgasenā (अनङ्ग सेना) some Piṅgala (पिङ्गला), some Padmākṣī (पद्माक्षी), others Bhānamatī (भानमती). In the भरतखण्ड अर्वाचीनकोष by Mr. R.B. Godbole, the name is stated to be पद्माक्षी ; she is also called there to be पिङ्गला on her being restored to life after death.
3. See our note on Stanza 2 (Nīti) ; also Todd's "Annals and Antiquities of Rajasthan" Vol. II. p. 369

Pingalā (पिङ्गला), with whom he soon became attached as before. One day having gone deershooting he saw that one of his *śikarīs* who had shot a buck being himself bitten by a venomous snake was soon laid a corpse on the ground. But the thing which struck him most was that the doe of the dead buck came to the spot and threw herself dead on her husband's antler; and similar to this was the case of the *śikarī's* wife who, on discovering the death of her hunband, burnt herself with her lord on her self made pyre. The Rājā ran home in amazement and explained to Pingalā the wonderful events of his day's excursion. But Pingalā, to his great surprise, coolly remarked that there was nothing strange and extraordinary in the story; for a true suttee could burn herself without having recourse to fire. Hushing up the matter for sometime, the king again went out shooting in the forest, and, to put to test the truth and fidelity of Pingalā, he sent one of his attendants to the queen with his clothes soaked in blood to report his death by a tiger. One hearing the sad tidings Pingalā, calmly (to all outward, appearance) took over the Rājā's bloody cloths, put them on the ground, made her last bow to her husband's accoutrements and rose no more. The Rājā, when he came to know the heart-rending catastrophe, was quie overwhelmed with grief, left the palace and went out to forest to lead the life of pious ascetic so admirably depicted by him in his Vairāgya Śataka.[1] There he met with the great Yogī Gōrakṣanātha (योगी गोरक्षनाथ) who initiated him into the secrets of Mysticism. It is generally believed here that Bhartṛhari, by his austere practice of yōga, attained to immortality.

[B] Bhartṛhari's Writings

The Three Śatakas on Nīti, Śṛṅgāra and Vairāgya, the Vākyapadīya (वाक्यपदीय, a grammatical commentary in terse

1. See Todd's "Annals & Antiquities of Rajasthan," Vol. II. p. 370.

and pithy Sanskrit prose), and the Bhaṭṭikāvya (भट्टिकाव्यम्, a Grammatical poem), are the works which are generally ascribed to Bhartṛhari. Almost all the scholars who have made their acquaintance with Bhartṛhari and his works are unanimous in their opinion that Bhartṛhari is the undisputed author of the Śatakas and he Vākyapadīya which furnishes us with a certain clue to the solution of the much disputed question of Bhartṛhari's age and authorship. But as to Bhartṛhari's authorship of the Bhaṭṭikāvya different persons hold different opinions. However erudite, discussions on the point by Messrs. Colebrooke, Telang, Peterson etc. have proved it beyond and shodow of doubt that Bhaṭṭikavi (भट्टिकवि) the author of the भट्टिकाव्य is quite a different person, and he cannot be identified with Bhartṛhari (भर्तृहरि) the author of the Śatakas. To make Bhartṛhari the author of the भट्टिकाव्य there is no stronger ground than the identity of name. Bharata (भरत) in his commentary on भट्टि gives the name of the author as भर्तृहरि, but says nothing more about it. In another commentary of भट्टिकाव्य which has been published in Calcutta, the author is described as the son of Śrī Svāmi (श्री स्वामि) and as a great Grammarian. This opinion is also corroborated by Colebrooke in his esseay on Sanskrit and Prākrit Poetry where he remarks—"The author was भर्तृहरि, not, as might be supposed from the name, the celebrated brother of विक्रमादित्य, but a Grammarian and poet who was son of श्रीधरस्वामी, as we are informed by one of his scholiasts विद्याविनोद।" According to Bohn, भर्तृहरि the Grammarian and author of भट्टिकाव्य is of a later date than भर्तृहरि the author of the Śatakas with whom he is erroneously confounded. Dr. Bhāu Dāji is of opinion that भट्टी was probably the son of भर्तृहरि. Dr. Rājendra Lal Mitra in his notices of Sanskrit Manuscripts Vol. VI. p. 145 concludes that भट्टि and भर्तृहरि are two distinct personages.

[C] An Estimate of the Śatakas

The Śatakas are not mere collections of elegent sayings from different authors as suggested by some, because a certain link of thought and diction connected the stanzas distinctly points to their being written by one and the same hand. Prof. Tawney remarks that the terse and epigrammatic character of these stanzas distinguishes them more and more in accordance with European canons of taste.

Prof. Lassen, in his 'Indische Alterthums kunde' (Vol. II, p. 174), expresses his opinion that this character "renders them conspicious among the productions of the Indian Muse. They place before us in terse and pithy language the Indian views about the chief aspirations of youth, manhood and old age; about love, about concern with the things of this world and about retirement from them into lonely contemplation. On account of the perfect art with which they are composed, these short poems are worthy of being ranked among the masterpieces of Indian Genius. Some of them are connected in sense, as the description of the seasons, others form a whole by themselves and may most fitly be compared to miniature paintings as presenting to us a complete picture in the narrow frame of one strophe."

II. WRITERS ON BHARTṚHARI

(A) Commentators, Critics etc.

1. In the "Asiatic Research" Vol. IX, p. 141, Bhartṛhari is said to have reigned for fourteen years and to have then been succeeded by his younger brother Vikramāditya. It is also maintained that Bhartṛhari himself founded the era.

2. Dr. Bhāu Dāji, in his paper on Kālidāsa, questions the contemporaneity of Bhartṛhari and Vikrama, and says—"He (Bhartṛhari) is commonly but erroneously supposed to be a brother of Vikarama, as the 5th couplet of Vairāgya Śataka shews, *viz.* : that the author was aneminent poet dissatisfied

with the reception he met with at the courts of several princes whom he visited in hope of reward."[1]

Dr. Bhāu Dāji also speaks of Bhartṛhari as one of the nine gems.[2]

At another place, confounding Bhartṛhari with Bhartṛmaindha (भर्तृमेंठ), he makes Bhartṛhari a contemporary of Kālidāsa.

3. Dr. Bohlen countenances the theory that the three Śatakas are mere compilations made by Bhartṛhari, a mere collection of "elegant entracts" from the works of previous writers.[3]

Von Bohlen accepts and identity of the Bhartṛhari of the Śatakas andthe Hari of the Vākyapadīya.[4]

On the authority of Roger, Bohlen relates that Bhartṛhari had 300 wives and was addicted to a voluptuous life. But having been severely reproved by his father for his dissolute conduct, he repudiated his wives, and collected, not composed, these Śatakas by making selections from older writers.

Von Bohlen published in 1833 at Berlin the first European Edition of the Śatakas.

4. According to Prof. Colebrooke, some other person than Bhartṛhari had probably put forth these Śatakas under Bhartṛhari's name.[5]

5. Pandint Durgā Prasād of Jeypore, in conjuction with Dr. P. Peterson, writes that Bhartṛhari the author of the

1. The couplet here alluded to is उत्खातं निधि etc., from a careful perusal of which we cannot, however, endorse the opinions of Dr. Bhāu Dāji. The point has also been elaborately discussed & refuted by Mr. Telang (See Bombay Sanskrit Series No. XI. p. 19).
2. For the enumeration of the "Nine gems", see our note on stanza 1 of Nīti.
3. See Bohlen's Praface to his edition of Bhartṛhari, p. VI.
4. See Bohlen's Preface, P. VI.
5. See Colebroke's Essays Vol. II

Śatakas and Vākyapadīya flourished in the middle of the 7th century A.D.

6. Mr. K.T. Telang adheres to the tradition of Bhartṛhari's full authorship of the Śatakas.[1]

In Telang's opinion Bhartṛhari probably[2] flourished somewhere later than Kālīdāsa and a good deal earlier than the beginning of the 6th century A.C. It is based on the following two reasons :—

(1) There is a stanza[3] in the Nītiśataka which is also found in the Pañcatantra which may safely be taken to have been composed not later than 500 A.C. Therefore, Bhartṛhari must have flourished at least half a century before that date.

(2) Again, from stanza 95 Nīti. Paraśurāma is regarded as in incarnation of Viṣṇu, but it is doubtful whether Kālidāsa held the same opinion.

Bhartṛhari must, therefore, be later in age than Kālidāsa.[4]

Mr. Telang again says :—Vikrama, the founder of the Saṁvat Era, flourished about 56 B.C. But granting Bhartṛhari to be the author of Vākyapadīya, we cannot accept him to be the brother of this Vikrama. Because, it is clear from the Vākyapadīya that it were Candrācārya (चन्द्राचार्य) and others who brought the great commentary of Pātañjali (पातंजलि) into general use and according to Rājātarañgini, Candrācārya and his colleagues flurished in the reign of King Abhimanyu (अभिमन्यु) *i.e.*, between 45 and 65 A.C.

Led by the observations of Dr. Kern, in his Preface to the Bṛhatsaṁhitā, where he argues that Vikramāditya according to the unanimous testimony of Hindu

---

1. See Bombay Sanskrit Series No. XXXI, p.74.
2. See Bombay Sanskrit Series Vol. XI, pp. VIII, & IX.
3. But we have shewn elsewhere that the Pañcatantra has got no less than 21 stanzas from Bhartṛhari's Śatakas.
4. See Bombay Sanskrit Seriest No. XI. pp. XII & XIV.

Astronomers, of the Arabian Astronomer Albiruni, of Kalhaṇa Paṇḍita (कल्हणपंडित), and of Hiouen Thsang, was commonly regarded as the founder of what is known as the Śākā (शाका), or Śālivāhana Era (शालिवाहनसंवत्), and as having flourished about 78 A.C., and not 56 B.C., Mr. K.T. Telant after remarking that this will enable us to reconcile the several statements which we receive from tradition, thinks as a conclusioin, grounded on a basis not very unstable, that Bhartṛhari flourished about the close of the first and the beginning of the second century of the Christian Era.[1]

7. Prof. Lassen is of opinion that the composition of the three hundred short poems, which by universal tradition are ascribed to Bhartṛhari, must be placed before the overthrow of the Gupta Dynasty. He further places the date of the author of these Śatakas at the end of the third century A.C., but he does not accept the tradition that he was Bhartṛhari.

8. Relying upon a Chinese tradition, Prof. Max Müller thinks Bhartṛhari to be a Buddhist.[2] The Professor also suggests that Kṣapaṇaka (क्षपणक) may be another name of Bhartṛhari.[3]

9. Dr. P. Peterson.

For Dr. P. Peterson's opinion see under Paṇḍit Durgā Prasāda (5).

10. M. Regnaud, in the Preface to his prose translation, contends that the legend connecting Bhartṛhari and

---

1. See Bombay Sanskrit Seriest No. XI, p. XVI.
2. The Buddhist flavour which Prof. Max Müller smells in the Śatakas, is however very difficult to be detected by us after a careful study of the poem. Moreover, the theory will utterly fall to the ground when we find in the body of the work of references to the Trinity (stanza 1 in the Śṛṅgara Śataka), to the ten incarnations of Viṣṇu (stanza 95 Nīti) to the Vedas, Smṛtis and Purāṇas (stanza 79 in the Vairāgya Śataka) and to the Vedāntic character of the whole poem especially to that of the opening stanza of Nīti.
3. See note on stanza 1. in Nīti.

Vikrāmaditya cannot be accepted, as some of the stanzas attributed to Bhartṛhari must be subsequent to the period of Śaṅkarācārya (शंकराचार्य).[1]

11. Abraham Roges.

For Roger's opinion on Bhartṛhari, see under Bohlen (3).

12. According to Mr. Śasghagiri Śāstri King Vikramāditya was the son of a Brahman named Candragupta (चन्द्रगुप्त) who took four wives, each of the four principle castes. Four sons, *viz* : Vararuci (वररुचि), Vikrama (विक्रम), Bhaṭṭi (भट्टी), and Bhartṛhari (भर्तृहरि) were born to him respectively by his Brahmin, Kṣatriya, Vaiśya and Śūdra wives. Vikramādiya became King, and Bhartṛhari served him as his prime minister.

13. After quoting the remarks of Lassen, Prof. Tawney says: —

"Considering the great uncertainty which attaches to Hindu Literary History, we may perhaps consider ourselves fortunate that there is something like a *consensus* as to the date of these poems. A century more or less is, after all, of trifling moment in Indian Chronology. The question of their authorship we must be content to leave in the midst in which it has been involved by the traditions of Indian sages and the conjectures of Western critics. So much at any rate is certain that our author, if not himself a king was thoroughly at home in the detail of Indian Court life."[2]

Prof. Tawney in his foot-note on the word 'परिजन' (which occurs in stanza 18 of the Vairāgya Śataka) thinks that this expression fall in with the legend that Bhartṛhari was a king and quitted his throne in a fit of disgust.

1. For the refutation this theory, see Bombay Sanskrit Serties No. XI pp. IX & X.
2. See Prof. Tawney's Two Centuries Bhartṛhari, p. IX.
3. See Prof. Tawney's Two Centuries Bhartṛhari, p. 60

14. Prof. Vaman Shivram Apte. M.A., at page 1192 of his Sanskrit-English Dictionary has the following : —

भर्तृहरि Author of the three Śatakas and of the Vākyapadīya. Mr. Telang gives it as his opinion that he must have flourished about the close of the first and the beginning of the second century of the Christian era. Tradition makes him brother of King Vikrama, and if this Vikrama be accepted as the same who defeated the Mlechhas in 544 A.D. we must suppose Bhartṛhari to have flourished in the latter half of the sixth century.

15. Prof. Wilson (in his Viṣṇu Purāṇa) elaborately argues that the earliest of the Purāṇas cannot have been written long before the 8th or 9th century of the Christian era. As Bhartṛhari clearly mentions the Purāṇas in stanza 79 of the Vairāgya Śataka, we are to inter that he must, therefore, be later than the 8th or 9th century A.D.[1]

(B) Translators etc.

The first translation of Bhartṛhari's Śatakas into any European tonge was that by a Christian missionary Abraham Roger who publisehd in 1651 A.D. 'A History of the Religion of the Brāhmaṇas' in which were contained two hundred proverbs of the sage Bhartṛhari, translated into Dutch. The stanzas on Nīti were styled by him as "the reasonable conduct of men," and those on Vairāgyas "the road which leads to heaven."

This work was subsequently translated into French in 1670 A.D.

---

1. In order to refute this theory we have to state that Śaṅkarācārya, who is generally and rightly acknowledged to have flourished in the 8th century A.D. has actually quoted the Purāṇas in his commentary on the 'Śvetāśvatara Upaniṣad. Besides this, the Purāṇas in general and the 'Vāyu-purāṇa' in particular are even referred to by Bāṇabhaṭṭa (बाणभट्ट) in this famous work "Kādambarī" (कादम्बरी) Bāṇa's age is now fixed about the beginning of the seventh century A.D. Prof. Wilson's argument is therefore untenable :

Prof. Tawney says that the Centuries of Bhartṛhari are also contained in the Sanskrit Anthology of Haeberlin M. Galanos translated the Nīti and Vairāgya Śatakas into Greek.

They were included by prof. Böhtlingk in his "Indische Sprüche St. Petersburg, 1863-65 A.D.

They were translated into French by M. Hippolyte Fanch in 1852 and by M. Regnaud in 1875 A.D.

Vāmana Paṇḍita has translated the stanzas into Marāṭhī.

In 1795 A.D. H.H. the Mahāraja Śawāi Pratap Singhji of Jeypore translated the three Śatakas of Bhartṛhari into Bhāṣā verse, under the title of नीतिमंजरी, शृंगारमंजरी and वैराग्यमंजरी chiefly consisting of the Chappya (छप्पय) verses, which make the translation go by the popular name of Partāpa Singhji's Chhappayas, ignoring altogether the few, Soraṭhās (सोरठा) and Dohās (दोहा) which also form its part.

Once Paṇḍit Rishabha Deve Śāstri of Jodhpore has recently translated the three Śatakas into Hindi. This book was published in 1894 A.D. by the Gyānsāgar Press, Bombay.

An anonymous translation of Bhartṛhari's Nīti and Vairāgya Śatakas into English prose was published in the Subodha Prakāsh Press at Bombay. The book is entitled 'The Proverbial Philosophy of Bhartṛhari."

Prof. Durgrā Prasād, Editor "Harbinger" of Lahore, has also translated in 1889 the aforesaid two Śatakas of Bhartṛhari into English prose. Both these Śatakas are published separately and called Maharāja Bhartṛhri's 100 couplets on Renunciation.

(C) Books About Bhartṛhari

Now we have come to that part which relates to those books which give us some account of Bhartṛhari's life. Had we been forturate in this we would not have much difficulty in fixing the chronology of Bhartṛhari and giving an authentic record of his life on the authority of stubborn facts. But, to the great disappointment of all, our information in this respect is limited to two sources *viz.*:—(1) BHARTṚHARI NIRVEDAṂ "भर्तृहरिनिर्वेदम्" and (1) Bhartṛhari's Khyālas (ख्याल)।

(1) BHARTṚHARI NIRVEDAṂ (भर्तृहरिनिर्वेदम्)

It is a dramatical work in Sanskrit by Hariharopādhyāya (हरिहरोपाध्याय). Unfortunarly, however, we do not know anything positively about Hariharopādhyāya's life except the fact of his being a Maithila Paṇḍita. As for the full information of the work, we would here subjoin a clear and succint synopsis of the Sanskrit play into English prose.

BHARATṚHARI NIRVEDA NĀṬAKAṂ
BY HARIHAROPĀDHYĀYA
ACT I

Bhartṛhari meets his Rānī Bhānumatī (रानी भानुमती) after long separation, for which the latter expostulates with him, and the Rājā makes some religious excuse for the prolonged absence from her. In the meanting, seeing a suttee mounting the blazing pyre of her dead husband, the Rājā extols her conduct to the skies before the Rānī; but she remarks that she does not see the propriety of a suttee's having recourse to real fire, when the fire of separation is quite sufficient to burn her immediately to ashes. Though a little incredulous, Bhartṛhari then agrees with his Rānī and takes his leave of her to go out shooting, to which she reluctantly and sorrowfully consents, on the condition of her being allowed to remain standing at the gate anxiously looking out the path of his speedy return.

ACT II

Opens with the dialogue of maid servants upon the sudden death of their Mistress (Rānī Bhānumatī), who, while standing at the gate, soon became lifeless on hearing the (false) news of Bhartṛhari beign slain by a tiger. The Rājā, on his return to the Capital, finds the scene full of great sorrow and grief, and on knowing the corpse being taken to the crematorioum hastens to that place and there mourns and weeps like a child and strictly forbids his men to set fire to the pyre on pain of precipitating himself into the burning logs.

ACT III

Sorrowing over the corpse of his Rāni, Bhartṛhari sees at a distance that a Yogī is excessively weeping over the breakage of his earthen dish. The Rājā goes to him and tries to pacify him by many wise cousels, but the Yogī is obdurate and goes extolling the virtues of his dish and bemoaning its irreparable loss more and more on account of his being himself the cause of its sudden destruction, for he dropped it down to test its strenght. The plot of the dialogue is so framed that all the arguments put into the mouth of the Yogī are applicable even more strongly to the Rājā for his grieving over Bhānumati's loss. Bhartṛhari, though he recognizes all this in his heart, yet still persists in consoling the Yogī by alluding to the transitoriness of all things in the world and the futility of man's grief over what he has no control. The Yogī there assails the Rājā with his own arguments and observes :—

परोपदेशे पाण्डित्यमिदम्मूढस्य गीयते।
तमः समाश्रितस्येव दीपस्यान्यप्रकाशनम्।।

Being struck with the congency of the remark Bhartṛhari then recognizes the Yogī to be no other than Gorakṣanātha (गोरक्षनाथ) himself, and the latter acknowledges himself to be the same, and to have intentionally assumed the character in order to dispel the unavailing sorrow from the Rājā's mind. Bhartṛhari soon lays himself prostrate at his feet and requests from him the easiest road to self-knowledge and to this Gorakṣanātha thus replies :—

विषयेभ्यः समाहृत्य मनः शून्ये निवेशय।
स्वयमानन्दमात्मानं स्वप्रकाशमुपैष्यसि।।

ACT IV

The prime minister is pleased to fine the Rājā joyfully sitting with the Yogī and then he ventures to ask his permission to cremate the corpse of Bhānumati. But strange to say that his master replies to have no concern with the world. Devatilaka (देवतिलक), the minister, then remonstrates with him but to no purpose.

ACT V

Opens with the meeing of Bhartṛhari with Bhānumati who is restored to life through the mystic powers of Gorakṣanātha. Bhānumati tries to embrace her husband but the Rājā runs and avoids her. She, thereupen, exerts her fair charms but in vain, and, failing in these, she resortes to the means of bringing her young son before the Rājā who is still indifferent to them.

The requests of the prime minister also prove fruitless. Gorakṣanātha then advises the minister to desist from his useless endeavours and to place the Rājakumāra on the Gaddi for wholse protection he will exert his own influence with that of the Rājā. He then consoles Bhānumati with the hope of again meeting (never to part from) her lord Bhartṛhari after his obtaining immortality and here the play ends in happiness to all.

The reader will see for himself how for the play coincides with our Bhartṛhari's life in the beginning, and in what partricular points it differs from it.

(2) Bhartṛhari' Streets Plays or Melodramas

These streets play are acted all over India and are very popular. They relate that King Bhartṛhari was very fond of his wife Piṅgalā (पिंगला). He one day went shooting the wild deer and made his mark on a big buck. His does, thereupon, remonstrated with the Rājā and entreated him to spare the buck and take instead the lives of as many of them as he pleases, because his death will make them all widows. But the Rājā turned a deaf ear to these requests and shot the buck dead on the spot. The exasperated does thereuopn uttered a *Shapt* (curse) against the Rājā that the days of his Rājya are numbered, for he shall have soon to abdicate the Kingdom and roam about in the forest as a hermit leaving his views no better than widows. His meeing with Gorakṣanātha is then related at length and the Yogi after fully testing the veracity of the Raja's request makes him his pupil. The plays also speaks of Bhartṛhari as king and a brother of the celebrated Vikramāditya.[1]

European scholars will no doubt laugh that I make much of these triffing plays. But I would beg permission to remark that the fact of their having survived so long must be a sufficient guarantee of their being founded on authenticated historic and real life. A lie cannot last long. The remarkable incidents of Bhartṛhari's life being framed into a play which is so popular with the general public speaks much of the high esteem and honor in which Bhartṛhari is still held by them.[2]

III

As for the different works wherein the Ślōkas from Bhartṛhari's Śatakas have been tracet out, we would only beg to draw the reader's attention to their respecive footnotes where full partculars have invariably been given of them. However, we have also thought it advisable to arrange them for brevity and clearness,' sake, in a tabular form which will enable the reader to make a prompt and ready references to them at a moment's time. It needs only be stated that the numbers given in this list will be found corresponding to those of the stanzas as arranges in the Nīti, Śṛṅgāra, and Vairāgya Śatakas of the present edition, and not to the numbers of the verses of the works or books to which they are traced.

1. The writer of these lines can himself attest to these vulgar plays being acted at many places in Rājputānā as at Jeypore, Jodhpore and Bikaner, generally during the months of the Spring.
2. In the शनिकथा or शंनिश्चरजी की कथा, a poetical narration in vernacular of Vikrama's calamities, Bhartṛhari is clearly and undoubtedly spoken of as the elder brother to Vikramāditya.

Alphabetical list of works wherein we find the following stanzas form Bhartṛhari's Satakas :

No. of works.	Works.	Stanzas from the Nītiśataka.	Remarks	Stanzas from the Śṛṅgāraśataka	Remarks	Stanzas from the Vairāgyaśataka.	Remarks	Total each number of stanzas in work.
1.	2.	3.	4.	5	6.	7.	8.	9.
1.	Abhinavagupta's Commentary on the Dhvanyālōka.	44	Quoted anony-mously					1
2.	Amaruśataka by Amarūka			14				1
3.	Alaṅkāra Śekhara by Keśava Miśra.					40	Quoted anony-mously	1
4.	Alaṅkāra sarva-sva by Ruyyānaka.	56	Quoted anony-mously					1
5.	Aṣṭaratna	56, 95				116		3
6.	Ātmānusaśāna-kāvya by Gunabhadā-cārya	88						1
7.	Udaharana-candrikā by Vaidyanātha	56	Quoted anony-mously	18,28	Qutoed anony-mously	40, 71	Quoted anony mously Quoted under भर्तृहरि	5
8.	Aucityavicāra carcā by Kṣemendra.			63	Quoted under Candraka.	12, 40, 54	Quoted under different authors.	4

1.	2.	3.	4.	5.	6.	7	8.	9.
9.	Kavikaṇṭhabharaṇa by Kṣemendra					38	Qutoed under Candraka.	1
10.	Kāvyaprakāśa by Mammaṭa.	56	Quoted anony-mously					1
11.	Kāvyapradīpa Govinda.	56	Quoted anony-mously	18, 28	Quoted anony-mously	40, 71	Quoted anony-mously	5
12.	Kāvyānuśāsana by Vāgbhaṭṭa.	29, 61	Do.	18, 64	Do.	38, 40	Do.	6
13	Kuvalayānanda by Appadikṣita	44, 64	Do.	81	Do.			3
14.	Guṇaratna by Bhavabhūti	20						1
15	Caturvargasaṅgraha by Kṣemendra					116		1
16	Cāṇakyaśataka	53						1
17.	Daśarūpā-kvalōka by Dhanañjaya,	27	Quoted under भर्तृहरि	18	Quoted anony-mously			2
18.	Dhvanyālōka by Ānandavardhana.			6	Do.			1
19.	Naṁsādhū's Commentary on Kāvyālaṅkāra.			63	Do.	13, 22	Quoted anony-mously	3
20.	Nītipradīpa by Vetālabhaṭṭa.	80, 91						2
21.	Pañcatantra by Viṣṇuśarmā.	27,30,31, 32, 40, 41, 42, 47, 48, 57, 58, 63, 67, 91, 106		64, 76, 80, 81, 86		113		21

Contd..

1.	2.	3.	4.	5.	6.	7	8.	9.
22.	Pañcaratna.	11, 21						2
23.	Prabodha-candrōdaya by Kṛṣṇa Miśra.			21, 71				2
24.	Bhojaprabhandha by Ballāla.	35, 40, 92						3
25.	Mahānāṭaka.							1
26.	Mudrārākṣasa by Viśākhadatta.	27						1
27.	Mṛcchakaṭika by Śūdraka.			21				1
28.	Rasaratnahāra by Śivarāma					49, 71	Quoted anony-mously	2
29.	Vasiṣṭhasāra	1						1
30.	Vairāgyaśataka by Padmānanda.	6		71				2
31.	Śantiśataka	9, 94		76, 98		7,10,13,16, 18,20,22,34, 41,43,51,62, 66,67, 71,74, 77,82,85,102,107		25
32.	Śārṅgadharapad-dhati by Śārṅga-dhara.	17,38,42,43, 50,80,91, 92, 99,104	Quoted anony-mously	11,13,20,22,43, 47,49,50,68, 80,92	Quoted anony-mously	91, 113	Quoted anony-mously	
		3,4,5,8,16, 18,24,29,33,39, 41,44,56,57,63, 75,77,84,90, 94,95,101,106	Quoted under भर्तृहरि	3,47,64,86,95	Quoted under. भर्तृहरि	11,12,13,14,19,20 23,30,31,36,37,40, 43,44,49,54,60, 66,71,81,85,86,87, 99,102, 108,110,114	Quoted under भर्तृहरि	87

1.	2.	3.	4.	5.	6.	7	8.	9
		53, 67	Quoted under different authors	28, 37,59,93	Quoted under different authors	97	Quoted under Vijjaka	
33.	Śṛṅgāratilaka by Kālidāsa			86				1
34.	Śṛṅgāravindu by Kālidāsa			81				
35.	Ṣaḍratna.	55						1
36.	Saptaratna.	62						1
37.	Sarasvatī Kaṇṭhābharaṇa by Bhojarāja	77	Quoted anony-mously			82	Quoted anony-mously	2
38.	Siṁhādevamaṇi's Commentary on Vāgbhaṭṭālaṅkāra.	2	Do.					
39.	Subhāṣitāvali by Vallabhadeva.	7,11,17,22,27,31, 32,33,42,43,44,48,59, 62,64,68,70,77,80,82, 83,84,85,88,91,94, 95,99,100,104,106.	Quoted anony-mously	2,6,9,10,11,13, 14,15,16,18,20, 24,25,26,31,46, 47,49,50,54,59, 63,66,67,73,74, 84,86,92.	Quoted anony-mously	2,5,7,9,12,13,22, 29,32,40,49,60,61, 66,70,87,89,91,97, 110,115	Quoted anony-mously	
		1,3,4,5,8,16, 54,61,66	Quoted under भर्तृहरि	43.	Quoted under भर्तृहरि			128.
		28, 29,30,33,38, 39,53,57, 68, 66,90,92,96,98,106	Quoted under different persons.	3,37,80,81, 95,96,53.	Quoted under authors	14,16,32, 36,75	Quoted under different authors	

Contd.

1.	2.	3.	4.	5.	6.	7	8.	9.
40.	Suvṛttatilaka by Kṣemendra.			52	Quoted under भर्तृहरि	22	Quoted under भर्तृहरि	2
41.	Sūktāvali	11,13,14,19, 20,61,83,104						8
42.	Sūktimuktāvali by Jalhaṇa.			20.	Quoted under Śakavṛddhi.			1
43.	Hitōpadāsa by Nārayaṇa.	3,30,31,32, 33,40,47,53, 63,73,91,106.						12.
43.	Total numbers							350.

From this diagram it will be easily seen that we have traced out a large number (which amounts to no lees than 350) of Bhartṛhari's Ślōkas to the 43 works enumerated above, where many of them have however figured more than once. Out of these books some have been unscrupulosouly acknowledged to be older than the 6th century of the Christian era. Taking the aforesaid 350 stanzas, we may safely point out that no less than 80 of them have expressly been *quoted under Bhartṛhari,* 40 have been *quoted* under different authors and 137 have been *quoted* anonymously. Now, adding them together we get a total of 256 stanzas which are *distinctly marked as quotations* either from Bhartṛhari for others, and thus there is left comparatively very small number (*viz.* 93) to be differently accounted for. Granting that the Aṣṭaratna, Guṇaratna; Nītipradīpa, Pañcatantra, Pañcaratna, Bhōjaprabandha, Śāntiśataka, Śṛṅgāratilaka, Śṛṅgāravindu, Ṣaḍratna, Saptaratna, Sūktāvali and Hitōpadāsa are mere compilations and not genuine compositions of their several authors and deducting the sum of 3, 1, 2, 21, 2, 3, 25, 1, 1, 1, 1, 8, and 12, (or 81) stanzas which occur respectively in them we have now to face only an insignifcantly small number of stanzas (*viz.* 12), of which 1 is found in the Amaruśataka, 1 in the Ātmānuśāsanakāvya, 1 in the Caturvargasaṅgraha, 1 in the Cāṇakyaśataka, 2 in the Prabōdhacandrodaya, 1 in the Mahānāṭaka, 1 in the Vasiṣṭhasāra and 2 in the Vairāgyaśataka, (Padmānanda's). Amongst, these twelve, 6 will be found to have been on other than those which have already been accounted for as quotations, and one as occuring twive, thus reducing the number ultimately to 4, of which 1 stands in the Prabōdhacandrōdaya, 2 in the Vairāgyaśataka of Padmānanda, and 1 in the Mṛcchakaṭika and Prabōdhacandrōdya both. Here I thing we may conveniently drop this point without further comment.

This line of arguments will, it is hoped, furnish some clue to the solution of Bhartṛhari's age, as well as to the conclusion of these Śatakas being considered a genuine composition or a mere compilation by Bhartṛhari.

To do full justice to the subject I cannot help bringing to the notice of the reader that leaving out the number of times a stanza has made its appearance in the foregoing table we may safely observe that out of the total of 326 stanzas as given in this edition no less than 182 have been found to exist in the 43 pieces enumerated above, and that of these 182 nearly 40 verses have figured from three to seven times in the diagram. This gives us a very distinct and indisputable proof of the proverbial and substantial popularity the Śatakas have so deservedly enjoyed from the very date of their production to the present day.

IV. SEQUEL

After writing so much in the preceeding portion of the Preface, it is not necessary to dwell at great length on giving out the conclusions we have arrived at, regarding the followeing questions of modern critics and scholars :—

(1) Are the Śatakas eigther a mere collection of elegant extracts from several writers or a genuine composition by a singly author?

(2) Who is the author of the Śatakas?

(3) What is the approximate date of the composition of this work?

(4) What other works are written by the author of the Śatakas?

(5) Was the author of the Śatakas himself a king and the brother of the celebrated Vīkramāditya, the founder of the Saṁvat Era?

In answering these questions we would beg the reader's indulgence to condense our views in as small a space as possible, for everything is to be based on previous data which have already been given in full.

(1) From the appearance of several Ślokas in many of the current Sanskrit works it is argued that the Śatakas are a mere collection of elegant extracts from numerous authors.

But if we study the point a little carefully we will find that most of the works in which they are met with are in themselves mere collections and not compositions e.g., the Pañcaratna, Ṣaḍratna, Saptaratna, Aṣṭaratna, Hitōpadeśa, etc. Whereas in others as काव्यानुशासनं, काव्यप्रदीप, काव्यालङ्कारः सुभाषितावलिः, शार्ङ्गधरपद्धतिः etc., the Ślōkas are merely quoted either anonymously or as Bhartṛhari's or as some others.' Again, there are a few, very few, say some twelve Ślōkas, which are found in works like the Amaruśataka, Mudrārākṣasa etc. These may harmlessly be considered as interpolations either in the Śatakas or in the works themselves. Besides, there is a certain threadlike thought which pervades them all and unites them into one whole. We are therefore in a position to say that the Śatakas are a genuine work from the pen of some particular person.[1]

(2) Having thus decided the first question, it is not very difficult to arrive at a definite conclusion upon the authorship of the Śatakas. When men like the authors of "दशरूपावलोकः" [27 नीति॰] (composed in the time of मुञ्ज uncle to राजभोज), "सुवृत्ततिलकम्" [22 वैराग्य॰, 52 शृंगार॰] (composed about the middle of the 11th century, A.D). "उदाहरणचन्द्रिका" [79 वैराग्य॰] and others have quoted some of the stanzas from these Śatakas distinctly as Bhartṛhari's, it is mere childlike obstainacy still to question the authorship of Bhartṛhari, because besides their extensive knowledge of Sanskrit Literature and the wide range of their information, they were unquestionably nearer than we to the author of the Śatakas by may centruries, the difference between us and him-being undoubtedly less nearly by 8 centuries in the case of the authors of Daśarūpāvaloka and Suvṛttatilaka. It is therefore proved beyond controversy, that Bhartṛhari is the author of these Śatakas.

1. For further discussion on this point see Preface I (C) and III.

(3) To give a precise answer to the third question is no way easy. But from a careful examination of the facts before us we shall try to fix the the date of these Śatakas as accurately as possible. Referring to the diagram put forward in part III of this preface we are able to assert that, many stanzas from these Śatakas are found quoted in the works of (1) Abhinavagupta (ध्वन्यालोक टीका), (2) Keśavamiśra (अलङ्कारशेखरः), (3) Ruyyānakka (अलङ्कारसर्वस्वम्), (4) Vaidyanātha (उदाहरण-चंद्रिका), (5) Kṣemendra (आचित्यविचारचर्चा, कविकण्ठाभरणम्, and सुवत्त तिलकम्) (6) Mammaṭa काव्यप्रकाशः), (7) Gōvinda (काव्यप्रदीपः), (8) Vāgbhaṭṭa (काव्यानुशासनम्), (9) Namisādhu (काव्यालङ्कारटीका), (10) Appayadīkṣta (कुवलयानन्दः), (11) Dhanañjaya (दशरूपा-वलोकः), (12) Ānandavardhana (ध्वन्यालोकः), (13) Viṣṇu Śarmā (पञ्चतंत्रम्), (14) Ballāla (भोजप्रबन्धः), (15) Śivarāma (रसरत्नहारः), (16) Śārṅgadhara (शार्ङ्गधरपद्धतिः), (17) Bhojarāja (सरस्वतीकण्ठा-भरणम्), (18) Vallabhadeva (सुभाषितावलिः), (19) Jalhaṇa (सूक्तिमुक्तावलिः) and Nārāyaṇa (हितोपदेशः). Of these authors Abhinavagupta flourished towards the end of the tenth, Kṣemendra and Nami Sādhu in the middle of the eleveneth, Dhanañjaya in the tenth, Ānandavardhana in the ninth and Bhōjarāja in the eleventh centuries of the Christian era. Excepting Viṣṇu Śarmā and Nārāyaṇa the remaining writers are comparatively later in age than these. Ānadavardhana is the oldest among them and besides quoting stanza 6 (शृं०) he even mentions भर्तृहरि by name.[1] This enables us to put the date of the Śatakas before आनन्दवर्धन, the author of ध्वन्यालोक *i.e.*, before the second half of the ninth century, because it is demontrated that Ānandavardhana flourished during the reign of King Avantivarmā (855-884 A.D.). Of the two writers mentioned above Viṣṇu Śarmā is universally acknowledged to be much older than Nārāyaṇa, and we shall therefore confine our remarks to him *i.e.*, विष्णुशर्मा. As we find no less

1. See ध्वन्यालोक, p. 47. (Kavyamala Series Bombay).

than 21 stanzas from these Śatakas in the Pañcatantra. Now, if we succeed in fixing the date of the Pañcatantra we shall at least be able to say something precisely about the chronology of the Śatakas.

The Pañcatantra quotes copiously from the Mahā-bhārata, Kāmandakīyanītisāra, Manusmṛti, Rāmāyaṇa and Cāṇakya. There are also two Ślokas in it (III. 27, and V. 14) which can respectively be traced to the Śiśupālabadha and Nāgānanda both of which are generally acknowledged to be later than the date usually assigned to the Pañcatantra. Besides naming Manu, Vṛshaspati, Vyāṣa, Vālmīki, Bhṛgu and Vātsyāyana, the Pañcatantra also mentions Cāṇakya (I. p. 2. 1.1) and Varāhamihira (I. p. 43, 1. 12), writers whose dates are pretty accurately known to us.

Of the two Ślōkas, one traceable to the Śiśupālabadha and the other to the Nāgānanda, we can easily dispose by thinking them either as later interpolations in the Pañcatantra or as unconscious plagiarism in the Śiśupālabadha and the Nāgānanda.

Cāṇakya as is is well known was the friends, guide and political adviser of the adventurous Candragupta, the contemporary of Selukus, and so he must be placed somewhere about 325 B.C.[1] Consequently there is nothing strange in the allusion of Cāṇakya's Arthaśāstra in the Pañcatantra.[2] But Varāhamihira's date is unanimously accepted as the sixth century of the Christain era. Here than lies the great difficulty we have to confront about the settlement of Pañcatantra's date.[3] However taking it for a historical fact of reliable authenticity that Pañcatantra is the original which was translated by "Buzerchemiher, the chief physician and afterwards Vizier of the great Anushirwān

1. See Hunter's Brief History of the Indian People pp. 76 and 77.
2. "ततो धर्मशास्त्राणि मन्वादी न्यर्थशास्त्राणि चाणक्यादानि।" (पंचतंत्रम्। कथामुखं)
3. According to the authority of the learned editors of the काव्यमाला Pañcatantra cannot be older than 750 A.D., because it quates the Śloka पर्यङ्केष्वास्तरणं etc. (Pañcatantra, I, 174) from the Kuṭṭinīmata of

(as Sir William Jones remarked at a meeting of the Society of the Asiatic Researches on the 26th Feburary 1876) we cannot help removing the date of the Pañcatantra to a time long before the reign of that illustrious monarch, and thinking the mention of Varāhamihira in it to be a mere interpolation by some later copyist of the work. Pañcatantra's date is therefore to be placed somewhere between that of Cāṇakya and that of Anushirwān or roughly speaking between 325 B.C. and 530 A.C. But as we learn from the preface of its first foreign translation that the work was rendered into that language after its obtaining a worldwide reputation, we cannot be far from right to allow about three centuries' time for the spread of its fame in those old days (bearing it in mind that the Indian princes in whose court the Pañcatantra had secured for itself a very exalted position of rank and honour, took the greatest possible care to conceal this rare gem from the foreigners). This will further push on the date of Pañcatantra's composition to somewhere about the second century of the Christian era.

As we find the 134th verse of the Pañcatantra, book II, expressly assigned to Vikramāditya (विक्रमादित्य)—whom tradition makes younger brother of Bhartṛhari (भर्तृहरि)—in the Śārṅgadharapaddhati of Śārṅgadhara, at No. 277, and the Subhāṣitāvali of Vallabhadeva at No. 507, and as there are no less than twenty-one stanzas from these Śatakas to be founde or the Pañcatantra, we can fairly infer that the author of the Śatakas lived a century or two earlier than Viṣṇu Śarmā the author of the Pañcatantra. This will go to prove the truth of the traditional history of Bhartṛhari as given in the beginning of ourk preface.

(4) There works are attributed to Bhartṛhari. Of these we take the Śatakas first of which we have acknowledged him to be the undisputed author.

Dāmodaragupta, the prime minister of king Jayāpīda (755-786 A.D.). See footnote at p. 111 of काव्य माला गुच्छक No. 3.

The second work generally ascribed to him is the वाक्यपदीय. But to my mind the identity rests merely on name. Nothing about the parantage or literary work of Bhartṛhari is told either in the वाक्यपदीय or the Śatakas. So, we are not authrorized by facts to think Bhartṛhari to be the author of the वाक्यपदीय. But the authority of tradition here countenaces the identiry of हरि of the वाक्यपदीय and Bhartṛhari (भर्तृहरि) of the Śatakas and we may do well to bow submissively to it untill we are able to set it aside by satisfactory evidence of facts and figures.

The third work which tradition assigns to Bhartṛhari is the भट्टिकाव्य.

But it has been already proved above in connection with the first and second parts of our Praface that the author of भट्टिकाव्य is a distinct personage from Bhartṛhari. Bhaṭṭikāvyaṃ is proved to have been composed in the 6th or 7th century A.D. (See Weber's Sanskrit Literature, p. 196 note).

(5) There is no internal evidence to prove that Bhartṛhari was himsẹlf a king and a brother of Vikramāditya. We have no authentic record about Vikramāditya, the found of the Saṁvat Era, being the younger brother of Bhartṛhari. Bhartṛhari himself does not say anything about it. The tradition is not corroborated by any reliable external evidence of unquestionable authority. Of course we learn from the Śatakas that, if not himself a king, Bhartṛhari is quite at home and well conversant with courtlife. Bhartṛhari is not doubt sopken of as King in the भर्तृहरिनिर्वेनाटक। The several street plays (ख्याल) on भर्तृहरि and गोपीचन्द also speak of Bhartṛhari as Maternal uncle to गोपीचन्द and brother to विक्रमादित्य and मैनावति mother of Gopicanda.

From what has been said above we may take it as pretty certain that Bhartṛhari is the author of the Śatakas and that his precise date, though involved in mystery, is belived to be about 50 or 60 A.D. From a careful study of the Śatakas we can also infer that he is a poet of no ordinary stamp, that he is quite at home in the delineation of Nīti, Śṛṅgāra and Vairāgya and therefore one who must have actually tasted the fruits of all three, and that from his frequent reference to king, king' surroundings and kingly enjoyments, he must have been, if not a king himself, one thoroughly conversant with a king's state and life.

I cannot, before concluding this part of my Praface, help adducing some plea for the acceptance of Bhartṛhari's tradition. When real authority is wanting, a people may justly be pardoned for accepting a tradition to generation, spreading over many centuries say 18 or 19, and which has not been thoroughly destroyed by the the canons of Western criticism. Putting aside the inconclusive theories of many a learned scholars who have written on or of Bhartṛhari, we may, therefore, be justified in heading the Preface with the traditional history of Bhartṛhari, adhering, though not quite wholly and without reserve, to what is preserved in men's minds about the writer of these Śatakas on Nīti, Śṛṅgāra and Vairāgya.

V. PLACES OF INTEREST RELATING TO BHARTṚHARI

Such places are numerous and spread all over India. We shall, however, confine ourselves to the description of these we have seen ourselves to the description of these we have seen ourselves or read about in any reliable work.

(1) "Bhartṛhari Gupha." A cave at Ujjain having within its centre a small alter at which Bhartṛhari is said to have made his daily offering, lighted his sacrificial fire and kindled his Dhūnī. It is also told that a subterranean passages which formerly connected this cave with Benares is now blocked up.[1]

(2) "Bhartṛhari's Gupha at Mount Abu."

On Mount Abu there are two caves pointed out as Bhartṛhari's. One is by the old footpath to Vasiṣṭhāśrama of Gaumukha which passes close to the Railway School leaving it on the left. A stream of water runs down the small rock in

---

1. Bombay Sanskrit Series No. XI, p. vi.

the rains. Once of the apertures in the recess of the cave is supposed to be subterraneously running as far as Kāśi. It is all dark within and nothing can however be positively ascertained about the substerraneous passage. But here I would beg permission to remark that such legends are quite common with many a cave of renowned sages and Yogīs throughout the land.

The other cave which is also spoken of as Bhartṛhari's is on a hill on the left side of the Acaleśvar Mandir (अचलेश्वर मंदिर) at Achalgarh. It is something like a proper Āśrama with one or two ragged *kuccha* sheds to give shelter to the residant Jogīs who live there. There men always keep a smoking fire or Dhūnī (धूनी) continually burning in one place which is sait to be the case from the time of Bhartṛhari downwards. They wear red or reddish (गेरुवा) clothes and keep no wives and profes themsevlees to be the followers of the royal ascetic Bhartṛhari.

(3) "Rājā Bhartṛhari kā Mahala." It is situated to the North of Schowan, a town on the right bank of the Indus and belonging to Hyderabad (Sind). The palace of Bhartṛhari, as it is called up to date, is still to be seen in the centre of a very ancient and extensive fortress where Bhartṛhari is said to have reigned when he was driven from Ujjain by his younger brother Vikramāditya.[1]

(4) "Bhartṛhari's Mandira". A temple to the south of Schwan which is held sacred both by the Hindus and Mohanmedans.[2]

(5) "Bhartewar." A town belonging to the Chief of Kānorh, one of the sixteen great Barons of Meywar. It was boasts of a high antiquity and Bhartṛhari the elder brother of Vikramāditya is said to be its reputed founder.[3]

1. For further particulars see footnote at page 369, Todd's Annals and Antiquities of Rajasthan Vol. II, popular edition Calcutta, 1884.
2. See Todd, p. 370, idem.
3. See Todd's Annals and Antiquities of Rajasthan, Vol. II p. 644, Popular Edition of Calcutta, 1884.

(6) "Bhartṛhari's Samādhiṣṭhānas." They are found in many places, but we shall enumerate those only to which we have been eyewitness.

(a) There is a small village in the midst of a group of hills to the west of Ulwar (Rājputānā), known by the name of Siriskā. Within a quarter of a mile from that place is situated Bhartṛhari's Samādhiṣṭhāna. Surrounded by dense forest the place abounds with wild beasts. A small rill flows through it during the rains and winter. There we find seven small domes or cupolās nearly a yard in height and a yard in diameter. The concave of these domes, which are situated not for from one another, is all hollow. At them I saw the place, six of the domes were close on all sides without any opening while the seventh had a small door having an Akhaṇḍa Dīpaka (अखण्डदीपक) or a small lamp continuously burning within it. There were also some *sindūra* tridents marked on both sides of the door. On enquiry I was told by the resident Jogis that Bhartṛhari has already taken his Samādhi in six of these cupolās, whereas the seventh containing the lamp represents Bhartṛhari's *Jyoti* ज्योति, where he is to come one day and take his seventh Samādhi as before. The mouth of this cupolā will also be closed at that time and an eight will be raised to represent his *Jyoti*. This will also be closed in time and a ninth and last will again sprint up to be similarly closed. Now, we speak of him as "राजा भर्तृहरि की जय" or "Victory to Rājā Bhartṛhari", but on his completing the ninth Samādhi, he will be included among the 'नवनाथ' or nine "Nāthas,' and then we shall speak of him as 'भर्तृहरि नाथ की जय' 'Victory to Lord Bhartṛhari'. It was also told by the Jogī that there is no specified time for Bhartṛhari's Samādhi-taking. He comes here when he likes *incognito,* but when he takes the Samādhi Bhartṛhari reveals himself in his true garb.

Needless to add that 'Samādhi-taking' is here unsed in the sense of burying oneself alive. When a *yogī* takes Samādhi, he is generally buried underground and a dome is raised on the spot to mark the event, but it is not unusual that he is again sen on the earth through his mystic powers of Yoga.

(b) Another Śamādhiṣṭhāna of Bhartṛhari is still pointed out at Cākṣu in Jeypore some 25 miles south of the Capital. Besides a cave and a yogī's shed and a *Mamuli* account of Bhartṛhari's Śamādhi taking at the place, there is nothing particular about it.

Apropose, I may also state that there exists a sect of Yogīs who hold Bhartṛhari in very high esteem and call themselves as 'भरतरी' or the followers of Rājā Bhartṛhari. I hear that annual fairs in honor of the royal ascetic Bhartṛhari are held at many places in Indian and they are frequented by numerous crowds of men and women of all castes and creeds. Bhartṛhari is said to be immortal and believed now and then to appear to those pious *Yogīs* who have renounced the world in right earnest.

Perhaps it will not be out of place to tell something about Gorakṣanātha (गोरक्षनाथ), the spiritual *Guru* of Bhartṛhari. He is acknowledged to be one of the नवनाथ *'Nine Nāthas'* or nine great Yogīs who are masters of the Yogaśāstra and who can reveal its wondrous secrets to whomsoever they please.[1] Some strange books, like the 'गोरक्षपद्धति' are attributed by the Gurkhas who hold him in great respect and reverence. The town of Gorakhpore some 55 miles west of Khatmandu (Nepal) is also called after the name of the reverend Yogī. In this town there is a cave known as Gorakhanātha's in which the great ascetic is said to have attained salvation.

VI. A PLEA FOR THE PRESENT EDITION

It was in June 1893, that a friend of mine who had come up Mount Abu on some business and put up with me in the

1. The nine Master Yogīs enumerated in the हठयोगप्रदीपिका are मत्स्येन्द्रनाथ, शाबरनाथ, आनन्दभैरवनाथ, चौरंगीनाथ, मीननाथ, गोरक्षनाथ, विरूपाक्षनाथ and तिलशयनाथ See हठयोगप्रदीपिका, 1।5।

Jeypore House, thus remarked to me in a friendly chat we were enjoying together in the cool evening : "I see that you are very light of work. Please not to while away yout time in idle pursuits and useless reading, but write out something which may do good to all of us." I could not deny the comparative ease of my position, and the earnestness with which the remark was made, led me to beg his excuse for my inability to put my hands to any serious useful composition. But my esteemed friend was not a man to easily put aside and he pressed me to give him a pledge of acting up to his counsel which was reluctantly accorded, but without the least idea of ever fulfilling the same. To render the "Three Centuries of Bhartṛhari" into English was his suggestion, and I gladly took the hint. Though I had not, as already noted, the least idea of keeping my word, still the auspicious moment in which the pledge was given led me on to set about the work in real earnest. The greater was my advance in the self-imposed task, the more hopful became the prospect. At last the translation was finished. I wrote to the energetic Secretary of the Bombay Theosophical Society for its publication, who undertook to do it on condition of the manuscript being approved by his European brothers. Consequently, the translation of the Vairāgya Śataka was sent him about the month of November. But the manuscript was kindly returned by him after a few days together with a printed pamphlet entitled the 'Proverbial Philosophy of Bhartṛhari' and a paper bearing the autograph note of Col., Olcott to whom the manuscripts and pamphlet were submitted for inspection. On reading the paper I found that the learned President of the Theosophical Society had remarked that both these needed corrections of idiom, the Pamphelt very much, the manuscript very little, and that he had no time to take it up for the present. Instead of being dejected by these remarks, I was very much gratified to see my first attempts being very near the point of being approved bythe redoubtable head of the Theosophical Society. Besides, a close comparision of my translation with the Pamphlet soon dispelled my fears and filled my hearts with great delight.

By the way, I may here state that up to that date I had never dreamt of any existing English Translation of Bhartṛhari. From that time downwards I gave myself heart and soul to bringk my translation to the necessary perfection by availing myself of the many books on and relating to Bhartṛhari. It may also be stated that this translated was submitted for his perusal Col. G.H. Trevor C.S.I, the then enlightened Agent to the Governor General for the States for the States of Rājputānā, in the beginning of March 1895. After goint through a considerable portion of the Nītiśataka he returened it with thanks and evinced his full sympathy and approbation of the undertaking.

H.H., the Mahārājādhirāja Savāi Pratāp Singhji's translation is in Hindi Poetry : Dohās, Soraṭhās and Chhappayas. It consists of three chapters on Nīti, Śṛṅgāra and Vairāgya and is very terse and pithy and hence difficult to grasp for an ordinary reader.

The Hindi prose Translation of the Śatakas by Pandit Rishabha Dutt Śāstrī of Jodhpore is neither correct nor good.

I have, therefore, thought it advisable to give here a correct translation in Hindi prose of the day which will be found quite easy, clear and idiomatic.

As for English Translations of the work I have before me the following :—

(I) The Proverbail Philosophy of Bhartṛhari : anonymous.

(II) The Two Centuries of Bhartṛhari : Prof. Tawney.

(III) Bhartṛhari's Nītiśataka and Vairāgya Śataka translated into English by Mr. Durgā Parasād of Lahore.

I. After the remarks of Col. Olcott it is needless to dwell more upon the merits of the first. It contains only the two Śatakss of Nīti and Vairāgya.

II. Prof. Tawney's is no doubt a very splendid and elegant translation. But as it is in verse, it is either more or less than the original. Moreover, there are to be found only the Nīti and Vairāgya Śatakas and the Śṛṅgāra chapter is quite left out in the edition.

III. It (Mr. Durgā Prasād's translation) is of course better than the Proverbial Philosophy of Bhartṛhari, but it is not quite up to the point. It this, too, the Śṛṅgāra Śataka is also wanting.

From these remarks it will not be quite difficult to see that the present edition is to fill up a necessary gap regarding the Śatakas of Bhartṛhari. Besides a large number of copious notes (both critical and explanatory) at the end of the volume, the original Sanskrit Text being immediately followed by Hindi and English translations, and variety of citations of parallel passages from Sanskrit and English authors, constitute a novel feature of the present edition. An English translation of the Śṛṅgāra Śataka is, I think, here presented for the first time to the public. There being really nothing which can properly be called obscene and immoral, I do not think that any apology is needed for the insertion of the Śṛṅgāra Śataka. On the contrary, the stanzas are to be found comparatively quite decent and innocent by the side of a number of novels and amorous poems in English. Moreover, if rightly understood, almost all the strophes of the Śṛṅgāra Śataka are intentionally composed to divert our attention from the banefull influence of women in particular and worldly enjoyments in general. So, if we are to leave out the noble thoughts of the Śṛṅgāra Śataka, we commit a great mistake in bringing out a very poor picture of the author's exalted and praiseworthy aim in the composition of this work.

In numbering the stanzas of the Nīti and Vairāgya Śatakas, I have generally followed the Nirnaya Sāgara (Bombay) Edition of Bhartṛhari's Śatakatrayaṃ, but in that of the Śṛṅgāra Śataka the plan adopted is mostly consistent with the Gyāna Sāgara Press Edition of Bhartṛhari's Śatakatrayaṃ.

As for the Table of Contents I have sticked to no particular copy or copies of the work but keeping in view almost all of them, I have independently worked out quite a new arrangement of the subjects from a careful study of the text. To make the edition as useful as possible, I have also appended to it an alphabetical list of all the ślōkas of these Śatakas. A full list of works and authors referred to in the compilation of this book isalso to be found in the present volume.

In the end I may remark, with Prof. Tawney that "translations are seldom popular either in prose or verse unless they depart widely from the spirit of the original. But a certain measure of fidelity to the original, even at the risk of making onself ridiculous is better than the studied dishonesty which characterises so many translations of oriental poets."

On the whole it can be safely said that if perused with care and attention the book will no doubt be found to be a very interesting and instructive reading. However, it being only the first juvenile attempt in the field of literary composition, the present volume cannot naturally be expected to be entirely free from all sorts of faults and drawbacks, but the reception accorded to it by the reading public and the impartial judgment passed on its merits and demerits by learned critics will ultimately decide whether the couple of years of hard labour and persevering industry spent in bringing it out have been well spent or not, and whether any other essay can again be usefully and successfully made inthis direction by its amateur editor.

Before concluding I may be permitted to pay my cordial and gratful thanks to those of my friends who have helped me any way by their valuable suggestions and appropriate encouragements not to give up the undertaking, nor to do it half heartedly and imperefectly but to carry it through to the best of my ability and power.

P. Gopinath

ABBREVIATIONS

Śp.	Śāraṅgadharapaddhati.
Sb.	Subhāṣitāvali.
Sk.	Sūktāvali.
Ks.	Kāvyānuśāsana.
Kl.	Kāvyālaṅkāra.
Kp	Kāvyapradīpa.
Ks.	Kāvyasaṅgraha.
N.	Nirṇayasāgara Press Edition.
G.	Gyānasāgara Press Edition.
T.	Telangs Edition.
H.	Hitōpadeśa.
P.	Pañcatantra.
Pdm.-Vś.	Padmānanda's Vairāgyaśataka.
Sarasvatī.	Sarasvatī Kaṇṭhābharaṇa.
Śś,	Śāntiśataka.
Nami.	Nami Śādhu's Commentary on Kāvyālaṅkāra.
Ud.	Udāharaṇacandrikā.
Rasa.	Rasaratnahāra.
Dh.	Dhvanyālōka.
Am.	Amaruśataka.
Kuvalaya.	Kuvalayānanda.
Śvindu.	Śṛṅgāravindu.
Śtilaka.	Śṛṅgāratilaka.
G. T.	Great Thoughts.
B. S. S.	Bombay Sanskrit Series.
Aucitya.	Aucityavicāracarcā.

NĪTIŚATAKAṂ

।। अथ नीतिशतकम् ।।

MORALITY

दिक्कालाद्यनवच्छिन्नानन्तचिन्मात्रमूर्तये ।
स्वानुभूत्येकमानाय नमः शान्ताय तेजसे ।। 1 ।।

भाषाटीका।

पूर्वादि दशदिशा और भूतादि तीन काल में अविनाशी, अनन्त चैतन्य स्वरूप, निज के अनुभव से प्रत्यक्ष होने वाले, शान्तिमय और प्रकाशरूप परमब्रह्म को नमस्कार है।

Bow to the calm and self-luminous Being whose image is entirely free from (or undefined by) the limits of Space, Time, etc., and is, therefore Infinite; and whose existence is only experienced by one's own conscience or whose sole (principal) essence is self-knowledge!

---

1. This Stanza which is quoted under *Bhartṛhari* (भर्तृहरि) in Ballabhadeva's *Subhāṣitāvali* (सुभाषितावलि) at No. 3 (Bombay Sanskrit Series XXXI) also forms the opening Śloka of the *Vasiṣṭhasāra* (वसिष्ठसार)।

यां चिन्तयामि सततं मयि सा विरक्ता
साऽप्यन्यमिच्छति जनं स जनोऽन्यसक्तः।
अस्मत्कृते च परितुष्यति काचिदन्या
धिक्तां च तं न मदनं च इमां च मां च।। 2।।

मैं जिसका निरन्तर चिन्तवन करता हूँ वह मुझ को नहीं चाहती किन्तु वह किसी अन्य पुरुष से प्यार करती है; और खेद का विषय है कि वह पुरुष किसी दूसरी ही स्त्री पर आसक्त हो रहा है। इस ही तरह कोई ऐसी स्त्री भी विद्यमान है जो हमसे बहुत ही प्रसन्न है। ऐसी दशा में इस स्त्री को, प्यारी के जारपुरुष को, प्यारी को, मुझ को और कामदेव को अत्यंत धिक्कार है।

She of whom I always think is indifferent to me, but, on the contrary, she likes another man, who, in his turn, is attached to a different woman. Again, there is some one else who takes much delight in me. With these facts before us we cannot help calling shame and censure upon her (the woman who loves me) him (my love's paramour), my love, myself, and Cupid (the real author of all these evils).

---

1. *Bhartṛhari* (भर्तृहरि) is here said to allude to the infidelity of his wife. See Note to this stanza.

2. This *Śloka* (श्लोक) is quoted anonymously by Siṁhadeva-maṇi in his conmmentary on *Vāgbhaṭṭālaṅkāra* (वाग्भटालंकार).

अज्ञः सुखमाराध्यः सुखतरमाराध्यते विशेषज्ञः।
ज्ञानलवदुर्विदग्धं ब्रह्माऽपितं नरं न रञ्जयति।। 3।।

हिताहित के न जानने वाले अज्ञपुरुष को (अनसमझ को) समझाना बहुत सहज है और युक्तायुक्त से परिचित ज्ञानवान् मनुष्य को संतुष्ट करना और भी सुगमतर है। परंतु ज्ञान के लेशमात्र से पंडित बने हुए मनुष्य को प्रसन्न करने के लिए स्वयं ब्रह्मा जी भी असमर्थ हैं।

To manage (conciliate) an ignorant person is quite easy, and easier still is the propitiation of the learned; but to please the conceited fellow whose head is turned by his little learning is surely an impossible task even for *Brahmā,* the Creator.

---

1. Quoted under *Bhartṛhari* (भर्तृहरि) in Ballabhadeva's *Subhāṣitāvali* (सुभाषितावलि) (No. 393, B.S.S. No. XXXI), and see *Sārṅgadharapaddhati* at No. 208. It also stands in the *Hitōpadeśa* IV. 104.

Cf. 2. *(a)* "Little learning is a dangerous thing;
Drink deep, or taste not the Pierian spring :
There shallow draughts intoxicate the brain."—
A. Pope's Essay on Criticism Part II.

(b) "ज्ञानी समुझत सहज में, पर जिन नर अभिमान।
मनरंजन तिनका कभी संभव नांहि सुजान।।"
(रसिक कवि)

प्रसह्यं मणिमुद्धरेन्मकरवक्त्रदंष्ट्रान्तरा-
त्समुद्रमपि सन्तरेत्प्रचलदूर्मिमालाकुलम्।
भुजङ्गमपि कोपितं शिरसि पुष्पवद्धारये-
न्नतुप्रतिनिविष्टिमूर्खजनचित्तमाराधयेत्।। 4।।

मगरमच्छ की दंष्ट्रा के अंतर्गत मणि को निकालने का उद्योग कोई भले ही करे, प्रचण्ड तरंग माला से व्याकुल समुद्र को तरण करने का प्रयत्न कोई भले ही करे, और कुपित हुए भीषण भुजंगम को पुष्प माला के समान मस्तक पर धारण करने को कोई भले ही सन्नद्ध हो, परंतु हठयुक्त मूर्ख मनुष्य के मन को संतुष्ट करने का साहस कोई कदापि ही न करे।

भावार्थ

दुराग्रही मूर्ख के मन को वश करना सर्वथा असंभव है।

You may even dare take out a precious gem from the pointed jaws of a dreadful alligator, or swim over the vast ocean whose waters are all disturbed by a series of furious rolling waves, or wear an enraged (offended) serpent upon your head, as if it were a flowery wreath; but, you should never undertake the fruitless task of conciliating the mind of a stupid fellow who is determined to hold obstinately to his own conviction whether right or wrong.

---

1. Quoted under *Bhartṛhari* (भर्तृहरि) in Ballabhadeva's *Subhāṣitāvali* (सुभाषितावलि) (No. 446. B.S.S. No. XXXI.), and also in the शार्ङ्गधरपद्धति at No. 416. *Cf.*—

"हालाहलं खलु पिपासित कौतुकेन, कालानलं परिचुचुम्बिषति प्रकामम्।
व्यालाधिपं च यततं परिरब्धुमद्धा यो दुर्जनं वशयितुं तनुते मनीषाम्।। 90।।"
(भामिनीविलासः। अन्योक्त्युल्लासः)

लभेत सिकतासु तैलमपि यत्नतः पीडय-
न्पिबेच्च मृगतुष्णिकासु सलिलं पिपासार्दितः।
कदाचिदपि पर्यटञ्छशविषाणमासादये-
न्नतुप्रतिनिविष्टमूर्खजनचित्तमाराधयेत्।। 5।।

यत्नपूर्वक मर्दन करते-करते शायद बालुका के कणों से भी तेल निकल सकता है, तृषार्त मनुष्य खोजते-खोजते शायद मरुस्थल में भी पानी का लाभ कर सकता है, और पृथ्वी पर भ्रमण करते-करते किसी समय में शायद शशश्रृंग भी किसी से दृष्टिगोचर हो सकता है। परंतु हठीले और दुराग्रही मूर्ख के मन को कोई मनुष्य भी कदापि अपने वश में नहीं कर सकता।

You may even succeed, by presistent endeavours to obtain oil by compressing the particles of sand, or to find out water to drink in the midst of a mirage; or sometimes in your wanderings you may even come upon the horns of a hare; but the propitiation of the impenetrable heart of a preverse fool is undoubtedly a useless undertaking for all your varied efforts.

---

1. Quoted under *Bhartṛhari* (भर्तृहरि) in Ballabhadeva's *Subhāṣitāvali* (सुभाषितावलि) (No. 446, B.S.S. No. XXXI.), and, also in the शार्ङ्गधरपद्धति at No. 415. *Cf.*—

अरण्यरुदितं कृतं शवशरीरमुद्वर्तितं, स्थलेऽब्जमवरोपितं सुचिरमूषरे वर्षितम्।
श्वपुच्छमवनामितं बधिकर्णजापः कृतः कृतान्धमुखमण्डना यदबुधो जनः सेवितः।।

(Ascribed to भर्तृहरि in the सुभाषितावलि)

व्यालं बालमृणालतन्तुभिरसौ रोद्धुं समुज्जृम्भते।
छेत्तुं वज्रमणीञ्छिरीषकुसुमप्रान्तेन सनह्यते।
माधुर्यं मधुबिन्दुना रचयितुं क्षाराम्बुधेरीहते, नेतुं
वाञ्छतियः खलान्पथिसतांसूक्तैः सुधास्यन्दिभिः।। 6।।

अपनी अमृतमय शिक्षाओं से दुष्ट पुरुषों को सन्मार्ग में लाने की अभिलाषा करना ऐसा ही अनुचित है जैसा कि कोमल कमलनाल से मत्तगजरा को रोकना, शिरीष पुष्प के सुकुमार अग्रभाग से कठोर वज्रमणि को छेदन करना, अथवा अमृत के बिंदु से अपार क्षार समुद्र को मधुर करने का साहस है।

The endeavours of a man to bring a blockhead to the right path by the influence of his wise and mellifluous words are no wise better than the fruitless efforts of one who ventures to keep an elephant fast bound by means of the delicate threads of a lotus stem, or to pierce a diamond by the tender fibres of *śiriṣa,* or to sweeten the saline waters of the vast ocean by pouring a single drop of nectar into its midst.

---

1. Also found in the *Vairāgya Śataka* (वैराग्यशतक) of *Padmānanda* (पद्मानंद कवि) at No. 54 *Cf.*—

(*a*) "दुर्जनः सज्जनीकर्तुं यत्नेनाऽपि न शक्यते। संस्कारेणापि लशुनं कःसुगन्धीकरिष्यति।।" (सुभाषितावलिः। 367। B.S.S. No. XXXI.).

(*b*) "न विषममृतं कर्तुं शक्यं प्रयत्नशतैरपि त्यजति कटुतां न स्वां निम्बः स्थितोऽपि पयोह्रदे।

गुणपरिचितामार्या वाणीं न जल्पति दुर्जनश्चिरमपि बलाध्माते लोहे कुतः-कनकाकृतिः।।" (Attribute to भर्तृहरि in the शार्ङ्गधरपद्धति। 377)।

स्वायत्तमेकान्तगुणं विधात्रा
विनिर्मितं छादनमज्ञतायाः।
विशेषतः सर्वविदां समाजे
विभूषणं मौनमपण्डितानाम्।। 7।।

विधाता ने मूर्खों की मूर्खता छुपाने का अर्थ मौन धारण करने का एक बहुत उत्तम उपाय निर्माण किया है और वह उपाय भी उसने मूर्खों के स्वाधीन ही रख दिया है। यह मौन केवल मूर्खता का आच्छादन करने वाला ही नहीं है किन्तु पंडितों की सभा में बैठे हुए मूर्खों का आभूषण भी है।

The best means (silence) by which ignorance can be concealed from the sight of others has been graciously left by god in the personal control of man who can use it as he pleases. Silence is an ornament of the illiterate, especially in the assembly of learned (all-knowing) people.

---

1. Quoted anonymously in Ballabhadeva's *Subhāṣitāvali* (सुभाषितावली) (No. 2382 B.S.S. No. XXXI) *Cf.*—

(*a*) "तावच्च शोभते मूर्खो यावत्किंचिन्न भाषते" (चाणक्यशतके 15)

(*b*) "Silence is the sanctuary of prudence." (Balthasar Gracian).

(*c*) "Silence is a virtue in those who are deficient in understanding."

(*d*) "By silence I hear other men's imperfections, and conceal my own." Great Thoughts Vol. XI. p. 527.

2. At page 2 of Indian Antiquary, Vol. IV Prof. Tawney quotes a Greek epigram as a parallel to this stanza.

यदाऽकिञ्चिज्ज्ञोऽहं द्विप इव मदान्धः समभवं
तदा सर्वज्ञोऽस्मीत्यभवदवलिप्तं मम मनः।
यदा किञ्चित्किञ्चिद्बुधजनसकाशादवगतं
तदा मूर्खोऽस्मीति ज्वर इव मदो मे व्यपगतः॥ 8॥

जब मैं बिल्कुल ही अज्ञान अर्थात् अनसमझ था तब मदोन्मत्त हस्ती के समान अभिमान में अंधा होकर अपने को सर्वज्ञ समझा करता था परंतु अब पंडितों की संगति से थोड़े से ज्ञान के होते ही वह सब उन्माद ज्वर वेग की तरह मेरे शरीर से इतना जाता रहा है कि मैं अपने आपको मूर्ख जानने लग गया हूँ।

When I knew nothing I behaved like a furious elephant in ruts, considering myself an omnicient being; but now when I have come to learn something from the wise I have discovered my own ignorance; and having shaken off the fever of vain conceit. I acknowledge myself to be a blockhead.

---

1. Quoted under *Bhartṛhari* (भर्तृहरि) in Ballabhadeva's *Subhāṣitāvali* (सुभाषितावलि) (No. 3456, B.S.S. No. XXXI), and the *Śārṅgadharapaddhati*) (शार्ङ्गधरपद्धति) at No. 4177.

2. This reading यदा ऽकिञ्चिज्ज्ञो ऽहं is far better than यदाकिञ्चिज्ज्ञोऽहं, and hence, it has been adopted here in preference to the latter.

कृमिकुलचितं लालाक्लिन्नं विगन्धि जुगुप्सितं
निरुपमरसं प्रीत्या खादन्नरास्थि निरामिषम्।
सुरपतिमपि श्वा पार्श्वस्थं विलोक्य न शङ्कते
नहि गणयति क्षुद्रो जन्तुः परिग्रहफल्गुताम्।। 9।।

जैसे अनेक कीड़ों से परिपूर्ण, लार से युक्त, दुर्गंध सहित, घृणायोग्य, अत्यंत विरस और मांसरहित मनुष्य की हड्डी को प्रीतिपूर्वक खाता हुआ कूकर अपने समीपवर्ती देवराज इंद्र की भी कुछ शंका (लाज) नहीं करता वैसे ही स्वार्थपरायण नीच मनुष्य भी परिग्रह की तुच्छता को कदापि नहीं जान सकता।

भावार्थ।

नीच और लोभी मनुष्य श्वान की तरह अत्यंत निंदनीय कर्म करते हुए भी कदापि नहीं लजाते।

Just as a dog is not ashamed of being seen by Indra, the lord of gods, when it is bent on joyfully eating a putrid and fleshless piece of human bone full of worms and saliva, and devoid of all juice and taste, so a mean fellow is never ashamed of accepting another worthless favour, charity or munificence.

PURPORT

No pursuit is ever considered as dishonest and derogatory by the mean.

---

1. This stanza is same as stanza 8 in *Śāntiśataka* Part II. (शांतिशतकं द्वितीयपरिच्छेदः).

2. अत्यंत विरस thought not exactly equivalent to निरुपमरसं of the text gives approximately the same idea.

शिरः शार्वं स्वर्गात्पतति शिरसस्तत्क्षितिधरं
महीध्रादुत्तुङ्गादवनिमवनेश्चापि जलधिम्।
अधोऽधो गङ्गेयं पदमुपगता स्तोकमथवा
विवेकभ्रष्टानां भवति विनिपातः शतमुखः।। 10।।

विष्णु भगवान् के चरणारविंदों से निकलने वाली गंगा प्रथम तो स्वर्ग से शिवजी के मस्तक पर और वहाँ से पर्वत पर, और ऊँचे गिरि शिखर से पृथ्वी तल पर, और फिर धरातल पर बहती हुई अंत में समुद्र में जा गिरती है। जैसे ऊँचे पद को छोड़ने पर बारंबार अधःपतन होते-होते गंगा के समान सुरनदी भी अत्यंत नीचे स्थान में आ जाती है वैसे ही ज्ञान मार्ग से भ्रष्ट हुए मनुष्य भी शतशः प्रकार की विपत्ति झेलते रहते हैं।

Those who have unfortunately lost the power of discerning right from wrong are sure to suffer a thousand falls like those of the Gaṅges that first falls from the heights of heaven upon the head of Śiva, and thence upon the lofty summits of the Himālaya, from which it again flows down to the plains below, and then empties its waters into the sea, being thus obliged to fall to the lowest level by gradual descent.

---

1. For the varied courses of the heavenly river—the Gaṅges—see our Notes on this stanza. One of the Sanskrit names of the Gaṅges (गंगा) is Tripathagā (त्रिपथगा) which means a river of three different paths or courses.

शक्यो वारयितुं जलेन हुतभुक्छत्रेण सूर्यातपो
नागेन्द्रोनिशिताङ्कुशेनसमदोदण्डेन गोगर्दभौ।
व्याधिर्भेषजसंग्रहैश्च विविधैर्मंत्रप्रयोगैर्विषं, सर्व-
स्यौषधमस्ति शास्त्रविहितंमूर्खस्यनास्त्यौषधम्।। 11।।

जैसे हम जल के द्वारा अग्नि को शमन कर सकते हैं, छत्र से सूर्य के तेज को रोक सकते हैं, मत्तगजराज को तीक्ष्ण अंकुश से वश कर सकते हैं, गौगर्दभादि पशुओं को लकड़ी की ताड़ना से भयभीत कर सकते हैं, अनेक प्रकार के रोगों को औषधियों से शान्त कर सकते हैं, और विष का प्रभाव नानाविध मंत्रादिकों से दूर कर सकते हैं। इस ही भाँति अन्यान्य सब उपद्रवों की भी यथोचित् औषधियाँ शास्त्र में विद्यमान हैं परंतु मूर्ख मनुष्य का मूर्खत्व नष्ट करने के निमित्त कहीं पर भी कोई औषधि दृष्टिगोचर नहीं होती ।

We can keep off fire by waters; the hot sun by an umbrella, a wild elephant in ruts by a sharpedged hook, the unrully cattle by the goading stick, a disease by collecting medicines, and the evil effects of a poison by the use of various charms (lit. Mantras). Every possible evil in the world has its apporpriate remedy prescribed by the *Śāstras*, but there is no effective cure of a blockhead throughout the vast range of the Scriptures.

---

1. This stanza is same as stanza 5 in the *Pañcaratna* (पञ्चरत्न)। It is also quoted anonymously in the *Subhāṣitāvali* (सुभाषितावलि) (No. 2943. B.S.S. No. XXXI). — The verse also occurs in the *Sūktāvali* (सूक्तावलि ।17।) *Cf.*—

"पोतो दुस्तरवारिराशितरणे दीपोन्धकारागमे निर्वाते व्यजनं मदान्धकरिणो दर्पोपशान्त्यै सृणिः।

इत्थं तद्भुवि नास्ति यस्य विधिना नोपायचिन्ता कृता मन्ये दुर्जनचित्तवृत्तिहरणे धाताऽपि भग्नोद्यमः।" (हितोपदेशः 2।151)

साहित्यसङ्गीतकलाविहीनः
साक्षात्पशुः पुच्छविषाणहीनः ।
तृणं न खादन्नपि जीवमान-
स्तद्भागधेयं परमं पशूनाम् ।। 12 ।।

जिस मनुष्य को साहित्य और संगीतशास्त्र का कुछ भी ज्ञान नहीं है वह निस्संदेह पुच्छ और शृंगार रहित पशु है। तृणादि भक्षण करने के बिना उसका जीवित रहना भी पशुओं का सौभाग्य सूचित करता है; क्योंकि यदि उसका जीवन भी घास पर ही निर्भर होता तो पशुओं को अपनी उदरपूरणा करने में बहुत ही कठिनता हो जाती।

One who is ignorant of literature and music is undoubtedly a tailless and hornless beast; and the fact of his being accustomed to live without grass affords a fortunate advantage to cattle that are thus secured to make a free use of their natural food.

---

1. The latter half of this Śloka—one of the most important sayings of Bhartṛhari—is often misinterpreted by commentators and translators. It is easy to see how much force it loses, and how non-sensical it becomes by the interpretation which renders it thus: Lower animals can subsist without grazing on grass and so they too are even better off than men."

येषां न विद्या न तपो न दानं
ज्ञानं न शीलं न गुणो न धर्मः।
ते मर्त्यलोके भुवि भारभूता
मनुष्यरूपेण मृगाश्चरन्ति।। 13।।

जिन मनुष्यों ने न तो विद्याध्ययन ही किया है, न तपश्चरण ही किया है, न दान ही दिया है, न ज्ञान ही संपादन किया है, न सुशील ही का आचरण किया है, न गुणोपार्जन ही किया है और न धर्मानुष्ठान ही किया है, वह इस मर्त्यलोक में केवल आकृति मात्र से मनुष्य कहलाते हैं; परन्तु वास्तव में वह साधारण मृगों की भाँति पृथ्वी माता के वृथाभाररूप हैं।

Those who have neither learning, nor devotion, nor charity, nor spiritual knowledge, nor good conduct, nor morality, nor religious faith are nothing less than mere useless burdens to mother earth, wandering over this mortal world like the wild deer in a human from.

---

1. Prof. Tawney cites a striking parallel to this stanza from the Illiad. See Tawney's Centuries of Bhartṛhari, p. 6.

2. The verse stands in the *Sūktāvali* (सूक्तावलि 8)

3. The point of the stanza seems to be that a man to prove his superiority to animals must give himself to learning, devotion, etc.

वरं पर्वतदुर्गेषु भ्रान्तं वनचरैः सह।
न मूर्खजनसम्पर्कः सुरेन्द्रभवनेष्वपि।। 14।।

व्याघ्रादि हिंसक जन्तुओं के साथ दुर्गम पर्वत और विषम वनादि के भ्रमण करना तो फिर भी किसी प्रकार अच्छा है परंतु मूर्ख जन का मिलाप तो इन्द्र भवन में भी श्रेष्ठ नहीं होता।

Roaming with wild beasts in dense forests and mountains is surely to be preferred to the company of a fool though it may take place within the palatial premises of the mighty Indra, the lord of gods.

---

1. It also stands in the *Sūktāvali* (सूक्तावलि । 20)

Cf. —न स्थातव्यं न गन्तव्यं दुर्जनेन समं क्वचित्।

(हितोपदेश 3।22)

2. In plain language the instruction conveyed by this stanza is that to live a poor and risky life is far better than to form an acquaintance of a fool. The temptation of a fool's friendship is invariably to be avoided at all costs and hazards.

3. The word पर्वतदुर्गेषु admits of two interpretations: (1) inaccessible mountains or (2) mountains and impassable lands, according to the two ways in which the word is compounded *i.e.*, either it is a तत्पुरुष or द्वन्द्व compound respectively.

शास्त्रोपस्कृतशब्दसुन्दरगिरः शिष्यप्रदेयागमा
विख्याताः कवयोवसन्तिविषयेयस्यप्रभोर्निर्धनाः।
तज्जाड्यंवसुधाधिपस्यकवयोह्यर्थंविनाऽपीश्वराः
कुत्स्याः स्युः कुपरीक्षकानमणयोयैरर्घतः पातिताः ।। 15 ।।

जिस राजा के राज्य में शास्त्रानुसार शुद्ध सुंदर भाषण करने वाले और वेदादि विद्याओं के पढ़ाने वाले सुप्रसिद्ध कविजन निर्धन होकर निवास करते हैं उस राजा के मूर्ख होने में किसी प्रकार का भी संशय नहीं, क्योंकि जैसे बहुमूल्य मणि का अल्पमूल्य अंकित करने से जौहरी ही कुपरीक्षक (या अनाड़ी) कहलाते हैं और मणिका वास्तव में वही मूल्य बना रहता है वैसे ही सत्कवियों का निरादर करने से भी राजा ही की मूर्खता प्रगट होती है, कवीश्वरों का यथार्थ में कुछ भी नहीं घटता क्योंकि वह तो धनादि न होने पर भी प्रभावशाली हैं।

The chief in whose territory the far-famed poets commanding a sweet and melodious speech saturated with deep learning of the *śāstras*, as well as a number of pupils of great erudition, cannot earn a substaintial livelihood, and hence drag on a poor miserable life is indeed to be stamped a veritable fool. The poets though suffering from penury are still to be thought as men of influence and power in the world; for, it is the sad mistake of the unfortunate jewellers who are misled to undervalue the precious gems which do not thereby lose a bit of their real worth.

1. Cf.—"Ability, and not riches, constitute worth." (*Saddi*).

हर्तुर्याति न गोचरं किमपि शं पुष्णातियत्सर्वदा
ह्यर्थिभ्यः प्रतिपाद्यमानमनिशंप्राप्नोतिवृद्धिंपराम्।
कल्पान्तेष्वपिनप्रयातिनिधनं विद्याख्यमन्तर्धनं
येषांतान्प्रतिमानमुज्झतनृपाः कस्तैः सहस्पर्धते।। 16।।

विद्या भी एक कैसा अपूर्व धन है कि जो (1) चौरादिक के दृष्टिगोचर नहीं होता, (2) विद्वानों का सदा काल कुछ न कुछ कल्याण साधन करता रहता है, (3) शिष्यादि अर्थिजनों को प्रदान करने से क्षय होने के बदले रात-दिन वृद्धि को प्राप्त होता है, और (4) जन्म-जन्मान्तर में क्या कल्पान्तर में भी जिसका कुछ नाश नहीं होता। ऐसा असामान्य विद्यारूप गुप्त धन जिन महात्माओं के पास है उन विद्वानों के समक्ष है राजाओ! अपने वैभव का अभिमान कदापि मत करो, क्योंकि इनकी बराबर करने में कोई भी समर्थ नहीं हो सकता।

Give up your vain pride, oh kings, before the learned and treat them fairly as your equals or even superiors; for who can ever compete with those whose hidden wealth of knowlege is (1) beyond the power of thieves to steal, (2) always a source of indescribable happiness to them, (3) so strange that instead of being lessened by distribution among its seekers (*i.e.* the students) it, on the contrary, ever grows more and more, and (4) is never subject to ruin not even at the end of Kalpa, *i.e.* on the day of universal destuction.

---

1. Quoted under *Bhartṛhari* (भर्तृहरि) in the *Subhāṣitāvali* (No.3459. B.S.S. XXXI.), and the *Sārṅgadharapaddhati* (शार्ङ्गधरपद्धति ।203) *Cf.*-

(*a*) "Education is a companion that no misfortune can depress, no disease destroy, no enemy alienate, no despotism enslave; at home a friend, abroad an introduction; in society an ornament in solitude a solace."

(*b*) "ज्ञातिभिर्वट्यते नैव चौरेणापि न नीयते। दाने नैव क्षयं याति विद्यारत्नं महाधनम्।। 11।।" (भवभूतेर्गुणरत्ने)

(c) "हर्तुर्न गोचरं याति दत्ता भवति विस्तृता। कल्पान्तेऽपि न या नश्येत्किमन्यद्विद्यया समम्।।" (सुभाषितरत्नभाण्डागार 44।4)

अधिगतपरमार्थान्पण्डितान्माऽवमंस्था-
स्तृणमिव लघु लक्ष्मीर्नैव तान्संरुणद्धि।
अभिनवमदलेखाश्यामगण्डस्थलानां
न भवति बिसतन्तुर्वारणं वारणानाम्।। 17 ।।

हे राजाओ! परमार्थ के जानने वाले विज्ञ पंडितों का अपमान कदापि मत करो, क्योंकि जिस तरह से अभिनव मद लेखा से श्यामलगंडस्थल वाले मदोन्मत्त हाथियों को वश करने के लिए कोमल कमलनाल समर्थ नहीं होते वैसे ही सूखे घास के तिनके के समान तुम्हारी तुच्छ लक्ष्मी भी उन विवेकी मनुष्यों को रोकने के हेतु किंचिन्मात्र भी सामर्थ्य नहीं रखती।

You should not show the least dishonour to those learned men who have obtained true spiritual knowledged; for, your worthless wealth is quite helpless to make them surrender to your power: the furious elephants whose temples have newly been marked with the black lines of rut can never be bound by the delicate tendrils of a lotus stem.

---

1. Quoted anonymously in the *Subhāṣitāvali* (सुभाषितावलि) at No. 2933, and also in the *Śārṅgadharapaddhati* (शार्ङ्गधरपद्धति) at No. 197.

2. "अधिगतपरमार्थान्" is also found in the 7th Śloka of *Rudraṭa's Kāvyālaṅkāra* Ch. 1.(रुद्रटस्य काव्यालङ्कारः । 1 अध्यायः।)

Cf.—"He who demands respect on account of his riches might as well demand that people should respect a mountain that contains gold." (Great Thoughts, Vol. XVII.).

अम्भोजिनीवननिवासिविलासमेव
हंसस्य हन्ति नितरां कुपितो विधाता।
न त्वस्य दुग्धजलभेदविधौ प्रसिद्धां
वैदग्ध्यकीर्तिमपहर्तुमसौ समर्थः।। 18।।

हंस पर कोप करके विधाता उसके कमल वन के निवास संबंधी विलास का नाश अलबत्ता कर सकता है, परंतु राजहंस की उस लोक-प्रसिद्ध सामर्थ्य का-जिसके द्वारा वह जल और दुग्ध को अलग-अलग छांट देता है-विधाता भी कदापि हरण नहीं कर सकता।

भावार्थ।

आनुषंगिक गुण का नाश भी अलबत्ता संभव है परंतु स्वाभाविक गुण का नाश कदापि हरण नहीं हो सकता।।

If the Creator be ever di · leased with the swan, He can of course deprive the wise bird of its pleasant luxury of living in the midst of a cluster of fair lotuses; but however wroth He may be He can never be successful to wrest from the sagacious fowl the enviable instinct of separating milk from water, with which it is openly credited all over the world.

PURPORT. No one can ever succeed to alter the natural propensities of the created nature.

---

1. The verse is quoted under भर्तृहरि in the शार्ङ्गधरपद्धति at No. 797.

For the point of the stanza, *cf.*—
"स्वभावः सर्वभूतानां सहजः केन वार्यते"।। 69।।
(क्षेमेन्द्रकृतदर्पदलनस्य द्वितीयविचारे).

2. For the natural instict of the swan (राजहंस) , *Cf.*—
"नीरक्षीरविवेके हंसालस्यं त्वमेव तनुषे चेत्।
विश्वस्मिन्नधनाऽन्यः कुलव्रतं पालयिष्यति कः।। 12।।"
(भामिनीविलासान्योक्त्युल्लासे).

केयूरा विभूषयन्तिपुरुषंहारानचन्द्रोज्जवला
नस्नानं नविलेपनंनकुसुमंनालङ्कृतामूर्धजाः।
वाण्येकासमलङ्करोति पुरुषं या संस्कृताधार्यते
क्षीयन्तेखलुभूषणानिसततंवाग्भूषणंभूषणम्।। 19।।

वाणीरूप भूषण सब भूषणों से उत्तम है, क्योंकि केयूरादि भुजबंध, चंद्रोज्ज्वलहार, स्नान, कुंकुमादि लेपन, पुष्प और सुंदर केशादि के भूषण क्षयी होने के कारण वाणीरूप अक्षय भूषण की बराबर कदापि नहीं कर सकते।

Properly speaking the person of man is neither adorned by armlets, nor by moonwhite necklaces, nor by bathing nor by ointments (*i.e.*applying perfumes), nor by flowers, nor by well-combed hair. The power of speech in a perfect and refined state is the only thing which can really add to the handsomeness of a man's person, for all other ornamets besides it are subject to decay whereas the gracefulness of speech lasts for ever.

---

1. It also stands in the *Sūktāvali* (सूक्तावतिः। 25)

Cf.—(*a*) नक्षत्रभूषणं चन्द्रो नरीरणां भूषणं पतिः।
पृथिवीभूषणं राजा विद्या सर्वस्य भूषणम्।। 8।।
(चाणक्यशतके)

(*b*) भूषण नर के हैं नहीं, वह हारादि अनेक।
सबसे उत्तम जानियो, वाणीभूषण एक।। (रसिक कवि)

विद्या नाम नरस्य रूपमधिकंप्रच्छन्नगुप्तंधनं
विद्याभोगकरीयशःसुखकरीविद्यागुरूणांगुरुः।
विद्या बन्धुजनो विदेशगमने विद्या परं दैवतं
विद्या राजसुपूजितानतु धनं विद्याविहीनः पशुः ।। 20 ।।

विद्या मनुष्य का सर्वोपरि सौंदर्य और अन्तर्हित गुप्त धन है, विद्या से मनुष्य को भोग विलास सुयश और सुख की प्राप्ति होती है, विद्या उपदेशकों की भी गुरु है, विद्या देश–देशान्तर में रहने वाले का बंधुजन है, और विद्या ही परमोत्कृष्ट देवता है। राजा महाराजा भी विद्या का जो सन्मान करते हैं वह धन का कदापि नहीं करते। विद्या के बिना मनुष्य पशु के समान है।

Knowledge is, no doubt, an additional beauty of man. It is a very hidden treasure. Knowledge brings enjoyment, fame, and happiness. Knowledge is the teacher of teachers. Knowledge substitutes a relative in foreign travels. Knowledge is the supreme god. Kings reverntly worship Knowledge and not wealth. One devoid of knowledge is a brute.

---

1. This stanza is same as stanza 3 in Bhavabhūti's गुणरत्नम्। It also stands in the Sūktāvali (सूक्तावलिः 14)

Cf.—(*a*) Without education man is but a splendid slave, a reasoning slave, vacillating between the dignity of an intelligence derived from God and degradation of passions participated in by brutes." (S. Coleridge).

(*b*) विहिताविहितविचारशून्यबुद्धेः श्रुतिविषयैर्विधिभिर्बहिष्कृतस्य।
उदरभरणमात्रकेवलेच्छोः पुरुषपशोश्च पशोश्च को विशेषः।।

क्षान्तिश्चेत् कवचेन किं किमरिभिः
क्रोधोऽस्ति चेद्देहिनां, ज्ञातिश्चेदनलेन
किं यदि सुहृद्दिव्यौषधैः किं फलम्।
किं सर्पैर्यदि दुर्जनाः किमु धनैर्विद्याऽ-
नवद्या यदि, व्रीडा चेत्किमु भूषणैः
सुकविता यद्यस्ति राज्येन किम्।। 21।।

क्षमा रहने पर कवच का, क्रोध् करने पर शत्रुओं का, स्वजातीय जन विद्यमान होने पर अग्नि का, सुहृद्वर्ग के रहने पर दिव्यौषधियों का, दुर्जनों के रहने पर सर्पों का, निर्दोष विद्या रहने पर धन का, लज्जा रहने पर आभूषणों का और सुंदर कविता शक्ति रहने पर मनुष्यों को राज्य का कोई प्रयोजन नहीं रहता।

भावार्थ—मनुष्यों को रक्षा के हेतु क्षमा, कलह के हेतु क्रोध, संताप के हेतु स्वजन, आरोग्यादि सुख के हेतु सुहृद्‌गण, कष्ट के हेतु दुर्जन, धन के हेतु विद्या, आभूषणों के हेतु लज्जा, और राज्य वैभव के हेतु सुंदर कविता शक्ति सर्वथा काफी समझना चाहिए।

The absence of armour, enemies, fire, good medicines, snakes, wealth, ornaments and kingdom are more than compensated respectively by one's forbearance, anger, relatives, friends, evil persons, profound (*lit.*unblamable) learning, modesty, and a high class poetical genius.

---

1. This stanza is same as stanza 4 in *Pañcaratna* (पंचरत्न).

2. The above stanza furnishes us with a very striking instance of Bhartṛhari's pithy and epigrammatic style. Every sentence is so laconic that it is sometimes not easy to know the sense at first sight.

दाक्षिण्यं स्वजने दया परजने शाठ्यंसदादुर्जने
प्रीतिःसाधुजने नयोनृपजनेविद्वज्जने चार्ज्जवम्।
शौर्यं शत्रुजने क्षमा गुरुजने नारीजने धूर्तता
ये चैवंपुरुषाः कलासुकुशलास्तेष्वेव लोकस्थितिः। 22।

लोकाचार की मर्यादा और स्थिति उन ही कलाकुशल नर रत्नों पर निर्भर है कि जो स्वजन के साथ उदारता, परजन में दयाभाव, दुर्जन के साथ कुटिलता, सत्पुरुष से प्रीति, राज सभा में नीति (अथवा राजा के आगे विनय), विद्वान् के आगे नम्रता, शुत्र के साथ पराक्रम, गुरुजन के आगे सहनशीलता, और स्त्री समाज में धूर्ततादि उत्तमोत्तम गुणों का समयानुसार बर्ताव कर सकते हैं।

Those persons who are well versed in showing politeness towards their relations, compassion towards strangers, wickedness towards the bad, love for the good, obedience to kings, humlity before the learned, valour against enemies, patient hearing and obedience to their elders, and shrewdness amongt women are no doubt the real cardinal points (main stops) on which the existence of the world mainly depends.

Purport. The world cannot go on as it does without the presence of such person of versatile capabilities.

---

1. Quoted anonymously in the *Subhāṣitāvali* (सुभाषितावलि) (No. 2946. B.S.S. XXXI.).

Cf. "माधुर्यं प्रमदाजनेषु ललितं दाक्षिण्यमार्ये जने शौर्य शत्रुषु नम्रता गुरुजने धर्मिष्ठता साधुषु।
मर्मज्ञेष्वनुवर्तनं बहुविधं मानं जने पण्डिते शाठ्यं पापिजने नरस्य कथिताः पर्यन्तमष्टौ गुणाः।। (बानर्यष्टके).

जाड्यं धियो हरति सिञ्चति वाचि सत्यं
मानोन्नतिं दिशति पापमपाकरोति।
चेतः प्रसादयति दिक्षु तनोति कीर्तिं
सत्सङ्गतिः कथय किं न करोति पुंसाम्।। 23।।

जिस सत्संगति के प्रताप से बुद्धि की जड़ता नष्ट हो जाती है, सत्य भाषण में अभिरुचि होती है, सन्मान की वृद्धि होती है, पाप दूर होता है, चित्त प्रसन्न होता है, और दश-दिशाओं में सुकीर्ति फैलती है; वह सत्संग मनुष्यों के लिए जो बात न कर सके वैसी संसार में कोई भी वस्तु नहीं है।

Good company is sure to drive out darkness from ignorant minds, water their words with truth, point them out the precise path of advancement, root out sinful propensities, enlighten their hearts, and winnow the fragrance of their fame throughout the four corners of the universe. There is nothing indeed which cannot be achieved by our communion with virtuous sages.

---

2. *Cf.*—(*a*) बुद्धिं वर्द्धयति श्रियं वितनुते वैदग्ध्यमामुञ्चति श्रेयः
पल्लवयत्यघानि दलयत्युन्मीलयत्युन्नतिम्।
विज्ञानं परिशोधयत्युपचिनोत्युच्चैः कलाकौशलं किं किं नारभते हरेरिव कथाऽजयं सतां संगतम्।। (सुभाषितरत्नभाण्डागारे 128 38)

(*b*) Value above all things the society of the wise.

(*c*) दूरीकरोति कुमतिं विमलीकरोति चेतश्चिरंतनमघं चुलुकीकिरोति।
भूतेषु किंच करुणां बहुलीकरोति सङ्गः सतां किमु न मङ्गलमातनोति।।"
(रसगङ्गाधरे).

(*d*) हरति कुमतिं भिन्ते मोहं करोति विवेकिनां वितरति रतिं सूते नीतिं तनोति विनीतमाम्।
प्रथयति यशो धत्ते धर्मं व्यपोहति दुर्गतिं जनयति नृणां किं नाभीष्टं गुणोत्तमसंगमः।।66।। (सोमप्रभाचार्यस्य सूक्तिमुक्तावली)

जयन्ति ते सुकृतिनो रससिद्धाः कवीश्वराः।
नास्ति येषां यशःकाये जरामरणजं भयम्॥ 24॥

सरस कविता के कहने वाले कवीश्वर संसार में सर्वोत्कृष्ट रहते हैं क्योंकि इनका सुयशमय शरीर जरामरणादि दुःख से बिल्कुल स्वतंत्र और निर्भय है।

यहाँ पर "रससिद्धाः" का प्रयोग दो अर्थों में किया गया है। (1) एक तो शृंगारादि नवरसों में प्रवीण और (2) दूसरे पारदादि सिद्धरसों के सेवन करने वाले।

The great poets who are perfect masters of the *Rasas* (*i.e.* the poetical styles) are indeed worthy of universal respect and glory; because the wonderfully composed state of their bodies being made up of pure immortal fame of quite free from the fearful influences of age and death.

---

1. *Cf.* — (*a*) उपेयुषामपि दिवं सन्निबन्धविधायिनाम्।
आस्त एव निरातङ्कं कान्तं काव्यमयं वपुः॥
(ध्वन्यालोकटीकायाम्)

(*b*) विशुद्धललिताकारा गुणालङ्कारशालिनी।
सरसा भारती यस्य स एवैकः प्रतिष्ठितः॥
(वेङ्कटनाथस्य सुभाषितनीवी)

(*c*) काव्यसंबन्धिनी कीर्तिः स्थायिनी निरपायिनी॥
(शार्ङ्गधरपद्धतिः । 150)

The verse is quoted under भर्तृहरि in the Śārṅgadharapaddhati (शार्ङ्गधरपद्धति) at No. 166. (Bombay Sanskrit Series).

सूनुः सच्चरितः सती प्रियतमा स्वामी प्रसादोन्मुखः
स्निग्धं मित्रमवञ्चकः परिजनो निष्क्लेशलेशं मनः।
आकारो रुचिरः स्थिरश्च विभवो विद्यावदातं मुखं
तुष्टे विष्टपहारिणीष्टदहरौ सम्प्राप्यते देहिना।। 25।।

सदाचारी पुत्र, सती स्त्री, प्रसादोन्मुख (प्रसन्नचित्त और हितैषी) स्वामी, वात्सल्यादि गुणयुक्त मित्र मण्डल, निष्कपट सेवक, क्लेशरहित मन, सुंदर आकार, स्थिर लक्ष्मी, और विद्या से सुशोभित मुख से सब उत्तमोत्तम सामग्री उस मनोवांछित फल के देने वाले श्रीजगदाधार विष्णु भगवान् के अनुग्रह के बिना किसी मनुष्य को भी प्राप्त नहीं हो सकती।

A son with good moral conduct, a chaste wife, a loving master, an affectionate friend, honest relatives, a mind free from all anxieties and cares, a handsome appearance, lasting (steady) prosperity, and an intelligent face can only be enjoyed by the special favour of Hari, the supporter of the universe and the granter of all desires.

---

1. *Cf.*—पुत्त पवित्त बहुत्त धणा भत्ति कुटुम्बिणि सुद्धमणा।
हक्कतरासइ भिच्चगणा कोकर वव्वर सग्गमणा।। 96।।
(प्राकृतपिङ्गलसूत्रे 2 परिच्छेदे)

A faithful and loving wife is indeed one of the greatest blessings of God.

Cf.— पतिव्रता पतिगतिः पतिप्रियहिते रसा।
यस्य स्यात्तादृशी भार्या धन्यः स पुरुषो भुवि।। (महाभारते)

प्राणाघातान्निवृत्तिः परधनहरणे संयमः सत्य-
वाक्यं, काले शक्त्या प्रदानं युवतिजनक-
थामूकभावः परेषाम्। तृष्णास्त्रोतोविभङ्गो
गुरुषु च विनयः सर्वभूतानुकम्पा, सामान्यः
सर्वशास्त्रेष्वनुपहतविधिः श्रेयसामेष पन्थाः।।26।।

प्राणी मात्र की हिंसा करने से निवृत्त रहना, दूसरों का धन हरण करने की इच्छा न रखना, सत्य भाषण करना, समयानुसार श्रद्धापूर्वक दान देना, पराई स्त्री को चर्चा करने और सुनने से दूर रहना, तृष्णा रूपी नदी के प्रवाह को रोकना, गुरुजनों के आगे विनय धारण करना और सब जीवों पर दया करना सर्व साधारण के लिए सर्वशास्त्रसंमत कल्याण का मार्ग है।

To avoid giving injury to living beings, to keep aloof from stealing the wealth of others, to tell the truth, to exercise due cahrity in time, to keep quiet on the gossips of others' wives, to cofine the desire of gain within proper limits, to behave with meekness before the elders, and to show mercy and kindness to all creatures are unanimously enjoined by the Scriptures to be the one unerring road leading to all sorts of good and happiness.

---

1. *Cf.*— सत्यं वाचि दृशि प्रसादपरता सर्वाशयाश्ववासिनी पाणौ
दानविमुक्तिरात्मजननक्लेशान्तचिन्ता मतौ।
संसक्ता हृदये दयैव दयिता काये परार्थोद्यमो यस्यैकः पुरुषः स जीवति भवे
भ्राम्यन्ति जीवाः परे।। (क्षेमेन्द्रस्य चतुर्वर्गसंग्रहे)

For "काले शक्त्या प्रदानम्" *Cf.*—"Liberality consists less in giving much than in giving at the right moment." (La Bruyere)

प्रारभ्यते न खलु विघ्नभयेन नीचैः
प्रारभ्य विघ्नविहता विरमन्ति मध्याः।
विघ्नैः पुनःपुनरपि प्रतिहन्यमानाः
प्रारभ्य चोत्तमजना न परित्यजन्ति।। 27।।

संसार में (1) नीच, (2) मध्यम और (3) उत्तम ये तीन प्रकार के मनुष्य होते हैं, जिनमें से (1) नीच मनुष्य तो आगन्तुक विघ्नों के भयमात्र से किसी कार्य का प्रारम्भ नहीं करते, और (2) मध्यम प्रकार के मनुष्य यद्यपि काम का समारम्भ तो कर देते हैं, किन्तु विक्षेप होने से बीच में अधूरा छोड़ देते हैं, परन्तु (3) उत्तम मनुष्य ऐसे धैर्यवान् होते हैं कि बारंबार विघ्न सहन करने पर भी अपने हाथ में लिए हुए काम को सम्पूर्ण किये बिना कदापि नहीं छोड़ते।

Bad men do not even begin a thing through fear of future obstacles; the mediocre after commencing it, give it up when they are confronted with real present evils; but good men never leave unfinished what they have once begun, notwithstanding the fact of their being repeatedly baffled and opposed.

---

1. Quoted anonymously in *Subhāṣitāvali* (सुभाषितावलि) (No. 544, B.S.S. No. XXXI). The stanza is also found in the *Pañcatantra* (पंचतंत्रम् । 3।177), the *Daśarūpāvaloka* (दशरूपावलोकः), and the *Mudrārākṣasa* (मुद्राराक्षसम् St. 17. Act. II.).

2. In the दशरूपावलोक it is given under भर्तृहरि.

3. For the point of the stanza, *Cf.*—

(*a*) आरब्धे हि सुदुष्करेऽपि महतां मध्ये विरामः कुतः?
(कथासरित्सागरे शशाङ्कवतीलम्बके 24 तरङ्गे 61 श्लोके).

(*b*) विहडन्तं पि समत्था ववसाअ पुरिसदुग्गमं णेन्ति वहम्।। 14।।"
(प्रवरसेनस्य सेतुबन्ध 3 आश्वासके).

असन्तो नाभ्यर्थ्याः सुहृदपि न याच्यः कृशधनः
प्रिया न्याय्या वृत्तिर्मलिनमसुभङ्गेऽप्यसुकरम् ।।
विपद्युच्चै स्थेयं पदमनुविधेयं च महतां
सतां केनोद्दिष्टं विषममसिधाराव्रतमिदम् ।। 28 ।।

दुष्टजनों की याचना कदापि न करना, तथा निर्धन अथवा अल्प धन वाले मित्र से किसी प्रकार की आर्थिक सहायता न चाहना, न्यायपूर्वक जीवनोपाय करने में अभिरुचि रखना, तथा प्राणनाश होने का भय रहते भी दुष्ट कर्म में कदापि प्रवृत्त न होना, विपत्ति काल में धैर्य रखना और गुरुजनों के मार्ग में गमन करना इस प्रकार के कठिन असिधारा व्रत को धारण करने के निमित्त सत्पुरुषों को यद्यपि किसी ने भी उपदेश नहीं दिया है, तथापि साधुजन स्वभाव ही से इसका अवलंबन किया करते हैं।

It is quite natural with good people to live upon their just earnings, never to do a sinful act not even at the time when there is a probability of losing their own lives, never to ask anything either from the evil or even from a poor friend short of money, to behave boldly and honourably in days of adversity, and always to follow the footsteps of the wise. No one has ever dictated this hard *Asidhārā* vow to the good, but its keeping is quite natural to them.

---

1. Quoted under *Jayāditya* (जयादित्य) in the *Subhāṣitāvali* (सुभाषितावलि) (No. 280. B.S.S. No. XXXI).

2. *Asidhārā* (असिधारा) literally means 'edge of a sword.' For further explanations see our Note.

क्षुत्क्षामोऽपि जराकृशोऽपि शिथिलप्रायोऽतिकष्टां दशामापन्नोऽपि विपन्नदीधितिरपि प्राणेषु नश्यत्स्वपि। मत्तेभेन्द्रविभिन्नकुम्भकवलग्रासैकबद्धस्पृहः किं जीर्णं तृणमत्ति मानमहतामग्रेसरः केसरी।। 29।।

जो मृगराज (सिंह) मानियों में अग्रगण्य है जो सदैव मदोन्मत्त गजराज का कुंभ स्थल भेदन करके अपना आहार संपादन करने की इच्छा करता रहता है वह चाहे कितना ही क्षुधातुर, जरावस्था से दुर्बल, बलहीन, अत्यंत दुःखी और तेजहीन क्यों न हो जाय, परन्तु प्राण संकट उपस्थित होने पर भी सूखा घास खाने को कदापि उद्यत नहीं हो सकता।

भावार्थ—अत्यंत दुःखित होने पर भी मानी जन अपने महत्व का परित्याग करके नीच कर्म करने को कभी उद्यत नहीं हो सकते।

Can the lion the foremost of the self-respecting and noble beings, who is always anxious to get a mouthful of the superb temples of wild elephants in ruts so much degrade himself as even to condescend to feed upon dry grass although he is lean and weak by hunger as well as by age, almost powerless, in a very painful condition, devoid of splendour and energy, and apt to lose his very life failing to get a morsel of food.

PURPORT. A man of self-reliance and respect can never degrade himself to do a mean and disgraceful act notwithstanding his too severely straitened circumstances.

Quoted under *Ratisena* (रतिसेन) in the *Subhāṣitāvali* (सुभाषितावलि) (No. 614, B.S.S. No. XXXI), under भर्तृहरि in the *Śārṅgadharapaddhati* at No. 907 (शार्ङ्गधरपद्धति 907), and anonymously in the *Kāvyānuśāsana of Vāgbhaṭṭa* (वाग्भट्टस्य काव्यानुशासनम्)।

Cf. —(*a*) मत्तेभकुम्भदलनाकुललोवल्गदन्तः क्वणत्करजवज्रशिखाभिघातः।
किं केसरी जगति मानभिधिस्तृणेन प्राणात्ययेऽपि कुरुते स्वशरीरयात्राम्।।
(सुभाषितवलिः)

(*b*) तनु तृणमुपभुङ्क्ते न क्षुधार्त्तोऽपि सिंहः पिबति रुधिरमुष्णं प्रायशः कुंजराणाम् (तत्रैव No. 266)

(*c*) व्याघ्र क्षुधितोऽपि भक्षयेन्न तृणम्।। 15।।
(दक्षिणामूर्तिविरचितलोकोक्तिमुक्तावलिः)

स्वल्पं स्नायुवसावशेषमलिनं निर्मांसमप्यस्थि
गोः श्वा लब्ध्वा परितोषमेति न तु तत्तस्य क्षुधाशान्तये।
सिंहो जम्बुकमङ्कमागतमपि त्यक्त्वा निहन्ति द्विपं सर्व कृच्छ्रग-
तोऽपि वाञ्छति जनः सत्त्वानुरूपं फलम्।। 30।।

थोड़ी-सी बची हुई वसा (चर्बी) और स्नायु से मलिन और मांस-रहित गवादि पशु के छोटे से हाड के टुकड़े की प्राप्ति होने पर-कि जिससे उसकी क्षुधा सर्वथा निवृत्त नहीं हो सकती।-कुत्ते को बहुत संतोष हो जाता है, परन्तु मृगराज सिंह को देखिये कि वह निजांक में आये हुए जंबुक को छोड़कर भी गजराज पर प्रहार करने को दौड़ता है। इससे प्रत्यक्ष है कि संकट में पड़े हुए प्राणियों के कार्य भी उनके बल और सामर्थ्य अनुसार ही हुआ करते हैं।

The dog is easily satisfied by securing a small piece of fleshless bone superficially dirty on account of a little fat and muscles, though it is quite insufficient to appease its hunger; but the lion is sure to throw off the body of a jackal already lying in his arms, so that he may prey upon an elephant. Notwithstanding his straitened circumstances every one is anxious to do what is becoming to his rank and position in life.

---

1. This stanza is found in the हितोपदेश (II 36), and the Panchatantra; and the author of *Subhāṣitāvali* (सुभाषितावलि) has also given it under the latter work, at No. 1025.

Cf.—(*a*) आत्मानुरूपं हि, फलं सर्वोऽपि वाञ्छति।
श्वा तुष्यत्यस्थिमात्रेण केसरी धावति द्विपे।। 36।।
(कथासरित्सागरे शक्तियशोलम्बके 4 तरङ्गे)

(*b*) उत्तुङ्गमत्तमाङ्गमस्तकंन्यस्तलोचनः।
आसन्नेऽपि च सारङ्गे न वाञ्छां कुरुते हरिः।।
(सुभाषितरत्नाभण्डागारे 382/9)

लांगूलचालनमधश्चरणावपातं
भूमौ निपत्य वदनोदरदर्शनं च।
श्वा पिण्डदस्य कुरुते गजपुङ्गवस्तु
धिरं विलोकयति चाटुशतैश्च भुङ्क्ते।। 31।।

कुत्ते को देखिए कि अपने स्वामी के समक्ष किस प्रकार पूँछ हिलाकर, पंजा बढ़ाकर और भूमि पर लोट कर अपने क्षुधातुर पेट के दर्शन कराता है, परन्तु उत्तम गजराज अपना आहार समर्पण करने वाले के सम्मुख किसी प्रकार की दीनता प्रगट न करके केवल धीरजता से ही नहीं देखता किन्तु खाने के लिए भी बहुत सी मनवारों (चाटुभाषण) के साथ उद्यत होता है।

A dog is given to wag his tail, fall at the feet of his master, and lie down flast on the ground to show his mouth and stomach to the man who feeds him; but such is not the case with the noble elephants who looks with a calm and steady glance upon the face of his master, and then condesceds to take his food after a series of soothing and flattering entreaties.

---

1. The stanza is also found in the *Pañcatantra* (पंचतंत्र) and the *Hitopadeśa* (हितोपदेश 2 137). It is quoted anonymously in the *Subhāṣitāvali* (सुभाषितावलि)(No. 641. B.S.S. No. XXXI.).

परिवर्तिनि संसारे मृतः
को वा न जायते।
स जातो येन जातेन
याति वंशः समुन्नतिम्।। 32।।

इस भ्रमणशील अस्थिर संसार में अगणित जीवों का जन्म और मरण सदा काल ही होता रहता है, परन्तु यथार्थ में जन्म लेना उस ही मनुष्य का सफल है कि जिसके जन्म लेने से उसके वंश के गौरव की वृद्धि हो।

Who is not born and dead on the face of this revolving planet? He alone is really said to be born by whose birth his family has risen to some great distinction.

---

1. This stanza which stands in the *Pañctantra* (पंचतंत्रम् 1 127) and the *Hitopadeśa* (हितोपदेशः। प्र0 13) is quoted anonymously in the *Subhāṣitāvali* (सुभाषितावलि) (No. 550. B.S.S. No. XXXI.).

Cf. (*a*) स पुमानर्थवज्जन्मा यस्य नाम्नि पुरः स्थिते।
नान्यामङ्गुलिमभ्येति संख्यायामुद्यताङ्गुलिः।।
(भारवेः किरातार्जुनीये XI. 62).

(*b*) किं तेन जातु जातेन मातुर्यौवनहारिणा।
आरोहति न यः स्वस्य वंशस्याग्रे ध्वजो यथा।
(पंचतंत्र 1 126)

2. The word परिवर्तिनि=is apt to change, inconstant, or ever-rolling.

कुसुमस्तबकस्येव द्वयी वृत्तिर्मनस्विनः।
मूर्ध्नि सा सर्व लोकस्य शीर्यते वन एव वा।। 33।

पुष्प के गुच्छे की तरह विचारशील मनुष्यों की स्थिति भी इस संसार में केवल दो ही प्रकार की होती है अर्थात् या तो वे सर्वसाधारण के शिरोमणि ही बनते हैं अथवा वन के वन ही में अपना जीवन व्यतीत कर देते हैं।

Like a bunch of flowers, there are only two alternatives or modes of existence open for noble souls: (1) either to be at the head of all men, or (2) to pine (fade) away in forest.

---

1. This stanza is quoted twice by Ballabhadeva in his *Subhāṣitāvali* (सुभाषितावलि) at No. 509 of which it is given anonymously, and at No. 201 it is put under the name of Ravigupta (रविगुप्त). In the *Sārṅgadharapaddhati* (शार्ङ्गधरपद्धति। 264) it is ascribed to *Bhartṛhari* (भर्तृहरि). It also stands in the *Hitopadeśa* (हितोपदेश: 1।101).

Cf. —(*a*) पुंसामुन्मत्तचित्तानां द्वयमेव सुखावहम्।
सर्वसंगनिवृत्तिर्वा विभूतिर्वा सविस्तरा।।

(सूक्तावलिः)

(*b*) होत मनस्वी लोक में, जनसमाज सिरताज।
अथवा वन में मर रहें, जग से खल रखत न काज।

(रसिक कवि)

सन्त्यन्येऽपि बृहस्पतिप्रभृतयः संभाविताः पञ्च-
षास्तान्प्रत्येष विशेषविक्रमरुची राहुर्न वैरायते।।
द्वावेव ग्रसते दिनेश्वरनिशाप्राणेश्वरौ भासुरौ भ्रातः
पर्वणि पश्य दानवपतिः शीर्षावशेषाकृतिः।। 34।।

यद्यपि सौर्यमण्डल में बृहस्पति को आदि लेकर और भी बड़े-बड़े पाँच नक्षत्र विद्यमान हैं; तथापि असामान्य पराक्रम में अभिरुचि रखने वाला दानवपति राहु इनके साथ अपना वैरभाव कदापि प्रगट नहीं करता, किन्तु अवसर आने पर प्रत्येक पर्व-तिथि में अर्थात् अमावास्या और पूर्णिमा के दिन दिवाकर (सूर्य) और निशानाथ (चंद्रमा) का ही ग्रास करने को उद्यत होता है।

Though there are some five or six well-known big planets like Jupiter, and others in the heavens, yet *Rāhu,* the headless demon, is never inclined to show the least cause of hatred to any of them; but being anxious to prove the superiority of his unusual valour he always tries to eat up or eclipse his real enemies the Sun (the lord of day) and the Moon (the beloved spouse of night).

PURPORT. The high-souleed are never inclued to wreak their vengeance upon others but their real enemies whether big or small.

Cf. — नैकमप्यरिमनन्तपत्तयोऽप्याहवेऽतगणयन्ति धीधनाः।
सत्सु तारकगणेषु राहुणा ग्रस्यते किमु न तारकाधिपः।। 22।।
(अमरचंद्रसूरेर्बालभारते उद्योगपर्वणि 2 सर्गे)

वहति भुवनश्रेणीं शेषः फलणाफलकस्थितां
कमठपतिना मध्ये पृष्ठं सदा स विधार्यते।
तमपि कुरुते क्रोडाधीनं पयोधिरनादरादहह
महतां निःसीमानश्चरित्रविभूतयः।। 35।।

चौदह भुवन को शेषनाग अपने फण पर धारण करता है और कच्छपराज ने अपनी पृष्ठ पर शेष नाग को धारण कर रखा है; परन्तु समुद्र ने इस कच्छपराज को भी एक हल्के से पदार्थ की तरह अपने अंक पर ले रखा है। इससे स्पष्ट है कि महापुरुषों के चरित्र का कोई पारावार नहीं हो सकता।

Śeṣanāga though he supports the entire universe upon the flat of surface of his thousand heads is always borne on back by the great tortoise; but he in his turn is easily sustained (as if it were the lightest and tiniest object in the world) on its lap by the storehouse of waters (*i.e.*, ocean). Oh, how infinite is the magnanimous conduct of noble souls!

---

1. The stanza is also found in the *Bhōjaprabandha* (भोजप्रबन्ध).

Cf.—विष्णुर्बिभर्ति भगवानखिलां धरित्रीं
तं पन्नगस्तमपि तत्सहितः पयोधिः।
कुम्भोद्भवस्तमपिबत्खलु हेलयैव सत्यं
न कश्चिदवधिर्महतां महिम्नः।।

(सुभाषितावलिः 993)

2. Mark that the beauty of each succeeding line of the stanza overshadows that of its predecessor, reaching the culminating point in the last foot.

वरं पक्षच्छेदः समदमघवन्मुक्तकुलिश-
प्रहारैरुद्गच्छद्बहलदहनोग्दारगुरुभिः ।
तुषाराद्रेः सूनोरहह पितरि क्लेशविवशे
न चासौ सम्पातः पयसि पयसां पत्युरुचितः ।। 36 ।।

हिमालय के पुत्र मैनाक के लिए देवराज इंद्र के वज्र प्रहारों से निकलती हुई जाल्वल्यमान ज्वाल मालाओं से दुःखित अपने पिता को महासंकट में छोड़कर प्राण रक्षा के निमित्त समुद्र में जाकर पतन करने की अपेक्षा विपत्ति काल में पिता के समीप रहकर निज पक्षों का छेदन कराना ही सर्वथा उचित था।

भावार्थ—पिता को कष्टावस्था में छोड़कर निज प्राण रक्षा के निमित्त अन्य स्थान में गमन करना मानी जनों के लिए सर्वथा निंदनीय है।

For the son of the Himālaya when his father was subjected to the severities of Indra's anger, the cutting of his own sides (wings) by the heavy strokes of proud Indra's thunderbolt giving out fire at every attack would have been much preferable to the mean effort of saving his person by leaving alone his venerable father in the midst of the sad plight and hastening to drown himself into the waters of the deep ocean.

---

1. *Cf.*—(*a*) क्रौंच विमुच्य पुत्रं च पितरं च हिमालयम्।
प्रविश्य जलधिं पक्षौ रक्षताऽनेन किं कृतम्।।
(मुरारिकृतानर्घराघवे)

(*b*) स्वस्थानादपि विचलति मज्जति जलधौ च नीचमपि भजते।
निजपक्षरक्षणमनाः सुजनो मैनाकशैल इव।। 682।।"
(गोवर्धनकृतार्यासप्तशती)

यदचेतनोऽपि पादैः स्पृष्टः प्रज्वलति सवितु-रिनकान्तः। तत्तेजस्वी पुरुषः परकृतविकृतिं कथं सहते।। 37।।

जब चेतनारहित सूर्यकांतमणि भी सूर्य किरणों का स्पर्श करते ही प्रज्वलित हो जाता है तो चैतन्ययुक्त तेजस्वी पुरुष दूसरों का अनादर कैसे सहन कर सकते हैं।

When it is possible even for a senseless and inanimate object like a sunstone to give out sparks of fire on his being touched by the rays (*lit.* feet) of the Sun, how can highsouled (irritable) person put up with the insulting encroachments of others?

---

1. *Cf.* — (*a*) रविमणिरपि निश्चेष्टः पादैस्तिग्मद्युतेर्भनाक् स्पृष्टः।
ज्वलतितरामिति को वा मन्युं सोढुं क्षमो मानी।।
(सुभाषितावलिः)

(*b*) न तेजस्तेजस्वी प्रसृतमपरेषां प्रसहते
स तस्य स्वो भावः प्रकृतिनियतत्वादकृतकः।
मयूखैरश्रान्तं तपति यदि देवो दिनकरः
किमाग्नेयग्रावा निकृत इव तेजांसि वमति।।
(उत्तररामचरिते)

2. The net point of the stanza seems to be this : a strong man of real worth cannot be expected to put up calmly with the insult of others.

सिंहः शिशुरपि निपतति मदम-
लिनकपोलभित्तिषु गजेषु।
प्रकृतिरियं सत्त्ववतां
न खलु वयस्तेजसो हेतुः ।। 38 ।।

सिंह का बच्चा छोटा होने पर भी उत्तम गजराज के मदांकित गण्ड स्थल पर प्रहार करता है। इससे जानना चाहिए कि तेजस्वी पुरुषों की शूरवीरता स्वाभाविक है। सच तो यह है कि अवस्था को निश्चयात्मकरूप में तेजस्विता का हेतु कदापि नहीं कह सकते।

The whelp of a lion though quite young is sure to fall upon a herd of ferocious elephants whose temples are soiled with secretious rut. Such action is quite natural with noble natures. That valour (तेज) is entirely independent of age is beyond controversy.

---

1. Quoted under *Vajrāyuddha* (वज्रायुद्ध) in the *Subhāṣitāvali* (सुभाषितावलि) (No. 593. B.S.S. XXXI.), and anonymously in the *Śārṅgadharapaddhati* (शार्ङ्गधरपद्धति) at No. 283.

Cf.— (*a*) शमयति गजानन्यान्गन्धद्विपः कलभोऽपि
सन्प्रभवतितरां वेगोदग्रं भुजंगशिशोर्विषम्।
भुवमधिगतिर्बालावस्थ्येऽप्यलं परिरक्षितुं
न खलु वयसा जात्यैवायं स्वकार्यसहो गुणः।। 18।।
(विक्रमोर्व्वशीये पंचमाङ्के)

(*b*) बालस्यापि रवेः पादाः पतन्त्युपरि भूभृताम्।
तेजसा सह जातानां वयः कुत्रोपयुज्यते।। (पंचतंत्रम्1 ।328)

(*c*) अणुरपि मणिः प्राणत्राणक्षमो विषभक्षिणां
शिशुरपि रुषा सिंहीसूनुः समाह्वयते गजान्।
तनुरपि तरुस्कन्धोद्भूतो दहत्यनलो वनं
प्रकृतिमहतां जात्यं तेजो न मूर्तिमपेक्षते।। (सुभाषितावलि ।325)

जातिर्यातु रसातलं गुणगणस्तस्याप्यधो गच्छ-
ताच्छीलं शैलतटात्पतत्वभिजनः संदह्यतां वह्निना।
शौर्ये वैरिणि वज्रमाशु निपतत्वर्थोऽस्तु नः केवलं
येनैकेन विना गुणास्तृणलवप्रायाः समस्ता इमे।।39।।

यदि जाति-पांति रसातल में चली जाय, नाना भाँति के गुण समूह उससे भी आगे प्रस्थान कर जायें, सुशीलता पर्वत शिखर से गिर जाय, उच्चकुल भी अग्नि से भले ही जल जाय, और इस वैरि शूर- वीरता पर भी शीघ्र ही वज्रपात हो जाय, तो कुछ चिंता नहीं, परंतु द्रव्य संचय में किसी प्रकार की बाधा नहीं होनी चाहिए, क्योंकि एक द्रव्य के होने से सारे गुणगण तृणकण के समान हो जाते हैं।

Let caste go down to the down-most depth of the nether world, and deeper still may sink the good qualities belonging to us; let morality be hurled down from a mountain, and respetability of birth be consumed into flames; let the thunderbolt of heaven soon fall upon the enemical physical valour; but let the gracious God leave us alone with our money by the single exception of which all these possessions are as worthless as straw.

---

1. Ballabhadeva in his *Subhāṣitāvali* (सुभाषितावलि) quotes it at No. 3037 under *Māgha* (माघ), but the śloka is not to be found in the *Śiśupālavadha* (शिशुपालवधं).

2. It is ascribed to भर्तृहरि in the *Sārṅgadharapaddhati* (शार्ङ्गधरपद्धतिः 1332).

Cf.—(*a*) धिगस्त्वेतां विद्यां धिगपि कवितां धिक्सुजनतां
वयो रूपं धिग्धिग्धिगपि च यशो निर्धनवतः।
असौ जीयादेकः सकलगुणहीनोऽपि धनवान्बहि-
र्यस्य द्वारे तृणलवनिभाः सन्ति गुणिनः।।
(सुभाषितरत्नभाण्डागारे 96।15).

(*b*) पण्डिताः कवयः शूराः कलावन्तस्तपस्विनः।
वैद्यस्येव सवित्तस्य वीक्षन्ते मुखमातुराः।।
(क्षेमेन्द्रस्य दर्पदलने द्वितीयविचारे 130)

तानीन्द्रियाणि सकलानि तदेव
कर्म सा बुद्धिरप्रतिहता वचनं तदेव।
अर्थोष्मणा विरहितः पुरुषः स एव
त्वन्यः क्षणेन भवतीति विचित्रमेतत्।। 40।।

यद्यपि ये सब इन्द्रिय ज्यों की त्यों बनी रहती हैं और कर्म, बुद्धि और वचन शक्ति भी मनुष्य की वैसी की वैसी ही विद्यमान रहती है, परन्तु एक द्रव्य के नष्ट हो जाने से मनुष्य क्षण भर में कुछ और का और ही हो जाता है यह निस्संदेह बहुत ही विचित्र है।

It is really wonderful that a man deprived of wealth (*lit.* the warmth of wealth) instantly becomes quite a different and changed being, notwithstanding his being still the master of his former senses, actions, and the same bright intellect and power of speech!

---

1. This stanza is also found in the *Bhojaprabandha* (भोजप्रबन्ध), the Pañcatantra (पंचतंत्रम् 5 I26) and the *Hitopadeśa* (हितोपदेशः 1 I97).

Cf.— जीवन्नप्यक्रियो निस्वः शवोऽप्यर्थेन सक्रियः।
दारिद्र्यं मरणं लोके धनमायुः शरीरिणाम्।। 26।।
(क्षेमेन्द्रविहितदर्पलनस्य द्वितीयविचारे)

2. It needs no explanation to prove that money is something like life to man. Instances are not wanting in the world to show that a rich man losing riches almost loses his life. Ed.

यस्यास्ति वित्तं स नरः कुलीनः
स पण्डितः स श्रुतवान्गुणज्ञः।
स एव वक्ता स च दर्शनीयः
सर्वे गुणाः काञ्चनमाश्रयन्ति।। 41।।

जिस मनुष्य के पास द्रव्य है वह निश्चय करके कुलीन, पण्डित, शास्त्रवेत्ता, गुणज्ञ, वक्ता और सुंदर कहा जाता है; इससे प्रत्यक्ष है कि सारे गुण द्रव्य ही के आश्रित हैं।

One who is wealthy is also considered as: (1) well born, (2) learned (3) a man of information, (4) a good judge of qualifications, (5) and able speaker, and (6) a handsome person. Everything good is invariably dependent upon gold (*i.e.*, money).

---

1. The śloka is also found in the *Pañctantra* (पंचतंत्रम्).

It is attributed to भर्तृहरि in the शार्ङ्गधरपद्धति at No. 333.

Cf.—(*a*) "Everything, vitue, glory, honour, things human and divine, all are slaves to riches." (Horace).

(*b*) यस्यार्थास्तस्य मित्राणि यस्यार्थास्तस्य बान्धवाः।
यस्यार्थाः स पुमांल्लोके यस्यार्थाः स च पण्डितः।।
(महाभारते शान्तिपर्वणि 8।19).

(*c*) The God of this world is riches, etc.
(M. Luther).

(*d*) यथा विहंगास्तरुमाश्रयन्ति नद्यो यथा सागरमाश्रयन्ति।
यथा तरुण्यः श्रियमाश्रयन्ति सर्वे गुणाः कांचनमाश्रयन्ति।।
(समायेचितपद्यमालिका)

दौर्मंत्र्यान्नृपतिर्विनश्यति यतिः सङ्गात्सुतो लालना-
द्विपोऽनध्ययनात्कुलं कुतनयाच्छीलं खलोपासनात्।
ह्रीर्मद्यादनवेक्षणादपि कृषिः स्नेहः प्रवासाश्रयान्मैत्री
चाप्रणयात्समृद्धिरनयात्त्यागात्प्रमादाद्धनम्।। 42।।

दुष्ट मंत्री से राजा, सांसारिक संग से संन्यासी, लाड़-चाव से पुत्र, विद्या न पढ़ने से ब्राह्मण, कुपुत्र से कुल, नीच मनुष्यों की संगति से सुशील, मदिरा पान से लज्जा, बिना संभाल से खेती, विदेश गमन से स्नेह, अप्रीति से मित्रता, अनीति से ऐश्वर्य और बिना विचारे खर्च करने से धन अवश्य ही नष्ट हो जाते हैं।

A king is ruined by evil counsel, an ascetic by worldly affections, a son by fond caresses, a Brāhmaṇa by not studying the Śāstras, a respectable family by wicked progeny, moral conduct by contact of the bad, modesty by drink, crops by negligence, love by separation, friendship by indifference, prosperity by injustice and riches by careless expenditure.

---

1. Quoted anonymously in the *Subhāṣitāvali* (सुभाषितावलि) (2945 B.S.S.No. XXX). and the शार्ङ्गधरपति at No. 1533

It also stands in the Pañcatantra (पंचतंत्रम्। 1।169).

For contempt of illiterate Brahmans, *cf.*—

"यथा काष्ठमयो हस्ती यथा चर्ममयो मृगः।
यश्च विप्रोऽनधीयानस्त्रयस्ते नाम बिभ्रांति।। 57।।"

(मनुस्मृतेर्द्वितीयाध्याये)

दानं भोगो नाशस्तिस्त्रो गतयो भवन्ति वित्तस्य।
यो न ददाति न भुंक्ते तस्य तृतीया गतिर्भवति।। 43 ।।

धन की केवल (1) दान (2) भोग और (3) नाश यह तीन ही गति होती हैं। जो मनुष्य न तो दूसरों को देते हैं और न स्वयं भोग करते हैं उनके धन की केवल तीसरी गति अर्थात् विनाश मात्र ही समझना चाहिए।

There are only three ultimate ends of money, *viz.*, munificence (charity), enjoyment, and waste; he who neither gives his riches in charity nor uses them for his own personal enjoyment is certainly doomed to the third condition *i.e.*, he is sure to lose them altogether.

---

1. Quoted anonymously in the *Śārṅgadharapaddhati* (शार्ङ्गधरपद्धति 390) and the *Subhāṣitāvali* (सुभाषितावली) (No. 478, B.S.S.No. XXXI). Also stands in the Pañcatantra II. 151. (पंचतंत्रम् 2-151)

Cf.—(*a*) दातव्यं भोक्तव्यं सति विभवे संग्रहो न कर्तव्यः।
पश्यामि मधुकरीणां संचितमर्थं हरंत्यन्य।।
(सुभाषितरत्नभाण्डागारे 100 I17).

(*b*) Riches without charity are nothing worth; they are a blessing only to him who makes them a blessing to other. (Fielding).

(*c*) अदानभोगोपहतं हि वित्त पुंसां परत्रेह च दुर्निमित्तम्।। 113 ।।"
(क्षेमेमन्द्रस्य दर्पदलने 2 विचारे).

(*d*) धनेन किं यो न ददाति नाश्नुते।
(हितोपदेशः I29)

मणिः शाणोल्लीढः समरविजयी हेतिनिहतो
मदक्षीणो नागः शरदि सरितः श्यानपुलिनाः।
कलाशेषश्चन्द्रः सुरतमृदिता बालललनास्तनिम्ना
शोभन्ते गलितविभवाश्चार्थिषु जनाः।। 44।।

खुरासान पर चढ़ी हुई मणि, हथियार से घायल विजयी योद्धा, मद के झराव से क्षीण (दुर्बल) हुआ हाथी, शरद ऋतु की शुष्क प्राय नदी, कला शेष द्वितीया का चंद्रमा, सुरत खेद से शिथिल हुई नवयौवना स्त्री और याचक जनों को धन लुटाकर दीनावस्था को प्राप्त हुए दानी अत्यंत कृश और क्षीण दशा में भी शोभा को प्राप्त होते हैं।

The gem when polished by a whetstone, the winner of a battle when wounded by a sword, the elephant when emaciated with the flow of rut, the wintry rivers whose banks (beds) are almost dry, crescent moon when rising anew with its waned splendour, charming young ladies when exhausted by amorous sports, and noble souls when they are reduced to poverty by charitably giving away their riches to the needy are all acknowledged to be extremely lovely and beautiful notwithstanding their tender and delicate physical appearance.

PURPORT. A person reduced to poverty on account of his charitably giving away his riches is all the more praiseworthy for that.

---

1. Quoted anonymously by Ballabhadeva in his *Subhāṣitāvali* (सुभाषितावलि No. 3457), by *Abhinavagupta* (अभिनवगुप्त) in his commentary of *Dhvanyāloka* (ध्वन्यालोक), and by अप्पयदीक्षित in his कुवलयानंद. It is ascribed to भर्तृहरि in the शार्ङ्गधरपद्धति at No. 1529.

परिक्षीणः कश्चित्स्पृहयति यवानां प्रसृतये स
पश्चात्सम्पूर्णो गणयति धरित्रीं तृणसमाम्।
अतश्चानैकान्त्याद्गुरुलघुतयाऽर्थेषु धनिनामवस्था
वस्तूनि प्रथयति च संकोचयति च।। 45।।

दरिद्री होने पर जो मनुष्य यव (जौ) के तुसों का संग्रह करने की वांछा किया करता हैं, वह धनाढ्य हो जाने पर संपूर्ण पृथ्वी को भी तृण समान समझने लग जाता है। इससे सिद्ध होता है कि सारे पदार्थों का लघुत्व और महत्त्व मनुष्यों के ऐश्वर्य और दारिद्र्य पर निर्भर है।

In straintened cirrcumstances a man is even anxious to collect the empty husks, but afterwards when he is master of enormous wealth he will attach no more importance to the whole earth than to a piece of dry straw. It is, therefore, quite clear that the value of a thing is altogether dependent upon the wealthy or penurious condition of man.

PURPORT.

Strictly speaking, things possess no absolute value in themselves, but they are valued more or less according to the straintened or affluent circumstances of their owners.

1. Cf.—छोटी मोटी जानियो, वस्तु न जग में तात।
उत्तम मध्यम जनदशा, साथ घटत बढ़ जात।
(रसिक कवि)

राजन्दुधुक्षसि यदि क्षितिधेनुमेतां
तेनाद्य वत्समिव लोकममुं पुषाण।
तस्मिंश्च सम्यगनिशं परिपोष्यमाणे
नानाफलैः फलति कल्पलतेव भूमिः।। 46।।

हे महाराज! यदि आप इस पृथ्वी रूप गौ को दोहना चाहते हैं तो प्रथम इसके लोक रूप वत्स का यथोचित् पोषण करें, क्योंकि प्रजा का समीचीनता से परिपालन करने से यह पृथ्वी कल्पलता की भाँति नानाविध मनोरथों को पूर्ण कर देती है।

Oh king! if thou art anxious to milk the cowearth, please not to fail to take the greatest possible care of her calf (the people); for, it is only by the proper nourishment of the people that the land can be made to suplly you with all your wants and luxuries like the famous plant of wondrous know as *kalpalatā*.

Cf.—(*a*) गोपालेन प्रजाधेनोर्वित्तदुग्धं शनैः शनैः।
पालनात्पोषणाद्ग्राह्यं न्याय्यां वृत्तिं समाचरेत्।

(पंचतंत्रम्। 2 ।218)

(*b*) सदानुरक्तप्रकृतिः प्रजापालनतत्परः।
विनीतात्मा हि नृपतिर्भूयसीं श्रियमश्नुते।।

(शार्ङ्गधरपद्धतिः)

सत्याऽनृता च परुषा प्रियवादिनी च
हिंस्रा दयालुरपि चार्थपरा वदान्या।
नित्यव्यया प्रचुरनित्यधनागमा च
वश्यांगनेव नृपनीतिरनेकरूपा।। 47।।

कहीं सत्य और कहीं मिथ्या, कहीं कठोरता और कहीं प्रिय भाषण, कहीं हिंसा और कहीं दयालुता, कहीं स्वार्थ साधन और कहीं दान, कहीं नित्यव्यय और कहीं धन संचय का व्यवहार करने वाली राजनीति भी वैश्या की भाँति अनेक प्रकार के रूप धारण कर लेती है।। 47।।

The policy of kings resembles a prostitute in its being both ture and false, cruel and kind, merciful and unmerciful, covetous and munificent, and expensive and lucrative (*lit.* full of plentiful resources).

PURPORT. The policy of kings is never constant and assumes innumerable masks like those of a prostitute as they serve their respective purposes.

---

1. Also stands in the *Pañcatantra* (1.425) and the *Hitopadeśa* (II. 166).

Cf.—(*a*) The very science of Government is the science of concealing truth." (Ernest Maltravers. Book IV. Ch. IV. By Lord Lytton).

(*b*) मुहुर्लक्ष्योद्भेदा मुहुरधिगमाभावगहना मुहुः संपूर्णाङ्गी मुहुरतिकृशा कार्यवशतः।।
मुहुर्नश्यद्बीजा मुहुरपि बहुप्रापितफलत्यहो चित्राकारा नियतिरिव नीतिर्नयविदः।।" (विशाखदत्तस्य मुद्राराक्षसे पंचमाङ्के)

For the everchanging masks of a prostitute, *cf.*—

(*a*) यत्किंचिद्व्यपदिश्य सनिदधते वेश्याः पुरः कामिनां गायन्त्यः कलमन्तरेव च ततस्तिष्ठन्ति दृग्गोचराः।
सव्याजश्लथनच्छलेन च मुहुः संदर्शयन्ति स्तनौ पश्चात्तान्व्रणस्पृशेव च दृशा दृष्ट्वा वशीकुर्वते।। 56।। (रामभद्रदीक्षितस्य शृंगारतिलकभाणे)

(*b*) गृध्री निर्भरमामिषेषु सरघा घोरा मधूनां भरे व्याघ्री तीक्ष्णनखक्षतेषु भुजगी दंशप्रकारेषु च।
उत्तानेषु निवर्तनेषु शफरी वित्तच्छले मूषकी वेश्या कामुकवंचनासु भवने रूपैरनेकैः स्थिता।। (सुभाषितावलि 2377)

आज्ञा कीर्तिः पालनं ब्राह्मणानां
दानं भोगो मित्रसंरक्षणं च।
येषामेते सद्गुणा न प्रवृत्ताः
कोऽर्थस्तेषां पार्थिवोपाश्रयेण।। 48।।

जिन पुरुषों ने (1) आज्ञा (अर्थात् दूसरो को आज्ञा देने और उसके पालन कराने की शक्ति), (2) सुयश, (3) ब्राह्मणों का पालन, (4) दान, (5) भोग और (6) स्वजन रक्षा ये सद्गुण संपादन नहीं किए उनकी राज सेवा निष्फल ही समझना चाहिए।

What for have they served the kings who have not learnt to cherish authority (or power to command), fame, charity, enjoyment, and the desire of protecting Brahmans and friends?

---

1. This stanza is quoted anonymously by Ballabhadeva in his *Subhāṣitāvali* (सुभाषितावलि) (No. 3229. B.S.S. No. XXXI.).

Cf. — दान भोग रक्षा सहृद, ब्राह्मणपालन और।
करन चहत यदि हे सुजन, नृपसेवा कर दौर।

(रसिक कवि)

यद्धात्रा निजभालपट्टलिखितं स्तोकं महद्वा धनं
तत्प्राप्नोति मरुस्थलेऽपि नितरां मेरौ ततो नाधिकम्।।
तद्धीरो भव वित्तवत्सु कृपणां वृत्तिं वृथा मा कृथाः
कूपे पश्य पयोनिधावपि घटो गृह्णाति तुल्यं जलम्।। 49।।

जो कुछ विधाता ने तेरे ललाट में लिख दिया है वह धन तो थोड़ा या बहुत जो कुछ है मरुस्थल में भी तुझ को अवश्य मिल जायेगा, परंतु उससे अधिक सुमेरु शिखर पर गमन करने पर भी कदापि हाथ नहीं लग सकता। इसलिए हे मित्र! धैर्य का अवलंबन कर और धनवानों के आगे वृथा दीनता मत करें; क्योंकि क्या तू नहीं जानता है कि घट को चाहे कूप में डालो चाहे समुद्र में डालो उसमें उतना ही जल आ सकता है कि जितना उसमें समा सके।

Thou art sure to get the quantity of wealth whether small or great according to thy preordained fortune; and it can never be more nor less no matter thou art case into the midst of a sandy desert, or on the ṭop of the famous golden mountain, the *Meru.* Thou shouldst therefore be patient and firm so as not to humiliate thyself before the wealthy. Can'st thou see that a pitcher can fetch only the same quantity of water without any regard to its being sunk into a well or sea?

---

1. *Cf.*—भुङ्ग्ध्वं यत्नविवर्जितं हुतवहे हुत्वा च दत्त्वाऽर्थिनै
भाव्यं पद्भवतां तदेव भविता तूष्णीं स्थितेऽपि स्वयम्।
संभ्रान्तैरपि सर्वतः क्षितितले नाभावि संलभ्यते
क्षिप्तोऽप्यम्बुनिधौ किमाढकजलं प्रस्थः प्रगृह्णाति हि।। 453।।
(दक्षिणामूर्तिविरचितलोकाक्तिमुक्तावलिः)

त्वमेव चातकाधारोऽसीति केषां न गोचरः।
किमम्भोदवरास्माकं कार्पण्योक्तिं प्रतीक्षसे।। 50।।

हे मेघराज! हम चातकों के आधार तो एकमात्र आप ही हैं यह बात संसार में सब कोई जानते हैं। इसलिए प्रार्थना है कि हमारी करुणासूचक विज्ञप्ति की प्रतीक्षा न करें और शीघ्र ही जल दान देकर हमारा मनोरथ पूर्ण करें।

भावार्थ।

अपने आश्रित जन की दीनोक्ति की प्रतीक्षा करना सर्वथा अनुचित है।

It is a well-known fact that thou alone art the only support of the *Cātaka*, why then, oh best of the rain-clouds, art thou now waiting to hear our humble requests in order to quench our thirst ?

PURPORT. It is no use waiting for the humble entreaties of our dependents.

---

1. The verse is quoted anonymously in the शार्ङ्गधरपद्धति at No. 782.

Cf.—(*a*) एक एव खगो मानी चिरं जीवतु चातकः।
म्रियते वा पिपासायां याचते वा पुरंदरम्।"
(उत्तरचातकाष्टके । 8).

(*b*) सन्ति कूपाः स्फुरद्रूपाः परितः सरितः शुभाः।
तथाऽपि चातकस्यैकः फलदो जलदोदयः।।
(सुभाषितावलिः । 686)

(*c*) पयोद हे वारि ददाति वा न वा त्वदेकचित्तः पुनरेष चातकः।
वरं महत्त्या म्रियते पिपासया तथाऽपि नान्यस्य करोत्युपासनाम्।
(उत्तरचातकाष्टके । 6)

रेरे चातक सावधानमनसा मित्र क्षणं श्रूयता-
मम्भोदा बहवो हि सन्ति गगने सर्वे तु नैतादृशाः।
केचिद्वृष्टिभिरार्द्रयन्ति वसुधां गर्जन्ति केचिद्वृथा यं यं
पश्यसि तस्य तस्य पुरतो मा ब्रूहि दीनं वचः ।। 51 ।।

हे चातक! सावधान होकर क्षणमात्र हमारे कथन को श्रवण कर। आकाश में अनेक प्रकार के मेघ हैं, परंतु संपूर्ण एक से नहीं होते। कितने ही तो ऐसे होते हैं कि वर्षा से सारी पृथ्वी को जलार्द्र कर देते हैं और कितने ऐसे भी हैं कि वृथा गर्जना मात्र करके रह जाते हैं। इसलिए हे मित्र! तुझ को उचित है कि जिस-जिस मेघ को देखे उस उसके आगे ही दीनता के वचन मत कहे।

भावार्थ।

मनुष्य को चाहिए कि बिना विचारे चाहे जिसके आगे ही दीनता न करे।

Friend Cātaka! please to cease crying for a moment and carefully listen to my counsel. Therefore are many clouds in the sky, but all are not alike; there are some which cover the entire earth with rain, whereas others thunder only in vain without giving a single drop of water; thou shouldst therefore be a little considerate in thy entreaties so as not to cry so pitiously before every cloud thou seest.

1. *Cf.*—(*a*) जलकणवितरणरहितः प्रकटितधवलितवेषः।
चातक रटसि वृथा किं जलदः शारद एषः।।
(सुभाषितरत्नावलिः । 685)
(*b*) कृच्छ्राद्दत्ते विरलविरलान्वारिबिन्दून्प्रवृद्धो गर्जत्येकं सरभसतरं पश्य तन्मात्रलाभात्।
नृत्यत्यन्योऽप्यतुलमहिमश्लाघ्यभूमिर्न जाने मध्यादाभ्यां विपुलहृदय-श्चातकः किं नु मेघः।। (सुभाषितावलिः 845)

अकरुणत्वमकारणविग्रहः
परधने परयोपिति च स्पृहा।
सुजनबन्धुजनेष्वसहिष्णुता
प्रकृतिसिद्धमिदं हि दुरात्मनाम्।। 52।।

किसी पर भी करुणा न करना, बिना कारण लड़ना, पर धन और पर स्त्री के निमित्त उत्सुक होना, और सज्जन और बंधु वर्ग की उन्नत्ति को सहना दुष्ट मनुष्यों के लिए स्वाभाविक बातें हैं।

Evil persons are naturally inclined to be cruel, quarrelsome without cause, ardently longing for the wealth and wife of others, and very envious of the prosperity of their relatives and friends.

---

1. *Cf.*—(*a*) अकस्मादेव कुप्यन्ति प्रसीदन्त्यनिमित्ततः।
शीलमेतदसाधूनामभ्रं पारिप्लवं यथा।। 225।।
(विदुरनीतौ)

(*b*) लरत हेतु बिन जोहि दया घट में नहिं राखत।
परकलत्रसँग प्रीति अन्यजनधनको ताक।।
सुजन बंधु से बैर करैं साधुन को आरत।
रसिक लेहु पहिचान लोक जिन दुर्जन भाखत।।
(रसिक कवि)

दुर्जनः परिहर्तव्यो विद्ययाऽलंकृतोऽपि सन्।
मणिना भूषितः सर्पः किमसौ न भयंकरः।। 53।।

विद्वान् होने पर भी दुष्ट मनुष्य तो सर्वथा परित्याग करने के योग्य है। क्योंकि जैसे मणि धारण करने से सर्प का भयंकरपन दूर नहीं हो सकता, वैसे ही विद्या संपादन कर लेने से दुर्जनों की स्वाभाविक दुष्टता का नाश भी कदापि नहीं होता।

An evil person though well educated ought always to be avoided by the wise. Is a venomous snake less dreadful than ever on account of its bearing a precious gem in its hood?

---

1. Quoted under Vālmīki (वाल्मीकि) in the *Subhāṣitāvali* (सुभाषितावलि । 355), and under चाणक्य in the *Śārṅgadharapaddhati* (शार्ङ्गधरपद्धति). It is also found in some copies of the *Hitopadeśa* (हितोपदेश) and the *Cāṇakyaśataka* (चाणक्यशतक).

Cf.—(*a*) निष्णातेऽपि च वेदान्ते साधुत्वं नैति दुर्जनः।
चिरं जलनिधौ मग्नो मैनाक इव मार्दवम्।। 82।।
(भामिनीविलासेऽन्योक्त्युल्लासे)

(*b*) दुर्जने कृष्णसर्पे च कुतो विश्वासतः सुखम्।। 154।।
(कथासरित्सागरे शक्तियशोलंबके 8 तरंगे)

(*c*) अविनयभुवामज्ञानानां शमाय भवन्नपि
प्रकृतिकुटिलाद्विद्याभ्यासः खलत्वविवृद्धये।
फणिभयमृतामस्तु च्छेदक्षमस्तमसामसौ
विषधरफणारत्नालोको भयं तु भृशायते।।
(मुरारेरनर्घराघवे । 4।12)

जाड्यं ह्रीमति गण्यते व्रतरुचौ दम्भः शुचौ कैतवं
शूरे निर्घृणता मुनौ विमतिता दैन्यं प्रियालापिनि।
तेजस्विन्यवलिप्तता मुखरता वक्तर्यशक्तिः स्थिरे
तत्को नाम गुणो भवेत्स गुणिनां यो दुर्जनैर्नांकितः।। 54।।

लज्जावान् को मूर्ख, व्रतोपवासादि करने वाले को ठग, पवित्र रहने वाले को धूर्त, शूरवीर को निर्दयी, मौनी को मतिहीन, प्रियभाषी को दरिद्री, तेजस्वी को अभिमानी, वक्ता (वचनचतुर) को वाचाल और धैर्यवान् को असमर्थ कहने वाले दुष्ट मनुष्यों ने गुणवानों के कौन से गुण को कलंकित नहीं किया है।

भावार्थ।

दुष्ट मनुष्य सत्पुरुषों के गुणों को येन-केन उपाय से कलंकित करना ही अपना कर्तव्य समझते हैं।

The bashful are considered as stupid, the devotee as hypocrite, the pious as deceitful, the brave as cruel, the considerate as foolish, the sweet-tongued as poor, the highsouled as proud, the eloquent as garrulous, and the contented as weak. What qualification of the good is there which is not stigmatised by the evil?

---

1. Quoted under *Bhartṛhari* (भर्तृहरि) in the *Subhāṣitāvali* (सुभाषितावलि) at No. 464.

Cf. —(*a*) Bad men give themselves no rest until they have done their utmost to make others as bad as themselves. (H.S. Brown)

(*b*) दोषान्वेषणमेव मत्सरजुषां नैसर्गिको दुर्ग्रहः
(श्रीकविभट्टकृते पद्यसंग्रहे)

(*c*) दुर्जनधिषणाभांक्ष्णे मृगयति दोषान्गुणेषु विलसत्सु
(श्रीकृष्णकवेर्भन्दारमकरन्दचम्पूः 86)

लोभश्चेदगुणेन किं पिशुनता यद्यस्ति किं पातकैः
सत्यं चेत्तपसा च किं शुचि मनो यद्यस्ति तीर्थेन किम्।
सौजन्यं यदि किं निजैः सुमहिमा यद्यस्ति किं मण्डनैः
सद्विद्या यदि किं धनैरपयशो यद्यस्ति किं मृत्युना।। 55।।

लोभ होने पर अवगुणों का, दुष्टा होने पर पातकों का, सत्य होने पर तप का, शुद्ध मन होने पर तीर्थ यात्रा का, सौजन्य होने पर स्वजनों का, सुयश होने पर आभूषणों का, उत्तम विद्या होने पर धन का और अपशय होने पर मृत्यु का होना न होना बराबर ही है। अर्थात् लोभादिक का होना ही अवगुणादिक होने के समान समझना चाहिए।

Any kind of vice is more than compensated by avarice, sin by deceit, penance by truth, pilgrimages by purity of heart, relatives by goodness, ornaments by fame, wealth by sound learning and death by disrepute.

---

1. This stanza which is quoted anonymously in the *Śārṅgadhara paddhati* (शार्ङ्गधरपद्धति । 1553) is also found in the *Shadratna* (षड्व 16)

For लोभश्चेदगुणेन किं, *Cf.* —

यशो यशस्विनां शुद्धं श्लाघ्या ये गुणिनां गुणाः।
लोभः स्वल्पोऽपि तान्हन्ति श्वित्रो रूपमिवेप्सितम्।।

(श्रीभागवते)

For "सुमहिमा यद्यस्ति किं मण्डनैः" *Cf.*—

Good name, in man and women,
Is the immediate jewel of their souls.

(Shakespeare, Othello, iii, 2.)

शशी दिवसधूसरो गलितयौवना कामिनी
सरो विगतवारिजं मुखमनक्षरं स्वाकृति।
प्रभुर्धनपरायणः सततदुर्गतः सज्जनो नृपाङ्गणगतः
खलो मनसि सप्त शल्यानि मे।। 56।।

दिवस काल का मलिन चंद्रमा, यौवन चले जाने पर शिथिल हुई स्त्री, कमलरहित सरोवर, विद्याहीन सुंदर रूपवान् मुख, कृपण धनवान्, दरिद्री सज्जन और राजसभा में प्रविष्ट हुआ दुर्जन ये सातों ही तीक्ष्ण कंटक के समान मेरे हृदय में सदा खटका करते हैं।

My mind is extremely pained at the sight of (1) the moon devoid of all glory in the course of a day, (2) a woman who has lost all charms of youth, (3) a tank without the presence of lotuses, (4) a handsome face without learning, (5) a master anxious to hoard up money, (6) a gentleman harassed with penury, and (7) a courtier disposed to do evil to others.

---

1. The reading स्वाकृति is here adopted from *Ruyyaka's Alaṅkārasarvasvaṃ* (रुय्यकस्यालङ्कारसर्वस्वम्).

This śloka which is quoted under भट्टवृद्धिः in the *Subhāṣitāvali* (सुभाषितावलि) of Ballabhadeva, at No. 3458, and anonymously in the *Kāvyaprakāśa* (काव्यप्रकाश) of Mammaṭa, the *Alaṅkārasarvasavaṃ*) (अलङ्कारसर्वस्वम्) of Ruyyānaka, the *Udāharaṇcandrikā* (उदाहरणचंद्रिका) of Vaidyanātha, and the *Kāvyapradīpa* (काव्यप्रदीपः) of Govinda, forms the 7th stanza of the *Aṣṭaratna* (अष्टरत्न). It stands under भर्तृहरि in the शार्ङ्गधरपद्धति at No. 1530.

Cf.— अविधेयो भृत्यजनः शठानि मित्राण्यदायकः स्वामी।
विनयरहिता च भार्या मस्तकशूलानि चत्वारि।। (सुभाषितावलिः)

न कश्चिच्चण्डकोपानामात्मीयो नाम भूभुजाम्।
होतारमपि जुह्वानं स्पृष्टो दहति पावकः।। 57।।

जैसे स्पर्श करने पर अग्नि अपने आहुति देने वाले को भी तत्काल जला देती है वैसे ही प्रचण्ड क्रोधवान् राजा लोग किसी को अपना आत्मीय नहीं समझते ।

Kings in their anger have as little regard for their kinsmen and friends, as fire can be said to have for those who feed it with sacrificial offerings.

PURPORT.

Kings when angry are never to be trusted by any, not even by their own kith and kin.

Quoted under *Bhartṛhari* (भर्तृहरि) in the *Śārṅgadharapaddhati* (शार्ङ्गधरपद्धति । 1376) and under the *Pañcatantra* (पञ्चतंत्र) in the *Subhāṣitāvali*, (सुभाषितावलि। 2799) The stanza is found in the Pañcatantra.

Cf.—(*a*) को नाम-राज्ञां प्रियः (षड्रत्ने)

(*b*) Be guarded with monarchs, for, they are like fire, which blazeth but destroyeth.

(*c*) किं विश्वसे द्विजिह्वस्य भुजगस्येव भूभुजः।। 109।।

(अमरचंद्रसूरिकृतबालभारते शान्तिपर्वणि 1 सर्गे)

(*d*) राजा मित्रं केन दृष्टं श्रुतं वा।

(पंचतंत्रम् 1।147)

मौनान्मूकः प्रवचनपटुर्वातुलो जल्पको वा
धृष्टः पार्श्वे वसति च तदा दूरतश्चाप्रगल्भः।
क्षान्त्या भीरुर्यदि न सहते प्रायशो नाभिजातः
सेवाधर्मः परमगहनो योगिनामप्यगम्यः।। 58।।

सेवाधर्म (पराई चाकरी) अत्यंत कठिन और बड़े-बड़े योगिराजों के भी अगम्य है। क्योंकि सेवक के कम बोलने पर मूक होने का, वचन चतुर होने पर वाचाल और लबार होने का, अति निकट रहने पर ढीठ होने का, दूर रहने पर लजालु होने का, सहनशील होने पर डरपोक होने का और असहनशील होने पर नीच जाति होने का कलंक सदैव लगाया जाता है।

The servant if keeping quiet is soon nicknamed as dumb, if eloquent he is accused of being talktive, if keeping too near to his master he is charged with impudence, if remaining at a distance he is blamed of bash fulness, if forbearing he is thought to be timid, and bold so as not to bear without a murmur the admonitions of his master he is sure to be stigmatised as a low-born fellow. We should therefore bear in mind that the art of serving another is extremely difficult being simply incompre-hensible even by learned philosophers.

The last line is also found in the *Hitopadeśa* (हितोपदेश) Verse 147, Book, II., and the *Pañcatantra* I. 285.

Cf.— क्षान्त्या भीरुः कोपयुक्तो सेवकमुच्यते।
रूपवांश्च भवेज्जारः सेवाधर्मोऽतिदुर्गमः।।

(समयोचितपद्यमालिका)

उद्भासिताखिलखलस्य विशृंखलस्य
प्राग्जातविस्तृतनिजाधमकर्मवृत्तेः ।
दैवादवाप्तविभवस्य गुणद्विषोऽस्य
नीचस्य गोचरगतैः सुखमाप्यते कैः ।। 59 ।।

अनेक अवगुणों की खान, मर्यादारहित, पूर्वजन्म के कुकर्म वश विस्तृत दुराचारी, देव कृपा से ऐश्वर्य पाने वाले और गुण द्वेषी दुष्ट मनुष्य के दृष्टि पथ में रहकर कोई भी मनुष्य कुछ सुख नहीं पा सकता।

भावार्थ।

नीच जन की सेवा कदापि सुखदायक नहीं होती।

No one can ever live with the least convenience and comfort in the service (*lit.*sigtht) of a wicked person who has (1) proved himself to be the fruitful source of all evils, (2) set himself quite free from the bonds of morality, (3) added a great deal to the store of vices done in his previous existence, (4) found himself, by a special grace of good fortune, in a sudden trun of affluent circumstances, and (5) given various proofs of his bitter hatred of all kinds of merits.

PURPORT. None can ever be happy in the service of an evil person.

---

1. Quoted anonymously in the *Subhāṣitāvali* (सुभाषितावलि) at No. 444.
2. For the point of the stanza, *cf.*—

"The low born wretch,
That from his mean degree rises at once
To unexpected riches, treats his slaves
With barbarous and unbounded insolence."
(The Plays of Aeschylus, p. 157)

आरम्भगुर्वी क्षयिणी क्रमेण
लघ्वी पुरा वृद्धिमती च पश्चात्।।
दिनस्य पूर्वार्द्धपरार्द्धभिन्ना छायेव
मैत्री खलसज्जनानाम्।। 60।।

दुर्जनों की मित्रता दिन के पूर्वार्द्ध की छाया के समान प्रारंभ में बड़ी फिर क्रमशः क्षयी होती है, परन्तु सत्पुरुषों की मैत्री दिन के उत्तरार्द्ध की छाया के समान प्रारंभ में कम और फिर क्रम-क्रम से वृद्ध होने वाली हुआ करती है।

The friendship of the wicked and the good is just like the changing shadow of the first and second halves of a day; for, in the former case it gradually diminishes from much to little, whereas in the latter it grows from little to much.

---

1. *Cf.* (*a*) खलसख्यं प्राङ्मधुरं वयोऽन्तराले निदाघदिनमन्ते।
एकादिमध्यपरिणति रमणीया साधुजनमैत्री।।। 193।।
(गोवर्धनस्यार्यासप्तशती)
(*b*) उत्तममध्यमनिकृष्टजनेषु मैत्री यद्वच्छिलासु सिकतासु जलेषु रेखा
(संस्कृतचंद्रिका Vol. I., No. 5)
(*c*) प्रारंभतोऽतिविपुलं भृशकृतमन्ते विभेदकृन्मलिनम्।
महिषविषाणमिवानृजु परुषं भयदं खलप्रेम।।
(सुभाषितावलिः)

मृगमीनसज्जनानां तृणजल-
सन्तोषविहितवृत्तीनाम्।
लुब्धकधीवरपिशुना
निष्कारणवैरिणो जगति।। 61 ।।

क्रमपूर्वक तृण, जल और संतोष पर अपने-अपने जीवन का निर्वाह करने वाले मृग, मत्स्य और सज्जनों से व्याध, धीवर और दुर्जन निष्कारण ही वैर भाव रखते हैं।

Though the deer, the fish and the good are respectively maintaining their peaceful lives by living upon grass, water, and contentmen; yet the huntsman, the fisher, and the bad (literally, cheat) are enemical to them without having any cause whatever for it.

---

1. Quoted under Bhartṛhari (भर्तृहरि) in the *Subhāṣitāvali* (सुभाषितावलि) at No. 422, and anonymously in the *Kāvyānuśāsana* (काव्यानुशासन) of Vāgbhaṭṭa. The verse also stans in the *Sūktāvali* (सूक्तावलि).

वाञ्छा सज्जनसङ्गमे परगुणे प्रीतिर्गुरौ नम्रता
विद्यायां व्यसनं स्वयोषिति रतिर्लोकापवादाद्भयम्।
भक्तिः शूलिनि शक्तिरात्मदमने संसर्गमुक्तिः खले
येष्वेते निवसन्ति निर्मलगुणास्तेभ्यो नरेभ्यो नमः ।। 62 ।।

सज्जनों से मिलने की अभिलाषा, दूसरों के गुणों में प्रीति, गुरुजनों के आगे नम्रता, विद्या की व्यसन, निज स्त्री में रति, लोकापवाद का भय, शिवजी की भक्ति, इंद्रिय मन की सामर्थ्य और दुर्जनों की संगति का पूर्ण परित्याग, ये सद्गुण जिन सत्पुरुषों में विद्यमान है उनके अर्थ नमस्कार है।

Bow to those good persons who are masters of the following merits *viz.* (1) to be anxious of mixing with gentlemen, (2) to be fond of good attributes in others, (3) to be humble before the elders, (4) to be ardently in love of knowledge, (5) to be satisfied with the enjoyment of their lawful wives, (6) to be afraid of getting a bad name in the world, (7) to be in sincere devotion of Śiva, (8) to be able to control their senses, and (9) to avoid the company of the bad !

---

1. This stanza which is quoted anonymously in *subhaṣitāvali* [सुभाषितावलि], at No. 2944 is also found in the *Mahānāṭaka* [महानाटक] and the *Saptaratna* [सप्तरत्न].

विपदि धैर्यमथाभ्युदये क्षमा
सदसि वाक्यपटुता युधि विक्रमः।
यशसि चाभिरुचिर्व्यसनं श्रुतौ
प्रकृतिसिद्धमिदं हि महात्मनाम्॥ 63॥

विपत्ति काल में धैर्य, ऐश्वर्य के समय में क्षमा, सभा में वचन चातुरी, युद्ध में पराक्रम, सुयश में प्रीति और शास्त्र में व्यसन महात्माओं के स्वाभाविक लक्षण हैं।

Fortitude in adversity, humbleness in prosperity, eloquence in council, bravery in war, strong desire for fame, and warm attachment to Śāstraic learning, are the natural attributes of noble-minded (great-minded) persons.

---

1. The *Śāraṅgadharapaddhati* (शार्ङ्गधरपद्धतिः। 209) quotes it under Bhartṛhari (भर्तृहरि), and the *Subhāṣitāvali* (सुभाषितावलिः 267) under *Meṇḍhaka* (मेण्ढक). The śloka is also found in Hitopadeśa (हितोपदेशः 1.124).

2. For the idea of the 1st line, *cf.*—
"To hold on with fortitude in one condition and sobriety in the other is a proof of a great soul."
(The Meditations of Marcus Aurelius, p. 17).

प्रदानं प्रच्छन्नं गृहमुपगते सम्भ्रमविधिः प्रियं
कृत्वा मौनं सदसि कथनं चाप्युपकृतेः।
अनुत्सेको लक्ष्म्या निरभिभवसाराः परकथाः
सतां केनोद्दिष्टं विषममसिधाराव्रतमिदम्।। 64 ।।

गुप्त रीति का दान, घर आए का सत्कार, पराया हित साधन करके मौन धारण करना, दूसरे के किए हुए उपकार का सभा में प्रकाश करना, लक्ष्मी का निरभिमान और निंदा रहित परकथा का संकीर्तन ये उत्तमोत्तम गुण सत्पुरुषों में स्वभाव ही से सिद्ध होते हैं, किसी के सिखाए हुए नहीं होते।

Who has ever taught the good (1) to conceal their charity from the public, (2) to show due respect and hospitality to their guests (3) to make no mention of the favours they have done to others, (4) to disclose to the world at large the obligations in which they have been placed by their fellowmen, (5) to feel no sort of pride in their being rich, and (6) to talk respectfully of others?

PURPORT. The aforeasaid *Asidhārā* (असिधारा) vow is quite natural with the good and virtuous.

---

1. Quoted anonymously in the *Subhāṣitāvali* (सुभाषितावलि 281), and the *Kuvalayānanda* (कुवलयानन्द)।

2. For "प्रदानं प्रच्छन्नं" *Cf.*—
"Let your chartitable gifts be anonymous gifts."
(Alexander Dumas).

3. For the 2nd line of the stanza, *cf.*—
"He who has received a kindness should remember it for ever, and he who has conferred it should instantly forget it, if the former would bear the character of a good man, and the latter avoid that of a paltry spirit."
(The Oration of Demosthenes upon the crown).

करे श्लाघ्यस्त्यागः शिरसि गुरुपादप्रणयिता
मुखे सत्या वाणी विजयिभुजयोर्वीर्यमतुलम्।
हृदि स्वच्छा वृत्तिः श्रुतमधिगतं च श्रवणयो-
र्विनाऽप्यैश्वर्येण प्रकृतिमहतां मण्डनमिदम्॥ 65॥

स्वाभाविक महत्पुरुषों के हाथ दान से, मस्तक गुरुचरणार- विंदों में प्रणति करने से, मुख सत्य भाषण से, विजयशील भुजबंध असामान्य पराक्रम से, हृदय शुद्ध वृत्ति से और कान शास्त्र श्रवण करने से ऐश्वर्य के बिना ही अत्यंत शोभा को प्राप्त होते हैं।

Without any regard to wealth, the hands of the good are naturally adorned by due charity, the heads by obedient bow to their elders, the mouths by speaking out truth, the ears by hearing the Śāstras, the victorious arms by matchless valour, and their hearts by good moral character.

---

1. *Cf.*—हस्तस्य भूषणं दानं सत्यं कंठस्य भूषणम्।
श्रोत्रस्य भूषणं शास्त्रं भूषणं किं प्रयोजनम्
(सुभाषितारत्नभाण्डागारें 58 (299)

सम्पत्सु महतां चित्तं भवत्युत्पलकोमलम्।
आपत्सु च महाशैलशिलसंघातकर्कशम्।। 66।।

समृद्धि के समय में महत्पुरुषों का चित्त कमल के समान कोमल हो जाता है, परन्तु आपत्ति काल में वही चित्त महान् पर्वत शिला के समान कठोरपन धारण कर लेता है।

In prosperity the heart of the great becomes as tender as a lotus flower, whereas in adversity is assumes the adamantine hardness of a mountain slab.

---

1. Quoted under *Bhartṛhari* (भर्तृहरि) in the *Subhāṣitāvali* (सुभाषितावलि), at No. 200.

Cf.—(*a*) सम्पत्तौ कोमलं चित्तं साधोरापादो कर्कशम्।
सुकुमारं मधौ पत्रै तरोः स्यात्कठिनं शुचौ।। 37।।

(कुसुमदेवस्य दृष्टान्तशतकम्)

(*b*) It is the part of the great mind to be temperate in prosperity, resolute in adversity.

(Seneca)

2. For the latter half of the stanza, *Cf.*—

पतिते व्यसने दैवाद्दारुणे दारुणात्मनि।
संवर्मयति वज्रेण धैर्यं हि महतां मनः।।

(अनर्घराघवे)

सन्तप्तायसि संस्थितस्य पयसो नामापि न ज्ञायते
मुक्ताकारतया तदेव नलिनीपत्रस्थितं राजते।।
स्वात्यां सागरशुक्तिमध्यपतितं तन्मौक्तिकं जायते
प्रायेणाधममध्यमोत्तमगुणः संसर्गतो जायते।।67।।

जैसे तपे लोहे पर पड़े वृष्टि के जल का तो नाम निशान भी नहीं रहता और कमल के पत्र पर पड़ा हुआ वहीं जल बिन्दु मोती के समान दृष्टि आने लगता है और वही जलबिन्दु स्वाति नक्षत्र में सागर शुक्ति के मुख में पड़ने से साक्षात् ही मोती बन जाता है वैसे ही अधम, मध्यम और उत्तम गुण भी संसार में प्रायः संसर्ग से ही उत्पन्न होते हैं।

A rain-drop if thrown upon a redhot iron is even deprived of its own existence, whereas if it happens to fall upon the leaf of a lotus plant it soon assumes the appearance of a beautiful pearl, and the same is again turned into a real pearl if it chances to drop into the mouth of a seashell in the auspicious time of the Svāti star. It is therefore to be inferred that the bad, mediocre, and good attributes of a thing are always to be traced to the company it keeps.

---

1. The verse stands in the Pañcatantra (पंचतंत्र ।1 ।250।।), and is quoted from that work by शार्ङ्गधर at No. 330.

Cf.—(*a*) पुण्यं स्वातिजलं सरित्सु पतितं शक्तासु मुक्ताजलं
कर्पूरं कदलीदलेषु गरलं व्याले स्थले कर्दमः।
क्षीरं क्षीरनिधौ तदम्बु पतितं क्षारोदकं सागरे
इच्छादानपरोपकारकरणं पात्रानुसारं फलम्।। (सुभाषितरत्नभाण्डागारे)

(*b*) "Would you judge a man? find out who his friends are." (Fenelon)

(*c*) "It I touch my hand to a board, there is only a blunt sound but if I touch it to the key of an instrument there is a musical sound. And the effect produced upon a person by that which he comes in contact depends upon what there is to be be touched." (H.W. Beecher)

(*d*) "A man is known by the company he keeps." (N.V. Bāpat's Beauties of English literature).

(*e*) There is a Spanish proverb which says, "Tell me who you live with and I will tell you who you are."

यः प्रीणयेत्सुचरितैः पितरं स पुत्रो
यद्भर्तुरेव हितमिच्छति तत्कलत्रम्।
तन्मित्रमापदि सुखे च समक्रियं
यदेत्त्रयं जगति पुण्यकृतो लभन्ते।। 68।।

अपने सच्चरित्र पिता को प्रसन्न करे वही पुत्र, भर्तार के आज्ञावर्ती रहकर उसका हित साधन करे वही स्त्री, और आपत्तिकाल तथा सुखावसर में समान बतार्व करे वही मित्र समझना चाहिये परंतु इन तीनों का लाभ संसार में विरले पुण्यवानों को ही प्राप्त होता है।

The name of a son is only deserved by him who pleases his father by his good actions; that of a wife by her who is entirely bent on looking after the welfare of her husband; and that of a friend by him who is equally sincere in adversity and prosperity, but the enjoyment of these three gifts (*i.e.*, an obedient son, a loving their wife, and a sincere friend) is only granted to virtuous persons.

---

1. Quoted anonymously in the *Subhāṣitāvali* (सुभाषितावलि) at No. 2929.

Cf.— "स सुहृद्व्यसने यः स्यात्सपुत्रो यस्तु भक्तिमान्।
स भृत्यो यो विधेयज्ञः सा भार्या यत्र निवृत्ति।। (पंचतंत्रम् 1।337)

2. For the 2nd line, *Cf.*—(*a*) "जा भत्तिमत्ता धम्मेकचित्ता।
सा होईणारी घणापिआरी।।"
(प्राकृतापङ्गलसूत्रे द्वितीयपरिच्छेदे । 37)

(*b*) "या सौन्दर्यगुणान्विता पतिरता सा कामिनी कामिनी"
(भवभूतिकृतगुणरत्नम् । 10)

For the 1st line *Cf.*—"कोऽर्थःपुत्रणे जातेन यो न विद्वान्न भक्तिमान्।"
(पंचतंत्रम्। 1।4।)

3. For the 3rd line, *Cf.*—(*a*) "A friend in need is a friend in deed"

(*b*) "Be the same to your friends in prosperity and adversity"
(Periander G.T.).

एको देवः केशवो वा शिवो वा
ह्येकं मित्रं भूपतिर्वा यतिर्वा।।
एको वासः पत्तने वा वने वा
ह्येका भार्या सुन्दरी वा दरी वा।। 69।।

इस संसार में मनुष्य की आराधना के निमित्त या तो विष्णु भगवान ही हैं और या शिव, मित्रता के अर्थ या तो राजा ही है या यति, निवास के लिये या तो नगर ही है या वन, और विलास के हेतु या तो सुंदर स्त्री ही है और या पर्वत की गुफा।

भावार्थ।

जैसे प्रवृत्ति मार्ग में गमन करने वाले के इष्टदेव विष्णु, मित्र राजा, निवास नगर और स्त्री सुंदर रूपवती होते हैं, वैसे ही निवृत्ति मार्ग में गमन करने वाले के इष्टदेव शिव, मित्र यति, निवास वन और भार्या पर्वत की कंदरा समझना चाहिये।

A wise man should worship either Viṣṇu or Śiva; make friends with a king or a hermit; inhabit a town or a forest; and sek the company of a handsome wife or a mountain den.

PURPORT. A man should either enjoy the world or give it up altogether. In the fomer case, he should worship Viṣṇu, befriend a king, inhabit a town, and marry a handsome woman; whereas in the latter, he should worship Śiva, befriend a hermit retire to forest, and live in a mountain cave.

Cf.— एको नेता क्षत्रियो वा द्विजो वा एका भार्या वंशजा वा प्रिया वा।
एका विद्याऽध्यात्मिकी वा त्रयी वा एकं मित्रं भूपतिर्वा यतिर्वा।।
(सरस्वतीकण्ठभरणम् 2 परिच्छेदः)

Mark that the 4th charana of this verse exactly corresponds with the 2nd charana of our text.

नम्रत्वेनोन्नमन्तः परगुणकथनैः स्वान्गुणान्ख्यापयन्तः
स्वार्थान्सम्पादयन्तो विततपृथुतरारम्भयत्नाः परार्थे।
क्षान्त्यैवाऽक्षेपरूक्षाक्षरमुखरमुखान्दुर्मुखान्दूषयन्तः सन्तः
साश्चर्यचर्या जगति बहुमताः कस्य नाभ्यर्चनीयाः ।। 70 ।।

नम्रता से उन्नत होने वाले, परपुरुषाक गुणानुवाद से निजगुण की प्रसिद्धि करने वाले, परहित साधन में दत्तचित होकर स्वार्थ संपादन करने वाले, निंदायुक्त कुवचन बोलने वाले दुष्ट पुरुषों के मुख को अपनी असाधारण क्षान्ति से कलंकित करने वाले, आश्चर्यजनक आचरणों से विभूषित और जगत् के माननीय सन्तजन किस मनुष्य के पूजन योग्य नहीं होते?

Where are they who do not worship the wonderful virtues of the good that prove their greatness by humility, disclose their merits by dwelling at large upon the qualifications of others, achieve their ends by helping the undertakings of their fellowmen, and throw back the blame entirely upon the shoulders of their detracting enemies with a patient heart?

Quoted anonymously in the *Subhāṣitāvali* (सुभाषितावलि) at No. 286.

Cf.—(*a*) सौजन्यामृतसिन्धवः परहितप्रारब्धवीरव्रता
वाचालाः परवर्णने निजगुणालापे च मौनव्रताः।
आपत्स्वप्यविलुप्तवीर्यनिचयाः संपत्स्वनुत्सेकिनो
माभूवन्खलवक्त्रनिर्गतविषज्वालातताः सज्जनाः।।

(सुभाषितारत्नभाण्डागारे 79 |21)

For the first line, *Cf.*—"गुणा नगृह्णन्सुजनो न निर्वृतिं, प्रयाति दोषानवदन्न दुर्जनः।" 7 (वीरनन्दिप्रणीते चन्द्रप्रचभरिते 1 सर्गे).

For the 3rd line of the stanza, *Cf.*—"In taking revenge, a man is but even with his enemy; but in passing it over, he is superior; for, it is a prince's part to pardon.

भवन्ति नम्रास्तरवः फलोद्‌गमे
नवाम्बुभिर्भूरि विलम्बिनो घनाः।
अनुद्धताः सत्पुरुषाः समृद्धिभिः
स्वभाव एवैष परोपकारिणाम्।। 71।।

जैसे फल आने के समय वृक्ष नीचे की ओर झुक जाते हैं, और वर्षा के जल से भरे हुए नवीन मेघ भी पृथ्वी पर झूमने लगते हैं वैसे ही सत्पुरुष भी समृद्धि के समय नम्रता ही प्रगट करते हैं। इससे प्रत्यक्ष है कि नम्रता धारण करना परोपकारी जनों का स्वाभाविक लक्षण है।

As trees bend downwards at fruiting season, and new clouds lower to earth when carrying rain, so good men instead of being proud of their affluence, naturally become meek and humble in prosperity. Humility is quite natural with the benevolent.

---

1. The indentical stanza occurs in the *Śakuntalā* (शकुन्तला) (K.T. Telang)

Cf.—(*a*) अप्यनावर्जिताः स्वेन फलभारेण संनताः।
अर्भकैरपि गृह्यन्ते साधुसंतानशाखिनः।। 2।।"
(वेङ्कटनाथस्य सुभाषितनीवी)

(*b*) फलसंपत्तीअ समीणोआइं तुङ्गाइं फलविपत्तीए।
(स्या) (यवतानि) (नि) (त्या)
हिअआइ सुपुरिसाणं महातरुणं व सिहराई।। 82।।
(हृदयानि) (रुषाणां) (णा मिव) (शिखराणि)
(सातवाहनस्य गाथासप्तशती 3 शतकम्)

श्रोत्रं श्रुतेनैव न कुण्डलेन
दानेन पाणिर्न तु कंकणेन।
विभाति कायः करुणापराणां
परोपकारैर्न तु चन्दनेन।। 72।।

करुणापरायण सत्पुरुषों के कानों की शोभा शास्त्र श्रवण करने से होती है कुण्डल धारण करने से नहीं होती, हाथों की शोभा दान देने से होती है कंगन पहनने से नहीं होती और इस ही प्रकार उनके देह की शोभा भी परोपकार करने से होती है चंदनादि के लेप करने से नहीं होती।

The body of those who are bent on sympathising with the misery of others is rendered beautiful by the performance of good to others and not by the application of sandal powder; the ears by hearing the Śāstras and not by the wearing of rings; and the hands by giving in charity to the needy and not by adorning them with a pair of bracelets.

---

1. *Cf.*— परोपकाराय फलन्ति वृक्षाः
परोपकाराय वहन्ति नद्यः।
परोपकाराय दुहन्ति गावः
परोपकारार्थमिदं शरीरम् (सुभाषितरत्नभाण्डागारः 108 । 11)

पापान्निवारयति योजयते हिताय
गुह्यानि गूहति गुणान्प्रकटीकरोति।
आपद्गतं च न जहाति ददाति काले
सन्मित्रलक्षणमिदं प्रवदन्ति सन्तः।। 73।।

अपने मित्र को पाप कर्म से बचाना, उसको हितयुक्त काम में नियुक्त करना, उसकी गुह्य बातों (अवगुणों) को गुप्त रखना, उसके गुणों को प्रगट करना और आपत्तिकाल में उसका परित्याग न करके यथोचित सहाय देना ये सब सत्पुरुषों के कहे हुए सन्मित्र के लक्षण हैं।

To keep off sin, to direct towards good, to conceal weaknesses, to proclaim merits, to help in adversity, and to give pecuniary assistance when necessary are the characteristic marks of a true and sincere friend as mentioned by the wise.

---

1. The stanza is also found in some copies of the *Hitōpadeśa* (हितोपदेश).

Cf.—(*a*) दूरीकरोति कुमतिं विमलीकरोति
चेतश्चिरंतनमघं चलुकीकरोति।
भूतेषु किं च करुणां बहुलाकरोति
संगः सतां किमु न मङ्गलमातनोति।। (रसगङ्गाधरे)

(*b*)—Of all felicities the most charming is that of firm and gentle friendship. It sweetens all our cares, dispels our sorrows, counsels us in all extremities . . . . . (Seneca).

(*c*)—To assist a fallen friend is instinctive with noble natures. (Beattie).

पद्माकरं दिनकरो विकचीकरोति
चन्द्रो विकाशयति कैरवचक्रवालम्।
नाभ्यर्थितो जलधरोऽपि जलं ददाति
सन्तः स्वयं परहितेषु कृताभियोगाः।। 74।।

जैसे सूर्य कमल को खिलाता है, चन्द्रमा कुमुद समूह को विकसित करता है और बिना याचना किए ही मेघ पृथ्वी पर जल की वर्षा करते हैं वैसे ही सन्तजन भी परोपकार करने के लिए स्वयमेव कटिबद्ध रहते हैं।

As the sun expands the petals of the lotus flowers, the moon blossoms the night lilies, and the rain cloud waters the whole world, all out of their own free will, so good men naturally help the interests of others without the slightest request being never made to their liberal hearts.

---

1. *Cf.*—*(a)* As the sun does not wait for prayers and incantations to be induced to rise, but immediately shines, and is saluted by all; so do you also not wait for clappings of hands and shout and praise to be induced to do good, but be a doer of good voluntarily, and you will be believed as much as the sun.

(Epictetus)

(b) सत्पूरुषः खलु हिताचरणैरमन्दमानन्दयत्यखिललोकमनुक्त एवा आराधितः
कथय केन करैरुदारैरिन्दुर्विकासयति कैरविणीकुलानि।। 73।

(भामिनीविलासे अन्योक्त्युल्लासे)

एके सत्पुरुषाः परार्थघटकाः स्वार्थं परित्यज्य ये
सामान्यास्तु परार्थमुद्यमभृतः स्वार्थाविरोधेन ये।
तेऽमी मानुषराक्षसाः परहितं स्वार्थाय विघ्नन्ति ये
ये निघ्नन्ति निरर्थकं परहितं ते के न जानीमहे।। 75।।

जो मनुष्य स्वार्थ का परित्याग करके परहित करते हैं वह निस्संदेह सत्पुरुष हैं, जो स्वार्थ की हानि न होने पर भी परोपकार कर सकते हैं वह साधारण पुरुष हैं और जो स्वार्थ के निमित्त परहित में विघ्न डालते हैं वह मनुष्यरूपी राक्षस हैं परन्तु जो मनुष्य निरर्थक ही परहित में हानि पहुँचाते हैं उनकी गणना किस श्रेणी में होना चाहिए सो हम नहीं कह सकते।

Virtuous persons sacrifice their own interests for the good of others; whereas ordianry men are inclined to benevolent acts when they do not clash their personal good. Wicked persons (literally, human demons) ruin the prospects of others in the hope of self-interest; but what are they who trouble others without any advantage to themselves is not known to me.

---

1. Quoted under (भर्तृहरि) in the (शार्ङ्गधरपद्धति) at No. 45.

Cf.—(*a*) To do an ill action is base ; to do a good one which involves you in no danger, is nothing more than common ; but it is the property of a truly good man to do great and good things though he risks everything by it. (Maurisius)

(*b*) सो जग जणमउ सो गुणमन्तउ जे कर परउअकार हसन्तउ। जो पुण परअआर विरुअइ तासु जणणि किंण थकइ वझइ।। 166।। (प्राकृतपिंगलसूत्रे 2 परिच्छेदे)

(*c*) परार्थप्रतिपन्ना हि नेक्षन्ते स्वार्थमुत्तमाः।। 92।। (कथासरित्सागरे पंचलंबके 2 तरंगे)

(*d*) Self-sacrifice for the sake of others is always divine. (Pomponia).

क्षीरेणात्मगतोदकाय हि गुणा दत्ताः पुरा तेऽखिलाः
क्षीरे तापमवेक्ष्य तेन पयसा स्वात्मा कृशानौ हुतः।
गन्तुं पावकमुन्मनस्तदभवद्दृष्ट्वा तु मित्रापदं युक्तं
तेन जलेन शाम्यति सतां मैत्री पुनस्त्वीदृशी।। 76।।

पानी के दुग्ध में मिलते ही दुग्ध ने अपने सब गुण पानी को दे दिये। इस ही हेतु दुग्ध का संताप देखकर पानी भी अपनी आत्मा को अग्नि में हवन करने लगा। निज मित्र जल की यह विपत्ति देख दुग्ध मन मलीन हुआ और अग्नि में पड़कर आत्मनाश करने लगा। इस उफनते हुए दुग्ध की फिर उस ही जल के प्रोक्षण से शान्ति हुई। सत्पुरुषों की मित्रता ऐसी ही होती है।

When water was mixed with milk, the latter gave all its qualites to it. Consequently, when water saw the distress of milk it began to burn itself. The sight of its friend's calamity much agitated milk and it went out of the pot to destroy itself on the burning embers. At this stage water came to its help and the milk soon became calm and cool. The friendship of the good is just like it.

---

1. For the general drift of the stanza, compare the noble lines of Dryden.

I had a friend that lov'd me :
I was his soul ; he liv'd not but in me ;
We were so close within each other's breasts,
The rivets were not found that joined us fast.
That does not reach us yet : we were so mix'd,
As meeting streams ; both to ourselves were lost.
We were one mass, we could not give or take,
But from the same; for he was I ; I He. (John Dryden).

इतः स्वपिति केशवः कुलमितस्तदीयद्विषा-
मितश्च शरणार्थिनः शिखरिणां गणाः शेरते।
इतोऽपि वडवानलः सहसमस्तसंवर्तकैरहो
विततमूर्जितं भरसहं च सिन्धोर्वपुः।। 77।।

अहो! समुद्र की सहनशीलता और उदारता भी कैसी आश्चर्यजनक और विचित्र है कि जिसके अन्तर्गत एक स्थान में शेषशायी विष्णु भगवान् शयन करते हैं और दूसरे में उनके शत्रुगण दानवों का परिवार वर्तमान है। यहां पर इंद्र वज्र से पक्षच्छेदन होने के भय से शरण आए हुए पर्वत शयन करते हैं और वहाँ पर प्रलयोत्पादक अग्नि समूह के सहित वडवानल विद्यमान है।

भावार्थ—महाजन सब के आश्रयभूत होते हैं।

The vastness, strenght, and power of endurance of the ocean are truly wonderful as evidenced by the following fact: Here in one place, sleeps into its bosom the god *Keśava* and there in another are seem the entire family of the demons, the hreditary enemies of His race; here under its hospitable roof are lying the refugee mountains who have sought its shelter from the fear of Indra's thunderbolt, and three again we find the *Badavā* fire together with *Saṁvartaka,* the fires of universal destruction.

PURPORT. The great and good shelter all.

---

1. Quoted under Bhartṛhari (भर्तृहरि) in the *Śārṅgadhara-paddhati* (शार्ङ्गधरपद्धति । 1093) and anonymously in the *Subhāṣitāvali* (सुभाषितावलि । 886). The verse is also found in the सरस्वतीकंठाभरण (चतुर्थपरिच्छेदः)

Cf.— मैनाकादिभिरद्रिभिर्मघवतः संत्रस्य यत्रास्यते
चण्डार्चिर्भगवानुदेति च यतो यत्रास्तमभ्येति च।
शेते क्वापि निलीय यस्य जगतां कुक्ष्यैकदेशे पति-
र्गाम्भीर्यश्रियमस्य कस्तुलयितुं वारांनिधेरर्हति। (सुभाषितावलिः)

तृष्णां छिन्धि भज क्षमां जहि मदं पापे रतिं मा
कृथाः सत्यं ब्रूह्यनुयाहि साधुपदवीं सेवस्व विद्वज्जनान्।
मान्यान्मानय विद्विषोऽप्यनुनय प्रच्छादय स्वान्गुणान्कीर्तिं
पालय दुःखिते कुरु दयामेतत्सतां लक्षणम्।। 78।।

तृष्णा का छेदन कर, क्षमा का अवलंबन कर, अभिमान का त्याग कर, पापकर्म में प्रीति मत रख, सत्य का भाषण कर, साधुजनों का अनुसरण कर, पंडितों की सेवा कर, मान्यजनों का समादर कर, शत्रु गणों को भी प्रसन्न कर, निज गुणों की प्रशस्ति मत कर, सुयश का पालन कर और दीन दुःखित मनुष्यों पर दया कर। ये सब सत्पुरुषों के लक्षण हैं।

To curtail the desire, to be forgiving to the faulty, to give up conceit, to dislike crime, to tell the truth, to walk on the right path, to serve the learned, to respect the honourable, to please even the enemies, to conceal one's merits, to be careful of fame, and to sympathise with the miserable, are the characteristic qualities of the good.

---

1. *Cf.*—साधु वही जिनके क्षमा, दया कीर्ति सत प्रीति।
मान पाप तृष्णा रहित, विद्यारसिक सुनीति।।
(रसिक कवि)

मनसि वचसि काये पुण्यपीयूषपूर्ण-

स्त्रिभुवनमुपकारश्रेणिभिः पूरयन्तः।

परगुणपरमाणून्पर्वतीकृत्य नित्यं निजहृदि

विकसन्तः सन्ति सन्तः कियन्तः।। 79।।

मन से वचन से और काया से सदा अमृत वर्षा करने वाले, लगातार उपकार से त्रिभुवन को पूर्ण करने वाले, और परमाणु मात्र दूसरे के गुणों को पर्वताकार विस्तृत मान कर शुद्धान्तःकरण से प्रफुल्लित होने वाले संतजन इस संसार में विरले ही होते हैं।

There are only a few of such good persons as being full of the nectar of virture can be equally candid in their hearts, words, and deeds; can please the three worlds by doing incessant good to others; and can, by extolling a particle of meritorious qualifications in their fellowmen, feel a consummate amount of happiness in their heart of hearts.

Cf.—(*a*) वदनं प्रसादसदनं सदयं हृदयं सुधामुचो वाचः।।
करणं परोपकरणं येषां केषां न ते वंद्याः।
(सुभाषितरत्नभाण्डागारः 71 । 90)

(*b*) भुवनान्युपकाराणां श्रेणिभिः प्रीणयन्ति ते। तत्रैव, 28
(श्रीकृष्णकवेमन्दारमरन्दचम्पः)

(*c*) यथा चित्तं तथा वाचो यथा वाचस्तथा क्रियाः।
चित्ते वाचि क्रियायां च साधूनामेकरूपता।।
(सुभाषितरत्नभण्डागारः 69 । 37)

किं तेन हेमगिरिणा राजताद्रिणा वा
यत्राश्रिताश्च तरवस्तरवस्त एव।
मन्यामहे मलयमेव यदाश्रयेण
कंकोलनिम्बकुटजान्यपि चन्दनानि।। 80।।

सुमेरु के सुवर्ण रूप और कैलास के रजतमय होने से संसार को किसी प्रकार का लाभ नहीं, क्योंकि इनके ऊपर उगने वाले वृक्ष अन्यान्य वृक्षों के समान ही बने रहते हैं। हमारी समझ में तो मलयाचल ही धन्य है कि जिसके आश्रय से कंकोल, निम्ब (नीम) और कुटज जैसे कटुवृक्ष भी चंदनतरु हो जाते हैं।

What advantage is there in the existence of either the *Sumeru* (the golden mountain) or the *Kailāsa* (the silver mountain) if trees growing on them are in no way superior to their class as found all over the earth? We, therefore, esteem the *Malaya* to be the best mountain in the world because it has the power and goodness to change even the bitterest trees of *Kaṅkola, Neem,* and *Kuṭaja* into those of the fragrant sandal.

---

1. This stanza which is quoted anonymously in the *Śārṅgadhara-paddhati* (शार्ङ्गधरपद्धति । 1067) and the *Subhāṣitāvali* (सुभाषितावलि 1006) forms the 12th śloka of *Vetālabhaṭṭa's Nītipradīpa* (वेतालभट्टकृतनीतिप्रदीप).

Cf.—*(a)* आत्मार्थं जीवलोकेस्मिन्को न जीवति मानवः।
परं परोपकारार्थं यो जीवति स जीवति।। (सुभाषिताभाण्डागार: 108 I6)

(b) रागिणि नलिने लक्ष्मीं दिवसो निदधाति दिनकर प्रभवाम्।
अनपेक्षितगुणदोषः परोपकारः सतां व्यसनम्।।
(हर्षचरितस्य पंचमोल्लासे)

(c) श्रीखण्डाचलगण्डशैलशिखरप्रान्ताटवीसंस्थिताः।
पाटीरानिभवन्ति शाल्मलिमुखा निःसारभूमीरुहाः।। 14
(मधुसूदनकवेरन्यापदेशशतके)

(d) Also the 48th stanza of the *Annyāpadeśaśataka.*

रत्नैर्महार्हैस्तुतुषुर्न देवा न
भेजिरे भीमविषेण भीतिम्।
सुधां विना न प्रययुर्विरामं
न निश्चितार्थाद्विरमन्ति धीराः।। 81।।

समुद्र मंथन करने से समय देवता नाना प्रकार के अमूल्य रत्नों का लाभ हो जाने से संतुष्ट न हुए और न वे तक्षक की भयानक विष ज्वाला से ही भयभीत हुए परन्तु जब तक उनको अमृत की प्राप्ति न हुई तब तक अविचल परिश्रम करते रहे और उन्होंने कुछ भी विश्राम न लिया। इस ही प्रकार धैर्यवान् मनुष्य भी अपने विचारे हुए कार्य को संपूर्ण किए बिना कदापि नहीं रहते।

At the time of churing the curd ocean the celestial beings were not satisfied merely with the possession of the precious jewels, but they continued in their difficult task without entertaining the least fear from the deadly poison of Bāsuki till they obtained the desired nectar. Resolute persons can never stop from their undertakings till they achieve their desired ends.

---

1. For the point of the stanza *Cf.*—

(*a*) प्रारब्धे ह्यसमाप्ते कार्ये शिथिलीभवन्ति किं सुधियः 115
(कथासरित्सागरे शशाङ्कवतीलंबंके 15 तरंगे)

(*b*) असिद्धार्था निवर्तंते नहि धीराः कृतोद्यमाः।। 114
(कथास॰ सा॰ चतुर्दारिक लंबके 3 तरंगे)

(*c*) आरब्धा ह्यसमाप्तैव किं धीरैस्त्यज्यते क्रिया ।। 234
(कथा॰ स॰ नरवाहनदत्तजननलंबके 2 तरंगे)

क्वचिद्भूमौ शायी क्वचिदपि च पर्यंकशयनः
क्वचिच्छाकाहारी क्वचिदपि च शाल्योदनरुचिः।
क्वचित्कन्थाधारी क्वचिदपि च दिव्याम्बरधरो
मनस्वी कायार्थी न गणयति दुःख न च सुखम्।। 82।।

निज कार्य के सिद्ध करने में कटिबद्ध हुए मनुष्य कभी तो भूमिशयन और कभी पर्यङ्कशयन, कभी शाक पात का आहार और कभी दाल–भात का उत्तम भोजन, कभी फटी पुरानी कंथा और कभी सुंदर–सुंदर वस्त्र अंगीकार करते हुए दुःख और सुख की ओर तनिक भी ध्यान नहीं देते।

Sleeping sometimes on the bare earth and sometimes on a luxurious sofa, sometimes living on the poor vegetables, and sometimes feasting on the delicious table of rice and other dainties, sometimes covering the body with worn out rags and sometimes adorning it with a costly apparel, a wise and strong minded man pays but little heed to the miseries and pleasures of the world when he is bent on accomplishing his heart's end.

---

1. Quoted anonymously in the *Subhāṣitāvali* (सुभाषितवलि) at No. 2940.

Cf. (*a*) त्रिविक्रमोऽभूदपि वामनोऽसौ स शूकरश्चेति स वै नृसिंहः।
नीचैरनिचैरातेनीचनीचैः सर्वैरुपायैः फलमेव साध्यम्।।
(घटकर्परस्य नीतिसारे)

(*b*) अपमानं पुरस्कृत्य मानं कृत्वा च पृष्ठतः।
स्वकार्यं साधयेद्धीमान् कार्यभ्रंशो हि मूर्खता।।
(सुभाषितरत्नभाण्डागारे 258 । 308)

2. The verse 4098 as given below is ascribed to भर्तृहरि in शार्ङ्गधरपद्धति।

क्वचित्कंथाधारी क्वचिदपि च दिव्याम्बरधरः।
क्वचिद्भुमौ शय्या क्वचिदपि च पर्यंकशयनः।
क्वचिद्भिक्षावृत्तिः क्वचिदपि च मिष्टाशनरुचि-
महात्मा योगज्ञो न गणयति दुःखं न च सुखम्।।

ऐश्वर्यस्य विभूषणं सुजनता शौर्यस्य वाक्संयमो
ज्ञानस्योपशमः श्रुतस्य विनयो वित्तस्य पात्रे व्ययः।
अक्रोधस्तपसः क्षमा प्रभवितुर्धर्मस्य निर्व्याजता
सर्वेषामपि सर्वकारणमिदं शीलं परं भूषणम्।। 83।।

ऐश्ववर्य का आभूषण सज्जनता, शूरवीरता का वाक्संयम, ज्ञान का शांति भाव, शास्त्र का विनय, धन का पात्र दान, तप का भूषण क्रोध का न होना, साामर्थ्यवान का क्षमा और धर्म का भूषण निष्कापट्य है। परन्तु सुशील सब मनुष्यों के लिए समस्त आभरणों का मूल कारण और उत्तमोत्तम आभूषण है।

The value of porsperity is much increased by gentlemanliness, that of personal valour by proper control of speech, that of knowledge by clamness, that of learning by humility, that of wealth by due charity, that of religious devotions by clamness (*lit.* absence of anger), that of power by forgivenes, and that of virtue by condour and sincerity of heart; but good conduct is the best ornament for all, because it heightens the worth of all the aforesaid merits.

---

1. Quoted anonymously in the *Subhāṣitāvali* (सुभाषितावलि) at No. 3054.

It also stands in the *Sūktāvali* (सूक्तावलि । 1)

Cf. —(*a*) वचो हि सत्यं परमं विभूषणं गजाङ्गनायाः कृशता कटौ तथा।
द्विजस्य विद्यैव पुनस्तथा क्षमा शीलं हि सर्वस्य नरस्य भूषणम्।।
(सुभाषितरत्नभाण्डागारः)

(*b*) किं भूषणाद्भूषणमस्ति शीलम्। 1
(शंकराचार्यकृतप्रश्नोत्तरमालायाम्)

निन्दन्तु नीतिनिपुणा यदि वा स्तुवन्तु
लक्ष्मीः समाविशतु गच्छतु वा यथेष्टम्।
अद्यैव वा मरणमस्तु युगान्तरेवा न्याय्यात्पथः
प्रविचलन्ति पदं न धीराः।। 84।।

नीति धुरंधर मनुष्य चाहे निंदा करे चाहे स्तुति, लक्ष्मी आये अथवा जाय, मृत्यु चाहे आज ही हो जाय या युगांतर में हो, धैर्यवान् मनुष्य न्याय मार्ग से इधर-उधर एक पद भी कदापि नहीं हो सकते।

No matter, whether the wise (or the moralists and politicians) may hate or praise, the goddess of wealth may come or go as she pleases, and death may happen either today or as far off as in remote ages, the good, intelligent and resolute persons can never deviate a step from the path of right they have chosen for themselves.

---

1. Quoted under *Bhartṛhari* भर्तृहरि in the *Śārṅgadharapaddhati* (शार्ङ्गधरपद्धति । 225), and anonymously in the *Subhāṣitāvali* (सुभाषिता-वलि । 278)

Cf.—(*a*) चलन्ति गिरयः कामं युगान्तपवनाहताः।
कृच्छ्रेऽपि चलत्येव धीराणां निश्चलं मनः।।
(सुभाषितरत्नभाण्डागारः 112। 2)

(*b*) त्यजन्त्युत्तमसत्त्वा प्राणानमपि न सत्पथम्। 42
(कथासरित्सागरे शशाङ्कवतीलंबके 25 तरंगे)

(*c*) अपि स्फुटति विन्ध्याद्रौ वाति वा प्रलयानिले।
गुरुशास्त्रानुगो मार्गः परित्याज्यो न धीमता।।
(योगवासिष्ठे)

भग्नाशस्य करण्डपीडिततनोर्म्लानेन्द्रियस्य क्षुधा
कृत्वाऽऽखुर्विवरं स्वयं निपतितो नक्तं मुखे भोगिनः।।
तृप्तस्तत्पिशितेन सत्वरमसौ तेनैव यातः पथा लोकाः
पश्यत दैवमेव हि नृणां वृद्धौ क्षये कारणम्।। 85।।

जीवन से निराश, पिटारे में बंद हुआ और शिथिल शरीर वाला सर्प जब क्षुधा से अत्यंत व्याकुल हो रहा था तब रात्रि के समय एक चूहा (मूषक) किसी खाद्य पदार्थ की आशंका से पिटारी छेद करके उसके भीतर गया और जाते ही उस सर्प का ग्रास बना कि जिसकी क्षुधा निवृत्त हुई और वह उस ही मार्ग से शीघ्र बाहर निकलकर स्वतंत्र भी हो गया। इसलिए हे मनुष्यो! तुम को उचित है कि अपनी वृद्धि और क्षय का कारण एकमात्र देव ही को समझते रहो।

One night a mouse cut out a hole into a bamboo basket, and thus entering into its interior, it became the morsel of a hungry serpent that had long been imprisoned there, and consequently, deprived of all power and hope of further life; but having appeased its hunger by the flesh of the mouse God had sent it, it now came out of its prison by the same path and became a free creature. Here you see that fate and fate alone is the real cause of good and evil to all men.

---

1. Quoted anonymously in the *Subhāṣitāvali* (सुभाषितावलि) at No. 3143.

Cf.—अभद्रं भद्रं वा विधिद्विखितमुन्मूलयति कः। (कथा सरित्सागरे)

In the *Bhartṛharinirveda* (भर्तृहरिनिर्वेद) the hero (*i.e.*, भर्तृहरि) is made to say :

भवितव्यता भगवती वस्तुप्रियमप्रियं वापि।
घटयितुमथ विघटयितुं प्रभवति पुरुषस्य को दोषः। (भर्तृहरिनिर्वेदम्)

आलस्यं हि मनुष्याणां शरीरस्थो महान्रिपुः ।।
नास्त्युद्यमसमो बन्धुः कुर्वाणो नावसीदति ।। 86 ।।

आलस्य, मनुष्यों के शरीर में बैठा हुआ बड़ा भारी शत्रु है और उद्यम उनका हितसाधन करने वाला असामान्य बंधु है। उद्यम करके कभी पछताना नहीं पड़ता।

भावार्थ।

आलस्य अत्यंत हानिकारक और उद्यम सर्वोत्तम सहायक है।

There can be no shadow of doubt that idleness is the greatest enemy of mankind, sitting within their own bodies. Industry is man's matchless friend, as no one can ever have the least cause for repentance and misery by being active or industrious.

PURPORT: To be idle is to be one's own enemy but to be active is equivalent to the possession of the best of friends.

---

1. For the point of the stanza compare the well-known English proverb—

God helps those who help themselves.

2. Though at first sight this will not appear an exact parallel to the text, yet a little reflection will convince a thoughtful reader of the precise similarity of the powerful thought of the above adage which lays it down that to be active is to secure the help of God, the best of friends.

छिन्नोऽपि रोहति तरुः
क्षीणोऽप्युपचीयते पुनश्चन्द्रः।।
इति विमृशन्तः सन्तः
सन्तप्यन्ते न ते विपदा।। 87।।

कटा हुआ वृक्ष फिर भी हरा-भरा हो जाता है और क्षीण हुआ कलाहीन चंद्रमा भी फिर वृद्धि को प्राप्त होता है। यह विचार करके सत्पुरुष अपनी विपत्ति से दुःखित नहीं होते।

When beset with difficulties the virtuous can pass them over with great patience without the least disturbance in their hearts; because they are conscious of the fact that a plant by being pruned is sure to grow up again with renewed vigour, and the crescent moon is certain to develop into her full splendour and glory.

---

1. *Cf.*—(*a*) We must not despair in sorrow, because it is only a prediction and an assurance that brighter days await us.

(Reynold's Loves of the Harem Vol. 11).

(*b*) आपत्सु च न मुह्यन्ति नराः पण्डितबुद्धयः। (विदुरनीतिः)

(*c*) What jars the thoughtless world to-day,
And drapes the land tomorrow,
May be Gods own paternal way.
Of blessings all tomorrow. (Whittier)

नेता यस्य बृहस्पतिः प्रहरणं वज्रं सुराः सैनिकाः
स्वर्गो दुर्गमनुग्रहः किल हरेरैरावतो वारणः।।
इत्यैश्वर्यबलान्वितोऽपि बलभिद्भग्नः परैः संगरे
तद्युक्तं ननु दैवमेव शरणं धिग्धिग्वृथा पौरुषम्।।88।।

बृहस्पति के समान गुरु (मन्त्री), वज्र के समान आयुध, देवताओं के समान योद्धा, स्वर्ग के समान दुर्ग, विष्णु के समान अनुग्राहक और ऐरावत के समान जिसके वाहन हैं वह अनुपम ऐश्वर्य का स्वामी इंद्र भी जब संग्राम में शत्रुओं से पराजित हो चुका है तो मनुष्यों का वृथा पौरुष तो सर्वथा धिक्कारयुक्त है। इस दशा में देव ही सबका शरण है।

When we see that Indra, the lord of gods and the special favourite of Hari, who was so fortunate as to have Mercury for his prime minister (*lit.* leader), lightning for his weapon, the celestial beings for his army, the havens for his citadel, and *Airāvat* for his elephant, was even defeated in battle by his enemies, the demons, it is proper for us to have full reliance on Fate, and relinquish the fruitless trust in our individual efforts.

---

1. This stanza which is, according to Dr. Peterson and Pandit Durga Prasada, also found in the *Ātmānuśāsanakāvyaṃ* (आत्मानुशासनकाव्य)is quoted anonymously in the *Subhāṣitāvali*, at Fo. 3151.

Cf.—(*a*) पाण्डउवंसिह जन्म करीजे संपअ अज्जिय धम्मक दीजे।
सा उ जुहिट्ठिर संकट पाआ देवक लेखिअ केण मिटाआ 102
(प्राकृतपिंगलसूत्रे 2 परिच्छेदे)

(*b*) When we reckon without Providence, we often have to Providence. (Madame De Senigne).

कर्मायत्तं फलं पुंसां बुद्धि कर्मानुसारिणी।।
तथाऽपि सुधिया भाव्यं सुविचार्यैव कुर्वता।। 89।।

यद्यपि यह सत्य है कि मनुष्य जैसा कर्म करता है वैसा ही फल पाता है और मनुष्यों की बुद्धि भी उत्तमाधम कर्मानुसार ही उत्तमाधम होती है तथापि मतिमानों को उचित है कि जो कार्य करें वह पूर्ण विचार के साथ ही करें।

Although the result of his actions is in accordance with his *Karma* or previous destiny, and the circuit of his intelligence is also defined by same, a wise man should still undertake to do a thing after carefull consideration.

---

1. For the first *charana* of the stanza, *Cf.*—

इह वा पूर्वभवे वा स्वकर्मणैवार्जितं फलं यद्यत्।
शुभमशुभं वा तत्तद्भोगोऽप्यप्रार्थितो भवति।। 72।।

(प्रबोधसुधाकरे)

2. For the point of the stanza, *Cf.*—

रसिक कार्य भल होय लघु, चाहे होय महान्।
पण्डित पूर्ण विचार कर, करत सदा धीमान्।।

(रसिक कवि)

खल्वाटो दिवसेश्वरस्य किरणैः सन्तापितो मस्तके
वाञ्छन्देशमनातपं विधिवशात्तालस्य मूलं गतः।।
तत्राप्यस्य महाफलेन पतता भग्नं सशब्दं शिरः
प्रायो गच्छति यत्र भाग्यरहितस्तत्रैव यान्त्यापदः।।90।।

सूर्य की किरणों से पीड़ित होकर एक खल्वाट (गंजे सर का मनुष्य) सूर्य के आतप से रहित शीतल स्थान को ढूँढ़ता–ढूँढ़ता देव योग से एक ताल वृक्ष के नीचे जा निकला, परन्तु वहाँ पर भी उसके भाग्य में सुख न था, क्योंकि उसके यहाँ पहुँचते ही एक ताल फल जोर के साथ उसके मस्तक पर गिरा कि जिससे उसका सिर फट गया। इससे प्रत्यक्ष है कि भाग्यहीन मनुष्य जहाँ जाता है विपत्ति भी प्रायः उसके साथ–साथ ही गमन किया करती है।

A baldheaded person being once pained with the scorching rays of the sun betook himself to the foot of a palmyra tree, but unfortunately when he reached its cool shade a bing cocoanut fell with a tremendous noise upon him, and thus broke his pate. It is therefore generally true that the feet of the unlucky are always dogged by misforunes.

---

1. Quoted under *Bhartṛhari* (भर्तृहरि) in the *Śārṅgadharapaddhati* (शार्ङ्गधरपद्धति । 2437) and under *Divira Devāditya* (दिविरदेवादित्य) in the *Subhāṣitāvali* (सुभाषितावलि), at No. 3141.

गजभुजङ्गमयोरपि बन्धनं
शशिदिवाकरयोर्ग्रहपीडनम्।।
मतिमतां च विलोक्य दरिद्रतां
विधिरहो बलवानिति मे मतिः।। 91।।

हाथी और सर्प का बंधन, चंद्र और सूर्य का ग्रहण और मतिमानों का दारिद्र्य देखकर मेरी यह संमति है कि विधाता की मति ही सब बातों में प्रबल है।

Seeing the eclipses of the sun and the moon, the capture of elephants and snakes, and the poverty of the wise, I am led to think that the power of fate is always supreme.

---

1. Quoted anonymously in the *Subhāṣitāvali* (3125) and the *Śārṅgadharapaddhati* (443). It forms the 4th śloka of *Vetālabhaṭṭa's Nītipradīpa,* (वेतालभट्टकृत नीतिप्रदीप). The stanza is also found in the *Pañcatantra* (पंचतंत्र ।2।19) and the *Hitopadeśa* 1.38, (हितोपदेश ।1238)

Cf.—(*a*) जातः सूर्यकुले पिता दशरथः क्षीणोभुजामग्रणीः
सीता सत्यपरायणा प्रणयिनी यस्यानुजो लक्ष्मणः।।
दोर्दण्डेन समो न चास्ति भुवने प्रत्यक्षविष्णुः स्वयं
रामो येन विडम्बितोऽपि विधिना चान्ये परे का कथा।। 10।।
(हलायुधस्य धर्मविवेके)

(*b*) अवश्यंभाविनो भावा भवन्ति महतामपि।
नग्नत्वं नीलकंठस्य महाहिशयनं हरेः।।
(सुभाषितरत्नभाण्डागारे, 36।28).

सृजति तावदशेषगुणाकरं
पुरुषरत्नमलङ्करणं भुवः।।
तदपि तत्क्षणभङ्गि करोति
चेदहह कष्टमपण्डितता विधेः।। 92।।

बड़े खेद का विषय है कि सारे गुणों की खान और पृथ्वी को शोभा देने वाले मनुष्य रत्न की रचना करके भी विधाता उसकी देह को क्षणभंगुर बना देता है, इससे निस्संदेह विधाता की मूर्खता ही प्रतीत होती है।

The ignoreance of Bidhi, the creator, is truly pitiable; for having created man, the storehouse of all merits and the ornaments of the whole terrestrial globe he sadly errs in making his life the most transitory of all.

---

1. Quoted anonymously in the *Śārṅgadharapaddhati* (शार्ङ्गधरपद्धति 4000) and under *Phalguhastinī* (फलगुहस्तिनी), in the *Subhāṣitāvali* (सुभाषितावलि) at No. 3126.

Cf.— भूभषण नररत्नकी, रचना करं पुनि भूल।
वाहि देह भंगूर करत, विधि मूरखता मूल।।

(रसिक कवि)

पत्रं नैव यदा करीरविटपे दोषो वसन्तस्य किं नोलू-
कोऽप्यवलोकते यदि दिवा सूर्यस्य किं दूषणम्।।
धारा नैव पतन्ति चातकमुखे मेघस्य किं दूषणं
यत्पूर्वं विधिना ललाटलिखितं तन्मार्जितुं कः क्षमः।। 93।।

यदि करीर (कैर) के वृक्ष के पत्र नहीं आते तो इसमें वसन्त का क्या दूषण है? यदि उलूक को दिन में नहीं दिखता तो सूर्य नारायण का क्या दोष है? और यदि चातक के मुख में जल धारा नहीं गिरती तो इसमें मेघ का क्या अपराध है? इन बातों से प्रत्यक्ष है कि विधाता ने जो कुछ ललाट में लिख दिया है उसे मिटाने को कोई भी समर्थ नहीं होता।

What fault can justly be attributed to (1) the spring, if the thorny plant of *Karīra* is not covered with leaves, or (2) the sun, if the owl is unable to see in broad day light, or (3) the raincloud, if the rain drops do not fall into the mouth of the *Cātaka*? What has been previously written in one's forehead can never be obliterated by his utmost efforts.

---

1. For the 1st Line, *Cf.*— प्रोप्त वसन्तामासे वृद्धि प्राप्नोति सकलवनराजिः
यन्न करीरे पत्रं तत्किं दोषो वसन्तस्य।। (सुभाषतावलिः)
2. For the 2nd line, *Cf.*—यस्मिन्नम्बुरुहणि जातसुदृढप्रेमाणि यस्मिन्घना-
नन्दं विंदति चक्रवाकपटली यस्मिन्प्रसन्ना दिशः।
तस्मिन्विश्वविकाशि तेजसि रवौ रज्यत्युलूको न
चेद्धानिः कैव तदा रवेः परमसौ हास्यास्पदं जायते।।
(मधुसूदनस्यान्यापदेशशतके)
3. For the 3rd line, *Cf.*—म्लानान्भूमिरुहोऽभिषिच्य परितः शुष्काः स्तवन्ती
पुनर्धाराभिः परिपूरय प्रतिदिशं संप्लावपोर्मीमिमाम्।
अंभोवाह परं त्वकीर्तितमिदं पानीयपानाशया
स्तोकोऽसौ भवदेकवृत्तिनिशं यद्रारटीत्याकुलः।। 20।।
(मधुसूदनकवेरन्यापदेशशतके)
4. For the 4th line, *Cf.*—यद्दैवेदन ललाटपट्टलिखितं तत्प्रोज्झितु कः क्षमः।।3।।
(वेतालभट्टस्य नीतिप्रदीपे)

नमस्यामो देवान्ननु हतविधेस्तेऽपि वशगा
विधिर्वन्द्यः सोऽपि प्रतिनियतकर्मैकफलदः।
फलं कर्मायत्तं किममरगणैः किंच विधिना
नमस्तत्कर्मभ्यो विधिरपि न येभ्यः प्रभवति।। 94।।

देवतागण यद्यपि हमारे वन्दनीय हैं परन्तु वह सब विधि के वशीभूत हैं, विधाता भी केवल प्रारब्धानुसार फल देता है और यह फल मनुष्यों के पूर्वसंचित शुभाशुभ कर्मानुसारी ही शुभाशुभ होते हैं। इसलिए हम को उचित है कि देवता और विधाता को छोड़कर उन कर्मों को ही प्रणाम करें कि जिनके प्रतिकूल विधाता भी कुछ नहीं कर सकता।

We bow respectfully to gods, but alas! they are all subject to *Bidhi* (Fate), who though worthy of worship is competent only to award according to a preordained destiny which is again the certain consequence of our own acts done in a series of former existences. We should, therefore, do well to give up our adorations for Gods and Fate, and take ourselves to the worship of our past actions over which Fate herself has not the least control.

---

1. Quoted anonymously in the *Subhāṣitāvalii* (सुभाषितावलि 3079) and the भर्तृहरि in the *Śārṅgadharapaddhati* (शार्ङ्गधरपद्धति । 436)

2. It also forms the opening stanza of the *Śāntiśataka* (शान्तिशतक)

Cf. — यत्कर्म बीजमुप्तं येन पुरा निश्चितं स तद्भुंक्ते।
पूर्वकृतस्य हि शक्यो विधिनाऽपि कर्तुमन्यथाभावः।। 80।।
(कथासरित्सागरे शशांकवतीलंबके 19 तरंगे)

ब्रह्मा येन कुलालवन्नियमितो ब्रह्माण्डभाण्डोदरे
विष्णुर्येन दशावतारगहने क्षिप्तो महासङ्कटे।।
रुद्रो येन कपालपाणिपुटके भिक्षाटनं कारितः
सूर्यो भ्राम्यति नित्यमेव गगने तस्मै नमः कर्मणे।।95।।

जिसके प्रभाव से ब्रह्मा इस ब्रह्माण्ड भाण्डोदर के मध्य में कुम्हार के समान काम कर रहे हैं, विष्णु भगवान् मत्स्यादि दशावतार ग्रहण करने के महासंकट में पड़े हुए हैं, रुद्र कपालपुट हाथ में लिए घर-घर भिक्षाटन कर रहे हैं और सूर्य नारायण नित्यप्रति आकाश में भ्रमण करते हैं उस कर्म को हमारा नमस्कार है।

Bow to that *Karma* (Past actions) through whose influence the Creator (Brahmā ब्रह्मा) is continually working like a potter into the interior of the vessel of the universe, the Protector (Viṣṇu विष्णु) is thrown into a series of misfortunes by assuming the well known ten incarnations, the Destroyer (Śiva शिव) is made to beg from door to door with a skull in hand, and the sun is compelled to revolve incessantly into the sky.

---

1. This stanza which stands as the 4th in the *Aṣṭaratna* (अष्ठरत्न) is quoted under भर्तृहरि in the *Śārṅgadharapaddhati* (शार्ङ्गधरपद्धति), at No. 435 and anonymously in the *Subhāṣitāvali* (सुभाषितावलि) at No. 3102.

Cf.— रामो येन विडम्बितो मृदुमयश्चंक्रः कलंकीकृतः
क्षाराम्बुः सरितांपतिश्च नहुषः सर्पः कपाली हरः।
माण्डव्यो मुनिशूलपीडिततनुर्भिक्षाभुजः पाण्डवा
नीतो येन रसातलं अलिरसौ तस्मै नमः कर्मणे।।

(सुभाषितरत्नभाण्डागार, 140।108)

नैवाकृतिः फलति नैव कुलं न शीलं
विद्याऽपिनैव न च यत्नकृताऽपिसेवा।।
भाग्यानि पूर्वतपसा खलु सञ्चितानि
काले फलन्ति पुरुषस्य यथैव वृक्षाः।। 96।।

शरीर की सुंदरता, कुल, शील, विद्या और यत्नपूर्वक की हुई सेवा ये कोई भी किसी काम नहीं आते, किन्तु अवसर आने पर पूर्व संचित प्रारब्ध ही वृक्षादि के समान मनुष्य को नाना प्रकार के फल देते हैं।

It is not the result of handsome person, nor that of his noble birth, nor that of his learning, nor that of attentive service of his master, but it is only the necessary consequence of a man's fortune as made up of his past good and virtuous actions that enables him to enjoy the pleasures and happiness of this world.

---

1. Quoted under *Aśvaghōṣa* (अश्वघोष)in the *Subhāṣitāvali* (सुभाषितावलि), at No. 3100.

Cf.—(*a*) विनाऽपि प्रोक्तनं कर्म न दाता कोऽपि कस्यचित्।
आगर्भाज्जन्तुरश्नाति पूर्वकर्मतरोः फलम्।। 109।।
(कथासरित्सागरे रत्नप्रभालंबके 6 तरंगे)

(*b*) भाग्यं फलति सर्वत्र न विद्या न च पूरुषम्।
समुद्रमथगल्लेभे हरिर्लक्ष्मी हरो विषम्।।

(*c*) जन्मान्तरे शुभमथाप्यशुभं यदेव यैरर्जितं स्वपरिणामवशेन कर्म।
तद्योग्यमेव फलमिष्टमनीप्सितं वा तैः प्राप्यते किमिति शोचसि हेतुहीनम्। (वीरनन्दिप्रणीतचंद्रप्रभचरितम् 3 सर्गः)

वरे रणे शत्रुजलाग्निमध्ये
महार्णवे पर्वतमस्तके च।।
सुप्तं प्रमत्तं विषमस्थितं वा
रक्षन्ति पुण्यानि पुरा कृतानि।। 97।।

वन, रण, शत्रु, जल, अग्नि और गहन समुद्र के मध्यवर्ती, अथवा पर्वत शिखर पर स्थित अथवा सुप्त, वा प्रमत्त वा संकटस्थ मनुष्य की रक्षा केवल प्राचीन जन्म के शुभ कर्मों से ही होती है।

It is only virtuous actions of his former lives which protect a man from injury and danger when he is thrown into the midst of a dense forest, a raging battle field, a crowd of enemies, a deep ocean, and burning fire; or when he is standing on the top of a mountain; or at the time when he is fast asleep, or drunk, or is placed in a dangerous or difficult position.

---

1. The idea is that in whatever place and in whatever circumstances one may be placed, the merit accumulated in a previous birth is always with its help. (K.T. Telang)

Cf.— निमग्नस्य पयोराशौ पर्वतात्पतितस्य च।
तक्षकनापि दुष्टस्य आयुर्मर्माणि रक्षति।।

(घटकर्परस्य नीतिसार: 20)

या साधूंश्च खलान्करोति विदुषो मूर्खान्हितान्द्वेषिणः
प्रत्यक्षं कुरुते परोक्षममृतं हालाहलं तत्क्षणात् ।।
तामाराधय सत्क्रियां भगवतीं भोक्तुं फलं वाञ्छितं हे
साधो व्यसनैर्गुणेषु विपुलेष्वास्थां वृथा मा कृथाः ।। 98 ।।

हे साधुजनो! यदि आप अपने मनोवांछित फल भोगने की इच्छा रखते हो तो अन्यान्य गुण समूह में वृथा आसक्त न होकर केवल सदाचार ही की आराधना करो कि जो दुर्जनों को सज्जन, मूर्खों की पंडित, शत्रुओं को मित्र, परोक्ष को प्रत्यक्ष और हालाहल को अमृत बनाने की तात्कालिक सामर्थ्य रखता है।

Oh ye good! if you wish to enjoy the pleasures and happiness of the world according to your heart's desires, then you should give up the vain efforts of acquiring all other merits and attributes, but take yourselves to the sincere devotion of the goddess of good conduct that is powerful enough immediately to change the evil into the good, the illiterate into the learned, enemies into well-wishers, invisible into the visible, and poison into nectar.

---

1. Quoted under *Śrīvardhana* (श्रीवर्धन)in the *Subhāṣitāvali* (सुभाषितावलि), at No. 3074.

Cf.—*(a)* The great high road of human welfare lies along the old pathway of steady welldoing; and those who are the most persistent, and work in the true spirit, will invariably be the most successful; success treads on the heels of every right effort.

(Samuel Smiles)

(*b*) What a rare gift is that of manners! How difficult to define; how much more difficult to impart! Better for a man to possess them than wealth, beauty or talent ; they will more than supply them all.

गुणवदगुणवद्वा कुर्वता कार्यमादौ
परिणतिरवधार्या यत्नतः पण्डितेन।।
अतिरभसकृतानां कर्मणामाविपत्तेर्भवति
हृदयदाही शल्यतुल्यो विपाकः।। 99।।

कोई कैसा ही क्यों न हो पंडितजन को प्रथम ही से उसके गुण, दूषण और परिणाम का विचार भली-भाँति कर लेना चाहिए, क्योंकि बिना विचारे और शीघ्रता से किए हुए कार्य का फल मरण-पर्यंत मनुष्य के हृदय को संतप्त करता रहता है।

Whether good or bad, a wise man should carefully consider the end of the action he takes in hand; for the result of our precipitate and inconsiderate doings invaribly becomes the source of constant pain to the end of our heart-rending existence.

---

1. This stanza is virtually the same as found in *Vallāla's Bhōjaprabandha* (वल्लालकृतभोजप्रबन्ध). It is quoted anonymously in the *Subhāṣitāvali* (सुभाषितावलि) at No. 2934, and the *Śārṅgadharaddhati* (शार्ङ्गधरपद्धति । 1391)

2. Cf.—(*a*) किं न म स्यादिदं कृत्वा किं नु मे स्यादकुर्वतः।
इति कर्माणि संचिन्त्य कुर्याद्वा पुरुषो न वा (विदुरनीतिः)

(*b*) Resolution without foresight, is but a temerarious folly; and the consequence of things is the first point to be taken into consideration.

(*c*) सहसा विदधीत न क्रियामविवेकः परमापदां पदम्।
वृणुते हि विमृश्यकारिणं गुणलुब्धाः स्वयमेव संपदः।। 30।।
(किरातार्जुनीये 2 सर्गे)

(*d*) In everything we do, we may be possbily laying a train of consequences, the operation of which may terminate only with our existence. (Bailey's Essays on the Formation and publication of Opinions.)

स्थाल्यां वैदूर्यमय्यां पचति तिलकणानिन्धनैश्चन्दनाद्यैः
सौवर्णैर्लाङ्गलाग्रैर्विलिखति वसुधामर्कमूलस्य हेतोः।।
छित्त्वा कर्पूरखण्डान्वृतिमिह कुरुते कोद्रवाणां समन्तात्प्रा-
प्येमां कर्मभूमिं न चरति मनुजो यस्तपो मन्दभाग्यः।। 100।।

जो मंदभागी इस कर्मभूमि (संसार) में जन्म लेकर तपश्चरण नहीं करता वह निस्संदेह उस मूर्ख के समान है जो तुच्छ तिलकणों को वैदूर्य मणि के पात्र में रखकर चंदनादि के सुगंधित ईंधन से पकाना चाहता है, अथवा अर्क की जड़ प्राप्त करने के हेतु सुवर्णमय लांगल से पृथ्वी का संशोधन करता है, अथवा सामान्य कोद्रव (कोदूं) के धान्य की रक्षा के निमित्त कपूर की बाड़ लगाता है।

Like those foolish and unfortunate beings who cook a quantity of sesamum in a canldron of Vaidūryamaṇi (वैदूर्यमणि or Lapsus lazule) by the fuel of sandal and other valuable woods; or who dig up the earth with a goldenedged plough in order to obtain the worthless root of the *Arka;* or protect the poor *Kodrava* grains by fencing its field with camphor pieces; the condition of the man who after being born into this world of trial does not observe the sacred rites of his religion is indeed very miserable and pitiable.

---

1. Quoted anonymously in the *Subhāṣitāvali* (सुभाषितावलि), at No. 3045.

Cf.— स्वर्णस्थाले क्षिपति सरजः पादशौचं विधत्ते
पीयूषेण प्रवरकरिणं वाहयत्येधभारम्।
चिंतारत्नं विकिरति कराद्वायसोड्डायनार्थं
यो दुष्प्रापं गमयति मुधा मर्त्यजन्म प्रमत्तः।। 5।।
(सोमप्रभाचार्यस्य सूक्तिमुक्तावली–धर्मप्रक्रमः)

**मज्जत्वम्भसि यातु मेरुशिखरं शत्रूञ्जयत्वाहवे
वाणिज्यं कृषिवेनादिः सकला विद्याः कलाः शिक्षतु।।
आकाशं विपुलं प्रयातु खगतत्कृत्वा प्रयत्नं परं नाभाव्यं
भवतीह कर्मवशतो भाव्यस्य नाशः कुतः।। 101।।**

चाहे समुद्र में गोता लगाओ, चाहे सुमेरु के शिखर पर चढ़ो, चाहे संग्राम में शत्रु को जीतो, चाहे व्यापार करो, चाहे कृषि कर्म और सेवादि सकल विद्या और कला को सीखो और चाहे बहुत प्रयत्न करके पक्षियों के समान आकाश में उड़ो परंतु प्रारब्ध के वश से न तो अनहोनी ही कभी हो सकती है और न होनहार ही कभी टल सकती है।

Notwithstanding his diving deep into the sea, or ascending by the peak of the *Meru* (मेरु), the famous golden mountain, or defeating his enemies in battle, or learning with proficiency the different sciences and arts of commerce, husbandry, and service; or crossing like a bird the endless sky; a man with all his efforts is quite unable to effect any thing contrary to his Fate; for, there is no doing against one's destiny whose course is wholly unavoidable.

---

1. Quoted under भर्तृहरि in the शार्ङ्गधरपद्धति at No. 433.

Cf.—(*a*) आकाशमुत्पततु गच्छतु वा दिगन्त-
मम्भोनिधिं विशतु तिष्ठतु वा यथेच्छम्।
जन्मान्तरार्जितशुभाशुभकृन्नराणां छायेव न त्यजति
कर्मफलानुबन्धः।।21।। (शान्तिशतकम् Part III)

(*b*) एवं प्राग्जन्मसंबधपरयत्तेषु जन्तुषु।
भावि को वस्त्वतिक्रामेत्को वा किं कस्य वारयेत्।।170।।
(कथासरित्सागरः सुरतमंजरी लंबकः 2 तरंगः)

(*c*) पातालमाविशतु यातु सुरेन्द्रलोकमारोहतु क्षितिधराधिपतिं च मेरुम्।
मंत्रौषधप्रहणैश्च करोतु रक्षां यद्भावि तद्भवति नात्र विचारहेतुः।।
(सूक्तावलिः)

भीमं वनं भवति तस्य पुरप्रधानं
सर्वे जनाः सुजनतामुपयान्ति तस्य।।
कृत्स्ना च भूर्भवति सन्निधिरत्नपूर्णा
यस्यास्ति पूर्वसुकृतं विपुलं नरस्य।। 102 ।।

जिस भाग्यवान् के प्राचीन संस्कार उत्तम हैं उसके लिए भयानक वन तो उत्तम नगर, सारे मनुष्य हितैषी और समस्त पृथ्वी अनेकानेक रत्नों की खान स्वयमेव हो जाते हैं।

The man who is fortunate in having done a lot of virtues in his former lives is able to turn out a dense and dreadful forest into a safe and beautiful capital, the whole of the human race into his true and sincere friends, and the entire mass of earth into a fruitful mine of invaluable gems.

---

1. *Cf.*—Before the fortunefavoured son of earth,
Apollo walks—and, with his jocund mirth,
The heart-enthralling Smiler of the skies :
For him gray Neptune smooths the pliant wave—
Charmed at his feet the crouching lion lies,
To him his back the murmuring dolphin gave.
(Schiller's The Fortune Favoured).

को लाभो गुणिसंगमः किमसुखं प्राज्ञेतरैः संगतिः
का हानिः समयच्युतिर्निपुणता का धर्मतत्त्वे रतिः ।।
कः शूरो विजितेन्द्रियः प्रियतमा काऽनुव्रता किं धनैर्विद्या
किं सुखमप्रवासगमनं राज्यं किमाज्ञाफलम् ।। 103 ।।

गुणी जनों की संगति के सिवाय लाभ, मूर्खों के संसर्ग के सिवाय दुःख, अवसर चूकने के सिवाय हानि, धर्मानुराग के सिवाय निपुणता, जितेंद्री की सिवाय शूरवीर, भर्तार के अनुकूल वर्तिनी स्त्री के सिवाय प्राण प्यारी, विद्या के सिवाय धन, जन्मभूमि के निवास के सिवाय सुख और आज्ञा करने की शक्ति के सिवाय राज्य कुछ भी वस्तु नहीं है।

What is gain but the society of the learned? What is misery but the company of the illiterate? What is loss but the missing of a favourable opportunity? What is perfection but faith in religious tenets? Who is a hero but he who can subdue his senses? Who is a beloved wife but she who implicitly obeys her husband? What is wealth but learning? What is happiness but residence in one's nativity? What is empire but the establishment of authority?

पातितोऽपि कराघातैरुत्पतत्येव कन्दुकः।।
प्रायेण साधुवृत्तानामस्थायिन्यो विपत्तयः।। 104।।

जिस प्रकार कराघात (हाथ के जोर) से फेंकी हुई गेंद शीघ्र ही ऊँची उठ आती है वैसे ही सदाचार युक्त साधु मनुष्यों की विपत्ति भी प्रायः अस्थिर ही हुआ करती है।

When a ball is struck against a floor it immediately rises up again. The miserable state of the good and virtuous is accordingly very unsteady and shortlived.

---

1. Quoted anonymously in the *Subhāṣitāvali* (सुभाषितावलि) at No. 222. and the *Śārṅgadharapaddhati* (शार्ङ्गधरपद्धति । 486) Also found in the सूक्तावलि No. 23.

Cf.—(*a*) उत्तमं सुचिरं नैव विपदोभिभवन्त्यलम्।
राहुग्रसनसंभूतक्षणो विच्छाययेद्विधुम्।। 80।।
(कुसुमदेवविरचितदृष्टान्तशतकम्)

(*b*) पातेन कन्दुक इव पतत्यार्यः पतन्नपि।
(सुभाषितावलिः No. 22)

अप्रियवचनदरिद्रैः प्रियवचानाढ्यैः स्वदारपरितुष्टैः।।
परपरिवादानिवृत्तैः क्वचित्क्वचिन्मण्डिता वसुधा।। 105।।

इस पृथ्वी को शोभा देने वाले ऐसे महज्जन किसी-किसी स्थान में ही होते हैं कि जो अप्रिय भाषण करने में दरिद्री, प्रिय भाषण में धनाढ्य, निज स्त्री सेवन से संतुष्ट और परनिंदा से पराङ्मुख हों।

It is only here and there that the earth is adorned with men who are poor of speaking harsh to others, rich in uttering sweet words to their fellow beings, content with the enjoyment of their lawful wives, and always averse to censure others.

Cf.— प्रियवाक्यप्रदानेन सर्वे तुष्यन्ति जन्तवः।
तस्मात्तदेव वक्तव्यं वचने का दरिद्रता।।
(समयोचितपद्यमालिका)

कदर्थितस्यापि हि धैर्यवृत्तेर्न
शक्यते धैर्यगुणः प्रमार्ष्टुम्।।
अधोमुखस्यापि कृतस्य
वह्नेनाधः शिखा याति कदाचिदेव।। 106।।

धैर्यवान् मनुष्य अत्यंत दुःखित होने पर भी अपने धैर्य का परित्याग कदापि नहीं करते। क्योंकि जलती अग्नि को उलटी कर देने से भी उसकी शिखा नीचे की ओर कभी नहीं होती।

As we cannot make a flame go downwards for a host of misfortunes to deprive a courageous man of his usual fortitude even by putting his patience to the severest test.

---

1. In the *Subhāṣitāvali* (सुभाषितावलि) this stanza is quoted under *Aśvaghoṣa* (अश्वघोष) at No. 528 and anonymously at No. 316. The *Śārṅgadharapaddhati* (शार्ङ्गधरपद्धति) at No. 227 gives it under भर्तृहरी। It also stands in the *hitopadeśa* (हितोपदेश । 61) and the *Pañcatantra* (पंचतंत्र)

Cf.— ते हि धीरा धरायां ये व्यसनेभ्यो न बिभ्यति।। 127।।
सत्त्ववंतो हि नात्मानं हापयन्ति विपद्गतम्।
उद्ग्रीवा इव धावन्ति पक्षच्छेदेऽपि वाजिनः।। 128।।
(अमरचंद्रसूरिकृतबालभारतम्। उद्योग पूर्वः 1 सर्गः)

कान्ताकटाक्षविशिखा न लुनन्ति
यस्य चित्तं न निर्दहति कोपकृशानुतापः।।
कर्षन्ति भूरि विषयाश्च न लोभपाशै-
र्लोकत्रयं जयति कृत्स्नमिदं स धीरः।। 107।।

स्त्रियों के कटाक्षरूपी बाणों से जिसका हृदय विदीर्ण न हो, क्रोध रूप अग्नि से जिसका अंतःकरण संतप्त न हो और विषयादिक के लोभ पाश से जिसका मन चलायमान न हो वह धैर्यधारी मनुष्य त्रिलोकी की विजय करने के हेतु समर्थ होता है।

That man who is neither pierced with the pointed arrows of famale glances, nor burnt with the scorching heat of anger, nor dragged into the tempting snares of sensual pleasures, is undoubtedly capable of conquering the three worlds.

---

1. *Cf.*—(*a*) प्रज्ञोऽतिधीरश्च शमोऽस्ति को वा
प्राप्तो न मोहं ललनाकटाक्षैः।। 12।।
(श्री शंकराचार्यस्य प्रश्नोत्तरमाला)
(*b*) कः शूरो यो ललनालोचनबाणैर्न विव्यथितः।।
(श्रीविमलाचार्यस्य प्रश्नोत्तररत्नमाला)

एकेनापि हि शूरेण पादाक्रान्तं महीतलम्।
क्रियते भास्करेणैव स्फारस्फुरित तेजसा।। 108।।

जैसे अकेला सूर्य देदीप्यमान किरणों से सारे जगत् को प्रकाशित करता है वैसे ही एक ही शूरवीर अपने असाधारण पराक्रम से इस अखण्ड भूमण्डल पर अपना प्रभाव प्रगट कर सकता है।

As the sun though alone illuminates the whole world by the spread of his dazzling light, so a single hero can also subdue the entire globe by dint of his matchless valour.

---

1. The word *pāda* (पाद) is here used in a sense, meaning both ray and foot.

2. *Tejas* (तेजस्) is also equivalent to (1) light and (2) influence or valour, the former as an attribute of the Sun and the latter as an attribute of a hero.

वह्निस्तस्य जलायते जलनिधिः कुल्यायते तत्क्ष-
णान्मेरुः स्वल्पशिलायते मृगपतिः सद्यः कुरङ्गायते।।
व्यालो माल्यगुणायते विषरसः पीयूषवर्षायते
यस्याङ्गेऽखिललोकवल्लभतमं शीलं समुन्मीलति।। 109।।

जो महापुरुष अखिल जगत् के मोहन करने वाले सुशील का स्वामी है उसके आगे अग्नि तो जल के समान, समुद्र नहर के समान, सुमेरु छोटी सी शिला के समान, मृगराज सिंह हरिण के समान, सर्प पुष्प माला के समान और विष अमृत के समान गुण धारण करते हैं।

One who possesses good conduct, the sole enchanter of the whole world, is enabled by virtue of his wonderful gift to convert fire into water, the ocean into a canal, the *Meru* (मेरु) into a deer, a snake into a flowery wreath, and poison into nectar.

---

1. Cf.—(*a*) तोयत्याग्निरपि स्रजत्यहिरपि व्याघ्रोऽपि सारङ्गति
व्यालोऽप्यश्वति पर्वतोऽप्युपलति क्ष्वेडोऽपि पीयूषति।
विघ्नोऽप्युत्सवति प्रियत्यरिरपि क्रीडातडागत्यपां
नाथोऽपि स्वगृहत्यटव्यपि नृणां शीलप्रभावाध्दुवम्।। 140।।
(सोमप्रभाचार्यस्य सूक्तिमुक्तावली)

(*b*) Good character is above all things else.

(*c*) अतीत्य हिं गुणान्सर्वान्स्वभावो मूर्ध्नि वर्तते।
(हितोपदेशः)

लज्जागुणौघजननी जननीमिव
स्वामत्यन्तशुद्धहृदयामनुवर्तमानाम्।।
तेजस्विनः सुखमसूनपि सन्त्यजन्ति
सत्यव्रतं व्यसनिनो न पुनः प्रतिज्ञाम्।। 110।।

सत्यभाषण करने वाले तेजस्वी मनुष्य अपनी प्रतिज्ञा भंग करने की अपेक्षा प्राण त्याग करने को श्रेष्ठ समझते हैं क्योंकि जो प्रतिज्ञा उनको लज्जादि उत्तम गुणों में प्रवृत्त करती है उसका पालन करना भी उनको अपनी माता के समान ही अभीष्ट है।

Lovers of truth, and men of spirit are always ready to abandon even life with ease rather than to swerve from their plighted faith which they cherish like their own mother; for, like her it tends to produce modesty and other virtues in them and keep their hearts full of purity and candour.

---

1. *Cf.*—(*a*) Live up to your engagements.

(*b*) एतदेव महत्त्वं च महतामुच्यते बुधैः।
प्रतिपन्नादचलनं प्राणानामत्ययेऽपि यत्।।

(कथासरित्सागरः शशाङ्कवतीलंबकः)

(*c*) If you make a promise be it a small or a great matter fulfil it. . . . .A promise shoule be kept as sacred as an oath.

(*d*) उदयति यदि भानुः पश्चिमे दिग्विभागे
विकसित यदि पद्मः पर्वताग्रे शिलायाम्।
प्रचट्ठति यदि मेरुः शीततां याति वह्निः
र्न चलति खलु वाक्यं सज्जनानां कदाचित्।।

(श्रीकविभट्टकृते पद्यसंग्रहे)

VARIANTS

As the subject of Variants has already been exhaustively dealt with by Mr. K.T. Telang (Vide Bombay Sanskrit Series No. XI) we shall only confine ourselves to such of the various readings as are not to be found there and advise our readers to refer to the aforesaid work for further information on the point: *(a), (b), (c)* and *(d)* are here used respectively to denote the first, second, third and fourth *caraṇas* of a stanza.

6. (a) रोद्धुं for व्यालं, मत्तेभ for रोद्धुंस; (b) भेत्तुं for छेत्तुं, ति for ते; (c) सतां for खलान्, खलान् for सताम् Pdm Vś.

11. (a) दहनश्छ for हुतभुक्छ, सूर्यप्रभा for सूर्यातपो; (c) प्रभावै for प्रयोगै; (d) सर्वेष्वौ for सर्वस्यौ Sk.

14. (b) भ्रमो for भ्रान्तं; (d) भुवने for भवने Sk.

17. (b) परिलघ्वीताम्रलक्ष्मी for लघुलक्ष्मी नैंवतान्सं Sb.; (c) मदमिलितमिलिन्द for अभिनवमदलेखा Sp.

19. (a) श्चंद्रप्रभा for न चंद्रोज्वला; (b) कुंचि for लंकृ; (c) एकावाणिर for वाण्येकासम; (d) चाक्षयं for भूषणं Sk.

20. (a) तुलं for धिकं; (b) वती for करी, सुखंवती for सुखकरी; (d) दुरितहा for नतुधनं Sk.

22. (a) तथा for सदा Sb.

28. (a) च्यो for च्य: Sb.

29. (a) न्वितो for कृशो Śp; (b) धीधृति for दीधिति Sb; (c) विशाल for विभिन्न, दलनव्यार for कवलग्रासैक Kś., दर्पाध्मातकरीन्द्रकुम्भदलनप्रेङ्खन्नखाग्राशनि: for मत्तेभेन्द्रविभिन्नकुंभकवलग्रासैकबद्धस्पृह: Sb.

30. (a) ल्प for ल्पं H., शुष्क for स्वल्पं Sb., सेक for शेष Sb., कं for गो: H.; (b) भवे for तुत H., ध: for धा Sb.

32. The Hitōpadeśa transposes the two halves of the stanza. In the Pañcatantra the 2nd caraṇa stands thus : जातस्तु गण्यते सो ऽत्र य: स्फुरत्यन्वयधिकम्.

33. (b) द्वे वृत्तीचम for द्वयी वृत्तिर्म ; (c) सर्वलोकस्य वा मूर्ध्नि वा सर्वछोकस्य; (d) विशिर्येतवनेऽथवा for शीर्यते वन एव वा H.

38. H. transposes (a) and (b).

39. शीलंशैलतटात्पतत्वभिजनो निर्दह्यतां वह्निना माश्रौषं जगति श्रुतस्यविफल क्लेशस्य नामाप्यम् for (a) and (b); (c) मे सर्वदा for नः सर्वदा; (d) बुस for लव; असौ for इमे Sb.

40. (a) ण्यवि for णिस H. P., नाम for कर्म H. P. ; (d) वाह्यः for त्वन्यः P.

43. (c) स्त्री for ह्री Sb.

44. Besides some of the Variants as given by Mr. K. T. Telang, Abhinavagupta in his commentary of Dhvanyālōka transposes (b) and (c).

48. (c) प्रचुरमित्र for प्रचुरनित्य H., भूरि for नित्य, वित्तध for नित्यध P.

50. (c) धिग for किम, यदस्यापि for वरास्माकं Sp.

53. (c) र्पो for र्पः; (d) भवेत्किं for किमसौ Sb.

54. (d) दुर्गुणवतां for त्सगुणिनां Sp.

57. (d) दहत्येवहि for स्पृष्टोदहति Sp.

59. (a) ह्ला for द्रा Sb.

61. (c) निःका for निष्का Kś Sk.

62. (c) ला for ले; (d) देतेयेषु for येष्वेतेनि Sb.

64. (a) सुच्छ for प्रच्छ; धि for धिः then comes with र for अ, प्यन for निर, and नीयाः for साराः ; then comes (b); (d) श्रुतेऽत्यन्तासक्तिःपुरुषमभिज्ञातं कथयति for (d) Sb.

66. (a) चेतो for चित्तं Sb.

68. Sb. reads (c) for (a), (a) for (b) and (b) for (c).

70. (a) पुष्णन्तः स्वीयमर्थं सतत कृतमहा for स्वार्थन्संपादयन्तो विततपृथुतरा Sb.

77. (b) पक्षिणः for णां गणाः Sarasvatī.

88. (c) श्रितानि for श्रयेण; (d) शाहोट for कंकोल Sb. The sp transpose the two halves of the stanza and reads शाखोट for कंकोल, अपि for न्यापि and नन्ति for नानि in our last caraṇa.

82. (b) मांसौ for शाल्यो ; (c) विचित्रा for च दिव्य Sb.

83. (a) पाण्डित्यस्य for ऐश्वर्यस्य, मधुर for सुजन Sb.; स्व for सु Sk.; (e) वतोध for वितुर्भ Sk.; Sb., र्वाच्य for व्याज Sk.; (d) सर्वस्यास्य पुन स्तथैव जगतः for सर्वेषामीपसर्वकारण मिदं Sb., कालसुभगं for कारणमिदं, वरं for परं Sk.

84. (a) अथवा for यदि वा; (b) परापर्तुतु for समाविशतुः (d) चलय for विचल Sb.

85. (c) लक्षण for सत्वर; (d) स्वस्थास्तिष्ठत for लोकाः पश्यत्, चोद्यतम् for कारणम् Sb.

88. (c) जि for भि, ग्नोऽसुरैः for ग्नः परैः Sb.

91. (a) रविनिशा for शशिदिवा P., (c) निरीक्ष्य for विलोक्य P.

94. (b) र्माप्त for मैंक Sb.

95. (a) एडान्त for एडोद Sb.; (b) क्षिप्तः सदा for क्षिप्तो महा Sp., रनिशं for पुटके, चरः कल्पितो for टनं कारिता; (d) भानुर्भ्र for सूर्योभ्रा, यद्वशेन for नित्यमेव Sb.

96. (b) सहस्त्रगुणिता for ऽपिनैव नचय, नचवाग्विशुद्धिः for त्रकृताऽपिसेवा; (c) कर्माणिपूर्वशुभसंचय for भाग्यानि पूर्वतपसाखलु Sb.

98. (a) धून्म्र for धूंम्र; (d) निन्गु for नैर्गु Sb.

100. The Sb. reads (c) for (b), and (b) for (c).

106. (a) महाशयस्य for हि धैर्यवृत्तेर् Sb.; (c) धः कृत for घोमुख तनूनपातो for कृतस्य वह्नेर् H. Sp.; (d) यान्ति for याति Sp. H. Sb.

NOTES

A. As to the first place being given to the नीतिशतकम् Kṛṣṇaśāstri Mahābala says: "इह खलु राजर्षिप्रवरः श्रीभतृहरिरुभयलोकसाधकं नातिशृङ्गारवैराग्याख्यशतकत्रयात्कं ग्रन्थं चिकीर्षुः सदाचरणस्य नीतिक्षानपूर्वकत्वात्तज्ज्ञानाय प्रथमं नीतिशतकमारभमाण इत्यादि".

B. नीति is a very comprehensive term including everything between the sciences of moral and political philosophies. Briefly speaking it is generally used for wisdom and prudence.

C. The word Nītiśatakam (नीतिशतकम्) is translated by Prof.

Tawney as Hundred stanzas on Ethics and Politics. At page XV of his preface, he says : "Though the word 'Nīti' is usually translated policy, most of the stanzas arranged under this head are rather of an ethical and social character. They inculcate maxims of worldly prudence, and seem designed to teach knowledge of men and individuals, rather than as members of political communities."

1. (a) "As Prof, Max Müller has suggested that Kṣapaṇaka may be a name of Bhartṛhari, it may, perhaps, be desirable to point out that in the अनेकार्थध्वनि मंजरी attributed to a महाक्षपणक we have the phrase स्वानुबोधकमानाय which seems to bear the same meaning as the phrase we have now discussed (*viz.*, स्वानुबोधैकमानाय). The stanza before us, however, is also given as the opening stanza of the Yogavasiṣṭhasāra in Aufrecht's Catalogue." (K. T. Telang).

Here I cannot help dissenting from the view held by the aforesaid learned scholars. First, because no Sanskrt writer has ever said anything about the identity of क्षपणक and भर्तृहरि; and, secondly, because the use of a single phrase स्वानुबोधैकमानाय by both the authors is merely a thing of pure accident which cannot logically lead us to infer that क्षपणक and भर्तृहरि were one and the same perosn.[1] Dr. Bhāu Dāji who thinks भर्तृहरि as one of the नवरत्न or nine gems probably confounds him with क्षपणक, The nine gems are thus enumerated in the following ślōka–

धन्वन्तरि क्षपणकामरसिंह शंकु वेतालभट्ट घटखर्पर कालिदासाः।
ख्यातो वराहमिहिरो नृपते सभायां रत्नानि वै वररुचि र्नव विक्रमस्य।।

(b) दिक्काल. Needless to say that Indian Science recognises ten दिशा's or directions (*viz.*, North, Northeast, East, Southeast, South, Southwest, West, Northwest, above or zenith, and below or nadir), and three काल's or thimes (*viz.* past, present, and furture).

2. (a) It is a general belief among learned Sanskritists that this stanza furnishes the keynote to the comoposition of this work, and especially to that of the last Chapter dealing with asceticism; and

1. The reader is here requested to refer to a number of phrases, from other works, similar to those of the śatakas, which are pointed out in the footnotes at their proper places in the course of this edition.

hence to my mind its appropriate place would have been there. However, as far as it is known to me, no edition of Bhartṛhari's Centuries has ever dared transfer it from Nīti to Vairāgya. Consequently, no apology would, I think, be needed for its present position.

(b) There is a tradition that once upon a time Bhartṛhari was presented with a wondroud fruit of divine virtues capable of bestowing immortality and everlasting youth upon one who ate it. The king who held wife even dearer to his own life thought it advisable to give this fruit to his beloved queen. However, the queen consort had no love for the magnanimous husband, and so, after receiving the aforesaid gift from the Rāja she gave it to her paramour who was passed it on the hands of a prostitute with whom he was in real love. The prostitute who had the highest regard and affection for Bhartṛhari came to him, and respectfully placed the miraculous fruit before her sovereign lord. But no sooner were his eyes cast upon it than the wise king did at once recognise it to be the same fruit with which a few days ago he was himself presented by a pious Brāhmaṇa. A strong suspicion immediately rose into his mind and he made full and prompt enquiries about the matter. The whole thing being soon clear he became much agrieved and distressed at heart. His affection for mundane objects thereby suffered a great deal and his heart was thus convinced of the utter impossibility of finding sincere love in women upon the surface of this terrestrial globe. This śloka has a covert reference to the aforesaid tradition.

3. ब्रह्मा is one of the Hindu Trinity. His special work is सृष्टिरचना *i.e.* bringing forth the creation.

5. Strictly speaking, a hare has no horns. To find out hare's horns therefore denotes an utter impossibility. The acquirement of oil from particles of sand, and that of water in the midst of a mirage are likewise impossible.

"On शशविषाणं the following stanza may be quoted : एष वंध्यासुतो याति खपुष्प कृतशेखरः। मृगतृष्णाम्भसिस्नातः शशशृङ्ग धनुर्धर।। which brings together the expression most in use to signify thing which do not exist". (K. T. Telang).

6. (a) Śirīṣa (शिरीष) A species of flower trees. The flower of Śirīṣa is generally regarded as the type of delicacy by Indian poets.

(b) क्षाराम्बुधि Ocean of salt water. It is worth noting in connection with this that according to Indian mythology the earth is surrounded with seven oceans, *viz.*— (1) क्षीरोदः, (2) इक्षुरसोदः, (3) सुरोदः, (4) घृतोदः, (5) दध्योदः, (6) क्षारोदः and (7) शुद्धोदः or oceans of milk, sugarcandy juice, wine, ghee, curdle, salt and drinkable water.

7. एकान्तगुणं means productive of extraordinary good एकान्ता अतिशयिता गुणा यस्मिन् तत्। अथातिशयोभरः तीव्रैकान्तनितान्तानि" इत्यमरः।

8. The late lamanted Pandit K. T. Telang says: "I am inclined to take यदाकिं as equal to यदाऽकिं to make distinctly that contrast with the third line." Needless to add that agreeing with him I have here adopted the suggested reading though I have not found it in any of the copies consulted for this edition.

9. The word निरुपमरसं which has here been rendered as 'devoid of all juice and taste,' literally means of incomparable taste', *i.e.* whose disgusting taste can stand no comparison whatever.

10. (a) The Gaṅges (गंगा). The rise of the Gaṅges is mythologically traced to the divine feet of Viṣṇu, whence after flowing through the heavens, she falls upon the head of Śiva ; and lastly, from the head of Śiva, she descends into the world and flowing down from the heights of the Himālayas empties here waters into the Bay of Bengal. The Gaṅges is described as having become arrogant in the Rāmāyaṇa (Bālakāṇḍa. XLIII., 6 Bomb. Ed.) and this fact will amply account for her successive falls.

(b) "How Bhāgiratha got the Gaṅges to Śiva's head, thence to the Himālaya, thence to earth and thence to the nether world; and how her waters there sanctified the offspring of Sagara is well known. For the whole story see Rāmāyaṇa *loc. cit.* According to that work (st 75) the Gaṅges गगनाच्छङ्कर शिरस्ततो धरणि मागता। शतमुख applies literally to the fall of to the river and to that of the man who is lost all sense of right and wrong; it applies in the sense of a variety of ways." (K. T. Telang)

(c) "Bhāgiratha, the son of Dilīpa and great-grandson of Sagara, king of Ayodhyā, brought the sacred Gaṅges from heaven to earth by the aid of Śiva, who is fabled to have received the stream on his head; he then conducted this river to the ocean in order to purify the ashes of his ancestors, the 60,000 sons of Sagara, who were reduced to ashes by Viṣṇu in the form of Kapila, when they dug through the earth in order to recover the sacrificial horse which had been stolen from their father." (Prof. Tawney).

12. The original text of the latter half of the stanza as herein given does not admit of the erroneous interpretation given to it by Mr. Durga Prasad of Lahore who translates it thus: " The superiority of his luck over the lower animals lies in his living without grazing grass."

13. धर्म–Mrs. Annie Besant in her translation of the Bhagvad Gītā Says: Dharma is a wide word, primarily meaning the essential nature of a thing; hence, the laws of its being, its duty; and it includes religious rites, appropriate to these laws. (*Vide* The Lord's Song by Annie Besant, p. 21).

16. (a) Kalpa (कल्प) generally means the end of the world or the universal destruction. It is a day of Brahmā consisting of 1,000 Mahāyugas each of which comprises the aggregate of the four Yugas or ages amounting to 4,320,000 years. The lenght of a Kalpa is therefore 4,320,000,000 years of mortals. At the end of each Kalpa the existing world is totally annihilated and its place is taken by a new one.

(b) The Hindus believe that knowledge never forsakes its fortunate owner throughout his successive births. Perhaps the belief in the Transmigration of souls does not need any special mention in the place.

On the immortality of knowledge Mr. K. T. Telang has the following.

"Comp. विद्याकुलजनबधुरिव जहाति नो जन्म जन्मा ऽ पि etc. ।।

and Kumāra I. 30."

17. परमार्थ–*Artha* (अर्थ) is interest or individual interest and *Paramārtha* (परमार्थ) is the highest interest or the interest of the soul.

18. (a) Haṁsa (हंस or swan)— This bird is generally believed as being gifted with the peculiar power of separating milk from water when they are mixed together and placed before it.

(b) "The meaning of the stanza is that the swan may be unfortunate, and not have a good dwelling place, but its great inherent qualities will still remain." (K. T. Telang).

However, to my mind, the real meaning of the stanza is this : "A learned man may be deprived of all his property, but no one can ever wrest from him his literary fame and reputation."

20. "On गुरूणांगुरु: the commentator has the following क्षुद्रगुरव: सर्वविद्यासम्पूर्णप्राज्ञं प्रष्टु मायान्ति स प्राज्ञो गुरूणामपि गुरु:।। अथा च गृणाति हित मुपदिशति इति गुरु रिति गुरुपदव्याख्यानमतो हित कर्त्री विद्यैव. This is too farfetched and not free from difficulties. गुरूणांगुरु: is simply greatest of the great." (K. T. Telang).

To me गुरूणां गुरु: is as clear as anything. I take it in its ordinary sense of Guru of Gurus (teacher of teachers) or the best teacher. गुरु is feminine. See Pāṇini IV. I. 44.

Kṛṣṇa Śāstri Mahābala also explains it as विद्यैव गुरूणा मुपदेष्टृणां गृणाति हित मुपदिशतीति गुरु रुपदेष्ट्री।

Prof. Tawney has left out the clause altogether.

21. To understand the clause 'ज्ञातिश्चेदनलन किम्' more clearly let us see what the Sanskrita commentator says upon it : ज्ञाति: स्वजाति: सन्निधावस्ति चेदनलेनाग्निाकिम् अग्निकृतं तापादिकं सैव करिष्यति।।

Mr. Durga Prasad translates it thus : he needs no fire to ruin him who hosts of relations to support.

24. (a) Here is a play upon the word रससिद्धा: which means (1) रसेषु पारदादिषु सिद्धा: सज्जा इत्यर्थ: as well as (2) रसेषु शृङ्गारादिषु सिद्धा: पूर्णा: कुशला इति। "रससिद्ध –perfect in the rasas or sentiments, masters of style, capable of ruling the passions and feelings of men." (K. T. Telang).

(b) Rasās (रसा:) The nine poetical styles (or Indian muses) as enumerated by the poets are : (1) the Śṛṅgāra of Erotic; (2) the Hāsya or Comic; (3) the Karuṇā or Elegiac; (4) the Vīra of Heroic ; (5) the Raudra of Tragic : (6) the Bhayaṅkara or Melancholic : (7) Vaibhatsa or Satiric ; (8) the Śānta : or Didactic ; and (9) the Adbhuta or Sensational.

26. Mr. Durga Prasada is far from being right and correct in translating the last line of the stanza. See Durga Prasad's English Translation of Bhartṛhari's Nātiśataka. Para 23.

28. Asidhārā vow (असिधाराव्रत) A vow to stand on the sharp

edge of a swrod ; or a vow to keep constant company with a young and handsome woman without ever dreaming of conjugal love.

30. The point of the stanza is not that the 'pariah' is not ashamed even to eat the fleshless bone of the cow (as Prof. Tawney seems to conclude) but the point is really this that the dog is not ashamed even to eat with great relish a piece of dry bone which has nothing at all to attract his attention.

"The poet's meaning certainly is that a special impurity attaches to eating the flesh of the cow. But Babu Rajendra Lāl Mitra has shown that this notion is of very recent origin. It does not appear to have been prevalent in time of Bhavabhuti, who is generally places in the eighth century. So, that this stanza seems to have been written at a far later date than that assigned by Prof. Lassen to the majority of Bhartṛhari's poems." (Prof. Tawney).

It will not be quite clear to the reader why have I quoted at length the above note of Prof. Tawney. But I will not tax his patience to tell the plain truth in the smallest possible space. There is a word गो: in the text, and this little monosyllabe has furnished the learned professor with a fine clue for the solution of the much debated quiestion of Bhartṛhari's period. However, I would beg to warn the general public to take it for what it is worth. Because it needs not be pointed out that in the first place the word गो: is put in merely for the sake of metre. If we take out गो: is put in merely for the sake of metre. It we take out गो: and put in some other word of equal measure (no matter, it qualifies अस्थि or not) the meaning of the śloka will remain substantially the same without losing the least and slightest force.[1] Secondly, the assumption that the notion of attaching a special impurity to eating the flesh of the cow is of later origin than the time of Bhavabhūti, is quite unfounded. The sanctity of the cow is al old as the Vedas. The Rāmāyaṇa and the Mahābhārata have numerous passage in praise of the sacred cow. "Kālidāsa in his Raghuvaṁśa says that Dilīpa the renowned

---

1. Mr. K.T. Telang has found कम् to exist for गो: in no less than seven different copies of the śatakas which he has consulted for his edition of भर्तृहरि: (Vide p. 9. B. S. Series No. XI). The copies of the Hitopadeśa, Pañcatantra, and the Subhāṣitāvali were the verse is quoted have also got क instead of गो: ।

ancestor of Rāmchandra, preferred giving his own life to seeing नन्दिनी (the sacrificial cow of वशिष्ठ) devoured by a lion.[1]

See also Mr. K. T. Telang's note at p. xii Bombay Sanskrit Series No. xi.

32. The radical meaning of the word संसार is also equivalent to what is always in motion संसरतीति संसारः।

"परिवर्तिनि– revolving, rotating. The allusion is to the ever-recurring birth and death in this world. पुनरपि जननं पुनरपि मरणं पुनरपि जननी जठरे शयनम् are familiar verses to the same effect. They are ascribed to Śaṅkarācārya. See Kāvya Saṅgraha 35." (K. T. Telang).

34. (a) Rāhu, (राहु)– Name of a demon, son of Vipracitti and Siṁhikā.

(b) For the story of Rāhu's vengeance on the sun and the moon, refer to the following note of Mr. F. S. Growse, from his Translation of the Rāmāyaṇa of Tulsidāsa vol. III :— The demon Rāhu having disguised himself as one of the gods, succeeded in securing a draught of the nectar which the gods had churned out of the ocean. The sun and the moon, who had detected the impostor, gave information to Viṣṇu, who thereupon cut off the monster's head and two of his forearms. As he could not rob him of the miiortality that the nectar had conferred, the severed head and tail were metamorphosed into heavenly bodies, under the names of Rāhu and Ketu, or the ascending and descending node; of which the former still wreaks vengeance on the sun and the moon by now and then swallowing them.

35. (a) Śeṣa (शेष)–Name of the celebrated serpent King Bāsukī. He is represented as supporting the entire world on his thousand heads of hoods. *Cf.* "ब्रह्माण्डकुम्भकारं भुजगाकारं जनार्दनं नौमि। स्फारेयत्फणचक्रे धरा शरावश्रियं वहति" (गोवर्धनस्यार्यासप्तशती 17).

(b) Kamaṭhapati (कमठपति). The lord of tortoises, Viṣṇu is represented as to have assumed the form of a tortoise in order to support the serpent King Bāsuki together with the entire world

1. सत्वं मदीयेन शरीरवृत्ति देहेन निर्वर्तयितुं प्रसीद।
दिनवसानोत्सुकबालवत्सा विसृज्यतां धेनुरियं महर्षेः।।

(रघुवंशम्।2।45)

upon his stalwart back. *Cf.* "यो धत्तेशेषनागं तदनुवसुमतीं स्वर्गपातालयुक्तां युक्तां सर्वैः समुद्रैर्हिमगिरिकनक प्रस्थमुख्यैर्नगेन्द्रैः। एतद्ब्रह्माण्ड मस्यामृत धरसदृशं भाति वंशे मुरारेः पायाद्वः कूर्मदेहः प्रकटितमहिमा माधवः कामरूपी।।"

36. It is told that the mountains were formerly furnished wit wings by which they were enabled to fly from one place to another. Every thing whether animate or inanimate being therefore afraid of being crushed to pieces by their fall, Indra was led to make a vow to deprive them all of this valued privilege. When he began to cut off their wings by his *Bajra* many had to save their lives by flying into the ocean. *Maināka,* the son of the Himālayas was one of those who retained their wings by drowining themselves into the ocean who kindly gave them the desired refuge. This story is told in the Sundarakāṇḍa of the Rāmāyaṇa.

37. (a) इनकान्त–Sun-gem. "A king of crystal cool to the touch, and supposed to posses fabulous properties, because like a glass lens it gave out heat when exposed to the rays of the sun."

(Monier Williams.)

(b) Mark the word *pāda* (पाद) in the text which means both foot and ray.

38. (a) " The idea of the last line finds frequent expression in Sanskrit Literature; तेजसा सह इतानां वयः कुत्रोपयुज्यते or Kālidāsa's तेजसां हि न वयः समीक्षते, or Bhavabhūti's गुणाः पुज्यास्थानं गुणिषु न च लिंगं न च वयः are other wellknown instances." (K. T. Telang).

(b) *Teja*— (तेजः) The word is susceptible of a wide range of interpretations. It is thus defined by Bharata the father of Sanskrit Drama:

अधिक्षेपापमानादे : प्रयुक्तस्य परेण यत्। प्राणत्ययेऽ प्यसह्नं तत्तेजः समुदाहृतम्।।

See Nāṭyaśāstram XXII. 39.

40. Mr. Charles Wilkins' interpretation of the verse runs as follows:—

"Those faculties are not injured." This is a mere saying. "The judgement is unimpaired." That also is but an expression; for the moment a man is deprived of the comfort of riches, he is quite another. Is not this curious? See Fables and Proverbs from the Sanskrit. Morley's Universal Library No. 30, p. 70.

46. *Kalpalatā* (कल्पलता) a creeper of Indra's paradise. This heavenly plant is supposed to be able to grant all desires and hence it is also called as the wish-yielding tree.

49. *Meru* (मेरु) See Note to stanza 80 (a) (Nīti).

50. *Cātaka* (चातक) a Species of partridge. Name of a bird which is supposed to live only on rain drops.

"The Cātaka is fabled never to drink except it be such drops as fall in the month of October, when the sun is in the same longitude as oreturus (Svāti), a time of the year when a shower is a very rare occurence. The same precious drops if they fact into the sea are transmuted into pearls." (Mr. Growse).

Allusion is made to the latter tradition in stanza 57. (Nīti.)

53. It is a general belief among the people of India that there exists a certain species of snakes which bear or carry invaluable gems upon their hoods.

58. It must be understood that the stanza refers to the service of evil masters.

64. See note to stanza 28 (Nīti).

67. See Note to stanza 50 (Nīti).

69. "The idea of stanza is that all should make their choice of the alternative stated. The two cannot be joined. *Cf.* also the quotation at Sarasvatī-kaṇṭhābharaṇa, p. 69. (Barooa's Ed.)" (Telang).

74. (a) *Padma* (पद्म) a species of lotus that expands in the day and closes at night.

(b) *Kairava* (कैरव) is the lily that blossoms in the night and fades at sunrise.

76. "This stanza gives a moral aspect to the physical phenomenon of boiling milk being prevented from overflowing by water being thrown upon it." (K. T. Telang).

77. *Keśava* (केशव)– One who sleeps in water. It is a name of *Viṣṇu* (विष्णु).

(b) For the lying of refugee mountains into the bomb of the ocean see our Note to stanza 36. *supra.*

(c) *Baḍavānala* (बडवानल)–The submarine fire is represented

in mythology as a being with a body of flame and the head of a mare whih sprang from the things of the partiarch *Urya* and fell into the ocean. *Baḍvānala* is a compound word meaning mare-fire.

(d) *Saṁvarataka* (संवर्तक)– a species of rains powerful enough to bring about the universal destruction by incessant downpour or heavy showers.

(e) "According to Hindu notions the fires that are to roll every thing together and destroy the world at the time of universal destruction, are concealed beneath the sea." See Prof. Tawney"s Three centuries of Bhartṛhari p. 31 Cal. Ed.

79. *Tribhuvana* (त्रिभुवन) The three spheres of the universe, comprising the earth, heaven, and hell.

80. (a) *Hemagiri* (हेमगिरि) or *Sumeru* (सुमेरु) The sacred mountain Meru. This celebrated golden mountain is supposed to be situated in the centre of the world, and around which the sun is said to make his daily revolutions.

(b) *Rajatagiri* (रजतगिरि) or *Kailāsa* (कैलास) is the name of mountain, which forms the northwestern peak of the Himālayas and the residence of *Śiva* and *Kuvera*. This peak of the abode of Ice is supposed to be made of silver. The name silver peak might possibly have been given to it on account of its silver-like appearance owing to the fact of its remaining covered over with ice all the year round.

(c) *Malaya* (मलय)–"Name of mountain range in Southern India, abounding in sandal trees. Poets usually represent the breeze from the Malaya mountain as wafting the odour of sandal trees and other plants growing, thereon, which peculiarly affects persons who are smit withlove." (Prof. V. S. Apte). Dr. Kielhorn says that Malaya is the name of a mountainous range on the Western coast of the Indian peninsula on which the best sandal wood trees grow.

(d) *Kaṅkōla* (कङ्कोल) a kind of plant "कोलकम्। कंकोलकं कोशफलम्" इत्यमरः। The commentator says कोलकं-कंकोलकं-कोशफलं त्रीणि कंकोल "गवला" इति ख्यातस्य।

(e) *Nimba* (निम्ब) is a kind of large tree very common in India. Its name is ordinary Hundustāni is Neema. Its bark, twigs, and leaves are all very bitter of taste.

(f) *Kuṭaja* (कुटज)– It is a king of forest plant of soury taste. Its Latin name as given by the Bhāṣākāra of the *Abhinavanighaṇṭu* is pongamia glabrā. See page 102 of अभिनवनिघंटु by Pandit Dattarāma Chaube.

81. (a) The churning of the ocean is one of the common place of Hindu poetry. With mount Mandara as a churning stick, the great serpent Bāsuki as a rope, and Narain himself in tortoise form as the pivot on which to work, the gods and demons combined to churn the Milky ocean." (Mr. Growse).

(b) The fourteen jewels churned out of the ocean are thus enumeraed in the popular stanza of the Maṅgalāśataka which is attributed to Kālidāsa लक्ष्मीः कौस्तुभ पारिजातक सुरा धन्वन्तरि श्चन्द्रमा। गावः कामदुधाः सुरेश्वरगजो रम्भादि देवाङ्गनाः। अश्वः सप्तमुखो विषं हरिधनुः शंखोऽमृतं चाम्बुधे, रत्नानीह चतुर्दश प्रतिदिनं कुर्युः सदा मङ्गलम्।। *i.e.* they are: (1) the goddess of wealth of beauty, (2) a gem worn by Viṣṇu, (3) the tree of paradise, (4) wine, (5) the physician of the gods, (6) the moon, (7) the cow of plenty, (8) Indra's elephant, (9) the heavenly nymphs, (1) the seven mouthed horse, (11) poison, (12) the bow of Viṣṇu, (13) the sacred conch and (14) nectar.

84. Yuga (युग) An age of the world. The yugas are four in number *viz.*, the Satyayuga (the golden age), the Tretāyuṇa (the silver age), the Dvāparayuga (the brozen age) and the Kaliyuga the iron age). The duration of each is said to be respectively 1,728,000; 1,296,000, 864,000; and 420,000 years of men. It is also supposed that the regularly descending length of the Yugas represents a corresponding physical and moral deterioration in the people who live during each age.

85. *Daiva* (दैव) "पूर्व जनम कृतं कर्म तद्दैव मिति कथ्यते।"

87. (a) *Vṛhaspati* (वृहस्पति) He is the regent of the planet Jupiter, and preceptor of the gods." (Prof. Tawney's Bhartṛhari, p. 35).

(b) *Airāvata* (ऐरावत) is the name of Indra's elephant, It is one of the fourteen jwewls. See note to stanza 81 (b). (Nīti).

89 *Karma* (कर्म) Here man's fate or the certain consequence of the acts done in a former life.

90. "The fact of the tree being the ताल (Palm) adds to the force of the lines as it gives little or no shade." (K. T. Telang).

93. (a) I think there is no necessity of pointing out that the Karīra bush has to leaves all the year round, that the owl is doomed not to see in day light and that the Cātaka is believed to drink no water except the drops of October showers.

(b) *Karīra* (करीर) a thorny plant in the woods eaten by camels and goats. It remains leafless at all seasons of the year.

(c) *Cātaka* (चातक) See note to stanza 50. (Nīti) believed by the Hindus to be Creator of the universe, Viṣṇu to have assumed the ten incarnations and Mahādeva to be an ascetic. The ten incarnations of Viṣṇu are those of Fish, Tortoise, Boar, Man-lion, Vāmana (Dwārf), Paraśurāma, Rāmacandra, Kṛṣṇa, Buddha and Kalki.

(b) The author in common with a large majority of Indian poets evidently beleives that it is the Sun who revolves round the Earth; but, on the contrary, scientific men both before and after him have proved it beyond doubt that the Earth revolves round the Sun and not vice versa.

(c) "ब्रह्माण्डभाण्डोदरे" is a common expression, Comp. Vīracarita, p. 17, or Sāhityadarpaṇa, p. 97. The allusion is to the story of Brahmā coming out of the primordial egg, the two halves of which then became Heaven and Earth. See Manu, Ist. 11, 12 13 and Matsya Purāṇa. II. 28, et seq. Prof. Tawney (Indian Antiquary, Vol IV., p., 264) refers to Aristophanes for the same idea. (See his Bhartṛhari, p. 38)". (K. T. Telang).

ब्रह्माण्ड means the egg of Brahman, *i.e.* the whole universe.

99. अविपत्तेः is rendered by Dr. Peterson as "to the bitter end."

100. (a) *Arka* (अर्क) plants generally abound in wild growth on the Indian soil.

(b) *Kodrava* (कोद्रव) is the *paspalum frilmentaceum* or *Scrobiculatum* which bears a small grain of inferior quality, eaten only by the poor.

(c) "कर्मभूमिः This world is often so called. The idea is somewhat similar to that of Bishop Butler, who calls this a world for man's probation. See Rāmāyaṇa (Bomb. Ed.) Ayōdhyākāṇḍa, CIX, 28 (p. 205), कर्मभूमिमिमां प्राप्य कर्तव्यं कर्म यच्छुभम्. See also Muir, V., 325 (Ed. 1870), कर्मभूमिरियं ब्रह्मन्फलभूमिरसौ मता which fixes the meaning precisely.......... The idea expressed in the several analogies in the first three line is that of good things misapplied. Thus तिलखली is a very worthless stuff to be cooked in a pot of the Vaidūrya-precious stone with sandal wood fuel; a golden ploughshare similarly is misapplied if used indigging up the ground for the अर्क root which is of little value, and so is a collection of कर्पूर trees if it is cut down to make a hedge around a field where कोद्रव is grown, this being a very coarse and poor sort of grain. This is exactly the idea of the fourth line also. The opportunities given by birth in this world are lost when तपस is not practised. The अर्क is mentioned in the familiar proverb "अर्के चेन्मधु विन्देते किमर्थं पर्वतं व्रजेत्." (K. T. Telang).

101. (a) *Meru* (मेरु)– See Note to stanza 80 (a) (Nīti).

(b) "A man may do the most difficult and dangerous things in order to do what is fated not to happen or to avoid what is fated to happen. But he will fail." (K. T. Telang).

109. *Meru* (मेरु)– See Note (a) no stanza 80 (Nīti).

ŚṚṄGĀRAŚATAKAṂ

।। अथ शृङ्गारशतकम् ।।

COITION

शम्भुस्वयम्भुहरयो हरिणेक्षणानां
येनाक्रियन्त सततं गृहकर्मदासाः ।।
वाचामगोचरचरित्रविचित्रताय
तस्मै नमो भगवते कुसुमायुधाय ।। 1 ।।

भाषाटीका।

जिस प्रभावशाली कुसुमायुध ने ब्रह्मा, विष्णु और महेश इन तीनों देवताओं को मृगनयनी सुंदरियों के गृहकार्य करने वाले दास बना रखे हैं। और जिसका चरित्र सर्वथा विचित्र और अकथनीय है उस कामदेव रूप भगवान् के अर्थ हमारा नमस्कार है।

Bow to the illustrious *Kusumāyudha* (कुसुमायुध), the holder of a flowery bow (*i.e., Cupid),* who compelled Svayaṁbhu or Brahmā (स्वयंभु or ब्रह्मा), the Creater, Hari or Viṣṇu (हरि or विष्णु), the Protector, Śambhu or Mahādeva (शंभु or महादेव), the Destroyer, of the Universe to be domestic servants of antelope-eyed, ladies, and whose strange deeds are far beyond the description of words!

---

1. *Cf.*—(*a*) सक एकस्त्रीणि जयति जगन्ति कुसुमायुधः।। (काव्यप्रदीपः)
   (*b*) अनङ्गेनाबलासंगाज्जिता येन जगत्रयी।
   स चित्रचरतिः कामः सर्वकामप्रदोस्तु वः।। (शार्ङ्गधरपद्धतिः)
   (*c*) जाहि प्रभाव महेश हरि, विधि मृगनयनी दास।
   ताहि जगत कुसुमषुके, वश हो लेत उसास। (रसिक कवि)

स्मितेन भावेन च लज्जया भिया
पराङ्मुखैरर्धकटाक्षवीक्षणैः।।
वचोभिरीर्ष्या कलहेन लीलया
समस्तभावैः खलु बन्धनं स्त्रियः।। 2।।

मंद-मंद मुस्कान, हाव-भाव, लज्जा, भय, पराङ्मुखता, अधखुले नेत्रों के कटाक्ष, वचन, ईर्ष्या, कलह और लीलाविलासादि सब प्रकार से ही स्त्रियों के बंधन रूप होने में कुछ भी संदेह नहीं है।

There is no doubt that women ensnare men by their smiles *Bhāvas* (भाव) or feelings and emotions, modesty, fear, turn of face, half-opened glances, words, jealousy, amorous quarrels and all other graceful sports.

---

1. Quoted anonymously in the *Subhāṣitāvali* (सुभाषितावलि) at No. 3383.

Cf.—(*a*) कुविआओ पसन्नाओ ओरण्णमुहोओ विहसमाणाओ।
कुपिताः प्रसन्ना अवरुदितमुखा विहसन्त्यः।
जह गहिओ तह हिअअ हरन्ति उच्छिन्तमहिलाआ
यथा गृहीताः तथा हृदयं स्वैरिण्यो महिलाः।।
(आनन्दवर्धनस्य ध्वन्यालोके)

(*b*) एता एव स्तृताः स्त्रीणां विप्रलम्भनवागुराः।
बद्धा यास्ववसीदन्ति तरुणा/हरिणा इव।।
(भर्तृहरिनिर्वेदम्)

भ्रूचातुर्याकुञ्चिताक्षाः कटाक्षाः
स्निग्धा वाचो लज्जिताश्चैव हासाः।।
लीलामन्दं प्रस्थितं च स्थितं च
स्त्रीणामेतद्भूषणं चायुधं च।। 3 ।।

यथोचित भ्रूभंगपूर्वक कुंचित नेत्रों के कटाक्ष, मधुर भाषण, लज्जायुक्त हास्य और लीला सहित मंदगति और स्थिति स्त्रियों के आभूषण और आधुय दोनों का काम देते हैं।

Side-long looks with contracted pupils and skilful display of eyebrows, honeyed and affectionate words, modest smiles, and artful slow movements and postures of their bodies equally serve as ornaments and weapons to women.

---

1. Quoted under *Bhartṛhari* (भर्तृहरि) in the *Śārṅgadharapaddhati* at No. 3954, and under Kaviputrau (कविपुत्रौ) in the *Subhāṣitāvali* (सुभाषितावलि), at No. 2227.

Cf.— भावस्थैर्मधुरकथैः सुभाषितैस्त्वं साटोपस्खलितविलम्बितैर्गतैश्च।
मानाढ्यैर्हरसि मनांसि कामुकानां सुव्यक्तं ह्यति जगती प्रहर्षिणीव।।
(भरतनाट्यशास्त्रम् 15 अध्यायः)

क्वचित्सुभ्रूभङ्गैः क्वचिदपि च लज्जापरिणतैः
क्वचिद्भीतित्रस्तैः क्वचिदपि च लीलाविलसितैः।।
नवोढानामेतैर्वदनकमलैर्नेत्रचलितैः स्फुरन्नी-
लाब्जानां प्रकरपरिपूर्णा इव दिशः।। 4।।

विषयासक्त मनुष्यों की दृष्टि में कहीं तो सुंदर भ्रूभंग, कहीं लज्जा से नम्रभाव, कहीं भय भीति और कहीं लीलायुक्त विलासादि सहित नवोढा नारियों के मुखारविंद को शोभा देने वाले प्रकाशमान नीलकमल के समान चंचल नेत्रों के समूह से संसार की दशों दिशा ही परिपूर्ण हो रही हैं।

भावार्थ।

संसारिक मनुष्यों के लिये संपूर्ण जगत् ही नवयौवना रमणियों के हाव-भावों से व्याप्त हो रहा है। यहां तक कि इस संसार में उनको ऐसा कोई भी स्थान दृष्टि नहीं आता कि जहाँ पर इस विघ्न से सुरक्षित होकर वे अपने आत्मोद्धार का सुखपूर्वक प्रयत्न कर सकें।

One who is ardently in love of women always finds the different directions of the world entirely filled with the charming glances of lotus-eyed *Navoḍhās* (young and newly married women) which are somewhere marked with the play of their fair eyebrows, somewhere with modesty or bashfulness, somewhere with fear, somewhere with sportive gracefulness and somewhere with the unsteady motions of their fickle eyes resembling the splendour of a dark blue lotus in its full blossom.

वक्त्रं चन्द्रविडम्बि पङ्कजपरीहासक्षमे लोचने वर्णः
स्वर्णमपाकरिष्णुरलिनीजिष्णुः कचानां चयः।।
वक्षोजाविभकुम्भविभ्रमहरौ गुर्वी नितम्बस्थली वाचो
हारि च मार्दवं युवतिषु स्वाभाविकं मण्डनम्।।5।।

पूर्ण चंद्रमा को लज्जित करने वाला मुख, कमलों का उपहास करने वाले विशाल नेत्र, सुवर्ण की कांति का निरादर करने वाली देह, भ्रमर पंक्ति का पराजय करने वाले केश, गजराज के गण्डस्थल का अपमान करने वाले उरोज, विस्तृत नितंबस्थल, मनोहर वचन और कोमलता स्त्रियों के स्वाभाविक भूषण हैं।

भावार्थ–प्रत्यक्ष रूप से तो इस श्लोक में स्त्रियों की असाधारण सुंदरता का वर्णन किया गया है। वैराग्य पक्ष में इसका भावार्थ इस प्रकार समझना उचित है। स्त्रियों की छवि स्वभाव ही से बहुत मनोहर है इसलिये इनसे अपनी आत्मा की रक्षा के निमित्त मतिमानों को सदैव सुसज्जित रहना चाहिये।

A face that can put to shame the splendour of the refulgent moon, a pair of eyes that can laugh at the beauty of a blooming lotus, a fair complexion of person outshining the lustre of gold, a luxurious growth of hair eclipsing the sootish colour of the black bee, a pair of heaving breasts apt to make us forget the frontal globes on the forehead of elephants, the rounded, and fully developed buttocks, and a sweet enchanting speech are the natural ornaments of young females.

---

1. *Cf.*—(*a*) कर्णोत्संगविसर्पिणी नयनयोः कान्तिर्वसन्तोत्पलं
लाक्षासंभ्रमनिर्व्यपेक्षमधुरं लावण्यमेवाञ्चति।
हारोऽस्याः स्मितचंद्रिकैव कुचयोरङ्गप्रभाकंचुकी
तन्व्याः केवलमङ्गहारमधुना मन्ये परं भूषणम्।। (नागानन्द)
(*b*) चकोरीपाण्डित्यं मलिनयति दृग्भङ्गिमहिमा हिमांशोरद्वैतं कवलयति वक्त्रं मृगदृशः।
तमोवैदग्ध्याति स्थगयति कचः किं च वचनं कुहूकंठोकंठध्वनिमधुरिमाणं तिरयति।। (काव्यप्रदीपकर्तुर्गोविन्दस्य)

स्मितं किंचिद्वक्त्रे सरलतरलो दृष्टिविभवः
परिष्यन्दो वाचामभिनवविलासोक्तिसरसः।।
गतीनामारम्भः किसलयितलीलापरिकरः स्पृश-
न्त्यास्तारुण्यं किमिह नहि रम्यं मृगदृशः।। 6।।

यौवनावस्था में प्रवेश करने वाली मृगनयनी तरुणियों की कौन-सी बात मनोहर और रमणीय नहीं होती? इनके मंदस्मित मुखारविंद, स्वाभाविक चंचल दृष्टिपात, अभिनव भोग विलास की कथा से सरस वाक्य प्रबंध और हाव-भावरहित गमन, सबके सब ही कामीजनों के मन को तत्क्षण हरण करते लेते हैं।

भावार्थ—शृंगार पक्ष का अर्थ तो उपरोक्त अनुवाद से स्पष्ट ही है परंतु वैराग्य पक्ष में भी हम इस श्लोक को इस प्रकार संगत कर सकते हैं इसलिये, इनसे रक्षा करने के निमित्त मुमुक्षुजनों को विशेष सन्नद्ध रहना चाहिये।

What is not handsome and enchanting in the persons of young and fair-eyed damsels just entering the outskrits of womanhood? The gentle smile of their faces, the naturally fickle glances, the sweet words drenched with the honey of artful references to their blooming youth and recent amors, and slow movements of their limbs like the soft wavings of lotus stems are one and all extremely charming and lovely.

---

1. Quoted anonymously in the *Subhāṣitāvali* (सुभाषितावलिः। 2236) and the *Dhvanyālōka* (ध्वन्यालोक).

Cf.— सविभ्रमस्मितोद्भेदा लोलाक्ष्यः प्रस्खलद्गिरः।
नितम्बालसगामिन्यः कामिन्यः कस्य न प्रियाः।। (ध्वन्यालोकः)

दृष्टव्येषु किमुत्तमं मृगदृशां प्रेमप्रसन्नं मुखं घ्रात-
व्येष्वपि किं तदास्यपवनः श्राव्येषु किं तद्व चः।।
किं स्वाद्येषु तदोष्ठपल्लवरसः स्पृश्येषु किं तत्तनुर्ध्येयं
किं नवयौवनं सुहृदयैः सर्वत्र तद्विभ्रमः।। 7।।

देखने योग्य पदार्थों में मृगनयनी सुंदरियों के प्रेम भरे प्रसन्न मुखारबिंद, सूँघने योग्य पदार्थों में उनके श्वास, श्रवण करने योग्य पदार्थों में उनके वचन, स्वादु लेने के योग्य पदार्थों में उनका अधरामृत, स्पर्श करने के योग्य पदार्थों में उनके कोमल शरीर और ध्यान करने के योग्य पदार्थों में उनके नवयौवन और विलास के सिवाय रसिकजनों के लिये इस संसार में और कुछ भी नहीं है।

भावार्थ–सानुरागी सांसारिक जनों के देखने, सूंघने, सुनने, स्वादु लेने, स्पर्श करने और ध्यान करने के लिए तो इस संसार में स्त्रियों के मुखारविंदादि के सिवाय और कुछ नहीं है परन्तु वैरागियों का (अर्थात् संसार से मुक्त होने की इच्छा करने वालों का) मार्ग इससे बिल्कुल ही निराला है।

For lovers, (1) the affectionate and pleasant countenance of their antelope-eyed sweethearts is the best sight to look at; (2) their sweet breath, the best perfume to smell; (3) their lovely speech, the best music to hear; (4) the ambrosia of their lips, the best delicacy to taste; (5) their tender bodies, the best thing to touch; and (6) their blooming youth and charming grace, the best objects to thing about and adore in the world.

---

1. *Cf.*— श्रुतं दृष्टं स्पृष्टं स्मृतमपि नराल्हादजनकं।
न रत्नं स्त्रीभ्योऽन्यत्क्वचिदपि कृतं लोकपतिना।।4।।
(वाराहीसंहिता 74 अध्यायः)

एताः स्खलद्वलयसंहतिमेखलोत्थ-
झङ्कारनूपुररवात्हृतराजहंस्यः।।
कुर्वन्ति कस्य न मनो विवशं तरुण्यो
वित्रस्तमुग्धहरिणीसदृशै कटाक्षैः।। 8।।

ढीले कटिभूषण और नूपुर के मधुर कलरव से राजहंसों का निरादर करने वाली तरुण सुंदरियाँ भोली-भाली भयचकित हरिणियों के समान कटाक्षों से किसका मन वशीभूत नहीं कर सकतीं?

There is none whose mind in not subdued by the artless glances—like those of frightened fawns—of those youthful and lovely women the melodious jingle of whose loose anklets and waist-belts has already put to shame the sweet-toned swans.

---

1. The comparison of the jingle of women's anklets to the melodious songs of swans is a fovourite idea with Sanskrit poets. In the 2nd act of *Vṛshabhānujā* (वृषभानुजा) Kṛṣṇa is made to say :—

वासन्तोमधुपानमत्तमधुपध्वानः किमुज्जृम्भते किंवा हंसकदम्बकूजितमिदं दूरात्समुत्पसर्पति।

आं ज्ञातं मणिनू पुरध्वनिरियं मद्वल्लभायाः स्फुटं दृश्यन्ते हि दिशस्तदङ्गकरुचा हेमाम्बुसिक्ता इव। (मथुरादासस्य वृषभानुजानाटिका)

2. For the point of the stanza, *Cf.* —

सद्वस्त्रसौष्ठवभवद्द्विगुणांगलक्ष्म्यो माणिक्यभर्मकृतभूषणभासमानाः।

वातेरिवाम्बुजविभाचयचारुनेत्राः कस्य स्त्रियो न पुरुषस्य मनो हरन्तिः।।

(गोस्वामिजनार्दनभट्टकृतं शृंगारशतकम्)

कुङ्कुमपङ्ककलङ्कितदेहा
गौरपयोधरकम्पितहारा ।।
नूपुरहंसरणत्पदपद्मा कं
न वशं कुरुते भुवि रामा ।। ९ ।।

कुङ्कुमार्चित देह, गौरवर्ण पयोधरों पर हिलते हुए हार, और नूपुररूपी राजहंस के कलरव से शब्दायमान चरण-कमल धारण करने वाली मनोहर स्त्री इस पृथ्वी पर किसको अपने वश में नहीं कर सकती?

The charms of a beautiful woman whose body is painted with saffron, whose hanging necklaces are gently trembling with the heaving of her lovely breasts, and whose lotus feet are sounding with the melodious notes of the goose-like anklets, are truly irresistible by man on this earth.

---

1. Quoted anonymously in the *Subhāṣitāvali* (सुभाषितावलि) at No. 1275 (B.S.S. No. XXXI).

Cf.— केसरचर्चित देह जिन, हिलत हार जिन अंग।
सुंदरि लखि किनके हृदय, होत नजन्म अनंग।।?

(रसिक कवि)

नूनं हि ते कविवरा विपरीतबोधा ये
नित्यमाहुरबला इति कामिनीनाम्।।
याभिर्विलोलतरतारकदृष्टिपातैः
शक्रादयोऽपि विजिता अबलाः कथं ताः।। 10।।

स्त्रियों को सदा अबला कहने वाले कवीश्वरों की बुद्धि निस्संदेह विपरीत हैं, क्योंकि जिन सुंदरियों ने अपने चंचल नेत्रों के कटाक्षों से इंद्रादिक महाबलियों का गर्व गंजन किया है वे कदापि ही अबला नहीं हो सकतीं।

There can be no doubt that the best poets have invaribly erred in calling women as weak; for, how can they be justly styled to be such (*i.e.*, weak) who have succeeded to hold absolute sway over the hearts of the mighty gods like Indra and others, by the mere glances of their charming eyes with ever-rolling pupils?

---

1. Quoted anonymously in the *Subhāṣitāvali* (सुभाषितावलि । 1287)

Cf.—(*a*) Can, with a single look, inflace.
The coldest breat, the rudest tame.

(Whittier)

(*b*) गुरुपत्न्यां निशाधीशो ब्राह्मण्यां पाकशासनः।
गतः पञ्चेषुलक्ष्यत्वं का कथाऽन्यस्य देहिनः।।

(*c*) कथमपि किल दृष्टे कामिनीलोकमात्रे परवशयति यूनां मानसं पंचबाणः। 26 (रामभद्रदीक्षितकृतशृंगारतिलकभाणः)

नूनमाज्ञाकरस्तस्याः सुभ्रुवो मकरध्वजः।।
यतस्तन्नेत्रसंचारसूचितेषु प्रवर्तते।। 11।।

उस सुंदर भौंह वाली रमणी का मीन केतन कामदेव निस्संदेह एक आज्ञावर्ती सेवक है, क्योंकि जहाँ पर उसके कटाक्ष पड़ते हैं यह भी शीघ्र ही वहाँ जा पहुँचता है।

भावार्थ–एक तो वह स्वयं ही सुलोचना है और दूसरे कामदेव जैसा महाबली उसका आज्ञावर्ती सेवक है। अतएव हे मुमुक्षुगण! आप उसके दृष्टिपथ में पड़ने से पूर्ण सचेत रहें।

It is quite true that *Makaradhvaja* (मकरध्वज Cupid) is an ever obedient servant of that beautiful lady who commands a pair of fair eybrows; for, we see that he is always ready to set on the man pointed out by the motion of her glancing looks.

---

1. Quoted anonymously in the *Subhāṣitāvali* at No. 1227 and the शार्ङ्गधरपद्धति at No. 3298.

Cf.—(*a*) यत्र यत्र चलते शनैः शनैः सुभ्रवो नयनकोणविभ्रमः।
तत्र तत्र शतपत्रधोरणी तोरणी भवति पुष्पधन्वनः।
(सुभाषितरत्नभाण्डागार 435।111)

(*b*) यत्र पतत्यबलाना दृष्टिर्निशिताः पतन्ति तत्र शराः।
तच्चपरोपिताशरो धावत्यासां पुरः स्मरो मन्ये।
(सुभाषितरत्नभाण्डागारः 416 । 26)

(*c*) यत्रैता लहरी चलाचलदृशो व्यापारयन्ति भ्रुवं
यत्तत्रैव पतन्ति संततममी कर्मस्पृशो मार्गणाः।
तच्चक्रीकृतचापसञ्जिशरप्रेङ्खत्करः क्रोधनो
धावत्यग्रत एव शासनधरः सत्यं सदासां स्मरः।।
(काव्यप्रदीपे उदाहृतम्)

(*d*) यतोयतः क्षिपन्यक्षि क्षिप्रमायतलोचना।
ततस्ततः प्रक्षिपति पंच पंचशरः शरान्।। (सुभाषितावलिः)

(*e*) जे तीय तिक्ख वल चक्खु तिहा अदिठ्ठ, ते कामचन्दमहु पञ्चममारणिज्जा।
जे संपुणो णिवडिआ सअला वि दिठ्ठी, चिठ्ठन्ति ते तिलजलञ्जलिदाण-जोग्गा 176 (प्राकृतपिङ्गलसूत्रे 2 परिच्छेदे)

केशाः संयमिनः श्रुतेरपि परं पारङ्गते लोचने
चान्तर्वक्त्रमपि स्वभाशुचिभिः कीर्णं द्विजानां गणैः।।
मुक्तानां सतताधिवासरुचिरं वक्षोजकुंभद्वयं चेत्थं
तन्वि वपुः प्रशान्तमपि ते क्षोभं करोत्येव नः।। 12।।

हे कृशांगि! संवारे हुए केश समूह, दीर्घ और विशाल नेत्र, स्वभाव शुद्ध धवल दंतपंक्ति से सुशोभित मुखारबिंद और मोतियों के हार से विभूषित कुचयुगल को धारण करने वाला तेरा शांतिमय शरीर भी हमारे मन में अनेकानेक विकार उत्पन्न करता है यह बड़े आश्चर्य की बात है।

खेद का विषय है कि इस श्लोक में "संयमिनः" आदि पदों का प्रयोग करके कवि ने जो चमत्कार दिखलाया है वह अनुवाद में स्पष्ट नहीं दिखलाया जा सकता। आशा है कि शुद्ध हिंदी के जानने वालों को इन पदों के निम्नलिखित दो–दो अर्थों के अवलोकन करने से कवि का आशय समझने में कुछ कठिनता न होगी। स्त्रियों के शरीर को शान्तिमय होने पर भी विकार उत्पन्न करने वाला कहने में इस श्लोक का चमत्कार है और इस शरीर को प्रशान्त कहने का कारण भी न इन पदों के दूसरे अर्थ से प्रत्यक्ष हो जायेगा।

(क) "संयमिनः" = 1 संवारे हुए और 2 जितेन्द्री।

(ख) "श्रुतेरपि पारङ्गते" = 1 कर्णान्तायत अर्थात् कानपर्यंत देखने वाले या विशाल और 2 वेद वेदान्तादि शास्त्रों में पारंगत।

(ग) "द्विजानां" = 1 दांतों और 2 ब्राह्मणों के।

(घ) "मुक्तानां" = 1 मोतियों के और 2 संसार में मुक्त हुए मनुष्यों के।

Oh delicate lady! though thy person fully resembles a calm and contented *Yogī* by thy well-combed hair, large eyes, regular set of naturally clear teeth, and a couple of heaving breasts adorned with beautiful wreaths or necklaces of excellent pearls, it is still causing a geat deal of internal distrubance in the midst of our hearts!

An ordinary English reader will not quite understand the exquisite beauty of this stanza as well as the reason which enables the poet to compare the person of women to that of Yogīs. But a fair Sanskrit scholar will find no difficulty in tracing the secret to the double interpretations of the words संयमिनः, श्रुतेः द्विजानाम् and मुक्तानाम् which equally mean well-combed or self-denying, of the ear or the Śāstras, of teeth or the twiceborn, and of pearls or emancipated souls. As the English tongue is here found to be incapable of such niceties of wordplay, the aforesaid words are above translated only in their former sense.

---

1. *Cf.*— नवविकसितकमलकरे कुवलयदललोचने सितांशुमुखि।
दहसि मनो यत्तत्किं रम्भागर्भोरुयुक्तं ते।। 22।।
(रुद्रटस्य काव्यालंकारे 8 अध्याये)

मुग्धे धानुष्कता केयमपूर्वा दृश्यते त्वयि।।
यदा विध्यसि चेतांसि गुणैरेव न सायकैः।। 13।।

हे मुग्धे! धनुष विद्या में ऐसी असाधारण प्रवीणता न मालूम तुझ में कहाँ से आ गई है कि बाण छोड़ने के बिना केवल गुणमात्र से ही दूसरों का चित्त सहज ही में हरण कर लेती है।

इस श्लोक में "गुण" शब्द का प्रयोग दो अर्थ में किया गया है (1) शील चातुर्य्यादि गुण और (2) रज्जु जिससे धनुष की दोनों कोटि बांधी जाती है।

Oh thou innocent young lady ! how is that thou art so uncommonly masterly in the pratice of archery; for thou canst pierce the hearts of others simply by touching the strings of the bow, without the use of a single shaft?

---

1. In the *Subhāṣitāvali* (सुभाषितावलि) this stanza is quoted anonymously at No. 2025. It is also given anonymously in the *Śārṅgadharapaddhati* (शार्ङ्गधरपद्धति) at No. 3654.

सति प्रदीपे सत्यग्नौ सत्सु तारारवीन्दुषु।।
विना मे मृगशावाक्ष्या तमोभूतमिदं जगत्।। 14।।

यद्यपि दीपक जल रहा है, अग्नि प्रज्वलित हो रही है, सूर्य, चंद्रमा और तारागण भी ज्यों के त्यों प्रकाशमान हैं, तथापि एक प्राण प्यारी मृगनयनी के बिना यह सारा संसार मुझको अंधकारमय प्रतीत होता है।

On account of the absence of my fawn-eyed love, the whole world appears to me to be wrapped in dense darkness notwithstanding its bright lamps, fire, sun, moon and stars.

---

1. This stanza which is quoted anonymously in the *Subhāṣitāvali* (सुभाषितावलि । 1235) stands 153rd in the *Amarū Śataka* (अमरूशतक).

Cf.—(*a*) पुत्रपौत्रवधूभृत्यैः संपूर्णमपि सर्वदा।
भार्याहीनगृहस्थस्य शून्यमेव गृहं मतम्।।

(सुभाषितरत्नभाण्डागार, 252।134)

(*b*) यः प्रदोषः प्रदीषोसौ कालः कालः किमुच्यते।
दोषा दोषाकरवती विना तन्व्याः समागमात्।।

(सुभाषितावलिः)

(*c*) "She was my life's unerring light :
That quenched, what beam shall break my night?" Byron's Poems of love.

उद्वृत्तः स्तनभार एष तरले नेत्रे चले भ्रूलते
रागाधिष्ठतमोष्ठपल्लवमिदं कुर्वन्तु नामव्यथाम्।।
सौभाग्याक्षरपङ्क्तिकेव लिखिता पुष्पायुधेन स्वयं
मध्यस्थाऽपि करोति तापमधिकं रोमावली केन सा।। 15।।

हे सुंदरी तुम्हारे पीनोन्नत कुचयुगल, चंचल नेत्र, चपल भ्रूभंग और बिंबफल के समान लाल होंठ रसिकजनों को दुःखित करते हैं वह तो ठीक, परंतु कामदेव के निज कर कमल से लिखी हुई सौभाग्यरूप अक्षरों की पंक्ति के सदृश यह रोमावली मध्यस्था होने पर भी न मालूम क्यों कर विशेष दुःखदायी हो रही है।

भावार्थ—कुचयुगल, नेत्र, भ्रूलता और ओष्ठपल्लव के दुःखदायी होने का हेतु तो उनके उन्नत, चंचल, चपल और लाल होने से स्पष्ट पाया जाता है परंतु यह रोमावली मध्यस्थ होने पर क्योंकर दुःख देती है सो कुछ समझ में नहीं आता। लोक में ऐसा प्रसिद्ध है कि जो मध्यस्थ हो वह संताप का हेतु नहीं होता।

Properly speaking there cannot be any justification in our complaint against the constant agitation of our passionate hearts by the separate and combined influences of thy rounded and developed breasts, fickle eyes, ever-moving arched brows, and rosy lips. However, we do not know why we are so sorely pained by the line of hair on they abdomen just above the navel, though it is occupying an intermediate position and though it looks like a special mark of good fortune written by the hand of *Puṣpāyudha* (पुष्पायुध), the wielder of flowery weapons!

---

1. Quoted anonymously in the *Subhāṣitāvali* (सुभाषितावलि) at No. 1345.

Cf.— भ्रूचपि निहितः कटाक्षविशिखो निर्मातु मर्मव्यर्था श्यामात्मा कुटिलः करोतु कबरीभारोऽपि मारोद्यमम्।

मोहे तावदयं च तन्वि तनुतां बिम्बाधरी रागावान्सद्धृतस्तनमंडलस्तव कथं प्राणैर्मम क्रीडति।। (गीतगोविन्दे तृतीयसर्गे)

गुरुणा स्तनभारेण मुखचन्द्रेण भास्वता।।
शनैश्चराभ्यां पादाभ्यां रेजे ग्रहमयीव सा।। 16।।

गुरु स्तन भार से, सूर्य के समान प्रकाशमान मुख चंद्र से और शनैश्चर (मंदगामी) चरणों से वह सुंदरी ग्रहमयी प्रतीत होती है।

इस श्लोक का चमत्कार "गुरुणा", "चंद्रेण", भास्वता" और "शनैश्चराभ्यां" के दोनों अर्थों के जानने से प्रत्यक्ष होगा।

(क) "गुरु" = 1 भारी अर्थात् पीनोन्नत और 2 बृहस्पति।

(ख) "चन्द्रमा" = 1 चंद्रमा सदृश और 2 चंद्रमा।

(ग) "भास्वान्" = 1 प्रकाशमान और 2 सूर्य।

(घ) "शनैश्चर" = 1 मंदगामी और 2 शनैश्चर।

With her full-developed Jupiter-like breasts, bright and sunny moonlike face and slow-moving Saturn-like limbs, the fairy form of that handsome woman resembles the brilliant constellation of the planets.

---

1. Quoted anonymously in the *Subhāṣitāvali* (सुभाषितवलि) at No. 1233.

Cf.—(*a*) गुरुणा स्तनभारेण हासेन श्वेतरोचिषा।
गमनेन सुमन्देन रेजे ग्रहमयवि सा।। 178

(श्रीकृष्णकवेर्भन्दारमकरन्दचम्पूः)

2. Mark that the first and fourth *Caraṇas* of this ślōka exactly correspond with those of our text.

(*b*) मास्वतालंकारेण, श्वेतरोचिषा स्मितेन, लोहितेनाधरेण, सौम्येन दर्शनेन, गुरुणा नितम्बेन, सितेन हारेण, शनैश्चरेण पादेन, विकचेन लोचनोत्पलेन, त्रिभुवनविजयकेतुना रूपेण ग्रहमयीव। (वासवदत्ता)

यस्याः स्तनौ यदि घनौ जघनं विहारि
वक्त्रं च चारु तव चित्त किमाकुलत्वम्।।
पुण्यं कुरुष्व यदि तेषु तवास्ति वाञ्छा
पुण्यैर्विना नहि भवन्ति समीहितार्थाः।। 17।।

हे चित्त! उस स्त्री के पीनोन्नत कुच युगल, मनोहर जघन स्थल और सुंदर मुख को देख-देखकर वृथा संतप्त क्यों हो रहे हो, क्योंकि यदि इस सुंदरी के पयोधरादि का भोग करने की तुम्हारी अभिलाषा है तो सुकृत करने के लिए तत्पर हो। पुण्य संचय के बिना मनोवांछित फल की प्राप्ति कदापि नहीं हो सकती।

भावार्थ।

पर स्त्री सौंदर्य को देखकर विकल होना सर्वथा अनुचित है।

Oh heart! what possible gain is there in thy painful sensation at the sight of her thick-set breasts, charming buttocks, and fairy face? If thou hast the least desire to enjoy the aforesaid things, thou must perform a series of virtuous actions. The fulfilment of one's hopes and wishes is entirely dependent upon piety and goodness.

---

1. *Cf.*—किंचिद्वक्रितकंठकंदलदलत्पीनस्तनार्वतनव्यायामाञ्चितकञ्चुक मृगदृशस्त-स्यास्तदालोकितम्। वाचस्ताश्च विदग्धभावचतुराः स्फारीभवन्मन्मथा हंहो मानस किं स्मरस्यभिमताः सिध्यन्ति पुण्यैः क्रियाः।।

(रुद्रभट्टकृतशृंगारतिलकोदाहरणम्)

मात्सर्यमुत्सार्य विचार्य
कार्यमार्याः समर्यादमिदं वदन्तु।
सेव्या नितम्बाः किमु भूधराणा-
मुत स्मरस्मेरनितम्बिनीनाम्।। 18।।

हे आर्यजनो! मत्सरता छोड़कर कर्तव्य कर्म के विचारपूर्वक शास्त्रीय प्रमाण सहित यह कहो कि इस संसार में जन्म लेकर मनुष्य को पर्वतों के मध्यवर्ती कंदरादि का सेवन करना श्रेष्ठ है अथवा कामोद्दीपन करने वाली मंदस्मित विलासवती तरुणियों के सुंदर जघन स्थल का उपयोग करना श्रेष्ठ है।

Oh ye learned Āryas (आर्याः) ! you must, after a careful consideration of the Śāstrās, at once make a candid and authetic (founded on authority) declaration, leaving aside your one-sided views or partiality, as to whether a man should renounce the world and take his abode into the caves of mountains, or should enjoy it in a right royal fashion and give himself up to the pleasures of lovely women with charming buttocks.

---

1. Quoted anonymously in the *Subhāṣitāvali* (सुभाषितावलि । 2229) the *Daśarūpāvalōka* (दशरूपालोक), the *Kāvyānuśāsana* (काव्यनु-शासनम्),the *Kāvyapradīpa* (काव्यप्रदीप), and the *Udāharaṇa-candrikā* (उदाहरणचंद्रिका).

Cf.— अधीतविद्यैर्विगते शिशुत्वे धनेर्जिते हारिणि यौवने च।
सेव्या नितम्बास्तु विलासिनीनां ततस्तदर्धं धरणीधराणाम्।।

(सुभाषितावलिः)

संसारेऽस्मिन्नसारे परिणतितरले द्वे गती पण्डितानां
तत्त्वज्ञानामृताम्भःप्लवलुलितधियां यातु कालः कदाचित्।।
नोचेन्मुग्धाङ्गनानां स्तनजघनघनाभोगसंसर्गिणीनां स्थूलो-
पस्थस्थलीषु स्थगितकरतस्पर्शलोलोद्यतानाम्।। 19।।

इस परिणाम में चंचल और असार संसार में पंडित जनों की केवल दो ही गति होती है, एक तो तत्त्व ज्ञान के अमृतमय सरोवर में बारंबार अवगाहन करके अपना समय व्यतीत करना और दूसरे मुग्ध युवतियों के विस्तृत कुच युगल और जघन स्थल के स्थूल उपस्थल का सकाम स्पर्श करके कंदर्प सुख का भोग करना।

In this worthless and changeable world, learned men should either (1) pass their days in drinking the nectar of Spiritual knowledge, or (2) devote themselves to the the pleasant enjoyment of youthful women whose breasts and buttocks are both hard and thick-set, and whose hips and loins are fully developed and extended.

---

1. *Cf.*—त्याग लोकसुख या रहें, मत्त परात्माध्यान।
रमणीरति में रत रहें, अथवा रसिक सुजान।।
(रसिक कवि)

मुखेन चन्द्रकान्तेन महानीलैः शिरोरुहैः।।

पाणिभ्यां पद्मरागाभ्यां रेजे रत्नमयीव सा।। 20।।

चन्द्रकान्त मुख से, महानील केश समूह से, पद्म रागसम कर-कमलों से वह स्त्री रत्नमयी प्रतीत होती है।

इस श्लोक का चमत्कार भी "चन्द्रकान्त", "महानील", "पद्मराग" के दोनों अर्थ जानने से ही प्रत्यक्ष होगा।

(क) 'चंद्रकान्त' = 1 चंद्रमा के समान कांति वाला और 2 चंद्रकान्त मणि।

(ख) 'महानील' = 1 बहुत नील और 2 नीलम या नीलमणि।

(ग) 'पद्मराग' = 1 पद्म के समान लाल और 2 लाल या लाल मणि।

The person of that beautiful woman can be fairly said to be made up of various precious gems, in as much as her face resembles the moonstone, her dark blue hairs the sapphires, and her reddish palms the rubies.

---

1. Quoted under *Śakavṛddhi* (शकवृद्धि) in the *Sūktimuktāvali* (सूक्तिमुक्तावलि), and anonymously in the *Subhāṣitāvali* (सुभाषितावलि) at No. 1236, and the शार्ङ्गधरपद्धति at No. 3371.

Cf.— नयने हि तरलतारे सुतनु कपोलौ च चन्द्रकान्तौ ते।

अधरोऽपि पद्मरागास्त्रिभुवनरत्नं ततो वदनम्।। 21।।

(रुद्रस्य काव्यालंकार 10 अध्यायः)

संमोहयन्ति मदयन्ति विडम्बयन्ति
निर्भर्त्सयन्ति यन्ति रमयन्ति विषादयन्तिः।।
एताः प्रविश्य हृदयं सदयं नराणां किं नाम
वामनयना न समाचरन्ति।। 21।।

हृदय में सदय (दयापूर्वक) प्रवेश करके मनुष्यों को मोहित कर लेने, मदोन्मत्त करने, तरसाने, धमकाने, प्रसन्न करने और दुःख देने वाली इन मृगनयनी सुंदरियों के लिए ऐसा कौन सा काम है जिसे वह न करती हों?।

भावार्थ।

मृगनयनी सुंदरियों के नेत्र मनुष्यों के हृदय में प्रथम तो मानो दया भाव से ही प्रवेश करते हैं, परन्तु एक बार प्रवेश करने के पश्चात् उनको नाना भाँति से कष्ट देने के लिए भी किसी प्रकार की त्रुटि नहीं करते?

After once entering the hearts of men, with apparent profession of kindness and sympathy clever (*lit.* crooked-eyed) women can either stupify or madden or mock, or threaten or gladden, or trouble them in a thousand different ways as it suits their whims.

---

1. The stanza is also found in the *Mṛchhakaṭika* (मृच्छकटिक) and the प्रबोधचंद्रोदय

Cf.—(*a*) धैर्यं ध्वंसयति श्रियं कवलयत्युन्माद्यस्यान्तरं
पादे पातयति प्रयच्छति रतस्यान्ते च कुत्सा मलम्।
औन्निद्रयं कुरुते विभाणयति च प्राणोमैर्बंधुभिः
संधत्ते अरसा युवानमपि तन्नारी क्व नारीधति।।

(भर्तृहरिनिर्वेदम्)

(*b*) What careth she for hearts when once possessed?
Byron's Chile Harold's Pilgrimage. II. 34.

विश्रम्य विश्रम्य वने द्रुमाणां
छायासु तन्वी विचचार काचित्।।
स्तनोत्तरीयेण करोद्धृतेन निवार-
यन्ती शशिनो मयूखान्।। 22।।

वन के वृक्षों की छाया में विश्राम ले-लेकर वह विरहिणी तरुणी अपने चीर को स्तन पर से उठाकर चंद्रमा की किरणों से निज कोमल शरीर की रक्षा करती हुई वन में विचर रही है।

इस श्लोक में कवि ने किसी विरहिणी स्त्री के कोमल शरीर की असाधारण सुकुमारता का वर्णन किया है कि जिसके कारण से वह सूर्य की प्रखर किरणों को ही नहीं किन्तु चन्द्रमा के शीतल प्रकाश को भी सहन नहीं कर सकती। प्रत्येक पद से श्लोकोक्त तन्वी की असामान्य सुकुमारता प्रत्यक्ष रूप से झलकती है।

Look at the delicate form of that fairy woman who is walking in cool moonlit night advancing step by step with a slow and cautious pace, resting occationally under the shade of forest trees and drawing up her veil across the moon so as to protect her face from the effects of lunar rays.

---

1. Quoted anonymously in the शार्ङ्गधरपद्धति at No. 3399. This Śloka is generally misinterpreted by translators.

अदर्शने दर्शनमात्रकामा
दृष्ट्वा परिष्वङ्गरसैकलोला।।
आलिङ्गितायां पुनरायताक्ष्या-
माशास्महे विग्रहयोरभेदम्।। 23 ।।

विशाल नेत्र वाली रमणी का जब तक दर्शन न हो तब तक तो दर्शन मात्रा ही की आकांक्षा बनी रहती है और दर्शन के पीछे उसका आलिंगन करने की लालसा उत्पन्न हो जाती है, परंतु आलिंगन के अनन्तर तो हमारी यह इच्छा हो जाती है कि किसी प्रकार से हम दोनों की देह कभी पृथक् ही न हो और हम दोनों में कोई भेद न रहकर इन दो शरीरों का एक ही शरीर हो जाय तो बहुत उत्तम हो।

भावार्थ

एक बार देख लेने पर स्त्रियों से बचना सर्वथा असंभव हो जाता है इसलिए मुमुक्षु जन को स्त्रियों का चिंतवन मात्र भी नहीं करना चाहिए।

As long as we do not see her, our only wish is to have a glance of her handsome person; but when this simple wish is gratified we are anxious to have her body in our loving embrace. However, when that boon is also granted we pray God that He may be gracious enough never to part us asunder but to keep our bodies inseparably closed to one another!

PURPORT

It is impossible not to fall into the snares of women after once seeing their faces. True, lovers of freedom of will and action should, therefore, avoid them from a distance.

मालती शिरसि जृम्भणोन्मुखी
चन्दनं वपुषि कुङ्कमाविलम्।।
वक्षसि प्रियतमा मनोहरा
स्वर्ग एष परिशिष्ट आगतः।। 24।।

मस्तक पर खिलती हुई मालती की माला धारण करना, केसर चंदन से अंग-राग करना और मनोहर प्राण-प्यारी को वक्ष-स्थल से लगाना पृथ्वी तल पर ही स्वर्ग मुख भोगने के समान समझना चाहिए।

Those who wear fragrant garlands of budding jasmine blossoms round their necks, rub the sweetscented saffron over their bodies, and press the handsome person of a beloved charming lady close to their hearts, can justly be said to obtain a portion of heavenly bliss even upon the surface of this wretched world.

---

1. Quoted anonymously in the *Subhāṣitāvali* (सुभाषितावलि) at No. 2223. For the idea of the latter half of the stanza. *Cf.*—

उत्स्तनीं समवलम्ब्य या रतिः सा न धातृभवनेऽस्ति मे मतिः।। 18 (वाराहीसंहिता 74 अध्यायः)

2. For the point of the Stanza *Cf.*—

"It Heav'n a drought of heavenly pleasure spare,
On cordial in this melancholy vale,
"Tis when a youthful, loving modest pair,
In other's arms breathe out the tender tale,
Beneath the milkwhite thorn that scents the evening gale."

Burn's. The cotter's Saturday Night.

प्राङ्मामेति मनागमानितगुणं जाताभिलाषं ततः
सव्रीडं तदनु श्लथीकृततनु प्रत्यस्तधैर्यं पुनः।।
प्रेमार्द्रं स्पृहणीयनिर्भररहः क्रीडाप्रगल्भं ततो
निःशङ्काङ्गविकर्षणाधिकसुखं रम्यं कुलस्त्रीरतम्।। 25।।

प्रथम ही प्रथम "नहीं-नहीं" के निषेध वाक्यों द्वारा कृतज्ञता रहित, पश्चात् थोड़ी-थोड़ी अभिलाषासूचक, पश्चात् लज्जापूर्वक अंग-प्रत्यंगों के शिथिल करने की चेष्टा सहित, पश्चात् अनुरागयुक्त, पश्चात् एकान्त क्रीड़ा की अतिशय वांछासहित, पश्चात् नानाविध केलि क्रीड़ा में प्रवीणता प्रगट करने वाला और तत्पश्चात् निर्भयपूर्वक अंगमर्दनादि के कारण असाधारण सुख देने वाला कुल स्त्री का रमण अत्यंत ही रमणीय है।

इस श्लोक में कवि ने अज्ञात यौवना नवोढा की दशा से प्रारंभ करके प्रौढावस्था पर्यंत को स्वीया नायिका के सुरत को प्रतिमूर्ति ज्यों की त्यों खींच दी है।

The enjoyment of one's own wife coming of a high and respectable family is indeed the best and highest pleasure on the face of the earth; for.......

Note—I abstain from translating the above stanza from fear of oversensitive crities who are sure to decry it as obscene. To me, it, however, presents nothing which can justly be taken as really repugnant to man's feelings in general.

---

1. Quoted anonymously in the *Subhāṣitāvali* (सुभाषितावलि) at No. 2242.

उरसि निपतितानां स्त्रस्तधम्मिल्लकानां
मुकुलितनयनानां किंचिदुन्मीलितानाम्।।
सुरतजनितखेदस्विन्नगण्डस्थलानामधर-
मधुवधूनां भाग्यवन्तः पिबन्ति।। 26।।

वक्षस्थल पर पड़ी हुई, बिखरे हुए केश वाली, कभी पलक लगाए हुए, कभी अधखुले नेत्रों से कुछ-कुछ देखती हुई और सुरत-जनित प्रस्वेद बिंदुओं को गण्डस्थल पर धारण करने वाली पत्नियों के अधरामृत का पान करना विरले भाग्यवान् मनुष्यों के ही प्रारब्ध में लिखा है।

The pleasure of drinking the labial nectar of their beloved wives who are are lying on their breasts with dishevelled hair, half opened eyelids, and rosy cheeks streaming with the sweat of recent coition is indeed reserved for the fortunate few.

---

1. Quoted anonymously in the *Subhāṣitāvali* (सुभाषितावलि) at No 2135.

Cf.—(*a*) रतिरभसनितान्तश्रान्तकान्ताकुवान्तश्चलदमलकराग्रा नाभिदेशेष्वधो वा।
स्मितमधुरमुखीनां ह्रीणसनेत्रोत्पलानामधरमधुवधूतां भाग्यवन्तः पिबन्ति।।

(शार्ङ्गधरस्य)

Mark that the last charan of this verse exactly coincides with that of our text.

(*b*) आलोलामलकावलीं विलुलितां बिभ्रच्चलत्कुण्डलं
किंचिन्मृष्टविशेष के तनुतरैः स्वेदभिसः सीकरैः।
तन्व्या यत्सुरतान्तान्नयनं वक्त्रं रतिव्यतत्यये
तत्त्वां पातु चिराय किं हरिहरब्रह्मादिभिर्देवतैः।। (अमरुशतके)

आमीलितनयनायां यत्सुर-
तरसो नु संविदंकुरुते।।
मिथुनैर्मिथोऽवधारितमवितथ-
मिदमेव कामनिर्वहणम्।। 27।।

अधर खुले नेत्र वाली स्त्रियों के साथ सुरत रस का साक्षात्कार करना ही कामीजनों के मनोवांछित पुरुषार्थ का अन्तिम परिणाम है कि जिसको क्रीड़ा करने वाले दोनों स्त्री-पुरुष ही भली-भाँति जान सकते हैं।

The enjoyment of women whose eyes are partly closed on account of the intensity of their passion is the highest pleasure that can be felt by the loving pair and constitutes the ultimate end of amorous sports.

---

1. For etiquette's sake it is most appropriate and proper to leave this stanza without any note whatever.

इदमनुचितक्रमश्च पुंसां यदिह

जरास्वपि मान्मथा विकाराः।।

यदपि च न कृतं नितम्बिनीनां

स्तनपतनावधि जीवितं रतं वा।। 28।।

वृद्धावस्था में भी कामदेव के विकारों का अनुभव करना मनुष्यों के लिए बहुत ही अनुचित है, विशेष करके इस कारण से कि सुंदर जघन स्थल वाली रमणियों के जीवन और सुरत की अविध उनके स्तनों के पतन होने के समय पर्यंत नहीं रखी गई है।

How unjustifiable and improper is the decree of fate which makes men succumb to the sentiments of love even when they are too old for them; especially when we see that the life of women is not limited to the contraction or fall of their heaving breasts?

---

1. Quoted anonymously in the *Kāvyapradīpa* (काव्यप्रदीप) and the *Udāharaṇacandrikā* (उदाहरणचंद्रिका)

Cf.— न शतेनापि वर्षाणामपैति मदनाशयः।
तत्राशक्त्या निवर्तन्त नराः।। 14।।

(वाराहीसंहिता 74 अध्यायः)

2. In the शार्ङ्गधरपद्धति at No. 564, the first half of this verse is ascribed to शीलाभट्टारिका, and the second half to भोजराज when both were playing chess with one another.

एतत्कामफलं लोके यदद्वयोरेकचित्तता।।
अन्यचित्तकृते कामे शवयोरिव सङ्गमः।। 29।।

इस संसार में सुरत के समय स्त्री-पुरुष का एकचित्त होना ही काम का फल समझा गया है, क्योंकि जब दोनों का एक चित्त ही न हो वह तो सुरत ही नहीं कहा जा सकता किन्तु शव संगम के समान है।

The true end of coition is the full union of the hearts of the enjoying persons; but when that aim is not accomplished, the intercourse is nothing different from a contact of corpses.

---

1. *Cf.*— सुरंते च समाधौ च मनो यत्र न लीयते।
ध्यानेनापि हि किं तेन किं तेन सुरतेन वा।।

(शार्ङ्गधरपद्धतिः)

Union of hearts is, in reality, the first requisite for true friendship. Where this is not the case there is neither love nor friendship. The poet expresses this idea very strongly in the above Śloka.

प्रणयमधुराः प्रेमोद्गाढा रसादलसास्तथा
भणितमधुरा मुग्धप्रायाः प्रकाशितसम्मदाः।।
प्रकृतिसुभगा विश्रम्भार्हाः स्मरोदयदायिनो
रहसि किमपि स्वैरालापा हरन्ति मृगीदृशम्।। 30।।

नम्रतापूर्वक मधुर, अनुरागपूर्ण शृंगारादि रस की आधिक्यता से शिथिल, रति संकेतिक वचनों से मधुर, अस्फुट, आंनदयुक्त, स्वभाव ही से सुंदर, विश्वास के योग्य और कामदेव को उत्पन्न करने वाला, मृगनयनी सुंदरियों का एकान्त स्थल का स्वेच्छ भाषण निस्संदेह सबके मन को हरण कर लेता है।

The words of women with entelope-like eyes which are: (1) sweet on account of their meekness, (2) full of affection, (3) slow on account of the intensity of their love, (4) agreeable to hear, (5) almost indistinct and unintelligible, (6) expressive of happiness, (7) naturally graceful, (8) trustworthy, (9) apt to excite passion, and (10) coming out of their own free will, if spoken in a lonely space are sure to enslave the hearts of those to whose they are addressed.

---

1. Cf.—(*a*) मुहुरविशदा विस्रभार्हा मुहुः स्मृतमन्यवो मुहुरसरलाः प्रेमप्रह्वा मुहुर्मुहुरस्थिराः। विततशपथोपालंभाङ्का मुहुर्मधुरा मुहुः परिववृधिरे निष्पर्यन्ता मिथो मिथुनोक्तयः।। (सुभाषितावलि)

(*b*) म्लानस्य जीवकुसुमस्य विकासनानि सन्तर्पणानि सकलेन्द्रियनन्दनानि। एतानि ते सुवचनानि सरोरुहाक्षि कर्णामृतानि मनसश्च रसायनानि।।

(भवभूतिकृतोत्तररामचरितम्)

आवासः क्रियतां गाङ्गे पापहारिणी वारिणि।।
स्तनद्वये तरुण्या वा मनोहारिणि हारिणि।। 31।।

या तो पाप मोचनी श्री गंगाजी के तट का सेवन करना ही श्रेष्ठ है और या तरुणी सुंदरियों के मनोहर स्तन मध्य का भोग विलास ही ठीक है।

भावार्थ।

मनुष्य को उचित है कि या तो जगत के जंजालों को छोड़कर श्री गंगा जी के तट का निवास करे या संसार में अनुरक्त होकर सुंदर युवतियों के साथ विहार करे।

You should either go go the Gaṅges and take your abode on her pious banks quite capable of purifying your soul of all previous sins, or you should devote yourself to the charming breasts or young women adorned with beautiful necklaces.

---

1. Quoted anonymously in the *Subhāṣitāvali* (सुभाषितावलि) at No. 3425. (B.S.S. No. XXXI).

2. The Hindus consider the Gaṅges as the most sanctifying stream on the surface of the globe. For the description of the Gaṅges, see our note elsewhere.

प्रियपुरतो युवतीनां तावत्पदमातनोतु हृदि मानः।।
वहति न यावच्चन्दनतरुसुरभिर्निर्मलः पवनः।।32।।

तरुणियों के हृदय में अपने प्राण वल्लभ के समक्ष मान की स्थिति जग तक ही रह सकती है कि तब तक चंदन तरु की सुगंध- युक्त निर्मल पवन का संचार न हो।

भावार्थ।

मलयाचल के शीतल, मंद, सुगंध पवन के चलते ही मानवती स्त्रियों के मान का तत्काल मर्दन हो जाता है।

In company of their lovers, jealous anger in youthful women's hearts can only exist until the blowing of a fresh breeze smelling of the sweet scent of sandalwood.

---

1. Sanskrit poetry is very full—rather overful—of the description of *Mana* or jealous anger of our lady loves. Fresh breezes saturated with the sweet scent of sandal are one of the many causes which help us to a considerable extent to put out their anger, to reinstate ourselves into their favours and to bring about the wished-for reconciliation with our sweethearts for sooner than it could have been under any other circumstance.

परिमलभृतो वाताः शाखा नवाङ्कुरकोटयो
मधुरविरुतोत्कण्ठा वाचः प्रिया पिकपक्षिणाम्।।
विरलसुरतस्वेदोद्गारा वधूवदनेन्दवः प्रसरति मधौ
रात्र्यां जातो न कस्य गुणोदयः।। 33।।

जिस समय में सुगंधयुक्त पवन चलने लगता है, वृक्षों की शाखा नवीन पत्रांकुरों से सुशोभित हो जाती है, कोयल उत्कंठायुक्त प्रिय कलरव करने लगते हैं और पत्नियों के मुखचंद्र पर सुरत जनित प्रस्वेद की तनिक=सी धार बहार देने लगती है ऐसे वसन्त ऋतु की रात्रि में कौन=सा ऐसा पुरुष है कि जिसके हृदय में कामदेव का उदय न होता हो?

Who is it that can avoid the excitement of passion in the midst of a lovely night of Spring when the air is full of agreeable smell, the boughs of trees are covered with fresh foliage, the sweet cooings of cuckoos are causing great sensation in the hearts, and the coition sweat is slightly perceptible on the cheeks of moon-faced ladies?

---

1. *Cf.*—(*a*) आकम्पितानि हृदयानि मनस्विनीनां वातैः प्रफुल्ल-सहकारकृताधिवासैः।

संबाधितं परभृतस्य मदाकुलस्य श्रोत्रप्रियैर्मधुकरस्य च गीतनादैः ।।33।।

(ऋतुसंहारः)

(*b*) अविरलकमलविकासः सकलालिमदश्च कोकिलानन्दः।

रम्योऽयमेति संप्रति लोकोत्कण्ठाकरः कालः।।83।।

(काव्यालङ्कार 7 अध्यायः)

मधुरयं मधुरैरपि कोकिला-
कलकलैर्मलयस्य च वायुभिः।।
विरहिणः प्रणिहन्ति शरीररिणो
विपदि हन्त सुधाऽपि विषायते।। 34।।

कोकिल के मधुर कलरव और मलयाचल के सुगंधित पवनों से विभूषित होने पर भी यह वसंत ऋतु विरहीजनों के प्राणों का हरण कर लेता है। अहो! क्या ही खेद का विषय है कि देवधारियों के लिए विपत्ति के समय में अमृत भी विष के समान दुःखदायी हो जाता है।

The hearts of lovers separated from their sweethearts are sorely pained by the lovely Spring, notwithstanding its sweet cooings of cuckoos, and the odoriferous air of the Malaya. True it is, that in man's misfortunes nectar is even changed into poison.

Cf.—(*a*) पाटीरद्रुभुजंगपुंगवमुखा याता इवातापिनी वाता वान्ति दहन्ति लोचनममी ताम्रा रसालद्रुमाः। एते हन्त किरन्ति कूजितमयं हालाहलं कोकिला बालावालमृणलकोमलतनुः प्राणान्कथं रक्षतु।। 57।।

(भामिनीविलासः । शृंगारे)

(*b*) उन्मीलन्मधुगंधलब्धमधुपव्याधूतचूताङ्कुरक्रीडत्कोकिलकिलाकलकिलकलैरुद्गीर्णकर्णज्वराः। नीयन्ते पथिकैः कथं कथमपि ध्यानावधनाक्षणप्राप्तप्राणसमासमागमरसोल्लासैरमी वासराः।।

(गीतगोविन्दः । प्रथम सर्गः)

आवासः किल किंचिदेव दयितापर्श्वे विलासालसः
कर्णे कोकिलकामिनीकलरवः स्मेरो लतामण्डपः।।
गोष्ठी सत्कविभिः समं कतिपयैः सेव्याः सितांशोः कराः
केषांचित्सुखयन्त्यवेहि हृदयं चैचो विचित्राः क्षपाः।। 35।।

जिस समय में, भोग-विलास से शिथिल होकर अपनी प्राण-प्यारी के निकट कुछ काल निवास करना, कोकिल कामिनियों के सुंदर शब्दों का श्रवण करना, प्रफुल्लित लतामण्डप का आनंद लूटना और उत्तमोत्तम कवीश्वरों की गोष्ठी और चंद्रमा की शीतल किरणों का सेवन करना आनंददायक होता है वैसी चित्र-विचित्र चैत्र की रात्रियाँ किसी-किसी भाग्यवान् मनुष्यों के हृदय को ही सुखी करती हैं।

There are only a few persons who can afford to delight themselves in the wonderfully pleasant nights of *Caitra* either by taking a slight rest from their amorous toils by the side of their beloved loves, or by hearing the sweet chirpings of female cuckoos, or by entering the interior of a lovely bower of creepers, or by conversing with good poets, or by enjoying the cool rays of the moon.

Cf.—(*a*) रम्यः प्रदोषसमयः स्फुटचंद्रभासः पुंस्कोकिलस्य विरुतं पवनः सुगन्धि। मत्तालियूथविरुतं निशि शीधुपानं सर्वं रसायनमिदं कुसुमायुधस्य ।। 34।।

(ऋतुसंहारे वसन्तवर्णने)

पान्थस्त्रीविरहानलाहुतिकथामातन्वती मञ्जरी
माकन्देषु पिकाङ्गनाभिरधुना सोत्कण्ठमालोक्यते।।
अप्येते नवपाटलापरिमलप्राग्भारपाटच्चरा वान्ति
क्लान्तिवितानतानवकृताः श्रीखण्डशैलानिकाः।। 36।।

इस वसंत काल में स्थान-स्थान में पथिकों की विरहिणी स्त्रियों की वियोगाग्नि से निकली हुई मंजरीरूपी शिखा प्रज्वलित हो रही है, आम्र के वृक्षों में कोयल उत्कंठा सहित अवलोकन कर रही हैं और नवीन खिले हुए पलाश के पुष्प समूह की सुगंधि चुराने वाले और मार्ग चलने के श्रम को दूर करने वाले मलयाचल के पवन चल रहे हैं।

इस श्लोक में कवि ने वसंत ऋतु की स्वाभाविक महिमा वर्णन की है।

The sight of mango stalks representing as it were the burning flame of the fire of separation from his beloved wife, the passionate looks of female cuckoos, and the sweet-scented breeze of the Malaya mountain blowing with the stolen odour of the newly blossomed *Pāṭalas* that can allay the fatigue of the way, all combine to add a great deal to the mental pangs of the unfortunate traveller away from home.

---

1. *Cf.*—(*a*) दरविगलितमल्लीवल्लिचंचत्परागप्रकटितपटवासैर्वासयन्काननानि।
इह हि दहति चेतः केतकीगंधबधुः प्रसरदसमबाणप्राणवद्गंधवाहः।।
(गीतगोविंदः प्रथमसर्गः)

सहकारकुसुमकेसरनिकरभरामोदमूर्छितदिगन्ते।।
मधुरमधुविधुरमधुपे मधौ भवेत्कस्य नोत्कण्ठा।। 37।।

जिस समय में आम के पुष्पों की केसर के अतिशय सुगंध से दशों दिशा व्याप्त हो जाती हैं और मधुर मधु के आस्वादन से सारे भ्रमर उन्मत्त हो जाते हैं उस वसंत ऋतु में किस मनुष्य के मन में कामोद्दीपन नहीं होता?

The advent of the lovely season of Spring when the whole atmosphere is quite saturated with the sweet perfume of copious mango blossoms, and the bee are almost maddened with drinking the flowery juice, is powerful enough to make us ardently long for the company of our beloved persons. To be sure, there is none who can successfully stand the irresistible force of Love in Spring.

---

1. Quoted under *Kapilarudra* in the *Subhāṣitāvali* (सुभाषितावलि) at No. 1666, and the (शार्ङ्गधरपद्धति) at No. 3787.

Cf.—(*a*) विकसितसहकारभारहारिपरिमलपुञ्जितगुञ्जितद्विरेफः।
नवकिसलयचारुचामरश्रीर्हरति मुनेरपि मानसं वसन्तः।।
(काव्यप्रदीपः)

(*b*) मलयानिलललनोल्बणमदकलकलकंठकलकलललामः।
मधुरमधुविधुरमधुपो मधुरयमधुना धिनोति धराम्।।
(काव्यालङ्कार, II. 30)

2. Mark that the 3rd *Caraṇa* of this stanza is similar to that of our text.

अच्छार्द्रचन्दनसार्द्रकरा मृगाक्ष्यो
धारागृहाणि कुसुमानि च कौमुदी च।।
मन्दो मरुत्सुमनसः शुचिहर्म्यपृष्ठं ग्रीष्मे
मदं च मदनं च विवर्द्धयन्ति।। 38।।

अत्यंत स्वच्छ चंदन के रस से आर्द्र हाथों वाली मृगनयनी सुंदरियाँ, जलयंत्र (हौज फव्वारे आदि), पुष्प, चन्द्रमा की निर्मल चाँदनी, मंदगामी सुगंधित पवन और सुंदर महल की छत ये सब ग्रीष्म ऋतु में आनन्द और कामदेव दोनों ही की वृद्धि करते हैं।

Hands of faireyed damsels drenched with the juice of pure sandal, houses furnished with artificial jets or fountains of water, flowers, moonlit nights, slow and sweet-scented breezes, and beautiful roofs of stately palaces are all conducive to strengthen high spirits and passion in Summer.

1. *Cf.*— निशा शशाङ्कः क्षत्तनीरराजयः क्वचिद्विचित्रं जलयंत्रमंदिरम्।
मणिप्रकारः सरसं च चदनं शुचौ प्रिये यान्ति जनस्य सेव्यताम्।।
(ऋतुसंहारः । ग्रीष्मवर्णमम्)

स्रजो ह्यद्यामोदा व्यजनपवनश्चन्द्रकिरणाः
परागः कासारो मलयजरजः सीधुविशदम्।।
शुचिः सौधोत्सङ्गः प्रतनुवसनं पङ्कजदृशो
निदाघार्ता ह्येतत्सुखमुपलभन्ते सुकृतिनः।। 39।।

ग्रीष्म के निदाघ से पीड़ित होकर मनोहर पुष्पमाला, पंखे का पवन, चंद्रमा की शीतल किरण, पुष्पों का पराग, सरोवर, चंदन की रज, उत्तम मदिरा, सुंदर महल की छत, बारीक वस्त्र और कमलनयनी प्राणप्यारी के उपभोग करने का सुख विरले भाग्यवान् मनुष्य ही लूट सकते हैं।

Beautiful garlands, fan-breezes, lunar rays, pollen dust, tank, sandal powder, pure wine, fine palaces, few (necessary) clothes of delicate fibre, and lotus-eyed women constitute a special privilege of the blessed few when they are pained with the excessive heat of summer.

---

1. *Cf.*— अत्यच्छं सितमशुकं मधु स्वामोदमच्छं रजः
कर्पूर विधूतार्द्रचन्दनकुवद्वन्द्वाः कुरङ्गीदृशः।
धारावेश्म सपाटलं विचकिलः स्त्रग्दामचन्द्रत्विषो
घातः सृष्टिरियं वृथैव तव न ग्रीष्मोऽभविष्यपद्यदि।।
(सुभाषितरत्नभांडागारः)

सुधाशुभ्रं धाम स्फुरदमलरश्मिः शशधरः
प्रियावक्त्राम्भोजं मलयजरजश्चातिसुरभि।।
स्रजो ह्यद्यामोदास्तदिदमखिलं रागिणि जने
करोत्यन्तःक्षोभं नतु विषयसंसर्ग विमुखे।। 40।।

लिपा-पुता स्वच्छ महल, चंद्रमा निर्मल प्रकाशमान चाँदनी, प्राण-प्यारी का मुख कमल, अत्यंत सुगंधित चंदन की रज और मनोहर पुष्पमाला कामीजनों के मन में बहुत क्षोभ उत्पन्न कर सकते हैं परंतु विषय-वासना से विरक्तजन के अंतःकरण में किसी प्रकार का विकार नहीं कर सकते।

A neat and clean house, the clear and refulgent moon, the lotus-like face of sweethearts, fragrant sandal dust, and charming garlands are able to cause a powerful storm into the hearts of the passionate; but, on the contrary, they are quite helpless to produce the least effect upon the calm and serene temperament of those who have resolutely turned their faces from sensual pleasures.

---

1. When we consider the point of the stanza we cannot fairly justify its place in the description of Summer. However, the poet seems apparantly bent on bringing the cooling effects of cleanliness, moon, ladies, sandal and flowers to the notice of his readers.

तरुणीवैषा दीपितकामा
विकसितजातिः पुण्यसुगन्धिः।।
उन्नतपीनपयोधरभारा प्रावृट्
कुरुते कस्य न हर्षम्।। 41।।

कामोद्दीपन करने वाली, प्रफुल्लित मालती लता से सुशोभित, उत्तम सुगंध से सुगंधित तथा उन्नत और सघन पयोधरों से युक्त वर्षा ऋतु तरुणी स्त्री के समान किस मनुष्य के हृदय को हर्षित नहीं करती।

कवि ने इस श्लोक में वर्षा ऋतु की तुलना तरुणी स्त्री के साथ की है। "दीपितकामा", "विकसितजातिः", "पुण्यसुगंधिः" और "उन्नतपीनपयोधरभारा" तरुणी और प्रावृट् दोनों ही के विशेषण हैं।

Who is not delighted at the sight of the rainy season which like a youthful lady is quite capable of exciting men's passions by the fragrant odour of full-blown *Jāti* flowers and the thick grathering of rising clouds loaded with rains?

---

1. In the following couplet we have got a very striking contrast to the idea of the text ; for, here, the poet *Vṛddhi* (वृद्धि) compares the rainy season to an old woman.

अपगतरजीविकारा घनपटलाक्रान्ततारकालोका।
लम्बपयोधरभारा प्रावृद्धिये वृद्धवनितेव।। (सुभाषितावलिः)

वियदुपचितमेघं भूमयः कन्दलिन्यो
नवकुटजकदम्बामोदिनो गन्धवाहाः।।
शिखिकुलकलकेकारावरम्या वनान्ताः
सुखिनमसुखिनं वा सर्वमुत्कण्ठयन्ति।। 42।।

वर्षा काल के मेघ पटल से व्याप्त हुआ आकाश, नवीन अंकुरों से युक्त भूमि स्थल, तत्क्षण खिले हुए कुटज और कदंब के पुष्पों की सुगंध से सुगंधित पवन और मयूर मण्डली के कलरव से रमणीय वन प्रदेश सुखी और दुःखी सब ही को उत्कंठित करते हैं।

The spirits of every person whether happy or unhappy are sure to be affected with ardent passion at the sight of the cloudy sky, the sprouting fields, the fragrant breeze blowing with the odour of newly blossomed *Kuṭaja* (कुटज) and *Kadamba* (कदम्ब) flowers, and the charming forests full of melodious noise of peacock flights.

---

1. *Cf.*—(*a*) उन्निद्रकन्दलदलान्तरलभ्यमानगुञ्जन्मदान्धमधुपे घनमेघकाले।
स्वप्नेऽपि यः प्रवसति प्रविहाय कान्तां, तस्मै विषाणरहिताय नमो वृषाय। (सुभाषितरत्नभांडागारः)

(*b*) गअणं च मत्तमेहं धारालुलिअज्जुणाइँ अ वणाइँ।
(गनं) (घं) (तार्जुनानि) (च) (नानि)
णिरहङ्कार मिअङ्का हरन्ति नीलाओ वि णिसाओ।
(नि) (मृगा) अपि (निशाः) (आनन्दवर्धनस्य ध्वन्यालोके)

(*c*) वियदलिमलिनाम्बुगर्भमेघं मधुकारके किलकूजितैर्दिशां श्रीः।
धरणिरभिनवाङ्कुराङ्कटङ्का प्रणति परे दयिते प्रसीद मुग्धे।।
(काव्यप्रदीपः)

उपरिघनं घनपटलं तिर्यग्गिरयोऽपि नर्तितमयूराः।।
क्षितिरपि कन्दलधवला दृष्टिं पथिकः क्व यापयतु।। 43।।

मस्तक के ऊपर तो मेघों की घट का घटाटोप हो रहा है, दोनों पार्श्व के पहाड़ों में मयूर मण्डली नृत्य कर रही है और चरणों के नीचे की भूमि नवीन कंदल से धवल हो रही है। इस दशा में बिचारे पथिक किस तरफ में दृष्टि करके संतुष्ट हो सकते हैं? क्योंकि वे जिधर देखते हैं उधर ही कामोद्दीपक पदार्थों से उनका अंतःकरण संतप्त होता है।

How can the mind of a wayfarer be not disturbed at the sight of his head being canopied with raining clouds, the sidelong hills being filled with peacocks dancing with pleasure, and the soil beneath his feet being covered with flowers and roots?

---

1. Quoted under *Bhartṛhari* (भर्तृहरि) in the *Subhāṣitāvali* (सुभाषितावलि), at No. 1744 and anonymously in the शार्ङ्गधरपद्धति at No. 3886.

2. The words "उपरि घनं घन पटलं" are also met with in the *Mudrārākṣasa* (मुद्राराक्षस 1।21)

Cf.— दलत्कंदलभाग्भूमिः सनवाम्बुदमम्बरम्।
वाप्यः पुफल्लाम्बुजयुजो जाता दृष्टिविषं मम।।

(काव्यानुशासनम्)

इतो विद्युद्वल्लीविलसितमितः केतकितरोः
स्फुरद्गन्धः प्रोद्यज्जलदनिनदस्फुर्जितमितः।।
इतः केकिक्रीडाकलकलरवः पक्ष्मलदृशां
कथं यास्यन्ते ते विरहदिवसाः संभृतरसाः।। 44।।

नहीं मालूम कि सुलोचना विरहिणी स्त्रियों के शृंगारादि रसों की वृद्धि करने वाले वियोग के दिन इस वर्षा काल में किस प्रकार से कटेंगे, क्योंकि एक ओर तो आकाश में बिजलियों ने झमाझम मचा रखी है और दूसरी ओर फूली हुई केतकी की महक उड़ रही है, तथा इधर तो बरसते हुए मेघों का समूह गर्जना कर रहा है और उधर मयूर मण्डली उन्मत्त होकर नाँचती हुई सुंदर कलरव कर रही हैं।

With what great difficulty will, the days of women, with strong and beautiful eyelashes and wellversed in the art of sensual enjoyments, be passed at the time of separation from their loving husbands when their hearts are sorely pained with the fire of passion continually brightened at the sight of a brilliant flash of lightning in the sky, on the one side, and the odorous air fraught with the strong scent of *Ketakī* (केतकी) flowers, on the other; as well as of the roaring of raining clouds, in this place, and the passionate cries of peacocks in that?

---

1. *Cf.*—(*a*) दिशाधारा हाराः शमितशमभाराः शमवतामसूचीसंचाराः कृतमदविकाराश्च शिखिनाम्। धृताध्वव्यापारास्तुहिनकणसारा विरहिणीमनःकीर्णाङ्गाराः किरति जलधारा जलधरः। (सुभाषितरत्नभाण्डागारः)

(*b*) मेघेर्व्योम नवाम्बुभिर्वसुमती विद्युल्लताभिर्दिशो धाराभिर्गगनं वनानि कुटजैः पूरैर्वृता निम्नगाः। एकां घातयितुं वियोगविधुरां दीनां वराकीं स्त्रियं प्रावृट्काल हताशवर्णयकृतं मिथ्या किमाडम्बरम्।। (सुभाषितावलिः)

(*c*) इतः केकीनादैस्तुदति शतकोटिप्रतिभटैरितः कामः कामं कठिमतरबाणैः प्रहरति। इतो गर्जत्युच्चैर्जलधरगाणो भीमनिनदैर्विना नाथं जाने न सखिभविता किं ननु मम।। (जनार्दनभट्टस्य शृंगारशतकम्)

असूचीसंसारे तमसि नभसि प्रौढजलद-
ध्वनिप्राये तस्मिन्पतति दृषदां नीरनिचये।।
इदं सौदामिन्याः कनककमनीयं विलसितं मुदं
च ग्लानिं च प्रथयति पथिष्वेव सुदृशाम्।। 48।।

जिस सांवन की महा अंधियारी रात में सूई के बराबर भी पगडण्डी नहीं सूझती और अत्यंत गर्जना करने वाली और मूसलधार बरसने वाली घटा से सारी पृथ्वी ओले और जल से व्याप्त हो रही है, उस समय की सुवर्ण के समान सुंदर बिजली की चमक सुलोचना विरहिणी स्त्रियों के अंतःकरण में हर्ष और ग्लानि दोनों का विस्तार करती हैं।

In the dark nights of *Nabhas* or *Śrāvaṇa* (नभस् or श्रावण) when rain and hail are falling upon the earth with a tremendous noise of roaring clouds, and when footpaths are quite impercetible to the eyes, the golden flash of lighting beautifully shining across the sky is at once a source of great delight and disturbance to fair-eyed ladies.

1. The downpour of rain is particularly smart and heavy during the month of Śrāvaṇa which generally falls in with July ; add to it the deafening roar of the clouds in a dark night ; and the miseries or fears of a lovely woman will be found really astounding.

आसारेण न हर्म्यतः प्रियतमैर्यातुं बहिः शक्यते
शीतोत्कम्पनिमित्तमायतदृशा गाढं समालिङ्ग्यते।।
जाताः शीतलशीकराश्च मरुतश्चात्यन्तखेदच्छिदो
धन्यानां बत दुर्दिनं सुदिनतां याति प्रियासङ्गमे।।46।।

जिस समय में मूसलधार वर्षा के कारण प्राण वल्लभ शयन मंदिर से बाहर नहीं जा सकते और शीत से काँपती हुई पूर्ण रूप से खुले हुए नेत्रों से देखने वाली प्राण-प्यारी गाढ आलिंगन करते हैं तथा शीतल जलकण को धारण करने वाली पवन सुरत के अत्यंत परिश्रम को मिटा देती है, वह वर्षा के दुर्दिन सौभाग्यशाली पुरुषों के लिए सुदिन का स्वरूप धारण कर लेते हैं।

For blessed persons, a foul rainy day is even changed in a pleasant and enjoyable one; for, when they are unable to go out of their bedrooms on account of the incessant downpour of rains, they gladly return to their loves who trembling with cold take them into their close embraces; as well as when the cool particles of water in the surrounding atmosphere give them a refreshing sensation, and allay the excess of fatigue they might have incurred in their sensual pleasures.

---

1. Quoted anonymously in the *Subhāṣitāvali* (सुभाषितावलि) at No. 1784.

2. No one needs be told that the company of those near and dear to us invariably lightens the bitter severities of a stormy and foul weather.

अर्द्धं नीत्वा निशायाः सरभससुरतायासखिन्नश्लथाङ्गः
प्रोद्भूतासह्यतृष्णो मधुमदनिरतो हर्म्यपृष्ठे विविक्ते।।
सम्भोगाक्लान्तकान्ताशिथिलभुजलतावर्जितं कर्करीतो
ज्योत्स्नाभिन्नाच्छधारं पिबति न सलिलं शारदं मन्दभाग्यः।। 47।।

जो पुरुष शरद की चाँदनी में आधी रात के समय शीघ्रतापूर्वक किए हुए सुरत के परिश्रम से शिथिल, असह्य तृष्णा से व्याकुल और मदिरा पान से उन्मत्त होकर स्वच्छ महल की छत पर बैठा हुआ संभोगजनित खेद से शिथिल भुजा वाली प्राणप्यारी के हिलते हुए हाथों में ली हुई हिलती हुई झारी से पड़ती हुई निर्मल जलधारा का पान नहीं करता वह निस्संदेह मंदभागी है।

One who after the lapse of the first half of night when having tired of the recent enjoyment of his wife, and pained with unbearable thirst on that account, is sitting in an intoxicated state on the lovely roof of a palace, does not avail himself of the pleasure of drinking clear autumnal water pouring out in a transparent stream in bright moonlight from the mouth of a beautiful waterpot held by the trembling hands of his beloved sweetheart whose strength has equally failed owing to the said coition, is no doubt a very unfortunate being.

---

1. Quoted under *Bhartṛhari* भर्तृहरि in the *Śārṅagadharapaddhati* (शार्ङ्गधरपद्धति । 3908) and anonymously in the *Subhāṣitāvali* (सुभाषितावलि 1824)

Cf.— इत्थं निर्मलकर्करीस्थमसहपालेथवाताहतं।
नाधन्याः प्रचुरं पिबन्त्यनुदिनं प्रोन्मुक्तधारं पयः।। (काव्यालंकारटीकायाम्)

हेमन्ते दधिदुग्धसर्पिरशना माञ्जिष्ठवासोभृतः
काश्मीरद्रवसान्द्रदिग्धवपुषः खिन्ना विचित्रैरतैः।।
पीनोरुस्तनकामिनीजनकृताश्लेषा गृहाभ्यन्तरे
ताम्बूलीदलपूगपूरितमुखा धन्याः सुखं शेरते।।48।।

हेमंत ऋतु के समय दही, दुग्ध और घृतादि का भोजन करने वाले, मंजीठ के रंगे हुए लाल वस्त्र पहनने वाले, सघन केसर के रस से शरीर को चित्रित करने वाले, नाना प्रकार के सुरतजनित खेद से शिथिल होकर पीनोन्नत उरुस्थल और स्तनों को धारण करने वाली कामवती स्त्रियों का आलिंगन किए हुए सुंदर तांबूल की वीटिका मुख में लिए जो पुरुष मंदिर के अभ्यंतर स्थान में सुखपूर्वक शयन करते हैं वह निस्संदेह धन्य हैं।

In winter, those persons are indeed very fortunate who can affored to (1) have plenty of milk and Ghee upon their tables, (2) wear deep red clothes upon their bodies, (3) enjoy the luxury of rubbing a thick layer of saffron juice over their handsome persons, (4) have the pleasure of tiring themselves with a variety of sensual enjoyment, (5) lie down into the close embraces of lovely women with thickset breasts, and (6) sleep with ease and comfort in the interior of their houses, chewing a leaf of piper-betel mixed areca nut and other spices.

1. It may be observed that the use of curd, milk, ghee, red clothes and saffron is specially recommended in the cold weather.

चुम्बन्तो गण्डभित्तीरलकवति मुखे सीत्कृतान्यादधाना
वक्षःसूत्कञ्चिकेषु स्तनभरपुलकोद्भेदमापादयन्तः ।।
अरूनाकम्पयन्तः पृथुजघनतटात्स्रंसयन्तोंऽशुकानि
व्यक्तं कान्ताजनानां विटचरितकृतः शैशिरा वान्ति वाताः ।।49 ।।

कामिनियों की अलकावलियुक्त कपोल स्थली का चुंबन करने वाले उनके मुख से शीताधिक्य के हेतु 'सी', 'सी' शब्द कराते हुए, कंचुकीरहित वक्षस्थल पर प्रकट हुई रोमावलि के कारण से दोनों कुच युगल का भेद बतलाने वाले, दोनों पेडुओं को कंपित करते हुए और भारी जंघाओं से वस्त्रों को दूर करते हुए शिशिर ऋतु के पवन प्रत्यक्ष रूप से स्त्रियों के साथ जार कर्म कर रहे हैं।

Kissing the cheeks, causing a shivering sound of their lips in the fairy faces upon which the luxuriant hair is falling in a wanton state, giving rise to the appearance of a distinct line of demarcation between their bare and heaving bre-asts, shaking the buttocks, and blowing aside the clothes from their bulky upper legs, the wintry winds are clearly playing the part of *Viṭas* or paramours with beautiful women in broad daylight.

---

1. Quoted anonymously in the *Subhāṣitāvali* (सुभाषितावलि) at No. 1855 and the *Śārṅgadharapaddhati* शार्ङ्गधरपद्धति at No. 3945.

Cf.— सीत्कारं शिक्षयति व्रणयत्यधरं तनोति रोमाञ्चम्।
नागरिकः किंतु मिलितो नहि नहि सखि हैमनः पवनः।।
(केशवमिश्रस्यालंकारशेखरे)

केशानाकलयन्दृशौ मुकुलयन्वासो बलादाक्षिपन्ना-
तन्वन्पुलकोद्गमं प्रकटयन्नङ्गेषु कम्पं गतैः ।।
बारंबाररमुदारसीत्कृतकृतो दन्तच्छदान्पीडयन्प्रायः
शैशिर एष सम्प्रति मरुत्कान्तासु कान्तायते ।। 50 ।।

केशों को इधर-उधर बिखेरते हुए, नेत्रों को बंद करते हुए, वस्त्रों को जोर से उड़ाते हुए, शरीर को रोमांचित करते हुए, सारी देह को कंपित करते हुए, शीत की अधिकता के हेतु मुख से बारंबार सीत्कार शब्द का उच्चारण कराते हुए और होठों का चुंबन करते हुए शिशिर ऋतु के पवन स्त्रियों के साथ प्रायः पतिका सा आचरण कर रहे हैं।

Dishevelling the hair, closing the eyelids, forcibly throwing away the clothes, causing a distinct thrill throughout the body, embracing their slightly trembling persons, making them repeatedly utter the low but audible sounds of fear and joy, and kissing the lips, the cool breezes of winter are frequently acting the part of wanton husbands or lovers with women.

---

1. Quoted anonymously in the *Subhāṣitāvali* (सुभाषितावलि) at No. 1854 and the *Śārṅgadharapaddhati* (शार्ङ्गधरपद्धति) at No. 3944.

असाराः सन्त्वेते विरतिविरसायासविषया
जुगुप्सन्तां यद्वा ननु सकलोदोषास्पदमिति।।
तथाऽप्यन्तस्तत्त्वे प्रणिहितधियामप्यतिबलस्त-
दीयोऽनाख्येयः स्फुरति हृदये कोऽपि महिमा।। 51।।

"संसार के विषय सब असार हैं। विरति उत्पन्न होने पर रस रहित हैं, और सारे दोषों के मूल कारण हैं" इत्यादि निंदा हम भले ही करें, तथापि विषयों की महिमा के अपार और प्रबल होने में कोई संदेह नहीं। क्योंकि परब्रह्म परमात्मा के तत्त्ववेत्ता विद्वानों के अंतःकरण में भी ये विषय कामाग्नि को संदीपन करने में सर्वथा समर्थ होते हैं।

Sensual pleasures are, no doubt, fruitless and a great hinderance to our renoucing the world. People may therefore hate them as they like, and stigmatise them as the source of all woe and misery. However, there is something very powerful and indefinable in their matchless might to cause a strong agitation even into the hearts of those who having forsaken mundane objects have entirely devoted themselves to the search of the First Principle or True Cause.

---

1. *Cf.*—(*a*) विवेकप्रध्वंसादुपचितमहामोहगहनो।
विकारः कोऽप्यन्तर्जडयति च तापं च कुरुते।। (मालतीमाधवे)
(*b*) अलमति चपलत्वात्स्वप्नमायोपमत्वा-
त्परिणति विरसत्वात्सङ्गमेनाङ्गनायाः।
इति यदि शतकृत्वस्तत्त्वमालोचयाम-
स्तदपि न हरिणाक्षीं विस्मरत्यन्तरात्मा।। (बिह्लणचरितम्)

भवन्तो वेदान्तप्रणिहितधियामाप्तगुरवो
विचित्रालापानां वयमपि कवीनामनुचराः।।
तथाऽप्येतद्ब्रूमो नहि परहितात्पुण्यमधिकं न
चाऽस्मिन्संसारे कुवलयदृशो रम्यमपरम्।। 52।।

आप तो वेदांति पंडितों के गुरु हैं और हम नाना प्रकार की सुंदर कविता कहने वाले कवीश्वरों के अनुचर हैं। तथापि हम सबको यह बात अवश्य कहनी पड़ती है कि इस संसार में परोपकार के सिवाय पुण्य और कमलनयनी सुंदरियों के सिवाय रमणीय और कुछ भी नहीं है।

You are the acknowledged preceptors of those who have given themselves to the study of Vedānta and we are the followers of poets whose words being never monotonous are always very beautiful and sweet; but let us make no secret of saying that upon the surface of this earth no other virtue is greater than that of doing good to others, and that nothing is more delightful here than lotus-eyed women.

---

1. This Śloka is quoted under *Bhartṛhari* (भर्तृहरि) by *Kṛemendra* (क्षेमेन्द्र) in his *Suvṛttatilaka* (सुवृत्त तिलक).

Cf.—(*a*) किं संसारे सारं बहुशोऽपि विचिन्त्यमानमिदमेव।
मनुजेषु दृष्टतत्वं स्वपरहितायोद्यतं जन्म।।
(विमलाचार्यस्य प्रश्नोत्तररत्नमाला)

(*b*) सन्तः शृणुध्वं हृदये निदध्वमुत्क्षिप्यं बाहुं परिराटीमि।
न सुभ्रुवां तुल्यमिहास्ति रम्यं न सुभ्रुवां तुल्यमिहास्ति रम्यम्।।
(सरस्वतीकण्ठभरणम् । द्वितीय परिच्छेदः)

किमिह बहुभिरुक्तैर्युक्तिशून्यैः प्रला-
पैर्द्वयमपि पुरुषाणां सर्वदा सेवनीयम्।।
अभिनवमदलीलालालसं सुन्दरीणां स्तन-
भरपरिखिन्नं यौवनं वा वनं वा।। 53।।

युक्तिरहित अनेकानेक बकवाद करने से क्या प्रयोजन है। इस संसार में आकर पुरुषों के सेवन करने योग्य दो ही पदार्थ हैं। (1) या तो अभिनव रस क्रीड़ा से शिथिल और स्तन भार से पीड़ित सुंदरियों का यौवन और (2) या वन।

What use is there in talking a great deal of non-sense and incoherent prattle? There are only two things worth the devotion of man in this world : (1) either the youth of beautiful women who are ever anxious of having a varietyof sensual enjoyments, tired as it were of the burden of their full developed breasts; or (2) the forest (to live as a hermit).

---

1. किमिबहुभिरुक्तैः is also found in the *Nāṭyaśāstra* of Bharata (भरतमुनिकृतनाट्यशास्त्रम् १५।६७) The *Subhāṣitāvali* quotes it under (भट्टोद्भट्ट), at No. 3453.

Cf.— रसिक सुनहु तुम कान दे, सब ग्रन्थनको सार।
योग भोग में इक बिना, यह संसार असारः।।

(रसिक कवि)

सत्यं जना वच्मि न पक्ष-
पाताल्लोकेषु सर्वेष्वतितथ्यमेतत्।।
नान्यन्मनोहारि नितम्बिनीभ्यो
दुःखस्य हेतुर्न हि कश्चिदन्यः।। 54।।

हे मनुष्यो! हम पक्ष-पातरहित सत्य-सत्य कह रहे हैं कि इस संसार में सुंदर नितंब स्थल धारण करने वाली युवतियों को छोड़कर न तो कोई मनोहर पदार्थ ही है और न कोई दुःखादि का हेतु ही है।

भावार्थ।

स्त्री को छोड़कर संसार में सुख-दुःख का हेतु और कोई नहीं है।

Oh my friends! I speak real and impartial truth when I say that the only cause of pleasure and pain (good and evil) in this world of ours is beautiful women of well developed buttocks.

---

1. Quoted anonymously in the *Subhāṣitāvali* (सुभाषितावलि 2233)

Cf.—(*a*) सन्तः शृणुध्वं हृदयं निदध्वमुत्क्षिप्यं बाहू परिराटीमि।
न सुभ्रुवां तुल्यमिहास्ति रम्यं न सुभ्रुवां तुल्यमिहास्त्यरम्यम्।।

(*b*) Alas ! the love of women! it is known
To be a lovely and a fearful thing.
Byron's Don Juan.

(*c*) जो जग में होती नहीं, वामलोचना वाम।
रसिक सुना जाता नहीं, कहीं दुःख सुख नाम।।
(रसिक कवि).

तावदेव कृतिनां हृदि
स्फुरत्येष निर्मलविवेकदीपकः।।
यावदेवं न कुरङ्गचक्षुषां
ताड्यते चपललोचनाञ्चलैः।। 55।।

ज्ञानवानों के हृदय में निर्मल विवेकरूपी दीपक का प्रकाश केवल तब तक ही रह सकता है कि जब तक उसके मृगनयनी तरुणियों के चंचल नेत्रों की पवन का झकोरा न लगे।

The lamp of clear sighted judgement and knowledge in the hearts of good and virtuous persons can burn only so long as it is not blown out by the clever and flickering glances of antelope-eyed women.

PURPORT.

Women destroys all discretion in man.

---

1. The idea of the stanza is a favourite point of oriental authors.

Cf.—(*a*) यावद्दृष्टिर्मृगाक्षीणां नो नरीनर्तिभङ्गुरा।
तावज्ज्ञानवतां चित्ते विवेकः कुरुते पदम्।

(*b*) प्रभवति मनसि विवेको विदुषामपि शास्त्रं संभवस्तावत्।
निपतन्ति दृष्टिविशिखा यावन्नेन्दोवराक्षणाम्।। (रसमंजरी)

(*c*) तदवधि कुशलोपुराणशास्त्रश्रुतिशतचारुविचारजो विवेकः।
यदवधि न पदं दधाति चित्ते हरिणकिशोरदृशो दृशोर्विलासः।।
(भामिनीविलासः शृङ्गारोल्लासः)

(*d*) कष्ट एव तरलस्तरुणीनां भावभंगुरदृगन्तनिपातः।
एष चेन्मनसि लब्धविपाकः किं करिष्यति विवेकवराकः।।
(भर्तृहरिनिर्वेदम्)

2. There is also a couplet *Sekha Sādi*, the wellknown Persian poet, which may thus be translated in Hindi : "विवेकियों के निर्मल प्रकाश का यश उसी समय तक रहता है जब तक वह स्त्रियों के चरित्रों से बचे रहें।"

भवति वचसि सङ्गत्यागमुद्दिश्यवार्ता
श्रुतमुखरमुखानां केवलं पण्डितानाम् ।।
जघनमरुणरत्नग्रन्थिकाञ्चीकलापं
कुवलयनयनानां को विहातुं समर्थः ।। 56 ।।

शास्त्र के पढ़े हुए चतुर पंडितों के मुख में वैराग्यसूचक उपदेश केवल कथन मात्र ही समझना चाहिये। क्योंकि कमलनयनी स्त्रियों की लाल रत्नों से जटित कांचि कलापयुक्त जंघा का परित्याग करने में वस्तुतः कोई भी समर्थ नहीं होता।

Men professing to be learned in the *Śāstras*, do not preach the doctrine of renouncement in real earnest, but simply with their tongue; for, no one in the world is ever able to give up the sight of lotuseyed women's beautiful buttocks adorned with belts of crimson precious gems.

---

1. *Cf.*—(*a*) येऽप्यङ्गनानां प्रवदन्ति दोषान्वैराग्यमार्गेण गुणान्विहाय।
ते दुर्जना मे मनसो वितर्कः सद्भाववाक्यानि न तानि तेषाम् ।। 5 ।।
(वाराहीसंहिता 74 अध्यायः)

(*b*) बुरी बुरी सब जग कहे, त्यागी किन से जाय?
नारि हृदय जिनके रसिक, ईश्वर प्रगटै आय।।
(रसिक कवि)

स्वपरप्रतारकोऽसौ निन्दति
योऽलीकपण्डितो युवतीः।।
यस्मात्तपसोऽपि फलं स्वर्गः
स्वर्गेऽपि चाप्सरसः।। 57।।

जो मिथ्याभिमानी पण्डित तरुण सुंदरियों की निंदा करते हैं वह स्वयं भी धोखा खाते हैं और दूसरों को भी धोखा देते हैं, क्योंकि अनेकानेक तपश्चरणों का फल तो स्वर्ग की प्राप्ति और स्वर्ग लाभ का फल अप्सराओं का भोग विलास है।

That learned man, who preaches the doctrine of hate against young women is indeed a false philosopher who having first deceived himself is deceiving others; for, the enjoyment of *Apsarās* or heavenly nymphs is the ultimate end of heaven, which, in its own turn, is again the result of a series of religious devotions and virtues.

---

1. *Cf.*—(*a*) क्रतुं धनानां फलमग्र्यमाहुः फलं क्रतूनामविवादि पुण्यम्।
पुण्यस्य पूर्ण फलमिन्द्रलोको द्विरष्टवर्षाः स्त्रिय एव नाकः।।
(चतुर्वर्गसंग्रहः ।३।३)

(*b*) अहो धाष्ट्र्यमसाधूनां निन्दतामनघाः स्त्रियः ।।15।।
(वाराहीसंहिता 74 अध्यायः)

2. According to the Mahomedan religion, Hoories are said to consititute prominent feature of the heavenly bliss of blessed souls.

मत्तेभकुम्भीदलने भुवि सन्ति शूराः
केचित्प्रचण्डमृगराजवधेऽपि दक्षाः।।
किन्तु ब्रवीमि बलिनां पुरतः प्रसह्य
कन्दर्पदर्पदलने विरला मनुष्याः।। 58।।

इस पृथ्वी पर मदोन्मत्त गजराज का कुंभस्थल दलन करने वाले बहुत से शूरवीर विद्यमान हैं, और ऐसे ही प्रचण्ड मृगराज सिंह का वध करने वाले मनुष्य भी बहुत मिल सकते हैं; परन्तु बलवानों के समक्ष हम यह बात जोर देकर कह सकते हैं कि कामदेव का गर्व गंजन करने वाले विरले ही मनुष्य होंगे।

Quite true that there are men on this earth who are able to break into pieces the frontal heads of wild elephants, as well as some who are skilful to take out the life of lions, the cruel and dreadful lords of the deer; but I can safely assert before the courageous, that persons who can successfully brave the attacks of Cupid and subdue the passion of love are undoubtedly very few.

---

1. *Cf.*—शूरान्महाशूरतमोऽस्ति कोऽवा मनोजबाणैर्व्यथितो न यस्तु।

(शंकराचार्यस्य प्रश्नोत्तररत्नमालायाम्)

2. Successful resistance of the charms of fair ladies is, no doubt, the most difficutl taks for the Sons of Adam.

सन्मार्गे तावदास्ते प्रभवति पुरुषस्तावदेवेन्द्रियाणां
लज्जां तावद्विधत्ते विनयमपि समालंबले तावदेव।।
भ्रूचापाकृष्टामुक्ताः श्रवणपथगता नीलपक्ष्माण एते
यावल्लीलावतीनां हृदि न धृतिमुषो दृष्टिबाणाः पतन्ति।।59।।

अपनी इन्द्रियों के सुमार्ग में प्रवृत्त रखने, लज्जा के धारण करने, और नम्रता के अवलंबन करने की अंतिम अवधि, विलासवती युवतियों के भौंहरूपी चाप से छोड़े हुए कर्णपर्यंत विशाल नील पलकों को धारण करने वाले और धैर्य का हरण करने वाले दृष्टि रूप बाणों के पुरुष के हृदय में लगने के समय तक ही समझनी चाहिए।

A man can walk in the path of righteousness, subdue his sences, preserve his modesty, and hold to his moral training, untill his heart is not pierced by the stupifying arrows of women's glances shot off from their arched brows and blue eyelashes.

---

1. The verse is quoted anonymously in the *Subhāṣitāvali* (सुभाषितावलि 2246) and under *Bāṇabhaṭṭa* (बाणभट्ट) in the *Śārṅgadaharapaddhati* (शार्ङ्धरपद्धति) at No. 3300. I Must add that I have not been able to trace out the verse either to कादम्बरी or to हर्षचरित, the two celebrated works of बाणभट्ट।

Cf.— न श्रुतेन न वित्तेन न वृत्तेन न कर्मणा।
प्रवृत्तं शक्यते रोद्धं मनोभर्वपथे मनः।।

(क्षेमेन्द्रकृतदर्पदलनम् 3 विचारः)

उन्मत्तप्रेमसंरम्भादारभन्ते यदङ्गना।।
तत्र प्रत्यूहमाधातुं ब्रह्माऽपि खलु कातरः।। 60।।

अतिशय अनुराग से उन्मत्त होकर स्त्रियाँ जिस कार्य को आरंभ कर बैठती हैं उसमें विघ्न डालने के निमित्त स्वयं ब्रह्मा जी भी भयभीत होते हैं।

Brahmā, the Creator, is Himself afraid of throwing an obstacle what has been undertaken by women in the hurry and excitement of their passionate love.

---

1. *Cf.*—What woman wills, heaven wills also.

(A. Dumas' Margurite de Valois)

2. For the verification of the poet's statement the reader is referred to the desperate actions of Portia, Juliet, Imogen, Rosalind and others which sometimes make the heroines of Shakespeare appear to be something more than ordinary women.

Cf.— कहा तिया नहिं कर सके, कामवती जब होय?
रसिक सास पति पुत्र सब, कर नसकै कछु कोय।।

(रसिक कवि)

तावन्महत्त्वं पाण्डित्यं विवेकित्वं कुलीनता।
यावज्ज्वलति नाङ्गेषु हन्त पञ्चेषुपावकः।। 61।।

बड़प्पन, पण्डिताई, कुलीनता और ज्ञान की स्थिति मनुष्य के हृदय में कामाग्नि संदीपन होने के समय तक ही रह सकती है।। ६१।।

भावार्थ।

कामदेव की अग्नि प्रज्वलित होते ही बड़ाई, पण्डिताई, विवेक और कुलीनता तत्काल नष्ट हो जाते हैं।

A man can preserve his greatness, learning, nobility and wisdom only so long as his frame is not set aglow with the burning passion of love caused by the fire of *Pañcheshu* (पञ्चेषु), the holder of the five *arrows (*i.e.,* Cupid).

---

1. *Cf.*—(*a*) तावद्धत्ते पुमान्धैर्यं विवेकं शीलमेव च।
यावत्पतति कामस्य सायकानां न गोचरे ।।204।।
(कथासरित्सागरः । अलंकारवतीलंबके 4 तरंगः)

(*b*) जबलग मानवके रसिक, काम न उपजै देह।
कुशल तभी तक जानियो, धन मन मति जन गेह।।
(रसिक कवि)

2. For the five arrows of Cupid, the reader is referred to our note on the word पञ्चेषु।

शास्त्रज्ञोऽपि प्रथितविनयोऽप्यात्मबोधोऽपि बाढं
संसारेऽस्मिन्भवति विरलो भाजनं सद्गतीनाम्।।
येनैतस्मिन्निरयनगरद्वारमुद्घाटयन्ती वामाक्षीणां
भवति कुटिला भ्रूलताकुञ्चिकेव।। 62।।

शास्त्र के जानने वाले, विनयशील और आत्म ज्ञानियों में से भी इस संसार में कोई बिरला ही पुरुष होगा कि जो सद्गति का लाभ कर सके, क्योंकि वामलोचन वाली स्त्रियों की कुटिल भ्रूलता- रूपी कुंजी से नरक द्वार के कपाट उनके लिए पहले ही से खुले रहते हैं।

Out of those who are well read in the *Śāstras,* who are renowned for their morality and who are favoured with the knowledge of self, a few persons can only be ever successful to attain to the state of eternal beatitude; for, the key of the arched brows of crooked-eyed women always opens the doors of hell for the passage of mortals.

---

1. *Cf.*—द्वारं किमेतन्नरकस्य नारी।।3।। (श्रीशंकराचार्यस्य प्रश्नोत्तरमाला)

Sanskrit poets when dwelling on the dark side of women generally take delight in describing them as the foremost obstacle in man's entrance into heaven.

कृशः काणः खञ्जः श्रवणरहितः पुच्छविकलो
व्रणी पूयक्लिन्नः कृमिकुलशतैरावृततनुः।।
क्षुधाक्षामो जीर्णः पिठरककपालार्पितगलः
शुनीमन्वेति श्वा हतमपि निहन्त्येव मदनः।। 63।।

अहो! कैसे कष्ट की बात है कि दुर्बल, काणा, खोड़ा, बूचा, बांडा, जख़्मी (घायल), दुर्गंध युक्त सहस्रशः कीड़ों से व्याप्त शरीर वाला, क्षुधातुर, जीर्ण और गले में मिट्टी के घड़े का गरगना धारण करने वाला कुत्ता भी कामान्ध होकर कुतिया के पीछे-पीछे दौड़ता फिरता है। हाय! इस निष्ठुर कामदेव को ऐसे मरे हुए प्राणी के मारने में भी कुछ लज्जा नहीं आती।

When we see that a wretched dog that is (1) lean, (2) one-eyed, (3) bald, (4) earless, (5) shorn of its tail, (6) wounded, (7) stinking, (8) covered with thousands of insects, all over the body, (9) pained with excessive hunger, (10) worn out with age and (11) wearing the circular head of a broken earthen pot around its neck, is even compelled to run passionately after a bitch, we cannot help crying unreserved shame upon the meanness and cruelty of the god of love who is not ashamed of trying his deadly arrows on such a miserable creature already dead of its own misfortunes.

---

1. The stanza which is quoted under *Candraka* in his *Aucityavicāracarcā* (औचित्यविचारचर्चा) by *Kṣemendra* (क्षेमेन्द्र) is given anonymously in *Nimisādhu's* commentary on *Rudraṭa's Kāvyālaṅkāra* (रुद्रटकृतकाव्यालङ्कार), and the *Subhāṣitāvali* (सुभाषितावलि) at No. 3390.

स्त्रीमुद्रांझषकेतनस्यपरमांसर्वार्थसम्पत्करींयेमूढाः
प्रविहाययान्तिकुधियोमिथ्याफलान्वेषिणः।।
तेनैवनिहत्यनिर्दयतरंनग्नीकृतामुण्डिताः केचि-
त्पञ्चशिखीकृताश्चजटिलाः कापालिकाश्चापरे।। 64।।

जो मूढ जन कामदेव की परमोत्तम और सब प्रकार की संपदा को देने वाली स्त्री मुद्रा का परित्याग करके बुद्धि भ्रष्ट हो मिथ्या फल ढूँढते फिरते हैं उनको मीन के तन ने भी बहुत कठोर दण्ड दिए हैं। कितने ही तो नग्न हुए, कितने ही रुण्ड मुण्ड, कितने ही पंचकेशों धारण किए, कितने ही जटाधारी बने हुए और कितने ही कपाल हाथ में लिए हुए, भिक्षाटन करते घर-घर मारे-मारे फिरते हैं।

भावार्थ–जैसे कोई राजा अपनी मुद्रा के उल्लंघन करने वालों को उचित दण्ड देता है वैसे ही कामदेव भी अपनी स्त्री मुद्रा के अनादर करने वालों को नग्नीकरणादि उचित दण्ड देता है।

The fools who have forsaken the great woman seal of the god of love (who has the design of a fish emblazoned on his standard) which can bring them every kind of success in their various pursuits, are indeed devoid of all sense and wisdom; for, they have voluntarily given up the only source of all happiness in this world and are now wandering about in fruitless search of the same. But, see, that they have met adequate punishments at the hands of Cupid who has doomed some to roam about in the world with naked bodies, some with cleanshaven heads, some with bushy and shaggy hairs growing all over the body, some with twisted and matted locks, and others with human skulls in their hands pegging alms from door to door.

Purport—As kings punish those who disobey the royal sear, so Cupid inflicts condign punishiments on those men who set at naught his women-seal.

1. Quoted anonymously by Vāgbhaṭṭa in his *Kāvyānuśāsana* (काव्यानुशासन), and quoted under भर्तृहरि in the शार्ङ्गधरपद्धति at No. 3082. The verse stands in the *Pañcatantra* IV. 34. (पंचतंत्रम् 4 तंत्रम् 34)

विश्वामित्रपराशरप्रभृतयो वाताम्बुपर्णाशनास्तेऽपि
स्त्रीमुखपङ्कजं सुललितं दृष्ट्वैव मोहं गताः।।
शाल्यन्नं सघृतं पयोदधियुतं भुञ्जन्ति ये मानवा-
स्तेषामिन्द्रियनिग्रहो यदि भवेद्विन्ध्यस्तरेत्सागरम्।। 65।।

जब कि पवन, जल और वृक्षादि के पर्ण (पान) का भक्षण करने वाले विश्वामित्र पराशरादि ऋषि गण भी स्त्रियों का सुंदर मुख-कमल देखकर मोहित हो गए तो घृत, दुग्ध और दधि सहित शाल्यादि अन्न के भोजन करने वाले मनुष्यों का इंद्रियमन करना तो विंध्याचल के समुद्र में तरण करने के समान बिल्कुल ही असंभव है।

When learned saints like Viśvāmitra (विश्वामित्र) Parāśara (पराशर) and others who supported themselves upon the simplest food of bare leaves of trees and water were even thrown into a state of confusion and unconsciousness at the sight of lotus-faced women, how can it then be ever possible for those men who eat the dainties of various grains as rice, wheat, etc. together with milk, ghee and curdle, to keep absolute control over their senses? The subjection of passion in worldly men is as much out of question as the swimming of the Vindhyā over sea.

---

1. *Cf.*—(*a*) त्यक्त्वाहारमथो वने स्थितिमताः पञ्चाग्निविद्यातपः
सेवातत्परमानसा दशदिशो वासोवसानाः पुनः।
सिद्धा दारुसमीकृताङ्गलतिकाः कान्ताकटाक्षाशुगा-
च्छिन्नान्तर्हृदयाः क्षणात्समभवन्कामो नृणां दुर्जयः ।।74।।
(गोपीनाथस्य रामसौभाग्यशतकम्)

संसारेऽस्मिन्नसारे कुनृपतिभवनद्वारसेवावलम्ब-
व्यासङ्गध्वस्तधैर्यं कथममलधियो मानसं संनिदध्युः।।
यद्येताः प्रोद्यदिन्दुद्युतिनिचयभृतो न स्युरम्भोजनेत्राः
प्रेङ्खत्काञ्चीकलापाः स्तनभरविनमन्मध्यभागास्तरुण्यः।। 66।।

यदि इस असार संसार में पूर्ण चंद्रमा की कान्ति के समान रूपवती, शब्द करती हुई कणगती को पहनने वाली और स्तन भार से नम्रीभूत कटि को धारण करने वाली कमलनयनी तरुणियाँ न होतीं तो निर्मल मतिमान पुरुष दुष्ट राजाओं की ड्योढी की सेवा के संबंधी नाना प्रकार के दुःखों को अधीर होकर कदापि नहीं सहते।

Had there been no youthful ladies with facial splendour of the refulgent moon whose eyes are beautiful like a lotus, whose buttocks are quite melodious with a sweet tinkling of bells attached to their belts, and whose waists are somewhat bent on account of the burden of their fullgrown bust, we could never have found, in the mortal world, learned men of bright intellectual powers giving up their natural wisdom, and pass like fools the miserable days of their menial lives at the doors of bad and evil kings.

---

1. Quoted anonymously in the *Subhāṣitāvali* (सुभाषितावलि) a No. 2245.

2. In nine cases out of ten men accept service simply for the sake of supporting their family.

सिद्धाध्यासितकन्दरे हरवृषस्कन्धावगाढद्रुमे
गङ्गाधौतशिलातले हिमवतः स्थाने स्थिते श्रेयसि।।
कः कुर्वीत शिरः प्रणाममलिनं म्लानं मनस्वी जनो
यद्वित्रस्तकुरङ्गशावनयना न स्युः स्मरास्त्रं स्त्रियः।।67।।

यदि इस संसार में भयचकित मृगशावक नयनी स्त्रियाँरूपी कामास्त्र न होते तो सिद्ध गंधर्वादि के निवास करने के योग्य कंदरा, शिवजी के वाहन वृषभ श्रेष्ठ के खाज खुजाने के वृक्ष और गंगाधार से पवित्र हुए शिलातल को धारण करने वाले हिमाचल के उत्तमोत्तम स्थानों को छोड़कर कोई भी मनस्वी दूसरों के आगे प्रणाम करके अपने मस्तक को मलिन नहीं करते।

भावार्थ—सुंदर स्त्री ही मनुष्यों के मानमर्दन और दीनता का कारण है।

Had there been no women with fawnlike eyes, the real invulnerable weapons of the god of love, no wise man in the world would have stained his head by making a reverential bow before his fellow beings; especially when he could have easily passed his days in the beautiful valleys of the Himālaya whose caves are inhabited by the Siddhās, whose trees are rubbed with the shoulders of *Nandī* (नन्दी), the divine ox of Śiva, and whose rocks are washed down by the sacred waters of the Gaṅges.

PURPORT—Women alone is the cause of man's humiliation in the world.

---

1. Quoted anonymously in the *Subhāṣitāvali* (सुभाषितावलि) at No. 2244.

संसारोदधिनिस्तारपदवी न दवीयसी।।
अन्तरा दुस्तरा न स्युर्यदि रे मदिरेक्षणाः।। 68।।

यदि मदोन्मत्त नेत्र वाली स्त्रियाँ इस जगत् में न होतीं तो हे संसार! तेरे परली पार जाने का मार्ग हमारे लिए कुछ भी कठिन न होता।

The safe passage over the ocean of existence would have been comparatively nothing had there been no women with bewitching eyes who constitute the only insurmountable barrier to that end.

---

1. Quoted anonymously in the शार्ङ्गधरपद्धति at No. 4193.

(*a*) रे रे चंचललोचनांचितरुचे चेतः प्रमुच्य स्थिर-
प्रेमाणं महिमानमेणनयनामालोक्य किं नृत्यसि।
किं मन्ये विहरिष्यसे बत हतां मुञ्चान्तराशामिमा-
मेषा कंठतटे कृता खलु शिला संसारवारांनिधौ।

(काव्यप्रदीपः)

(*b*) जो होती नहिं नार, मदमाती मृगलोचनी।
जगके परली पार, गमन न दुर्गम कछुक था।।

(रसिक कवि)

राजंस्तृष्णाम्बुराशेर्न हि जगति गतः कश्चिदेवावसानं
को वाऽर्थोऽर्थैः प्रभूतैः स्ववपुषि गलिते यौवने सानुरागे।।
गच्छामः सद्म यावद्विकसितनयनेन्दीवरालोकिनीनामा-
क्रम्याक्रम्य रूपं झटिति न जरया लुप्यते प्रेयसीनाम्।।69।।

हे राजा! इस जगत् में आकर तृष्णारूपी समुद्र का पार तो किसी ने भी नहीं पाया। इसलिए शरीर के अङ्गाङ्ग शिथिल हो जाने पर और प्रीति युक्त यौवनावस्था के व्यतीत हो जाने पर बहुत-सा धनसंचय भी किसी प्रयोजन का नहीं रहता। अतएव जब तक विकसित इंदीवर के दल समान विशाल नेत्र वाली प्राण-प्यारियों का रूप लावण्य वृद्धावस्था के आक्रमण से लुप्त न हो जाय उससे पहले-पहले ही हमारा भी घर चला जाना सर्वथा उचित है।

Oh king! no one has ever succeeded in crossing over to the next shore of his ocean of desires. Of what ultimate use are hoards of riches, provided we pine away our youth without the enjoyment of our beloved wives? Let us therefore make haste to go our homes so as to reach them before the time when the beauty of our beloved loves is completely snatched away by the hand of age.

---

1. *Cf.*—किं यौवनेन विरहो यदि वल्लभायाः।।

Admitting that man is induced to sell his freedom of action to others only for the sake of his family, it is quite natural that he should long for due enjoyment of his happy home.

रागस्यागारमेकं नरकशतमहादुःखसम्प्राप्तिहेतुर्मोह-
स्योत्पत्तिबीजं जलधरापटलं ज्ञानताराधिपस्य।।
कन्दर्पस्यैकमित्रं प्रकटितविविधस्पष्टदोषप्रबन्धं
लोकेस्मिन्न ह्यनर्थव्रजकुसुमवनं यौवनादन्यदस्ति।। 70।।

अनुराग का एकमात्र घर, नरक की नानाविध महायातनाओं का हेतु, मोह की उत्पत्ति का बीजकारण, ज्ञानरूप चंद्रमा का आवरण करने वाला मेघ पटल, कामदेव का मुख्य मित्र और नाना प्रकार के प्रत्यक्ष दोषों को प्रगट करने वाले यौवन के सिवाय सारे अनर्थ समूह का उपवन इस लोक में दूसरा कोई दूसरा नहीं है।

No other evil is more disastrous to the Interests of man in this world than his own youth which is at once the storehouse of affection, the cause of dreadful agonies in hell, the seed of ignorance and illusion, the thick gathering of clouds for hiding the moon of knowledge, the one great friend of Cupid, the evident source of a series of manifold calamities, and the park of innumerable evils.

---

1. The rājā (Bhartṛhari) in *Bhartṛharinirveda* thus speaks of youth :

कामं दुर्विषहज्जवरं जनयति व्याघूर्णयत्यक्षिणी
गात्राण्यूरुनितम्बगण्डहृदयान्युच्छूनयत्युल्बणम्।
तां तां दुर्विकृतिं करोति सुहृदो गाढं व्यथन्ते यया
व्याधिर्यौवमात्मनाशनियतः के ते ग्रहण्यादयः।।

(भर्तृहरिनिर्वेदम् । पंचमोऽङ्कः)

शृंगारदुमनीरदे प्रचुरतः क्रीडारसस्त्रोतसि
प्रद्युम्नप्रियबान्धवे चतुरतामुक्ताफलोदन्वति।।
तन्वीनेत्रचकोरपार्वणविधौ सौभाग्यलक्ष्मीनिधौ धन्यः
कोऽपि न विक्रियां कलयति प्राप्ते नवे यौवने।। 71।।

शृंगाररूपी वृक्ष के सींचने वाले, क्रीड़ा रस के परिपूर्ण स्रोत, कामदेव के प्रियमित्र, चातुर्यरूप मुक्ताफल के समुद्र, कामिनी- गण के नेत्ररूपी चकोरों के पूर्णचन्द्र और सौभाग्य लक्ष्मी के निधान, यौवन का लाभ करके भी जो महाशय कामदेव के विकारों के वशीभूत नहीं होते वह निस्संदेह बड़े ही बड़भागी हैं।

That person who can keep a strict control over his senses at the critical time of his youthful manhood, the waterer of the tree of love, the vigorous streak of sensual pleasures, the beloved friend of Cupid, the ocean of the pearls of prudence, the full moon of women's *Cakora*-like eyes, and the mine of all happiness and wealth is indeed very fortunate and blessed.

---

1. Also stands as 17th in the *Vairāgya Śataka of Padmānandakavi* (पद्मानंदकविकृतवैराग्यशतक)

2. For further explanations of the words शृंगार and चकोर see our notes.

कान्तेत्युत्पललोचनेति विपुलश्रोणीभरेत्युत्सुकः
पीनोत्तुंगपयोधरेति सुमुखाम्भोजेति सुभ्रूरिति।।
दृष्ट्वा मुह्यति मोदतेऽभिरमते प्रस्तौति विद्वानपि
प्रत्यक्षाशुचिपुत्तिकां स्त्रियमहो मोहस्य दुश्चेष्टितम्।। 72 ।।

अहो! इस मोह की भी कैसी दुश्चेष्टा है कि बड़े-बड़े विद्वान् मनुष्य भी इस प्रत्यक्ष रूप से अशुचिकी पूतलीमय स्त्री को देख करके मोहित हो जाते हैं, बड़ा आनंद मानते हैं और प्रसन्न होते हैं, तथा उत्कंठित होकर प्राण-प्यारी, कमलनयनी, विपुल नितंब स्थल के धारण करने वाली, पीनोन्नत पयोधर वाली, कमलमुखी और सुंदर भौंह के धारण करने वाली इत्यादि संबोधनों से स्तुति करने लगते हैं।

How great and wonderful is the evil influence of delusion that notwithstanding his firm conviction of the fact that women is evidently the cause of all impurities and misfortunes, a learned man is even led to fondly address her in such tender language : "oh charmer, thy large eyes are like the waterlily, thy buttocks are fullgrown and round, thy protuberant breasts are thickset and heaving, thy face is beautiful and lotus like and thy eyebrows are fair and elegant!" Viewing her in this picturesque light he takes a considerable delight in seeing, enjoying and praising her handsome person.

---

1. The verse also stands in the प्रबोधचंद्रोदय (4 अङ्क).

Cf.—आलोकनं च ववनं च निगूहनं च यासां स्मरन्नमतवत्सरसं कृशस्त्वम्।
तासां किमङ्ग पिशितास्रपुरीषपात्रं गात्रं विचिन्त्य सुदृशां न निराकुलोऽसि। 56
(वाग्भट्टालंकारः)

स्मृता भवति तापाय दृष्टा चोन्मादकारिणी।।
स्पृष्टा भवति मोहाय सा नाम दयिता कथम्।।73।।

जो स्त्री चिन्तवन करने मात्र से चित्त को संताप देती है, दृष्टिगत होने से उन्माद की वृद्धि करती है और स्पर्श करने से सारे विवेक का नाश करके पूर्ण मोह का कारण हो जाती है वह स्त्री न मालूम प्राण-प्यारी क्योंकर कहलाती है?।

How can she deserve the name of a sweetheart or beloved when her very though is entailed with pain, sight with mental excitment, and touch with total stupfaction of the senses?

---

1. Quoted anonymously in the *Subhāṣitāvali* (सुभाषितावलि) at No. 1225.

Cf.— दर्शनाद्धरते चित्तं स्पर्शनाद्धरते बलम्।
संभोगाद्धरते वीर्यं नारी प्रत्यक्षराक्षसी।।

(समायोचितपद्यमालिका)

2. How pointed and perfect is the poet's ironical attack on the use of the word दयिता (beloved) for our lady loves !

Cf.— बिन देखे देखन चहत, देखे तृप्ति न होय।
नारी नरदुखदायिनी, प्यारी कैसे सोय?

(रसिक कवि)

तावदेवामृतमयी यावल्लोचनगोचरा।।
चक्षुःपथादपेता तु विषादप्यतिरिच्यते।। 74।।

स्त्री की भी कैसी विचित्र लीला है कि, जब तक हमारे नयनगोचर है तब तक तो निस्संदेह अमृतमय प्रतीत होती है, परन्तु ज्यों ही वह हमारी दृष्टि से अंतर्हित होती है त्यों ही विष से भी विशेष दुःखदायक हो जाती है।

A women is indeed the personification of pure nectar as long as she lies within the scope of our vision; but no sooner she is out of our sight than she is invariably worse than poison.

---

1. Quoted anonymously in the *Subhāṣitāvali* (सुभाषितावलि) at No. 1244.

2. To be in company of our beloved wives is indeed delightful: but separation from them tells as badly upon our health as poison.

3. *Amṛta* (nectar) and *Viṣa* (poison) are two of the fourteen precious things churned out of the ocean. For enumeration of the 15 gems see or note on the word रत्नानि।

नामृतं न विषं किंचिदेकां मुक्त्वा नितम्बिनीम्।।
सैवामृतलतारक्ता विरक्ता विषवल्लरी।। 75।।

सुंदर नितंब को धारण करने वाली स्त्री को छोड़कर इस संसार में न तो कोई अमृत है और न कोई विषय है, क्योंकि अनुराग युक्त होने पर यहाँ अमृत लता और विरक्त होने पर यही विष वेली के समान गुणागुणः धारण कर लेती है।

There is nothing ambrosial or poisonous in the world excepting woman; for, when she is attached to her lover she is no less than a nectareous creeper; but when she is indifferent to him, she is really equal to a poisonous plant.

---

1. *Cf.*—(*a*) नूनं स्त्री नाम सृष्टेपममृतेन विषेण च।
अनुरक्तामृतं सा हि विरक्ता विषमेव सा ।। 178।।
(कथासरित्सागरः : मदनमंचुकालंबकः 8 तरंगः)

(*b*) स्निग्धं भवत्यमृतकल्पमहो कलत्रं
हालाहलं विषमिवापगुणं तदेव।
(वामनस्य काव्यालंकारसूत्राणि)

(*c*) नामृतं विषं किंचिदेकां मुक्त्वा नितम्बिनीम्।
यस्याः सङ्गेन जीव्येत म्रियेत च वियोगतः।।
(पंचतंत्रम् 4 तंत्रम् 32)

2. Mark that the first half of this verse is exactly the same as that of our text.

आवर्तः संशयानामविनयभवनं पत्तनं साहसानां
दोषाणां सन्निधानं कपटशतमयं क्षेत्रमप्रत्ययानाम्।।
स्वर्गद्वारस्य विघ्नो नरकपुरमुखं सर्वमायाकरण्डं
स्त्रीयंत्रं केन सृष्टं विषममृतमयं प्राणिनामेकपाशः।।76।।

सारे संदेहों का भंवर, अविनय का घर, साहसों का नगर, दोषों का कोष, शतशः प्रकार के कपटों से सहित अविश्वासों का क्षेत्र, स्वर्ग द्वार की अर्गला, नरक पुर का द्वार, सब तरह के माया जाल की मोहन करने का एकमात्र पाश न मालूम किसने बनाया है?

Who is it that has created the ambrosial poison of woman, the whirlpool of confusion, the home of immorality, the town of adventurous undertakings, the source of sin and crime, the embodiment of hundreds of deceits, the field of faithlessness, the barrier across the doors of heaven, the gate of the infernal city (hell), the magical basket of all illusionary tricks, and the one unfailing snare for enticing men?

---

1. The verse is virtually the same as ślōka 3 in the *Śāntiśataka* II. (शान्तिशतकम् 2 परिच्छेदः). It also stands in the *Pañcatantra* I.

Cf.— अंतर्विषमया ह्येता बहिश्चैव मनोरमाः।
गुञ्जाफलसमाकारा योषितः केन निर्मिताः।।
(पंचतंत्रम् 1.196)

सत्यत्वेन शशांक एष वदनीभूतो न वेन्दीवरद्वन्द्वे
लोचनतां गते न कनकैरप्यंगयष्टिः कृता।।
किं त्वेवं कविभिः प्रतारितमनास्तत्त्वं विजानन्नपि
त्वङ्मांसास्थिमयं वपुर्मृगदृशां मन्दो जनः सेवते।।77।।

यदि पक्षपात छोड़कर सत्य-सत्य विचार करें तो मृगनयनी स्त्रियों के मुख को चंद्रमा, नयन युगल को नील कमल और शरीर को सुवर्ण से बने हुए कदापि न कहेंगे। परंतु कवियों की असत्य उक्तियों से वंचित होकर यथार्थ तत्त्व का परिचय होने पर भी हम लोग मूर्खता से स्त्रियों की त्वचा, मांस और अस्थिमय शरीर के सेवन करने में आसक्त हो रहे हैं।

To tell the truth, the face of woman is not made up of moon, the eyes are not the embodiment of a pair of lotus flowers, and the body is not realy constructed of gold; but foolish men being deceived by false exaggerations of poets are still led to devote a great deal of attention to females whose forms like those of all other beings are simply made up of skin, flesh, and bone.

---

1. *Cf.*—(*a*) त्वङ्मांसरुधिरस्नायुभेदोमज्जास्थिसंहतौ।
विण्मूत्रपूये रमतां कृमीणां कियदन्तरम्।।
(सुभाषितरत्नभांडागारः 636।125)

(*b*) क्व कफार्तं मुखं नार्याः क्व पीयूषनिधिः शशी।
आमनन्ति तयोरैक्यं कामिनो मंदबुद्धयः।।77।।
(पद्मानन्दकविकृतवैराग्यशतकम्)

लीलावतीनां सहजा विलासास्त
एव मूढस्य हृदि स्फुरन्ति।।
रागो नलिन्या हि निसर्गसिद्धस्तत्र
भ्रमत्येव मुधा षडंघ्रिः।। 78।।

जैसे कमलिनी के पुष्प की स्वाभाविक लाली देखकर मूर्ख भ्रमर वृथा ही आनंदमग्न हो उसके चारों ओर गूंजने लगता है, वैसे ही लीलावती स्त्रियों के सहज विलासों को लखिकर मूढजन भी फूले अङ्ग नहीं समाते हैं।

Notwithstanding the fact that redness is merely a natural attribute of lotuses, the black bee is yet misled to take it for a sure sign of their love towards it, and so being mad with joy it hovers continually around the flowers; just in the same way, though amorous and graceful acts are quite natural with sportive women, yet they go to make indelible impressions upon the hearts of fools who take them for all in all as to their (women's) sincere attachment to them.

---

1. The radical meaning of the word *Ṣaḍanghri* (षडंघ्रि) is six footed. But the application of the word is confined to the bee.

2. Flirtations are generally natural to the fair sex and we must not always take them for real love.

यदेतत्पूर्णेन्दुद्युतिहरमुदाराकृतिधरं
मुखाब्जं तन्वंग्याः किल वसति यत्राधरमधु।।
इदं तत्किं पाकद्रुमफलमिदानीमतिरसं व्यतीते-
ऽस्मिन्काले विषमिव भविष्यत्यसुखदम्।। 71।।

इस कटिकेहरी का पूर्ण चंद्रमा की कांति को हरण करने वाला और उदार आकार का धारण करने वाला यह मुख कमल जहाँ पर अधरामृत का निवास है इस समय यद्यपि अतिशय रसमय प्रतीत होता है, परन्तु यौवन व्यतीत होने पर यही मुख पककर के सड़े हुए द्रुम फल के समान विष के सदृश दुःखदायी हो जाएगा।

After the lapse of that lovely period of youth, the same lotus-like face of slender-bodied women, which resembles to the splendour of a full moon, contains the ambrosia of lips, and is full of such excellent juice at the present time, will undoubtedly be deprived of all its flavour, and will begin to taste of bitter poison like the rotten fruit of a pomegranate.

---

1. The simile may be extended to the regular set of teeth of a woman's mouth to the wellset seeds of a pomegranate fruit, both of which are seen to lose their charm when they are long past the period of maturity.

जल्पन्ति सार्द्धमन्येन पश्यन्त्यन्यं सविभ्रमाः ।।
हृदये चिन्तयन्त्यन्यं प्रियः को नाम योषिताम् ।। 80 ।।

जो विलासवती स्त्रियाँ बातें तो किसी और ही के साथ करती हैं, और देखती किसी ओर ही की ओर हैं, और अंतःकरण में किसी और ही का चिंतवन कर रही हैं उन युवतियों का अनुराग किसी विशेष पुरुष पर कदापि ही स्थिर नहीं रह सकता।

No one can be said to be really loved by women, who talk with one, glance at another, and think of a different person, all at one and the same time.

PURPORT. Women are generally faithless and inconstant in love.

---

1. Quoted under *Śrī Vyāsamuni* in the *Subhāṣitāvali* (सुभाषितावलि 2771), and anonymously in the (शार्ङ्गधरपद्धति) at No. 1497.

2. The verse also stands in the *Pañctantra* I. (पंचतंत्रम् । 1 तंत्रम् 135)।

Cf.—(*a*) अन्यं मनुष्यं हृदयेन कृत्वा, अन्यं ततो दृष्टिभिराह्वयति।
अन्यत्र मुञ्चन्ति मदप्रसेकमन्यं शरीरेण च कामयन्ते।।
(सुभाषितरत्नभाण्डागारः 596 । 69)

(*b*) नयनविकारैरन्यं वचनैरन्यं विचेष्टितैरन्यम्।
रमयति सुरतेनान्यं स्त्री बहुरूपाणि जायते कस्याः।।
(सुभाषितरत्नभांडागारः 596 । 60)

(*c*) अन्य प्रियालापपथं नयन्ते किञ्चित्कटाक्षैरपरं स्पृशन्ति।
अन्यं हृदा कञ्चन मंत्रयन्ते धिग्योषिता चञ्चलचित्तवृत्तिम् ।। 84 ।।
(पद्मनन्दस्य वैराग्यशतकम्)

मधु तिष्ठति वाचि योषितां
हृदि हालाहलमेव केवलम्।।
अत एव निपीयतेऽधरो
हृदयं मुष्टिभिरेव ताड्यते।। 81।।

स्त्रियों के वचनों में अमृत और हृदय में हालाहल भरा हुआ है। इसी कारण से पुरुष उनके अधरामृत का पान और वक्ष स्थल का मर्दन किया करते हैं।

While the words of women are saturated with nectar their hearts are exlusively filled with poison. It is, therefore, quite reasonable that men should eagerly drink the lips of ladies with their mouths, and beat (rub) the breasts with their fists.

---

1. Quoted under *Kālidāsa Māghau* (कालिदासमाघौ) in the *Subhāṣitāvali* (सुभाषितावली) at No. 3380. Also found in the *Pañcatantra* (पंचतंत्र 1। 189), *the Kuvalayānanda,* (कुवलयानन्द), and the *Śṛṇgārabindu* (शृङ्गारबिन्दु)

2. How exquisitely the poet accounts for men's kissing women's lips and rubbing their breasts! It is not natural that one should eagerly advance towards the place which contains nectar so as to drink it off without delay? It is not that poison is a fit object of man's abhorrence, and does not deserve a severe rubbing (beating) which contains the deadly bane?

अपसर सखे दूरादस्मात्कटाक्षविषानला-
त्प्रकृतिविषमाद्योषित्सर्पाद्विलासफणाभृतः ।।
इतरफणिना दष्टः शक्यश्चिकित्सितुमौषधैश्च-
तुरवनिताभोगिग्रस्तं त्यजन्ति हि मंत्रिणः ।। 82 ।।

हे मित्र ! इस कटाक्ष रूप विषाग्नि को धारण करने वाले, स्वभाव ही से विषम और विलासमय फणधारी स्त्रीरूपी सर्प का दूर ही से परित्याग कर, क्योंकि अन्यान्य सर्प के काटे हुए का इलाज तो औषधियों से हो सकता है परंतु चतुर स्त्रीरूप सर्प के डसे हुए मनुष्यों को असाध्य जानकर गारुडी लोग भी कुछ चिकित्सा नहीं करते।

Oh friend ! you should carefully avoid from a distance the contact of a woman-serpent that is deadly poisonous from its very nature, commanding the fiery arrows of side glances and wearing the hood of graceful and amorous sports; for, those who are bitten by ordinary snakes are liable to cure by use of medicines, but persons bitten by serpentine ogles of clever women are entirely incurable even through the skill of renowned charmers.

---

1. *Cf.*—"Oh woman, woman! thou art more baneful to the happiness of man than the poisonous dragon of the desert."
(*Sketches of Persia*, Ch. XX).

विस्तारितं मकरकेतनधीवरेण
स्त्रीसंज्ञितं बडिशमत्र भवाम्बुराशौ।।
तेनाचिरात्तदधरामिषलोलमर्त्य-
मत्स्यान्विकृष्य स पचत्यनुरागवह्नौ।। 83।।

कामदेवरूप धीवर ने इस संसार समुद्र में स्त्रीरूप जाल को बिछा रखा है जिसके द्वारा वह अधरामिष के लोभ से फंसे हुए पुरुषरूप मत्स्यों को शीघ्रतापूर्वक खैंच-खैंचकर अनुराग की अग्नि से पकाता रहता है।

Makaraketana (मकरकेतन) or Cupid, the wonderful fisherman, has thrown his woman-net into the ocean of existence, and through the offer of a tempting bait of labial flesh he is soon able to drag out the human fish and then to roast him alive into the fire of passionate love.

---

1. What a nice metaphor do we find here? We have got the fishermen, his net, his hook, his bait and everything else ready for immediate use. Not content with all this he has also provided against the last chance of escape of the poor things by keeping at hand a burning fire in which, roasts the fishes caught by him. When once into the snares of love, escape is out of question.

कामिनीकायकान्तारे कुचपर्वतदुर्गमे।।
मा संचर मनः पान्थ तत्रास्ते स्मरतस्करः।। 84।।

हे मनरूपी पथिक! कुचरूपी पर्वतों से दुर्गम कामिनी के शरीररूप गहन वन में तुम कदापि मत जाइयो, क्योंकि कामदेव- रूपी तस्कर वहाँ पर घात लगाए हुए निरंतर बैठा रहता है।

Oh my heart! you should never go into the dense forest of woman's body which is rendered quite impassable by the high mountains of her heaving breasts, and the stealthy presence of the god of love who frequents the place like a thief.

---

1. Quoted anonymously in the *Subhāṣitāvali* (सुभाषितावलि) at No. 1256.

Cf.—(*a*) Hast thou not found each woman's breast
(The land where thou hast travelled)
Either by savages possesst,
Or wild and uninhabited?
Lust, the scorching dogstar, here
Rages, with immoderate heat ;
... ... (Cowley)

(*b*) मृगक्षणा नूनमसावसीमा, भीमाटवी बुद्धिमतामतीत्या।
यद्बाहूवल्लीभिरनङ्गभिल्लो बद्ध्वा नराँल्लम्भयते न मुक्तिम्।।
(सोमप्रभाचार्यकृतशृङ्गारवैराग्यतरंगिणी 41)

व्यादीर्घेण चलेन वक्रगतिना तेजस्विना भोगिना
नीलाब्जद्युतिनाऽहिना वरमहो दष्टो न तच्चक्षुषा।
दष्टे सन्ति चिकित्सा दिशि दिशि प्रायेण धर्मार्थिनो
मुग्धाक्षीक्षणवीक्षितस्य नहि मे मन्त्रो न चाप्यौषम्।। 85।।

अत्यंत विशाल, चंचल, वक्रगति वाले, तेजस्वी और नील कमल के समान कांति वाले स्त्री के नेत्रों से डसे जाने की अपेक्षा पूर्वोक्त विशेषणों से विशिष्ट भयंकर सर्प से डसा जाना सर्वथा श्रेष्ठ है, क्योंकि सर्प के काटे हुए की धर्मार्थ चिकित्सा करने वाले वैद्य प्राय: स्थान-स्थान में विद्यमान् हैं परन्तु मुग्धा सुंदरी के नेत्ररूपी बाणों से घायल हुए पुरुष के इलाज के लिए न तो कोई मंत्र है और न औषधि है।

The bite of a big, swift-footed, crooked-moving, ferocious, hooded, and jetblack serpent is indeed to be preferred to that of the large, unsteady, crooked, brilliant, lovely, and dark-blue eyes of a young and beautiful woman : because skillful doctors for a charitable treatment of sankebites are plentifully found all over the world; but there are neither Vaidyas nor medicines to effect a perfect cure of him whose heart is pierced by the glances of ladies possessing the aforesaid qualifications.

---

1. Charmers cure snakebites, not only without talking anything from the patients but also at a great personal sacrifice to themselves.

मत्तेभकुम्भपरिणाहिनि कुङ्कुमार्द्रे
कान्तापयोधरतटे रसखेदखिन्नः ।।
वक्षो निधाय भुजपञ्जरमध्यवर्ती
धन्यः क्षपां क्षपयति क्षणलब्धनिद्रः ।। 86 ।।

जो पुरुष शृंगारादि रस के खेद से शिथिल होकर मदोन्मत्त गजपुंगव के कुंभस्थल के समान विस्तीर्ण और कुंकुम लेप से आर्द्र हुए निज प्राण-प्यारी के पयोधर रूप तट पर उसकी भुजलता के मध्य में अपना वक्षस्थल रख तनिक निद्रा का लाभ करके रात्रि व्यतीत करता है वह निस्संदेह धन्य है।

One who can afford to pass the night by taking a little snap as if to refresh himself from his amorous toils by reclining his head on the beautiful and cage-like arm-cushions of his beloved wife resting over her broad and globular breasts resembling the forehead of a wild elephant, and wetted with the application of saffron juice, is indeed blessed.

---

1. The verse which also stands in the *Pañcatantra* (पंचतंत्र) is quoted anonymously in the *Subhāṣitāvali* (सुभाषितावलि) at No. 1222, and under भर्तृहरि in the शार्ङ्गधरपद्धति at No. 3693. It is also found in the शृंगारतिलक of कालिदास at No. 22.

Cf.— असौ धन्यो यूनां यदुरसि विशाले मृगदृशः।
स्तनाभ्यां संक्रान्तो दृढतरपरीम्भसमये।। 27 ।।
(रामभद्रदीक्षितस्यं शृंगारतिलकभाणे)

न गम्यो मंत्राणां न च भवति भैषज्यविषयो

न चापि प्रध्वंसं व्रजति विविधैः शान्तिकशतैः।।

भ्रमावेशादङ्गे किमपि विदधद्भङ्गमसमं स्मरा-

पस्मारोऽयं भ्रमयति दृशं घूर्णयति च।। 87।।

कामदेवरूपी अपस्मार नाम रोग से पीड़ित हुए मनुष्य की व्यथा न तो मंत्र-तंत्र से दूर होती है, न औषधियों के प्रयोग से जाती है और न शांति पाठ आदि के कराने से ही शांत हो सकती है, किन्तु जब-जब इसका दौरा होता है तब-तब रोगी के अंग में न्यूनाधिक भाव से एक प्रकार की असह्य वेदना उत्पन्न हो जाती है कि जिससे उसका शरीर टूटने लगता है, मन फिरने लगता है, और दृष्टि घूमने लगती है।

The epilepsy of love is incurable either by *Mantras*, or medicines, and it can never be put to an end by the application of variety of sooting balms (or by reading of several *Śāntipāṭhas* 'शान्तिपाठ' *i.e.*, propitiatory texts); but whenever the patient is seized by its fits he suffers an indescribable pain which makes his limbs burn with passion and his eyes roll incessantly in a peculiar way.

---

1. *Cf.*— मनोरागस्तीव्रं विषमिव विसर्पत्यविरतं
प्रमाथो निर्धूमो ज्वलत विधुतः पावक इव।
हिनस्ति प्रत्यद्गं ज्वर इव गरोयानित इतो
न मां त्रातुं तातः प्रभवति न चाम्बा न भवति।।

(मालतीमाधवे)

जात्यन्धाय च दुर्मुखाय च जराजीर्णाखिलाङ्गाय च
ग्रामीणाय च दुष्कुलाय च गलत्कुष्ठाभिभूताय च।।
यच्छन्तीषु मनोहरं निजवपुर्लक्ष्मीलवश्रद्धया पण्य-
स्त्रीषु विवेककल्पलतिकाशस्त्रीषु रज्येत कः।।88।।

जन्मांध, कुरूप, जरासे जीर्ण शिथिल शरीर वाले, ग्रामीण (गँवार), नीच कुल में जन्म लेने वाले और कोढ़ झरते हुए घृणा योग्य पुरुष को थोड़े से धन के लोभ से जो वेश्या अपनी मनोहर देह को समर्पण कर देती है उस विवेक रूप कल्पलता के छेदन करने वाली गणिका से किस विद्वान का अनुराग हो सकता है?

What wise man can ever take delight in loving a prostitute—the moving scythe of the heavenly creeper of knowleddge—who, through the mere hope of getting a small amount of money, can even sell her lovely person to the disgusting embraces of a miserable creature that is born blind, ugly, worn out with age, rustice of low origin, and whose very sight is wholly unbearable on account of the stinking flow of his leprous scars?

---

1. *Cf.*— वित्तेन वेत्ति वेश्या स्मरसदृशं कुष्ठिनं जराजीर्णम्।
वित्तं विनापि वेत्ति स्मरसदृशं कुष्ठिनं जराजीर्णम्।।

(क्षेमेन्द्रः)

Prostitutes love money, but not men.

वेश्याऽसौ मदनज्वाला रूपेन्धनसमेधिता।।
कामिभिर्यत्र हूयन्ते यौवनानि धनानि च।। 89।।

वह वेश्या सौंदर्यरूपी ईंधन से प्रज्वलित होने वाली कामदेव रूप प्रचण्ड अग्नि है जिसमें कामीजन अपने यौवन और धन का निष्प्रयोजन हवन करते हैं।

A prostitute is the fire of love which strengthens through the fuel of beauty, and burns to ashes the youth and wealth of the libidinous.

---

1. Besides its being identical in sense the following verse is almost alike with the above stanza in its verbal construction :

अयं च सुरतज्वालाकामाग्निः प्रणयेन्धनः।
नराणां यत्र हूयन्ते यौवनानि धनानि च।।

(सुभाषितरत्नभांडागारः)

Cf.— रूपिणी कुसृतिः सृष्टा धनप्राणापहारिणी।
आढ्यानां यौवनान्धानां वेश्या नामेह वेधसा।।

(कथासरित्सागरः। शशाङ्कवतीलंबकः 1 तरंगः)

2. The poet's intention in the above stanza of the texts is apparently to strike a succesfful blow at immorality by holding to derision the figure of a harlot in darkest colours.

कश्चुम्बति कुलपुरुषो वेश्याधरपल्लवं मनोज्ञमपि।।
चारभटचौरचेटकनटविटनिष्ठीवनशरावम्।। 90।।

दूत, पामर, चौर, दास, नट और जार पुरुषों के थूकने के शराब (सरावा) रूप वेश्या के अधरोष्ठ का चुंबन अत्यंत मनोहर होने पर भी कोई कुलीन मनुष्य कर सकता है?।

What respectable person can ever condescend to kiss the lips of a prostitute which though very lovely are in reality a disgusting tray or dish constantly spit by spies, soldiers (mercenaries), thieves, slaves, actors, and sensual cheats?

---

1. The point of the stanza may be thus summarised:— Prostitutes are generally enjoyed by the dregs and rubbish of mankind, and therefore they are not in the least the fit objects of social intercourse of the gentry.

2. For futher explanations of the words विट etc. see our note on this stanza.

धन्यास्त एव चपलायतलोचनानां
तारुण्यदर्पघनपीनपयोधराणाम्।।
क्षामोदरोपरिलसत्त्रिवलीलतानां दृष्ट्वा-
ऽकृति विकृतिमेति मनो न येषाम्।। 91।।

चंचल और विशाल नेत्र वाली, यौवन के अभिमान रूप सघन और स्थूल पयोधर धारण करने वाली और अत्यंत सूक्ष्म उदर भाग पर त्रिवलीलता से विभूषित, तरुण स्त्रियों के सौंदर्य को देख करके जिन पुरुषों के मन में किसी प्रकार का विकार नहीं होता वह निस्संशय प्रशंसनीय हैं।

Those people are indeed blessed whose hearts are never agitated at the sight of beautiful ladies with (1) unsteady, bug and large eyes, (2) youthful, lovely, thickset, and heaving breasts and (3) charming lines upon their tender abdomen.

---

1. The word त्रिवली means threefolds. It is epecially applied to the threefold wrinkles of skin just above the navel of healthy and wellformed women. The poet here speaks of them as creepers on account of their zigzag appearance.

प्रोद्यत्प्रौढप्रियङ्गुद्युतिभृति विदलत्कुन्दमाद्यद्विरेफे
काले प्रालेयवातप्रचलविकसितोद्दाममन्दारदाम्नि।।
येषां नो कण्ठलग्ना क्षणमपि तुहिनक्षोदरक्षा मृगाक्षी
तेषामायामयामा यमसदनसमा यामिनी याति यूनाम्।।92।।

जिस काल में सुंदर प्रियंगु वृक्ष अपनी पूर्ण शोभा को दिखा रहे हैं, विकसित कुंद पुष्पों पर मदोन्मत्त भ्रमर गुञ्जार कर रहे हैं और पूर्ण रूप से खिले हुए मंदार वृक्षों का समूह शीतल वायु के झोखे से झकोरे ले रहा है, उस समय में शीतकाल के शीत को निवारण करने वाली मृगनयनी को जो पुरुष क्षणमात्र भी अपने वक्ष स्थल से नहीं लगा सकता उस युवा (जवान) की रात्रि शीघ्र व्यतीत न होकर यमराज के भवन के समान अत्यंत दीर्घ और भयंकर हो जाती है।

At the time when *Priyuṅgu* (प्रियंगु) creepers are in their full maturity, and the bees are humming with maddened joy on a cluster of blooming jasmines (कुंद), and when a series of ripe *Mandāras* (coral trees) in blossoms, are gently trembling by the blowing of a cool breeze, those who are unable to embrace the cold dispersing persons of beautiful ladies to the close of their bosoms are sure to feel the long watches of night as fearful as the palace of Yama, the god of death.

---

1. Quoted anonymously in the *Subhāṣitāvali* (सुभाषितावलि) at No. 1843, and the शार्ङ्गधरपद्धति at No. 3924.

सुधामयोऽपि क्षयरोगशान्त्यै नासाग्रमुक्ताफलकच्छलेन।।
अनङ्गसञ्जीवनदृष्टिशक्तिर्मुखामृतं ते पिबतीव चन्द्रः।।93।।

हे प्यारी! यह चंद्रमा सुधामय होने पर भी अपने क्षय रोग की शांति के लिए तेरी नासिका के अग्र भाग में लटकते हुए मोती के छल से तेरे अधरामृत का पान कर रहा है।

Although she is herself the embodiment of nectar, and engenderer of passionate love in the hearts of people, the moon has yet availed herself of the happy opportunity of assuming the form of a big pearl to adorn the point of thy acquiline nose, and thus to drink off the ambrosia of thy lips in order to cure herself of her periodical wanings.

Needless to say that the poet has here represented the pearl of a woman's nose-ring as a full moon drinking the ambrosia of her lips.

---

1. Quoted under वैद्यनाथ in the शार्ङ्गधरपद्धति at No. 3335.

Cf.— प्रिये सुधाकर रोग निज, क्षयी निवृत्ति उपाय।
चन्द पिबत मधु अधरका, नथ मोती मिस आय।।

(रसिक कवि)

शुभ्रं सद्म सविभ्रमा युवतयः श्वेतातपत्रोज्ज्वला
लक्ष्मीरित्यनुभूयते स्थिरमिव स्फीते शुभे कर्मणि।।
विच्छिन्ने नितरामनङ्गकलहक्रीडात्रुटत्तन्तुकं मुक्ता-
जालमिव प्रयाति झटिति भ्रश्यद्दिशोदृश्यताम्।। 94।।

जब तक मनुष्यों के प्राचीन पुण्य का प्रभाव बना रहता है तब तक सुंदर भवन, विलासवती युवतियाँ और छत्रचामरादि ऐश्वर्य की विभूति सब कुछ ही स्थिर रहते हैं परंतु पूर्वसंचित शुभकर्म के क्षय होते ही ये सब वैभव रस केलि की कलह में टूटी हुई मुक्ताफल की लड़ी के समान शीघ्र ही विलायमान हो जाते हैं।

भावार्थ—शृंगार का उद्बोध करने वाले सुंदर गृहादिकों की स्थिति मनुष्य के भाग्योदय पर्यंत ही रहती है।

The enjoyment of splendid palaces, graceful young ladies and spotless wealth and power together with their necessary symbols can only last with the definite term of our past virtues; for, when the influence of our previously accumulated good is no longer in force then all these gifts are soon scattered away and lost to the winds like a string of pearls broken in the course of an amorous quarrel.

PURPORT—The duration of worldly enjoyment synchronize with that of man's good fortune.

Cf.— धनयौवनप्रभृति सर्वमनुगतमिदं शरीरिणाम्।
न क्षणमपि भवति स्थितिमन्निजपूर्वजन्मकृतपुण्यसंक्षये ।।68।।
(वीरनन्दिकृतचन्द्रप्रभचरितम् 17 सर्गः)

अजितात्मसु संबद्धः समाधिकृतचापलः।।
भुजङ्गकुटिलः स्तब्धो भ्रूविक्षेपः खलायते।। 95।।

अजितेंद्रियों से संबंध रखने वाले, समाधि में विघ्न डालने वाले, सर्प के समान तिरछी चाल चलने वाले और गर्विष्ठ, स्त्रियों के भ्रूभंग का आचरण पूर्वोक्त विशेषणों से विशिष्ट दुर्जन के समान होता है।

A woman's glance is generally comaparable to a wicked person; for, it attaches itself to those who have no control over their senses, diverts the concentration of mind, moves in a crooked path like a venomous snaks, and maintains a proud and lofty bearing.

Quoted *ūrjita* (ऊर्जित) in the *Subhāṣitāvali* (सुभाषितावलि) at No. 1490.

किं गतेन यदि स न जीवति
प्राणिति प्रियतमा तथाऽपि किम्।।
इत्युदीर्य नवमेघमालिकां न
प्रयाति पथिकः स्वमन्दिरम्।। 96।।

घर जाने की लालसा रखने वाला पथिक, प्रस्थान समय में आकाश में उठी हुई नवीन मेघमाला की ओर दृष्टि करे यह तर्क करता है कि, यदि अब तक प्राण-प्यारी जीवित ही नहीं है तो मेरे वहाँ जाने से क्या प्रयोजन है? और यदि वह जीवित भी है तो भी मेरा इस समय का प्रयाण तो सर्वथा निरर्थक है, क्योंकि यह घनघोर घटा मुझ को सकुशल घर पर कब पहुँचने दे सकती है। इस प्रकार का तर्क-वितर्क करके वह बेचारा घर जाने का साहस कदापि नहीं करता।

Seeing the gathering of rain clouds just forming into the sky, a man who is away from his nativity is compelled to give up his immediate intention of returning home with the though that (1) in case his beloved wife is already dead of the pangs of separation it is no advantage in his going there, or (2) if she be still surviving the shock it is also useless to undertake the journey when the monsoon is about to set in.

---

1. Quoted under (उतिमित्र) in the *Subhāṣitāvali* (सुभाषितवलि) at No. 1748, and under भर्तृहरि in the शार्ङ्गधरपद्धति at No. 3885.

एको रागिषु राजते प्रियतमादेहार्धहारी हरो
नीरागेष्वपि यो विमुक्तललनासङ्गो न यस्मात्परः।।
दुर्वारस्मरबाणपन्नगविषज्वालावलीढो जन शेषः
कामविडम्बितो हि विषयान् भोक्तुं न मोक्तुं क्षमः।।97।।

जैसे अनुरागियों में पार्वती का अर्धांग में धारण करने वाले शिव जी ही सबके शिरोमणि हैं वैसे ही विरागियों में भी संसार के भोग विलास का सर्वथा त्याग करने वाले महादेव जी ही सब में अग्रगण्य हैं, क्योंकि कामदेव के बाणरूप सर्पों की असह्य विषाग्नि से संतप्त हुए अन्य जन जो मदन की चेष्टा से विडम्बित होकर न तो विषयादिकों का यथेच्छ भोग ही कर सकते हैं और न उनका त्याग ही कर सकते हैं।

Before His marriage with *Pārvatī* (पार्वती) Śiva succeeded in maintaining a complete indifference to the charms of women, and He went even so far as to reduce to ashes the god of love who had unfortunately once conspired with Spring to excite His latent passion; but after His espousing that beautiful lady as the mistress of His heart, He became so much attached to her that He was unable to part with her even for the slightest moment, and to ensure this He assumed the wonderfully composite form which is half man and half woman. Śiva is therefore the only one who stands conspicuous both among (1) the worldlings and (2) the ascetics; for once tasting the poisonous fire of Cupid's serpentine arrows, and always led astray by passionate lust, man is quite unable either to enjoy the sensual pleasures or abandon them altogether.

वैराग्ये संचरत्येको नीतौ भ्रमति चापरः।।
शृङ्गारे रमते कश्चिद्भुवि भेदाः परस्परम्।। 98।।

कोई मनुष्य वैराग्य में विचर रहे हैं, कोई नीति मार्ग में भ्रमण कर रहे हैं और कोई शृंगार ही में रम रहे हैं पृथ्वी तल पर इस प्रकार कितने ही भेदाभेद दृष्टि आते हैं।

The mental tendencies of people on the face of the globe are quite different from one another, *e.g.*, some are indifferent to the world and are engaged in the devotion of the Supreme Being; some are passing their days in the study of morality and politics; and some have turned their attention to the sole enjoyment of sensual pleasures.

---

1. It also occurs as stanza 3 in the *Śāntiśataka* Chapter II (शान्तिशतकम् 2 परिच्छेदः)

Cf.— On life's vast ocean diversely we sail,
Reason the cord, but passion is the gale.
(Pope's Essay on man Epistle ii.)

विरहोऽपि सङ्गमः खलु
परस्परं संगतं मनो येषाम्।।
यद्धृदयविघटितः स संगमो-
ऽपि विरहं विशेषयति।। 99।।

जिनका मन परस्पर संलग्न है उनका वियोग भी संयोग ही के समान समझना चाहिए और जो एक साथ रहकर भी मन में अंतर रखते हैं उनका संगम भी वियोगसे विशेष दुःखदायी है।

When the hearts of lovers are flowing in a perfect mental union, though quite apart from each other they are still to be considered as enjoying each other's society; but, on the contrary, when they cannot agree between themselves the actual company is even more painful than separation.

---

1. *Cf.*— दूरस्थोऽपि समीऽपस्थो यो यस्य हृदि वर्तते।
यो यस्य हृदये नास्ति समीपस्थोऽपि दूरतः।।
(सुभाषितारत्नभाण्डागारः 27. । 621)

2. All the copies of the text now before me give the third चरण of the stanza as यद्धृदय विघटितः which reading being short of two *Mātrās* is faulty in meter. I have therefore ventured to put in सः after it which make it alright without disturbing the sense.

इमे तारुण्यश्रीनवपरिमलाः प्रौढसुरत-
प्रतापप्रारम्भाः स्मरविजयदानप्रतिभुवः।।
चिरं चेतश्चौरा अभिनवविलासैकगुरवौ विलास-
व्यापाराः किमपि विजयन्ते मृगदृशाम्।। 100।।

यौवन की नवीन शोभा की सुगंध से सुगंधित, अतिशय सुरत-संबंधी प्रभावों के प्रारंभ सूचक, कामदेव विषयक विजयदान देने में समर्थ, चित्त के चुराने वाले और अभिनव रस के लिए एक मात्र गुरु, मृगनयनियों के भोग-विलास सर्वोत्कृष्टता से सदैव विद्यमान रहो!।

The amorous sports of antelopeeyed ladies which savour of the immence beauty of their youthful persons, consist of their incresing skill in the performance of sexual intercourse, command the power of conquering the god of love, and possess the charms to steal away the hearts of men and which are the only real masters to teach the mysteries of the first enjoyments of budding beauties and indeed indescribable !

VARIANTS

2. (a) हा भा; (b) क्षितैः for क्षणैः Sb.

3. (a) त्कु for कु Śp. तान्ताः for ताक्षाः Sp. Sb.; र्यं for र्या Sb.; (b) हावा for वाचो Sp. Sb.; लज्जिता न्ता श्च for लज्जिताश्चैव N. Sb.; (c) सस्मितं for चस्थितं N.

4. (a) गतैः for णतैः N.; (c) नवोढानामेमि for G. Ks., लसितैः for चलितैः N.; (d) ह्लीलालीना for न्नलिब्जाना Ks., कीर्णा for पूर्णा N., दृशः for दिशः Ks. G.

5. (a) विकासि for विडम्बि Ks. G.; (c) संभ्रम for विभ्रम G. Ks.; (d) वाचां for वाचो G. Ks.

6. (a) न्मुग्धं for द्वक्त्रे Sb. Dh., तरलमधुरो for सरलतरलो Sb. Dh.; (b) स्प for ष्य N. Sb. Dh., स्य for ष्य Ks.; (c) ता for ती Sb. Dh.; (d) व हि न for ह न हि Sb. Dh.

7. (a) इ for द Ks., (c) खा for स्वा Ks., दे for द्ये G., दो for दौ Ks. G., स्पर्शे स्पृश्ये for N.; (d) स for सु Ks.

8. (a) एताश्च for एताः स्ख N. (b) हंसाः for हंस्यः Ks.; (d) विश्वस्त for वित्रस्त Ks., शाक्षिपातैः for शैः कटाक्षैः N.

9. (b) लम्बि for कम्पि Sb.; (d) वशो for वश G. Sb. Ks.

10. (a) वाचो for बोधा Sb.; (d) स्त्वलाः for अबलाः G. Ks.

11. (b) भगो for भ्रुवो Sb.

12. (b) वक्र for वक्त्र G. Ks., गणाः for गणैः Ks.; (c) द्वय for द्वयं Ks. G., मित्थं for चेत्थं G. Ks.

13. (a) धतुष्मतो for धातुष्कता Ks.; (b) मपूर्वापिचदृश्यते for (b) Ks., मपूर्वा त्वयि दृश्यते for (b) G., तव दृश्यते for दृश्यते त्वयि Sp. Sb.; (c) यथा for यदा G. Ks., यया for यदा Śp. Sb. हरसि for विध्यसि G., बद्धंसि for विध्यसि Ks.

14. (b) मणो for रवी; (c) विरामे for विनामे; (d) स्त for त Sb. Am.

15. (a) यद्वृत्तः for उद्वृतः Ks. G.; (b) रागान्धेषु तदोष्ठ for रागाधिष्ठितमोष्ठ Ks. G.; (c) पंक्तिरेव for पंक्तिकेव Ks. G., मालि for पंक्ति Sb.; (d) भे for सा Sb.

17. (a) तस्याः for यस्याः Ks. G.

18. (b) मुदाहर for मिदंवद Kp. Ud., न्ति for न्तु Ud.; (c) किल for किभु G. Kp. Ud.; (d) विलासिनीनाम् for नितम्बिनीनाम् Ks. G. Kp. Ud., विलोचना for नितम्बिनी Sb.

19. (b) प्लुतललित for प्लवलुलित G.; (c) संभोगिनीनाम् for संसर्गिणीनाम् G.; (d) मा for ता N.

22. (a) वन for वने Ks. G. Sp.; (c) तन् for स्तनो Sp.

23. (b) दृष्टा for दृष्ट्वा Ks., लोलाः for लोला N.

24. (b) कूंकुमान्वितम् for कुंकुमाविलम् G.; (c) दालसा for नोहरा Sb.

25. (a) नागत for मानित SB.; (b) श्लथोद्यतमनु for श्लथीकृततनु G., श्लथोद्यममनु for श्लथोकृततनु Sb.; (c) प्रेमार्द्र for प्रेमार्द्रं G., प्रगल्मा for प्रगल्भं G.; (d) सङ्गा for शङ्का Sb., विघ for विक Sb., दि for धि G.

26. (a) परि for रसि Sb.; (c) समर for जनित Sb., स्वार्द्र for स्विन्न, G., लीं for ला G.

27. (b) यः for यत् G.

28. (b) थो for था, and रः for राः Kp. Ud.; (c) तदपि for यदपि G., इदमपि for यदपि च Śp.

31. (a) नि for आ Sb.; (b) पापवारिणि for पापहारिणि G. Sb.; (c) मध्ये for द्वये G., द्वन्द्वे for द्वये Sb., मृगाक्ष्या for तरुण्या Sb.

32. (c) भवति for वहित G.N.

33. (b) विरतो for विरुता Cs. G.

35. (b) कावुली for कामिनी Ks. G.; (d) सुखयन्ति नेत्रहृदये for सुखयन्त्यवेही हृदयं Ks. G.

36. (a) कला for कथा Ks. G.; (c) परिमलाः for परिमल Ks. G.

38. (a) अच्छाच्छ for अच्छार्द्र Ks. G.

39. (b) सिन्धु for सोधु Ks.; (d) निदाघेतूर्णंतत् for निदाघार्ताह्येतत् Ks.G.

41. (a) वेशा for वैषा Ks., चैषा for वैषा G.: (b) विकसज्जाति पुष्प for विकसितजातिः पुण्य Ks., जाती for जातिः G.; (d) तनुते for कुरुते N.

42. (c) एव for राव Ks.

43. (c) वसुधा for क्षितिरपि Ks. G.; (d) तुष्टिं for दृष्टिं Ks. G. पातयतु for यापयतु Ks. Śp. Sb., यातु संत्रस्तः for यापयतु G.

45 (b) प्राप्ते for प्राये Ks. G.

46. (a) आसारेषु for आसारेण Ks. यदा for बहिः Ks.; (c) जालैः for जाताः Sb., शोकरशीतला for शीतलशीकरा Sb., मरुतो वा for मरुतश्चा Ks. G., मरुतोर for मरुतश्चा Sb.

47. (a) सुप्त्वा for नीत्वा Sp., सुप्तो for नीत्वा Sb., सन्न for खिन्न Śp. Sb.; (b) विरतौ for निरतो, विबुद्धः for विविक्ते Śp. SB.; (c) तर्जितं for वर्जितं Ks. G., गर्गरो for कर्करी Śp.; (d) धरांशं for च्छधारं Ks., न पिवति for पिवति न Sb.

48. (a) धृताः for भृतः Ks.; (c) पीनारुःथल for पीनोरुस्तन Ks. G., रं for रे G.

49. (a) शी for सी Ks.; (b) वक्षस्युत्कं for वक्षःसूत्कं Ks.; (d) भृतः for कृतः Sb. Sp.

50. (a) कु for क Sp., दृशो for दृशौ Ks., G.; (b) न्नालिंग्य कम्पञ्छनैः for न्नङ्गेषु कम्पं गतैः Ks. G., न्नावेग for न्नङ्गेषु Sp. Sb., ते for तैः Śp. Sb.; (c) शीं for सी Ks., रवैर्द for कृतोद, दं for दान् Śp. Sb.

51. (a) सत्वोमी for संत्वेते Ks.

52. (a) यां सन्तु for यामाप्त Ks., मत्र for माप्त Aucitya.; (b) विदग्धा for विचित्रा Ks. G.; (c) द्ब्रूमौ for द्ब्रूमो G., द्बूमौ for द्बूमौ ks., बंदब्रू for तद्ब्रु Aucitya, मपरं मधिकं Aucitya.

53. (b) मिह for मपि Ks. G.; (c) लेखा for लोला Sb.

54. (b) प्तस्व for वेंष्व Sb., षुच for ष्वत्ति Ks. G.; (d) दुःखैक for दुःखत्य Ks. G., च for हि Ks. G. Sb.

55. (a) नामपि for नां हृदि Ks. G.

56. (a) वचसि for भवति, भवति for वचसि Ks. G. ; (b) श्रुति for श्रुत Ks. G.

57. (d) स्वर्गस्यापि फलं तथाप्सरसः for स्वर्गऽपि चाप्सरसः Ks. स्वर्गस्तस्यापि फलं तथाप्सरसः for स्वर्गः स्वर्गेऽपि चाप्सरसः G.

59. (a) च नर for पुरुष Ks. सनर for पुरुष G.; (c) जुषो for गता Sp, Sb.; (d) हृदि न for न हृदि Śp. Sb.

60. (b) पदं जनाः for यदंगनः Ks.

61. (b) कुलिनत्वं for विवेकित्वं, विवेकिता for कुलीनता Ks. G.; (d) स्वतः for हत Ks.

62 (d) कुटिल for कुटिला G.

63. (a) विकलः for रहितः, रहितः for विकलो Sb., गलि for रहि T., Śp. Aucitya. Nami read (c) for (b) and *vice versa;* (b) णैः for णी, ति for य त्रैः for त्रः Nami, परिवृतै for कुलशतै Aucitya, चितः for शतैः स्वाप बहुलः for

रावृततनुः Nami., ति for य T.; (c) वृद्धः for जीर्णः Śp. Nami., रूक्षः for जीर्णः Aucitya, र्दि for र्पि Nami. Aucitya, करः for गलः Śp., जीर्णोऽपि करके for जीर्णः पिठरक G., रज्ज for रक T.; (d) भ्ये for न्वे Sb. तमपिमदयत्ये for हतमपि निहन्त्ये Sb. Aucitya.

64. (a) कुसुमायुधस्य for झषकेतनस्य Śb., जननीं for परमां Ks., G., महतीं for परमां P. Kś.; (b) कला for फला Ks. (c) मुण्डीकृतालुञ्चिताः for नग्नीकृतामुण्डिताः Kś.; (d) द्रक्तपटी for त्पंचशिखी Śp. P., नः for लाः Kś.

66. (a) कलङ्क for वलम्ब Sb.; (b) व्यस्त for ध्वस्त Ks; G. Sb., धैर्याः for धैर्यं Ks. वि for नि Ks. G. Sb.

67. (a) Śp. reads the first half of (b) for that of (a) रुग्ण for गाढ Sb.; (b) ति for तः Sb.; (c) पर for शिं Sb, मानं for म्लानं Ks. G., मान्यो for म्लानं Sb., (d) यद्यत्रस्त for यद्वित्रस्त Ks. G., द्यु for हि Sb.

68. (a) रतव for रोदणि Ks. G., दुष्पार for निस्तार Śp.

69. (b) वाथोच्चै for वार्थोऽर्थेः Ks., सानुरागः for सानुरागे N.; (c) ताव for याव G., कुमुदे for नयने Ks., नान for नीना G.; (d) यावच्चा for माक्रम्या G.

70. (d) नर्थें निजकुलदहनं for नर्थव्रजकुसुमवनं Ks. G.

71. (a) बहुतर for प्रचुरतः Ks. विसृमर for प्रचुरतः N., सृमर for चुरतः Pdm. Vś.; (b) वाङ्मु for तामु Pum. Vś.; (c) पारण for पार्वण Ks. G.

72. (c) माद्यति for मुह्यति Ks. G., ऽति for ऽभि Ks. G. जानन्नपि for विद्वानपि Ks. G.; (d) मसि for शुचि n., पुत्रिकां for पुत्तिकां N. Ks.

73. (a) श्रुता for स्मृता Ks; (b) वर्द्धिनी for कारिणी Ks. G.

74. (b) गोचरः for गोचरा N., रे for रा Sb.; (c) चक्षुस्पथादतीता for चक्षुः पथादपेता Sb., दपगता for दपेतातु Ks. G.

76. (c) दुर्ग्राह्यं यन्महद्भिर्नरवरवृषभैः for स्वर्गद्वारस्य विघ्नोनरकपुरमुखं P.; (d) लोके for सृष्टं P. धर्मनाशायसृष्टं for प्राणिनामेकपाशः P., नां मोहपाशः for नामेकपाशः Ks. G.

77. (a) न सत्येन for सत्यत्वेन Ks.; (b) द्वंद्वं for द्वंद्वे G. गतं for गते G. (c) किन्त्वेकं for किन्त्वेवं G., मन for मना G.

78. (a) स्वभावा for विलासा N.; (b) स्ता for स्त ks.; (d) मुदा for मुधा Ks. G.

79. (a) दुदारा for मुदारा Ks. G.; वरं for घरं Ks. G.; (b) तत्रा for यत्रा Ks. G.; (c) तावत् for तत्किं Ks. G., मिवातीवविरसं for मिदानीमतिरस Ks. G.

80. (b) मम् for मा: Sp.; (c) हृद्गतं for हृदये P. Śp. Sb.; (d) न स्त्रीणामेकतो रतिः for प्रियः कोनाम योषिताम् Śp.

81. (a) अमृत्तं वचनेषु for मधुतिष्ठति वाचि. Kuvalaya. Śvindu; (b) हालाहलं महद्विषम् for हालाहलमेवकेवलम् P.

82. (c) दष्टाः for दष्टः Ks. G., शक्या for शक्य Ks. G.

83. (c) येना for तेना Ks. G.; (d) पचती for सपच Ks. G.

84. (d) सित for सते Sb.

85. (b) महं for महो N. G. Ks., दृश्यो for दष्टो Ks.; (d) वैद्यो for मंत्री G. वैद्या for मंत्रो G., Ks.

86. (b) युगे for तटे for तटे Śp. Stilaka., रति for रस Śtitaka.

87. (c) विदधद्भव्य for विदधद्भङ्ग Ks. G.

88. (c) गच्छन्तीषु for यच्छन्तीषु G.

91. (a) तरला for चपला Ks. G.; (b) पूर्ण for दर्प Ks., रूप for दर्प G.

92. (a) ढारविन्द for ढप्रियंगु Śp.; (c) द for र Sp.Sb.; (d) मियामा for मयामा Sp. Sb.

94. (a) सद्रस for सद्मस Ks; (b) चिरमनुस्यूते for स्थिरमिवस्फीते T.

95. (a) सि for जि Sb. समुत्पन्नः for सुसंबद्धः Sb; (b) विष्कृ for धिकृ Sb.; (c) निसर्ग for भुजङ्ग Sb., लस्तस्या for लः स्तब्धो Sb.

96. (c) क्ष्य for य Sp. Sb.

97. (b) नीरागेषु जनो for नीरागेष्वपि यो T., (c) व्याविद्धमुग्धो for ज्वालावलीढो T.; (d) तान्न for तोहि T.

NOTES

A. As to the second place being given to the Śṛṅgāraśataka Kṛṣṇa Śāstri Mahābala says :—

श्रीमद्राजर्षिप्रवरो भर्तृहरिः शृङ्गाररससेवनमपि नीतिपूर्वकमेव कर्तव्यं न तद्विरुद्धमिति सूचयन् प्रथमं नीतिज्ञानाय नीतितशकं कृत्वा ततः शृङ्गाररसस्य परिणामे वैराग्यजनकत्वात्क्वचिद्धेयत्वेने क्वचिदुपादेयत्वेनादौ तं वर्णयित्वा पश्चाद्वैराग्यं वर्णयिष्यामीति मनसि निधाय शृङ्गारशतकं प्रारिप्सुरित्यादि–

B. Śṛṅgāra (शृङ्गार)– "पुंनार्योरन्योन्यरक्तयो रातप्रकृतिः शृङ्गारः।" See रुद्रटकृतकाव्यालङ्कारः XII.5. It is thus defined in the Rasaratnahāra of Śivarāma :

"स्त्रीपुंसयोर्मिथो रागवृद्धिः शृङ्गार उच्यते" See श्रीत्रिपाठि शिवराम प्रणीत रसरत्नहारः 6।

According to another authority Śṛṅgāra is defined as follows:—

रम्यदेशकलाकालवेशभोगादिसेवनैः। प्रमोदात्मारतिः सैव यूनोरन्योन्य सक्तयोः।।
प्रहृष्यमाणा शृङ्गारो मधुराङ्गविचेष्टितैः। अयोगो विप्रयोगश्च संभोगश्चेति स त्रिधा।

See Sāhityasārasaṅgraha, by Moreshwara Rāmchandra Kāle, B.A., p. 55.

Śṛṅgāra is derived thus : भृंगं हि मन्मथोद्भेदस्तदागमनहेतुकः। पुरुषप्रमदाभूमि : शृङ्गार इति गीयते।

To Sum up all these, we have to say that Śṛṅgāra or the Erotic deals with the rise, growth and development of mutual love and attachment between man and woman.

1. (a) Brahmā, Viṣṇu and Śiva form the Hindu Trinity. Brahmā is generally known as the Creator, Viṣṇu, the Protector, and Śiva the Destroyer of the world.

(b) *Kusumāyudha* (कुसुमायुध)– Name of the god of love, so called on account of the fact of his weapon being made of flowers.

2. *Bhāva* (भाव)– Generally speaking Bhāvas are the different kinds of feelings and emotions that rise into the minds of women at the time of seeing youthful persons of the opposite sex. In dramatic science or in poetic composition generally, Bhāvas are either (स्थायिन्) primary or (व्यभिचारिन्) subordinate.

According to Bharata वागङ्गसत्वोपेतान्काव्यार्थान्भावयन्तीति भावाः। तत्राष्टौ भावाः स्थायिनः। त्रयस्त्रिंशद्व्यभिचारिणः। अष्टौ सात्विकाः। एवमेते काव्यरसाभिव्यक्तिहेतव एकोनपञ्चाशद्भावा : प्रत्यवगन्तव्याः। एभ्यश्च सामान्यगुणयोगेन रसा निष्पद्यन्ते। See भरतमुनि प्रणीतनाट्यशास्त्रम्। 7 अध्यायः।

Mr. Moreshwara Rāmchandra Kāle says :— Bhāva is the complete pervasion of the heart by any feeling whether of pleasure or of pain arising from the objects under sight. It is derived from भावन or वसन scent, i.e. that which gives its own smell to other things etc. See Moreshwara R. Kāle's Sāhityasāra Saṅgraha. p. 44.

3. *Līlā* (लीला)– Sportive manner. Līlā is one of the three physical embellishments of a yound lady. The other two are *Bhāva* (भाव) and *Hāva* (हाव).

4. Diśā (दिशा:)– The ten directions of the world See our Note to stanza 1 (b) Nīti.

6. Vilāsa (विलास)– Conversation with a smiling face. Also refer to Note on stanza C. *infra.*

10. (a) *Abalā* (अबला) means powerless. It is a special designation of women. Compare the use of the epithet 'weaker sex' in English.

(b) *Indra* (इन्द्र) was smitten with love at the sight of *Ahalyā* (अहल्या) the wife of *Gautama* (गौतम). The story is told both in the Bhāgavata and the Rāmāyaṇa.

11. मकरध्वज is the god with the emblem of makara (मकर), a kind of sea animal generally a fish. It is an epithet of Cupid.

12. The real beauty of the ślōka lies in the nice pun upon the words संयमिन:, श्रुते: द्विजानां and मुक्तानां. Also see our foot-note to the stanza.

Besides the words explained at the foot-note to this verse, the word पारंगते is also susceptible of two interpretations : (1) have gone to the extreme end of, and (2) have mastered completely.

13. (a) *Mugdhā* (मुग्धा) is a special epithet applied to young ladies blooming into youth. It is thus defined by a well known writer on Śṛṅgāra— मुग्धा नववय: कामा रतौ वामा मृदु: क्रुधि।

(b) The exquisite beauty of the stanza lies in the ingenious play on the word गुणै: which equally stands for (1) bow-strings, and (2) mental, moral and personal qualifications.

14. The learned editors of the *Subhāṣitāvali* (Bombay Sanskrit Series No. XXXI) remark on this couplet that the old reading तारारवीन्दुषु introduces the sun, which has no business here. However, I would like to adhere to the reading तारारवीन्दुषु, because the thought would thereby be considerably stronger and more beautiful and poetical, inasmuch as one away from his lady is naturally inclined to take the world to the full of darkness both in day and night.

Night is really dark in comparison with day, and there is neithere poetry nor beauty in alluding to its gloom. The sense would be much weakened by confining the idea of darkness to night with which it is always associated. The lins "तद्विश्लेषरुजान्धकारितमिदं दग्धं दिनं कल्पितं" in Kālidāsa Vikramorvaśi supports our view by keeping the word दिनं in the stanza.

15. Here too we find a very ingenious pun upon the words (उद्वृत्तः, तरले, चले, राग,—and मध्यस्था which may either be taken in their in their literal or secondary senses.

16. In this stanza the author has availed himself of the double meanings of the words गुरु, चन्द्र, भास्वन्, and शनैश्चर, which respectively mean both Jupiter and weighty, moon and bright, sun and luminous, and Saturn and slowmoving. Without fully understanding the double meanings of these words, the poet's exquisite comparison of woman with the well known planetary group will be quite obscure and nonsence.

18. (a) Ārya (आर्य)–Generally speaking it means an Āryan. But in its special sense it is confined to an inhabitant of Āryāvarta or India proper in contradistinction to the aboriginies. In Sanskrit compositions आर्य is usually applied to a man of learning and respectable family. Here it stands for a learned man. Pandit Vaidyanātha in his *Udāharaṇacandrikā* (उदाहरणचन्द्रिका) when commenting on this stanza explains आर्याः by विद्वांसः *i.e.* learned men.

(b) Vaidyanathā in his *Udāharaṇacandrika* (उदाहरणचन्द्रिका) after explaning the stanza adds : अत्र वाच्यः संशयः। व्यङ्ग्यस्तु शान्त शृंगार्यन्यतर गत निश्चय इति स्वरूपवैलक्षण्यम्।

19. Tattvajñāna (तत्त्वज्ञान)– knowledge of the Essence of things.

20. (a) Here again we meet the same ingenious play upon the words चन्द्रकान्त, महानील and पद्मराग which respectively mean both moonstone or moonlike sapphire or dark-blue and ruby or rosy.

(b) It may be noted with pleasure that Varāhamihira goes even a step further when the asserts that it is the women who adorn gems, and not the gems that adorn women; because women can enslave the herts of men without the help of gems, but gems can never be said to posses a like power without the company of women's handsome persons. The original text runs as follows :—

रत्नानि विभूषयन्ति योषा भूष्यन्ते वनिता न रत्नकान्त्या।
चेतो वनिता हरन्त्यरत्ना नो रत्नानि विनाऽङ्गनाऽङ्गसङ्गात्।।

Vide वाराहीसंहिता। LXXII. 2.

21. (a) *Vāmanayanā* (वामनयना)– Women are generally so called on account of their natural habit of looking at men with side glances.

(b) Dr. J. Taylor in his translation of the *Prabodhacandrōdaya* (प्रबोधचंद्रोदयः) renders the verse as follows :—

When a women by deceitful glances penetrates the tender heart of a man, what power does she not possess! She facinates him, she sports with him, teases him, frowns on him, fills him with eager desires and mocks him.

22. In this stanza the poet speaks of a delicate lady separated from her lover. Every word is so dexterously put as to successfully impress the extraordinary tenderness of her delicate frame. Not to speak of the sun, she is even unable to bear the rays of the moon. She walks very slowly, her paces are guided by here feminine strength, she stops and takes rest in the shade of trees, and in order to protect her uncommonly delicate face from the effects of the moon's rays she draws up her well against them.

24. *Svarga* (स्वर्ग) is heaven or Indra's paradise.

29. (a) Govinda in his Kāvyapradīpa and Vaidyanātha in his Udāharaṇacandrikā say that कृतं is अधिक, *i.e.* more than justified by the छन्द of the stanza.

(b) Under the particulars in which the stanza is cited by Sārṅgadhara in his Sārṅgadharapaddhati one would be led to agree with him in taking the verse to be the joint production of शीलाभट्टारिका and भोजराजः– I shall therefore prefer to read इदमपि for यदपि च in the 3rd caraṇa.

32. Māna (मान) is anger excited by jealousy (especially in women).

33. (a) Henceforward the poet begins to describe the six well-known seasons of the year : *viz.*, (1) *Vasanta* or Spring, (2) *Gīṣma* or Summer, (3) *Varṣā* or Rains, (4) *śarat* or Autumn, (5) *Hima* or winter, (6) *śiśira* or Early Spring respectively giving 5, 3, 6, 1, 1, and 2 stanzas to each of them.

(b) मधौ=चैत्रे। "स्याश्चैत्रे चैत्रको मधुः" इत्यमरः। As it (मधु) is one of the two months of Spring, it here stands for the whole of that lovely season.

35. (a) चैत्र is the first month of the Vikramī Saṁvat.

(b) It may be confidently noted here that the description we find in the stanzas numbered 35, 38, 39, 40 and 48 very strongly corroborates the belief that their author must either be a king or one wellconversant with kingly surroundings.

36. (a) *Pāṭala* (पाटल) "is the Bignonia or Stereospermum Sneneolem, a large tree common in South India, with dark dull crimson, exquisitely fragrant flowers." (Mr. Growse)

(b) श्रीखण्डशैल is another name of Malayācala. According to Prof. Apte it is one of the seven principal chains of mountains in India. It is most probably to be identified with the southern portion of the Ghātas running from the south of Mysore, and forming the eastern boundary of Travancore. See also our note to stanza 80 (c) in the Nītiśataka.

41. (a) The poet here compares the rainy season to a youghful woman. All the attributes are so chosen as to qualify both the rainy season and a young lady.

(b) *Jātī* (जाति or जाती)– A species of flowerplant known as the Jasmine.

42. (a) *Kuṭaja* (कुटज)– A kind or large tree with beautiful fragrant flowers. It blossoms in the rains. Hence, it is spoken of by poets as budding at the roaring of thunder clouds.

44. *Ketakī* (केतकी)– Name of a plant usually growing near water. The scent of its flowers usually called Śirā is very strong and lasting. It usually puts forth its blossoms in the beginning of the rainy season.

45. *Nabhas* (नभस् or श्रावण) is the fifth month of the Vikramī Samvat. श्रावण together with भाद्रपद the month next following it, forms the rainy season.

49. *Viṭa* (विट)– Generally speaking a paramour or voluptuary or sensualist. In dramatic literature Viṭa is the companion of a prince or dissolute young man, or of a courtizan. he is described as being skilled in the arts of singing, music and poetry, and as a parasite

on familiar terms with his associate to whom he nearly serves the purpose of *Vidūṣaka* (विदूषक).

50. सीत्कार is the making of an inarticulate sound by drawing in the air between the closed lips.

51. अन्तस्तत्व is the all pervading essence of things, *i.e. Brahma*—

52. *Vedānta* (वेदान्त) literaly means the end of the Vedas. Vedānta refers to that system of philosophy which deals with the ultimate end of the Vedas, teaches the pantheistic creed of the Hindus, and preaches the profound doctrine that *Brahma* is the only Truth and that the world is a mere delusion.

54. *Lōkas* (लोक)– The *lōkas* (worlds or spheres) are fourteen in number, seven above and seven below. See note to stanza 22 (c) in the Vairāgyaśataka.

57. The *Apsarās* or the heavenly nymphs are one of the fourteen jewels that were churned out of the ocean. Also refer to our Note to stanza 81 (b) in the Nitīśataka. The radical meaning of the word अप्सरा is a dweller of water, hence a Naiad. The names of the principal *Apsarās* are उर्वशी, मेनका, रम्भा, तिलोत्तमा etc.

59. Dr. Peterson in his note on stanza 2246 of the *Subhāṣitāvali* says that this verse is quoted in the *Hitōpadeśa* (हितोपदेश:) but the verse is nowhere to be found in that work. Strange it is that it cannot be traced out even in his own edition of the Hitōpadeśa.

60. *Brahmā* is the Creator. See also Note on stanza. 1 (a) *supra*.

61. *Pañceṣu* (पञ्चेषु)– Name of the god of love, so called on account of his being represented as the holder of five arrows.

Cf.—"अरविंदमशोकं च चूतं च नवमल्लिका। नीलोत्पलं च पञ्चेते पञ्च बाणा: प्रकीतिता:।।" or "संमोहनोन्मादनौ च शोषणस्तापनस्था। स्तंभनश्चेति कामस्य पञ्च बाणा: प्रकीतिता:।।"

In other words the five arrows of Cupid are thus enumerated by poets either to be the flowers of the lotus, aśōka, mango, Jasmine and blue lotus; or the acts of ravishing, maddening, drying up (or emaciating) heating (or paining) and stupifying.

64. At page 74 of the Bombay Sanskrit Series No. 1, Dr. G. Būller, C.I.E., has the following note on his stanza : नग्नीकृता मुण्डिता:, these two words describe the Jain and Baudha ascetics— रक्तपटीकृतां,

'(have been dressed in red rags.' Red clothes are also the marks of Smārta ascetics. कापालिका: 'scurl wearers.' This is the name of certain disreputable worshippers of Devi, see H. H. Wilson's Works, Vol. 1. pp. 21 and 264. The verse satirically represents asceticism as a consequence of the anger of Cupid.

65. (a) *Viśvāmitra* (विश्वामित्र) – Name of an illustrious sage, who though born a Kṣatriya attained ब्रह्मत्व by virtue of his hard penances. He was smit with love at the sight of *Menakā* (मेनका) who was sent by Indra to spoil his rigid devotions. *Menakā* bore him a daughter afterwards known as Śakuntalā the story of whose love and marriage with *Duṣyanta* forms the subject of Kālidāsa's immortal drama entitled "Śakuntalā."

(b) *Parāśara* (पराशर) – Name of celebrated sage, the father of Vyāsa, the well-known compiler of the Vedās. *Parāśara* is said to have fallen in love with a fisherwoman named Satyavatī who bore him the celebrated Vyāsa before her marriage to Śāntanu *Parāśara* is the author of a *smṛti* called after him *Parāśarasmṛti.*

(c) *Vindhya* (विन्ध्य) – Name of the great mountainous range known as the Vindhya mountains separating the Dekkan from India proper.

67. (a) *Siddha* (सिद्ध) A semi-divine being supposed to be of great purity and holiness, and said to be particularly characterized by eight supernatural faculties called *Siddhis.*

"The miraculous powers that can be acquired by perfect saints or *Siddhas*, are reckoned as eight in number, and are called, *Aṇimā, Mahimā, Garimā, Laghimā, Prāpti, Prākāmya, Iśhitva,* and *Vāṣitva.* The words denote the faculty–1st of becoming infinitely small : 2nd of becoming infinitely great, 3rd of becoming infinitely heave; 4th of becoming infinitely light; 5th of obtaining whatever one wishes; 6th of doing whatever one wishes; 7th of absolute supremacy; and 8th of absolute subjugation." (Mr. Growse).

(b) हरवृष is the bull of Hara, *i.e.* Śiva. Its most popular name is *Nandī* (नन्दी) and it is the vehicle of Śiva.

70. नरकं is hell or the region of Pluto. Mythology believes in numerous hells, and hence the phrase नरकशत etc. in the text. Each peculiar hell has its peculiar punishments, horrors, and pains

especially designed for the particular class of sinners that are doomed to enter it. Different authorities give different numbers of hells. But their number is popularly confined to twenty-one.

71. (a) *Śṛṇgāra* (शृङ्गार)– See our Note B. *supra.*

(b) *Cakōra* (चकोर)– The *cakōra* or partridge is supposed to be very fond of looking at the resplendent moon. It is therefore generally spoken of as drinking the mellifluous nectar of the lunar rays.

72. "Inflamed by passion, even wise men beholding woman, who is the daugher of impurity, address her in tender language : 'O Cahrner, thy large eyes are like the water-lily; thy lips are full and round; thy protuberant breasts touch each other; thy beautiful mouth resembles the lotus and elegant are thine eyebrows'. Viweing her in this manner, their pasions are inflamed, they are transported with desire and follow the dictates of lust". See Dr. J. Taylor's Prabōdhacandrōdaya, p. 50.

76. (a) स्वर्गद्वार is gate of heaven to the Indra's paradise.

(b) नरकपुर region of hell. Also refer ot our Note on stanza 70. *supra.*

78. Here again we have a very ingenious play upon the word राग which equally means red colour and affection.

80. In this stanza the poet has given us a very graphic description of the fickleness of woman's love.

81. On हृदयं मुष्टिभि रेव ताड्यते Dr. Keilhorn remarks as follows:—

'The heart is beaten with fists' (as it were to punish it for its malignancy and venomousness.

82. मंत्रिण: In India there is to be found a certain class of persons reputed to possess the Gāruḍi Vidyā by which they can cure snake-bites merely by the repetition of some charms or Mantras. They are generally known as snake-charmers or Gāruḍis. It must be known the Garuḍa (the eagle) is the deadly enemy of all sorts of snakes.

83. (a) Here we have got a very beautiful and striking metaphor in which the god of love is represented as a skinful fisherman, woman as his net, world as sea, female lips as tempting bait, men as fish and love as fire.

(b) *Makaraketana* (मकरकेतन)– See Note to stanza 11. *supra*. It is also necessary to say that *Ketu* and *Dhvaja* are equivalent in sense.

85. The words व्यादीर्घेण etc. which are adjectives qualifying अहिना (अहि snake) are also to be taken as attributes of चक्षुषा (चक्षु=eye). An attempt is made in the translation of the stanza to clear the simile by using appropriate separate epithets for serpent on the one hand and eye on the other.

88. In Sanskrit a prostitute is very appropriately called a पण्यस्त्री or marketwoman, because she cells her person to her customers.

90. (a) चेट–According to Bharata, *Ceṭa* is thus defined.

कलाप्रियो बहुकथो विरूपो गन्धसेवकः। मान्यामान्यविशेषज्ञाश्चेटो ह्येवं विधः स्मृतः। See Bharata's Nāṭya Śāstra XXIV. 107.

(b) *Viṭa* (विटः)– "वेश्योपचार कुशलो मधुरो दक्षिणः कविः ऊहा पोह क्षमो वाग्मी चतुरश्च विटो भवेत्।" (भरत नाट्यशास्त्रम्। 24 ।104)

Also refer to our note on stanza. 49. *supra*.

92. (a) *Priyaṅgu* (प्रियङ्गु) Name of a creeper which is said to put forth blossoms at the touch of women's feet.

(b) *Kunda* (कुन्द) a kind of Jasmine (white and delicate).

(c) मन्दार is the coral tree. It is one of the five trees in Indra's paradise. The word *Mandāra* is also used for *Arka* and Dhattūra plants.

(d) *Yamasadana* (यमसदन)– The palace of Yama, the god of death is spoken of as extending over many leagues in the Garuḍa-purāṇa.

94. The same note as that appended to stanza 35 (b) may appropriatety be repeated here with increases confidence.

95. Here is a very ingenious play upon all the adjectives of भ्रूविक्षेप (play of the eyebrows); for, they can also be applied to the word खल (a perverse person). But unfortunately the beauty of the original cannot be preserved in the translation.

97. (a) Wife is generally considered by men as the other half of her husband. Compare the often quoted lines of Milton in the 4th book of his Paradise Lost where Adam thus addresses Eve:

"Hom fly'st thou? whom thou fly'st, of him thou art,
His flesh, his bone; to give thee being I lent

Out of my side to thee, nearest my heart,
Substantial life, to have thee by my side
Henceforth an individual solace dear;
Part of my soul, I seek thee and thee claim,
My other half."

(b) "प्रियतमा etc. alludes to the idea that *Śiva* and *Pārvatī* form a single body, one half of which is male and the other half female. न यस्मात्परः= to whom there is no superior. The two lines mean that Śiva though he is so far under the dominion of Love as to have his wife as one-half of himself, is also the first to withstand love. *Cf.* Kirāta. XVIII. 31." (K. T. Telang).

(c) पार्वती literally means the daughter of a mountain. It is one of the several names of Durgā.

Cf. 'उमा कात्यायनी गौरी काली हैमवतीश्वरी। शिवा भवानी रुद्राणी शर्वाणी सर्व मङ्गला।। अपर्णा पार्वती दुर्गा मृडानी चण्डिका म्बिका।।' इत्यमरः

98. (a) *Vairāgya* (वैराग्य) is asceticism or detachment from the world. See also our Note B in the Vairāgyaśataka.

(b) *Nitī* (नीति) is motives of policy and prudence including morality. See also our Notes B and C in the Nītiśataka.

(c) *Śṛṇgāra* (शृङ्गार) is the first and most important of the nine Rasas and deals with man and woman and their mutual love, as members of the opposite sexes.

(d) The point of the stanza evidently is this : people generally differ very widely in their delights and pursuits.

Here we may also refer to the often quoted passage from the Mahābhārata which runs as follows :—

वेदा विभिन्नाः स्मृतयो विभिन्ना नासौ मुनिर्यस्य मतं न भिन्नम्।
धर्मस्य तत्वं निहितं गुहोयां महाजनो येन गतः स पंथाः।।

100. (a) *Vilāsa* (विलास) is thus defined by Bharata : स्मितपूर्वमथालापो विलास इति कीर्तितः। *See* Bharata's Nāṭyaśāstra. XXII. 33.

(b) The real meaning of the stanza seems to be that the amorous sports and lovely conversations of youthful ladies are always powerful to charm men.

VAIRĀGYAŚATAKAṂ

अथ वैराग्यशतकम्

ASCETICISM

चूडोत्तंसितचारुचन्द्रकलिकाचञ्चच्छिखाभास्वरो
लीलादग्धविलोलकामशलभः श्रेयोदशाग्रे स्फुरन्।
अन्तः स्फूर्जदपारमोहतिमिरप्राग्भारमुच्चाटयञ्चेतः-
सद्मनि योगिनां विजयते ज्ञानप्रदीपो हरः ।। 1 ।।

भाषाटीका।

मस्तक को भूषित करने वाली सुंदर चंद्रकला की देदीप्यमान शिखा के समान शोभायमान, कामदेवरूपी चंचल पतंग को अनायास ही दग्ध करने वाले और सब प्रकार के कल्याणों के निधान ज्ञानदीपक स्वरूप महादेव अंतःकरण में प्रकाश होने वाले अपार मोह के प्राग्भार का विनाश करते हुए योगि राजों के हृदय मंदिर में सर्वोत्कृष्टता से विराजमान है?

May the god Śiva (whose person is resplendent with luminous rays of crescent moon adorning the luxuriant locks of hair on His head; who reduced to ashes, quite in a sportive manner, the god of love, as if it were a mere moth; and who is the abode of all good), the lamp of perfect knowledge, long burn brightly into the mental abodes of Yogīs driving away the dense cloud of ignorance which is covering their conscience with a thick layer of darkness?

1. Mark the appropriateness of the author's bow to Śiva before commencing his Thoughts on Asceticism. It is an established fact beyond controversy that Śiva is the father, propagator and master of the Yoga Philosophy.

2. For । लीलादग्धविलोलकामशलभः। *Cf.*—यं पश्यन्दीपदर्शं सपदि मनसिजः कीटनाशं स नष्टः। (अप्पयदीक्षितस्य चित्तमीमांसायाम्)

बोद्धारो मत्सरग्रस्ताप्रभवः स्मयदूषिताः।
अबोधोपहताश्चान्ये जीर्णमङ्गे सुभाषितम्।। 2।।

जानने वाले तो दोष ढूँढ़ने की अभिलाषा से मत्सरता धारण कर बैठे हैं कि उनको कहना ही उचित नहीं, विभवशाली अपने ऐश्वर्य के अभिमान में मदोन्मत्त हैं कि वह किसी की सुनते ही नहीं और इतर जन (शेष मनुष्य) अज्ञानरूपी रोग से ग्रस्त हो रहे हैं कि उनको कहने को जी ही नहीं चाहता, इस दशा में जो सुभाषित हम कह सकते हैं वह संसार में प्रगट न होकर हमारे शरीर के शरीर ही में नष्ट हो रहे हैं।

The learned are fault-finding, the properous are proud of their fortunes, and the rest are mere fools devoid of all understanding; my good words (instruction) being thus unappreciated by men have pined away with the body.

---

1. Quoted anonymously in the *Subhāṣitāvali* (सुभाषितावलि) at No. 139.

Cf.—(*a*) Never hold any one by the button or the hand in order to be heard out ; for, if people are unwilling to hear you, you had better hold your tongue than them.

(Lord Chesterfield).

(*b*) रसिक कुटिल मतिमान हैं, मतवाले धनवान।
ज्ञानरहित समुझैं नहीं, किन ते करें बखान।।

(रसिक कवि)

न संसारोत्पन्नं चरितमनुपश्यामि कुशलं
विपाकः पुण्यानां जनयति भयं मे विमृशतः।।
महद्भिः पुण्यौघैश्चिरपरिगृहीताश्च विषया महान्तो
जायन्ते व्यसनमिव दातुं विषयिणाम्।। 3।।

यथार्थ रूप से विचार किया जाय तो यह सांसारिक व्यवहार किसी प्रकार से भी सुखदायी नहीं हाते और इस ही भाँति पुण्य-कार्यों का विचार करने से मुझे भयभीत ही होना पड़ता है। अनेकानेक पुण्यकर्म के प्रताप से चिरकाल पर्यंत भोगे हुए विषयादि विषयी मनुष्यों को केवल दुःखदायक ही हुआ करते हैं।

I see that worldly life is not altogether well; I am afraid of thinking upon the ultimate end of virtuous actions (for, at the cessation of our virtues we are again hurled down from the heavens). Pleasures when long enjoyed through lots of piety really increase in bulk as enjoyed through lots of piety really increase in bulk as if it were to give pain to the luxurious.

---

1. Quoted under *Bhartṛhari* (भर्तृहरि) in the *Subhāṣitāvali* (सुभाषितावलि), at No. 3455.

Cf.— न जातु कामः कामानामुपभोगेन शाम्यति।
हंविषा कृष्णवर्त्मेव, भूय एवाभिवर्द्धते।। 13।।
(मनुस्मृतिः 2 अध्यायः)

उत्खातं निधिशङ्कया क्षितितलं ध्माता गिरेर्धातवो
निस्तीर्णः सरितांपतिर्नृपतयो यत्नेन सन्तोषिताः।।
मंत्राराधनतत्परेण मनसा नीताः श्मशाने निशा प्राप्तः
काणवराटकोऽपि न मया तृष्णेऽधुना मुञ्च माम्।। 4।।

गड़े हुए खजाने की आशंका से पृथ्वी तल को खोद डाला, रसायन क्रिया से सुवर्णादि बनाने को अनेक धातु भी फूंक दिए, नदीनाथ समुद्र का भी जैसे-तैसे तरण किया, राजाओं को भी यत्नपूर्वक सेवा में प्रसन्न कर लिए, मंत्राराधन में निश्चल मन लगाकर श्मशान में बैठे हुए कई एक रात्रि भी व्यतीत कर दीं परंतु एक फूटी कौड़ी का लाभ भी मुझको न हुआ। इसलिए हे तृष्णा! अब तो (कृपा करके) तू मेरा पीछा छोड़ दे (तो श्रेष्ठ है)।

To obtain treasures, I have dug out the bowels of (mother) earth, smelt or melted various minerals, crossed the deep waters of the lord of rivers (*i.e* ocean), secured the favour of kings with great effort, and with a mind wholly absorbed in repeating Mantras, passed solitary nights in a cremtory; but unfortunately, I have not yet secured a single worthless (*lit.* broken) cowrie to myself. On greed, I would therefore implore thy favour to leave me alone now!

---

1. *Cf.*—दुर्भरजठरनिमित्तं समुपार्जयितुं प्रवर्तते चित्तम्।
लक्षावधि बहुवित्तं तथाऽप्यलभ्यं कपर्दिकामात्रम्।। 46।। (प्रबोधसागरः)

2. The point of the stanza seems to be that there is no use struggleing against fate.

भ्रान्तं देशमनेकदुर्गविषमं प्राप्तं न किंचित्फलं
त्यक्त्वा जातिकुलाभिमानमुचितं सेवा कृता निष्फला।।
भुक्तं मानविवर्जितं परगृहेष्वाशङ्कया काकवत्तृष्णे
दुर्मति पापकर्मनिरते नाद्यापि सन्तुष्यसि।। 5।।

अनेकानेक दुर्गम और विषम देश परदेश में भी फिरे, उच्चकुल और जाति का यथोचित् अभिमान त्याग करे निष्प्रयोजन दूसरों की सेवा भी की और परघर पड़े-पड़े भयभीतर होकर अपमान सहित दूसरों के दिए हुए टुकड़ों से पेट पालना भी किया परन्तु किसी कार्य से भी कुछ फल प्राप्त न हुआ। इसलिए हे दुर्मति धारण करने वाली पापिनी तृष्णा! तू अब तक भी संतुष्ट न हुई इसका क्या कारण है?

I have travelled over may rough and impassable countries, but all in vain. Having laid aside the natural pride of my (high) caste and family, I have served (others), but that to without any advantage to me. Trembling with fear like a crow, I have eaten dishonourable bread in another's house. But oh stupid and sinful Avarice! thou art not satisfied even now.

---

1. Quoted anonymously in the *Subhāṣitāvali* (सुभाषितावलि) at No. 3262.

Cf.—भ्रान्तं याचनतत्परेण मनसा देहीति वाक्प्रेरिता भुक्तं मानविवर्जितं
परगृहे साशाङ्कितं काकवत्। साक्षेपं भृकुटीकटाक्षकुटिलं दृष्टं
खलानां मुखं तृष्णे देवि यदन्यदिच्छसि पुनस्तत्रापि सज्जा वयम्।।
(सुभाषितरत्नभाण्डागार: 112 138)

2. Note that the 2nd line of this verse is almost the same as the 3rd of our text.

खलोल्लापाः सोढाः कथमपि तदाराधनपरैर्नि-
गृह्यान्तर्बाष्पं हसितमपि शून्येन मनसा।।
कृतश्चित्तस्तंभः प्रहसितधियामञ्जलिरपि त्व-
माशे मोघाशे किमपरमतो नर्तयसि माम्।। 6।।

दुष्ट मनुष्यों की सेवा करते हुए उनके खोटे खरे कटु वचन भी जैसे-तैसे सुने, तथा आंतरिक अश्रु प्रवाह को रोक कर सुन्नसान (शून्य) चित्त से उनके उपहास भी सहे और मन को निस्तब्ध करके अपने उपहास करने वालों को प्रणाम भी किया, परन्तु है निष्फल आशा! तू तो अब भी मेरा पीछा नहीं छोड़ती इसलिए नहीं मालूम कि मुझको इससे भी अधिक और क्या-क्या नाँच नचायेगी?

When serving my evil and cruel masters, I have somehow borne their harsh words with great patience, kept the natural rush of tears forcibly imprisoned within the eyes, thoughtlessly assumed a laughing countenance, and subduing all mental agitation bowed myself with clasped palms before the haughty persons of those senseless fellows who had scornfully laughed at my poverty. But what more disgraceful acts with thou, oh fruitless greed, still compel me to do I cannot precisely say?

---

1. Quoted under *Bhartṛhari* (भर्तृहरि) in the *Subhāṣitāvali* (सुभाषितावलि) at No. 3261.

Cf.— दृष्टं दुर्जनचेष्टितं परिभवो लब्धः समानाज्जनात्पिंडार्थे धनिनां कृतं श्वलडितं भुक्तं कपालेष्वपि। पद्भ्यामध्वनि संप्रयातमसकृत्सुप्त तृणप्रस्तरे यच्चान्यन्न कृतं कृतान्त कुरु हे तत्रापि सज्जा वयम्।।

(सुभाषितावलिः)

आदित्यस्य गतागतैरहरहः संक्षीयते जीवितं
व्यापारैर्बहुकार्यभारगुरुभिः कालो न विज्ञायते।।
दृष्ट्वा जन्मजराविपत्तिमरणं त्रासश्च नोत्पद्यते पीत्वा
मोहमयीं प्रमादमदिरामुन्मत्तभूतं जगत्।। 7।।

अहो! बड़े कष्ट की बात है कि यह जगत् मोहमयी प्रमादरूपी मदिरा का पान करके कैसा उन्मत्त हो रहा है कि सूर्य के उदय अस्त के साथ-साथ प्रतिदिन अपने जीवन का क्षय होना भी कोई नहीं देखता, नानाविध कार्यभार से व्यग्र हो सांसारिक व्यवहारों में लगे हुए समय का व्यतीत होना भी कोई नहीं जानता और जन्म, जरा, विपत्ति और मरण को देखकर भी कोई भयभीत नहीं होता!

Having durnk the intoxicating wine of delusion the people (world) have got quite mad and senseless; for, they do not see that their life is gradually shortended with the daily rising and setting of the sun; for, they cannot know that time is rapidly passing away, on account of their being seriously engaged with a variety of affairs; and, for, they are not frightened even at the sight of birth, old age, misfortunes, and death of others.

---

1. The verse which stands as 24th in the *Śāntiśataka*, Part VI, is quoted anonymously in the : *Subhāṣitāvali* at No. 3327.

Cf.— दिवसरजनीकूलच्छेदैः पतद्भिरनारतं
वहति निकटे कालस्रोतः समस्तभयावहः।
इह हि पततां नास्त्यालम्बो न चापि निवर्तनं
तदिह महतां कोऽयं मोहो यदेष महाविलः।।2।।

(शान्तिशतकम् । 3 परिच्छेदः)

2. For the first half of the stanza *Cf.*—"To those who are employed and busy, time flies with great rapidity."

दीनादीनमुखैः सदैव शिशुकैराकृष्टजीर्णाम्बरा
क्रोशद्भिः क्षुधितैर्निरन्नविधुरा दृश्येत चेद्गेहिनी।।
याच्ञाभङ्गभयेन गद्गदगलत्त्रुट्यद्विलीनाक्षरं को
देहीति वदेत्स्वदग्धजठरस्यार्थे मनस्वी जनः।। 8।।

अन्न के अभाव से विकल हुई अपनी स्त्री के फटे पुराने वस्त्रों को खींचते हुए, क्षुधातुर, अत्यंत दीन और रोते हुए, बाल-बच्चों को देखना तो भले ही अंगीकार कर लें, परन्तु अपने पापी पेट के भरने को याचना निष्फल जाने के भय से गद्गद स्वर में टूटते हुए अक्षरों से दूसरों के आगे (हमको दान) "दीजिये" पद का उच्चारण करना कोई भी मनस्वी स्वीकार नहीं कर सकता।

भावार्थ–विचारशील मनुष्य पूर्वार्धोक्त विशेषण विशिष्ट भार्या को देखकर भी इस दुष्ट जठर के भरण-पोषण करने को किसी की याचनाा नहीं करते।

Notwithstanding his seeing the pitiably miserable state of his wife whose threadbare clothes are continually dragged by her wretched and pale-faced children weepinjg incessantly at the corroding pain of their excessive hunger, no high-souled man can ever condescend, for the sake of his wretched stomach, falteringly to ask for alms at the hand of his fellowbeings, fearing that his request may be retused by them.

Purport—However straitened his circumstances may be no considerate man will ever ask alms of others in order to fill his wretched belly.

---

1. Quoted under *Bhartṛhari* (भर्तृहरि) in the *Subhāṣitāvali* at No. 3196.

Cf.— दारिद्र्येण समीरिताऽपि बहुशः कण्ठं समालम्बते
कण्ठात्कष्टशतैः कथंकथमपि प्राप्नोति जिह्वातलम्।
जिह्वाकीलककीलितैव सुदृढं तस्मान्न निर्यात्यसौ
वाणी प्राणपरिक्षयेऽपि महतां देहीति नास्तीति च।

(सुभाषितरत्नभाण्डागार 99।561)

निवृत्ता भोगेच्छा पुरुषबहुमानो विगलितः
समानाः स्वर्याताः सपदि सुहृदो जीवितसमाः।।
शनैर्यष्ट्युत्थानं घनतिमिररुद्धे च नयने अहो
धृष्टः कायस्तदपि मरणापायचकितः।। 9।।

विषय भोग करने की इच्छा यद्यपि बिल्कुल जाती रही है, जाति बिरादरी के मनुष्यों ने यद्यपि पहले के समान आदर करना छोड़ दिया है, समान अवस्था वाले यद्यपि परलोक के निमित्त प्रयाण कर चुके हैं, मित्रगण भी यद्यपि शीघ्र ही मरने वाले हैं, बहुत धीरे और लकड़ी के सहारे मात्र से ही यद्यपि उठा जाता है, नेत्रों के कोयों पर यद्यपि सघन अंधकारमय पटल फिर गया है, परन्तु यह ढीठ और निर्ल्लज शरीर मरने के नाम से अब भी कैसा चौकन्ना-सा हो जाता है।

Though the desire of sensual has ceased to exist in his mind, though he is no longer held in the same high esteem by his fellowmen, though his equals in age are already gone to heaven, though his friends are also at the point of death, though he can hardly support himself on his staff, though his eyesight is fast dimmed with a thick veil of darkness, the impudent and shameless person is still surprised at the mention of his approaching death!

---

1. Quoted anonymously in the *Subhāṣitāvali* at No. 3398.

Cf.—(*a*) दन्ता विश्लथदन्ताः केशा काशप्रसूनसङ्काशाः।
नयनं तमसामयनं तथपि चित्तं धनाङ्गनायत्तम्।। (सुभाषितरत्नभाण्डागारः)

(*b*) गतं तरुण्यं तरुणिहृदयानन्दजनकं
विशीर्णा दन्तालिर्निजगतिरहो यष्टिशरणा।
जडीभूता दृष्टिः श्रवणरहितं कर्णयुगलं
मनो मे निर्लज्जं तदपि विषयेभ्यः स्पृहयति।।
(सुभाषितरत्नभांडागारः 111।26)

(*c*) चक्षुष्यन्धे चलति दशने श्मश्रुणि श्वेतमाने
सीदत्यङ्गे मनसि कलुषे कम्पमाने कराग्रे।
दूतैरेतैर्दिनकरभुवः शश्वदुद्बोध्यमानास्तातुं
देहं तदपि भिषजामेव सान्त्वं वदामः।। 11।।
(नीलकण्ठदीक्षितशान्तिविलासः)

हिंसाशून्यमयत्नलभ्यमशनं धात्रा मरुत्कल्पितं
व्यालानां पशवस्तृणाङ्कुरभुजः सृष्टाः स्थलीशायिनः।।
संसारार्णवलङ्घनक्षमधियां वृत्तिः कृता सा नृणां याम-
न्वेषयतां प्रयान्ति सततं सर्वे समाप्तिं गुणाः।। 10।।

विधाता ने सर्पों के लिए पवन का भक्षण कैसा नियत किया है कि जिसे हिंसा करने के बिना वह सहज ही में लाभ कर सकते हैं, और इस ही प्रकार पशुओं को भी तृण का भक्षण करने वाले और जमीन पर शयन करने वाले बनाए हैं कि जिससे उनको किसी तरह का कष्ट नहीं होता, परन्तु संसार समुद्र का तरण करने की सामर्थ्य रखने वाले मनुष्यों की वृत्ति विधाता ने ऐसी दुर्लभ बनाई है कि जिसके संपादन करने में इनके सारे गुण समाप्त हो जाते हैं।

Snakes are made to live on air which is obtained very easily, and without causing the least harm to other creatures; cattle are made to live on grass and lie down on bare earth; but the food of man whose intellect can enable him to cross over the wordly ocean is made so difficult of attainment that all his abilities are generally of little avail to find it out.

---

1. Quoted under *Bhartṛhari* (भर्तृहरि) in the *Subhāṣitāvali* (सुभाषितावलि) at No. 3139.

2. The verse stands as 13th in the *Śāntiśataka* Part 1.

Cf.— घृतलवणतैलतण्डुलशाकेन्धनचिन्तयाऽनुदिनम्।
विपुलमतेरपि पुंसो नश्यति धीर्मन्दभिवत्वात्।।

न ध्यातं पदमीश्वरस्य विधिवत्संसारविच्छत्तये
स्वर्गद्वारकपाटपाटनपटुर्धर्मोऽपि नोपार्जितः।।
नारीपीनपयोधरोरुयुगलं स्वप्नेऽपि नालिङ्गितं
मातुः केवलमेव यौवनवनच्छेदे कुठारा वयम्।। 11 ।।

संसार से मुक्त होने के निमित्त विधिपूर्वक श्रीपरमेश्वर के चरणारविंदों का ध्यान भी न किया, स्वर्ग द्वार के किवाड़ों को खोलने वाले धर्म का उपार्जन भी न किया, तथा स्त्रियों के पुष्ट पयोधर और उरुयुगल का आलिंगन स्वप्न में भी हमने न किया। इनमें से किसी कार्य के न करने से हमने अपनी माता के पेट में जन्म लेकर उसके यौवन का वृथा ही नाश किया है।

Neither we have devoted ourselves to the due meditation of God for the final redemption of our souls; nor have we done any virtuous action in order to ensure our free entrance into the gates of heaven; nor have we ever embraced, even in a dream, the heaving....... and rounded.......... of lovely ladies. We have therefore done nothing, but have only been something like a scythe to mow dawn the youthforest of our mothers.

---

1. It is needless to remark that a woman loses her youth by delivery.

2. The verse quoted under भर्तृहरि in the शार्ङ्गधरपद्धति at No. 4152.

भोगा न भुक्ता वयमेव भुक्ता-
स्तपो न तप्तं वयमेव तप्ताः।।
कालो न यातो वयमेव याता-
स्तृष्णा न जीर्णा वयमेव जीर्णाः।। 12।।

विषयादि का भोग नहीं किया किन्तु हम भी भुगत गए, तपश्चरण भी नहीं किया किन्तु हम स्वयं ही संप्तप्त हुए, समय नहीं गया किन्तु हम ही गए गुजरे और तृष्णा शिथिल नहीं हुई किन्तु हम खुद ही बुढ़ा हो गए।

It is we who are exhausted but not the pleasures; it is we who are done up but not the penances; it is we who are gone but not the time; and similarly, it is we who have grown old but not the desire of gain.

---

1. Quoted under *Parivrājaka* परिव्राजक in the *Aucitya Vicāra carcā* (औचित्यविचारचर्चा), and anonymously in the *Subhāṣitāvali* (सुभाषितावलि) at No. 3396. The verse stands under भर्तृहरि in the शार्ङ्गधरपद्धति at No. 4150.

2. For the idea of the 1st line of our text, compare, *Bhartṛhari's* words in the *Bhartṛharinirveda* (भर्तृहरिनिर्वेद):—

भुज्यन्ते विषया मयेति भवति भ्रान्ता मतिर्देहिन-
स्तत्सिद्ध्यै कथमन्यथस्य विषयेष्विच्छा न विच्छिद्यते।
भुज्यन्ते पुरुषाः परन्तु विषयैरेवेक्षुवन्मन्मते
यत्तृप्ता इव सन्त्यजन्ति विरसान्निष्पीड्य वृद्धानमी 15

(भर्तृहरिनिर्वेदम् । चतुर्थोऽङ्कः)

क्षान्तं न क्षमया गृहोचितसुखं त्यक्तं न संतोषतः
सोढा दुःसहशीतवाततपनक्लेशा न तप्तं तपः।।
ध्यातं वित्तमहर्निशं नियमितप्राणैर्न शंभोः पदं
तत्तत्कर्म कृतं यदेव मुनिभिस्तैस्तैः फलैर्वञ्चितम्।। 13।।

बहुत से क्लेश भी सहन किए परन्तु क्षमापूर्वक न सहे, गार्हस्थ्य सुख का परित्याग भी किया परन्तु संतोष के हेतु नहीं किया परन्तु संतोष के हेतु नहीं किया, शीत, पवन और तपन के असह्य दुःख भी सहे परंतु तपश्चरण नहीं किया और निश्चल मन से रात-दिन धन का ध्यान भी किया परंतु शिवजी के चरणारविंद का चिंतन कभी न किया। अतएव मुनिजनों के करने योग्य सब कर्म करने पर भी हम उनके यथार्थ फलों से वंचित ही रहे।

We have borne insults, but not with a patient or forgiving spirit; we have given up the pleasures of home, but not through contentment; we have put up with unbearable cold, wind, and heat, but we have not undertaken the pains of a religious penance; we have attentively thought of wealth day and night, but we have not meditated on the sacred feet of Śiva; in short, we have done all that is generally done by saints and hermits, but alas ! we have not obtained the good results of the aforeasaid action (because they were not actuated by virtuous motives).

---

1. The stanza which stands as 9th in the *Śāntiśataka* Part, I. is quoted under *Bhartṛhari* in the *Śārṅgadharapaddhati* and anonymously in the *Subhāṣitāvali* and *Namisādhu's* commentary on *Rudraṭa's Kāvyālaṅkāra*.

बलिभिर्मुखमाक्रान्तं पलितैरङ्कितं शिरः।।
गात्राणि शिथिलायन्ते तृष्णैका तरुणायते।। 14।।

मुख पर झुर्रियाँ पड़ गई हैं, शिर के बाल श्वेत हो गए हैं और सारे अंग यद्यपि शिथिल हो गए हैं, परन्तु एक तृष्णा अब भी ज्यों की त्यों ही नहीं किन्तु प्रतिदिन तरुण होती जाती है।

The face is marked ove with wrinkles, the head is covered with hoary hair, and the limbs (members of the body) are all weak and worn out with age ; yet strange to say, that the desire of gain is still acting as youthfully as ever.

---

1. Quoted under *Vyāsamuni* (व्यासमुनि) in the *Subhāṣitāvali* (सुभाषितावलि) at No. 3242, and *Bhartṛhari* भर्तृहरि in the *Śārṅgadhara-paddhati* (शार्ङ्गधरपद्धति) at No. 419.

Cf.—(*a*) यौवनं जरया ग्रस्तमारोग्यं व्याधिभिर्हतम्।
जीवितं मृत्युरभ्येति तृष्णैका निरुपद्रवा।।

(सुभाषितावलिः)

(*b*) अङ्गं गलितं पलितं मुण्डं दशनविहीनं जातं तुण्डम्।
करधृतकम्पितशोभितदण्डं तदपि न मुञ्चत्याशापिण्डम्।। 15।।

(श्रीशङ्कराचार्यकृतमोहमुद्गरे)

(*c*) जीर्यन्ते जीर्यतः केशा दन्ता जीर्यन्ति जीर्यतः।
चक्षुः श्रोत्रे च जीर्येते तृष्णैका तरुणायते।।

(पंचतंत्रम् 5 तन्त्रम् । 16)

(*d*) "Like our shadows,
Our wishes lengthen as our sun declines".
(Young's Night Thoughts V)

येनैवाम्बरखण्डेन संवीतो निशि चन्द्रमाः।।
तेनैव च दिवा भानुरहो दौर्गत्यमेतयोः।। 15।।

अहो! चंद्रमा और सूर्य की भी कैसा दुर्गति है कि जिस मेघ खण्ड से रात्रि के समय चन्द्रमा संवेष्टित रहता है उस ही मेघ से दिन में सूर्य का भी आच्छादन हो जाता है।

The same piece of cloud which covers the moon is night also covers the sun in day. What a great misfortune is it to which both the powerful lumminaries are thus subjected ?

The meaning is : How pitiable is the penurious condition of sun and moon who both cover themselves with the same piece of cloud respectively sharing it in day night !

PURPORT. It is useless to wail and weep over one's own misfortunes.

---

1. *Cf.*—(*a*) कं वाच्यं सूर्य शशिनोर्दारिद्रयं महतां पुरः।
दिनरात्रिविभागेन परिधत्तो यदम्बरम्।।

(*b*) वही मेघ क्रम से रवी, शशि ओढत दिन रात।
रसिक दीन अति इन दशा, जगकी तब को बात?

(रसिक कवि)

अवश्यं यातारश्चिरतरमुषित्वाऽपि विषया वियोगे
को भेदस्त्यजति न जनो यत्स्वयममून्।।
व्रजन्तः स्वातन्त्र्यादतुलपरितापाय मनसः स्वयं
त्यक्त्वा ह्येते शमसुखमनन्तं विदधति।। 16।।

चाहे कितने ही दिन तक क्यों न रहें विषयादि एक दिन अवश्य जाने वाले हैं इसलिए हम स्वयं उनका त्याग करें अथवा वह हमारा त्याग करें। उनके हमारे वियोग में तो किसी प्रकार का संशय नहीं, परंतु संसारी मनुष्य फिर भी स्वयं इनका परित्याग नहीं करते। जब अपनी इच्छा से विषयादि हमारा त्याग करते हैं तो हमारे मन को अत्यंत दुःख होता है परन्तु जो हम स्वयं इनका परित्याग कर दें तो अनंत शांति सुख का लाभ कर सकते हैं।

To whatever lenght may sensual pleasures be ever prolonged, they are sure to end some day or other ; then, how is it that men are not willing to give them up ? When they go away themselves they are undoubtedly the cause of immense troubles to the mind, but when we can leave them of our own free will we may rest assured of reping everlasting contentment and happiness from the noble step.

---

1. The verse which stands as 3rd in the *Śāntiśataka* Part III. is quoted under *Jayāditya* in the *Subhāṣitāvali* at No. 3386.

Cf.—(*a*) स्वातंत्र्याद्विषयाः प्रयान्ति यदमी शोकायते स्युश्चिरं
सन्त्यक्ताः स्वयमेव ते शमसुखं निःश्रेयसं तन्वते।। 84।।
(प्रबोधसुधाकरः)

(*b*) यामीमाज्ञां हा वयं भावयन्तो भोगैस्याज्या एव राज्यादिभिश्चेत्।
न त्यज्यन्ते वञ्चयन्तः स्वयं ते कस्मादेवं तावदस्माभिरेव।। 28।।
(भर्तृहरिनिर्वेदम् । पञ्चमोऽङ्कः)

विवेकव्याकोशे विदधति शमे शाम्यति तृषा-
परिष्वङ्गे तुङ्गे प्रसरतितरां सा परिणतिः ।।
जराजीर्णैश्वर्यग्रसनगहनाक्षेपकृपणस्तृषापात्रं
यस्यां भवति मरुतामप्यधिपतिः ।। 17 ।।

ज्ञान के प्रकाश करने वाली शांति को धारण करने पर और तृष्णा का उन्नत शिखर शांत हो जाने पर, मनुष्य को उस विशेष सुख का अनुभव हो जाता है कि जिसकी दीर्घ काल तक विविध ऐश्वर्य भोगते रहने के कारण देवराज इंद्र भी सदैव लालसा किया करता है।

When the bud of knowledge begins to blossom, and the rise of high aspirations and desire of gain are entirely subsided, we are sure to attain that sort of supreme contentment which is even coveted by Indra, the lord of gods, who, through advancement of age, has grown too much addicated to his love of wealth and livelihood.

---

1. This stanza has been explained in different ways by different translators. But the text at it stands here cannot have another interpretation but that which we have given above.

भिक्षाशनं तदपि नीरसमेकवारं शय्या
च भूः परिजनो निजदेहमात्रम्।
वस्त्रं च जीर्णशतखण्डमयी च कन्था
हाहा तथाऽपि विषया न परित्यजन्ति।। 18।।

भिक्षाटन करके नीरस भोजन से पेट पालन करते हैं और वह भी दिन में एक बार मिलता है, कोरी पृथ्वी पर शयन करते हैं, निज देहमात्र को ही अपना परिवार समझते हैं, और शतशः फटे-पुराने टुकड़ों से बनी कंथा से शरीर को ढंकते हैं, परंतु बड़े ही खेद का विषय है कि विषय वासना अब भी हमारा परित्याग नहीं करते।

Though he has no other food than tasteless alms obtained only once a day, no other couch but the bare earth, no other dependents but his own body, and no other clothes than a wallet patched of hundreds of worn out rags, yet, alas ! he is not forsaken by worldly enjoyments !

---

1. This verse stands as 23rd in the *Śāntiśataka,* Part-1. (शान्तिशतकम्। 1 परिच्छेदः)

Cf.— आकर्ण्यन्ते तपनतनयग्रामसंलापघोषा
मन्दं मन्दं ग्रसति नियतः कालपाशोऽपि कण्ठे।
आपृच्छ्यन्ते कृतजिगमिषासम्भ्रमाः प्राणवाता
नैवेदानीमपि विषयवैमुख्यमभ्येति चेतः।। 10।।
(नीलकण्ठदीक्षितकृतशान्तिविलासः)

स्तनौ मांसग्रंथी कनककलशावित्युपमितौ
मुखं श्लेष्मागारं तदपि च शशाङ्केन तुलितम्।।
स्त्रवन्मूत्रक्लिन्नं करिवरकरस्पर्द्धि जघनमहो
निंद्यं रूपं कविजनविशेषैर्गुरु कृतम्।। 19।।

अहो! कैसे आश्चर्य की बात है कि सब तरह से अत्यंत निंदनीय स्त्रियों के रूप की कविजनों ने कितनी बड़ी प्रशंसा की है कि मांसग्रंथिरूपी स्तनों को सुवर्ण कलशों की उपमा देते हैं, श्लेष्मा के आगाररूपी मुख को चंद्रमा के तुल्य बतलाते हैं और झरते हुए मूत्र से आर्द्र हुए जघनस्थल को गजपुंगव के शुंडादण्ड के समान वर्णन करते हैं!

How strange and contemptible is it that the censurable person of women is so much extolled by poets, that their fleshy and bulbous..... are even compared to golden jars, their mouth though full of phlegm is equalled to moon ; and their.... though stained with the flow of ...... are always spoken of as something better than the trunks of the best elephants ?

---

1. Quoted under भर्तृहरि in the शार्ङ्गधरपद्धति at No. 4147.

Cf.—(*a*) समाश्लिष्यत्युच्चैः पिशितघनपिण्डं स्तनधिया
मुखं लालापूर्णं पिबति चषकं सासवामिति।
अमेध्यक्लेदार्द्रे पथि च रमते स्पर्शरसिको
महामोहान्धानां किमपि रमणीयं न भवति।। 29।।
(शान्तिशतकम् 1)

(*b*) लालां वक्त्रासपं वेत्ति मांसपिण्डौ पयोधरौ।
मांसास्थिकूटः जघनं जनः कामग्रहातुरः।। (सुभाषितरत्नभाण्डागारः)

(*c*) गण्डाख्यां न रुजं जिघृक्षति करः किं स्थूलमांसं कुचं
गर्ते चेन्न कफास्थिचर्मनिचिते वक्त्रे कुतश्चुम्बनम्।
भस्त्रा न श्वसनोद्गमागमवती कायः किमालिंग्यते
कुत्सा चेन्मलमूत्रभाजि नरके नार्यां न कार्या कुतः।।
(भर्तृहरिनिर्वेदम्)

अजानन्माहात्म्यं पततु शलभो दीपदहने
स मीनोऽप्यज्ञानाद्बडिशयुतमश्नातु पिशितम्।।
विजानन्तोऽप्येतान्वयमिह विपज्जालजटिलान्न
मुंचामः कामानहह गहनो मोहमहिमा।। 20।।

अग्नि का प्रभाव न जानकर पतंग जलते हुए दीपक में जा पड़ता है और इस ही तरह धीवर के कटप यंत्र से अजान हो मछली भी लोभवश कांटे में अटके हुए मांस को खाने के लिए दौड़ती है कि जिसमें हमको किसी प्रकार का आश्चर्य नहीं होता, परन्तु मनुष्य तो जान–बूझकर भी नाना विपत्ति के जालों से व्याप्त विषयादि का परित्याग नहीं करते यह बात वास्तव में बहुत ही शोचनीय है और इससे प्रत्यक्ष है मोह की महिमा अपार और दुर्निवार्य है।

It is quite true that a moth throws itself down into the burning flame of a lamp, and a fish devours the meat of deadly bait attached to the fishing-hook; but we must admit, that both the moth and the fish are entirely ignorant of the fact that this step of theirs will lead to their utter destruction. Whereas, on the contrary, we human beings cannot give up the temptations of sensural pleasures, notwithstanding the fact, that we are fully conscious of their being the inextricable snares of all our calamities and misfortunes in the world ! The influence of worldy delusion is, no doubt, tremendously great and mysterious !

1. The ślōka stands as 8th in the *Śāntiśataka*, Part I. it is quoted under भर्तृहरि in the शार्ङ्गधरपद्धति at No. 4156.

Cf.—पाशे कुरङ्गनिवहो न पतत्यविद्वान्दाहात्मतामकलयन् शलभः प्रदीपे।
जानन्नहं पुनरमूकन्करिकर्णलोहान्भोगांस्त्यजामि न तथापि क एव मोहाः ।। 78।।
(पद्मानन्दकविकृतवैराग्यशतकम्)

फलमलमशनाय स्वादुपानाय तोयं
शयनमवनिपृष्ठे वल्कले वाससी च।।
नवधनमधुपानभ्रान्तसर्वेन्द्रियाणाम-
विनयमनुमन्तुं नोत्सहे दुर्जनानाम्।। 21।।

जबकि खाने के लिए निर्मल फल, पीने के लिए मीठा जल, सोने के लिए धरणी तल और पहनने के लिए वल्कल विद्यमान हैं तो नवीन संचित धन रूप मदिरा के पान से मदोन्मत्त मनुष्यों का दुराचरण मनस्वी जन किस प्रकार से सह सकते हैं।

When we have nice fruits for our food, fresh water for our drink; the surface of earth for our bed, and the barks of trees for our clothes; why should we ever condescend to hear disgraceful taunts at the hands of proud men of fortune whose heads have turned mad through the intoxicating drinks of a small quantity of riches ?

Cf.— चीराणि किं पथि न सन्ति दिशन्ति भिक्षां
नैवांघ्रिपाः फलभृतः सरितोऽप्यशुष्यन्।
रुद्धा गुहाः किमजितोऽवति नोपपन्नान्क-
स्माद्भजन्ति कवयो धनदुर्मदान्धान्।।
(सुभाषितरत्नभाण्डागार: 109।16)

विपुलहृदयैर्धन्यैः कैश्चिज्जगज्जनितं पुरा
विधृतमपरैर्दत्तं चान्यैर्विजित्य तृणं यथा।।
इह हि भुवनान्यन्ये धीराश्चतुर्दश भुञ्जते
कतिपयपुरस्वाम्ये पुंसां क एष मदज्वरः।। 22।।

ब्रह्मा जैसे उदारचित्त महात्माओं ने इस जगत् को उत्पन्न किया है, विष्णु जैसे महानुभावों ने धारण किया है, परशुराम जैसे शूरवीरों ने दिग्विजय करके तृण समान जानकर ब्राह्मणों को दान कर दिया है और बलि राजा जैसे ऐश्वर्यवान अब भी इसके चतुर्दश भुवनों के साम्राज्य का भोग कर रहे हैं। इस दशा में जो मनुष्य थोड़े से ग्रामों का राज्य लाभ करके इतना अभिमान करते हैं वह सर्वथा अनुचित है।

When we see that there had been such magnanimous souls as Brahmā who have created the world; others as Viṣṇu who have repeatedly preserved it from utter destruction ; others as Paraśurāma (परशुराम) who after conquering have charitably given it away to the Brāhamaṇas, as if it were a mere straw; and others, as Bali (बलि) who have been holding undivided sway over the fourteen spheres; we cannot find the least possible ground for the vain conceit of those who can claim only a few small villages as their own.

---

1. The verse which stands as 13th in the *Śāntiśataka,* Part II is quoted under *Bhartṛhari* in the *Subhāṣitāvali* and *Suvrittatilaka.*

2. The third line "इह हि भुवनान्यन्ये धीराश्चतुर्दश भुञ्जते" is also quoted under *Bhartṛhari* by Namisādhu in his commentary on *Rudraṭa's Kāvyālaṅkāra.*

त्वं राजा वयमप्युपासितगुरुप्रज्ञाभिमानोन्नताः
ख्यातस्त्वं विभवैर्यशांसि कवयो दिक्षु प्रतन्वन्ति न।।
इत्थं मानद नातिदूरमुभयोरप्यावयोरन्तरं यद्यस्मासु
पराङ्मुखोऽसि वयमप्येकान्ततो निःस्पृहाः।। 23।।

आप राजा हैं वैसे हम भी श्रीगुरु महाराज की उपासना से पाई हुई प्रज्ञा शक्ति से समन्वित हैं, आप जैसे गजाश्वादि के ऐश्वर्य से विख्यात हैं वैसे हमारा यश भी कविजन दशों-दिशाओं में फैलाते हैं। इसलिए हे अपमान करने वाले राजा! आप में और हममें कुछ विशेष अंतर नहीं है, सो यदि आप हमारा यथोचित् सत्कार करने से मुँह मोड़ते हैं तो हमको भी आपके आदर की कोई वाञ्छा नहीं है।

Thou art a king, and we are the masters of profound learning as taught by our revered preceptors; thou art famous by thy fortunes, whereas the fame of our good name is spread by poets throughout the world. Thus, oh proud chief, that darest insult the learned, where does lie the great difference beween our respective positions, that thou turnest thy face so proudly against us for we too are quite regardless of thy favours ?

---

1. Quoted anonymously in the *Subhāṣitāvali* (सुभाषितावलि । 3473), and under भर्तृहरि in the *Śārṅgadharapaddhati* (शार्ङ्गधरपद्धति । 204).

For the point of the stanza, *Cf.*:—
निरीहाणामीशस्तृणमिव तिरस्कारविषयः।

(मुद्राराक्षसम् । तृतीयांङ्कः)

अभुक्तायां यस्यां क्षणमपि न यातं नृपशतैर्भुव-
स्तस्या लाभे क इव बहुमानः क्षितिभुजाम्।।
तदंशस्याप्यंशे तदवयवलेशेऽपि पतयो विषादे
कर्तव्ये विदधति जडाः प्रत्युत मुदम्।। 24।।

शतशः राजाओं ने जिस पृथ्वी को क्षणमात्र भी अभुक्त नहीं छोड़ी उस अनेक भूपालों की भोगी हुई भूमि लाभ करके भूमि पालों का इस कदर अभिमान करना सर्वथा अनुचित है, परन्तु कष्ट का विषय है कि इस सारी पृथ्वी के अंशांश के छोटे से अंश के एकमात्र खण्ड के स्वामी भी आज दिन मूर्खता के हेतु विषाद करने के बदले फूले अंग नहीं समाते हैं!

What magnanimous chiefs can pride over the possesion of this poor earth which has been continually enjoyed from its very existence by hundreds of kings that are now no more ? But, alas! those who can claim only a nominal portion of a part of its part to do now delight in calling themselves as kings. From this we must infer that the foolish are generally prone to be happy where, on the contrary, they ought to be sadly grieved.

---

1. Quoted under *Bhartṛhari* in the *Subhāṣitāvali* at No. 533.
Cf.— का रतिर्भूरिभोग्यायां गणिकायामिव क्षितौ।
भाग्यहीनं पतिं त्यक्त्वा रज्यते भाग्यभाजि या।। 14।। (बालभारतम् । उद्योगपर्वः । 2 सर्गः)

The same thought is again enlarged upon in verses 9 to 11 of the 2nd Sarga of the *Udyōgaparva*.

At page 20 of the Notes, the learned editors of the *Subhāṣitāvali* remarks that with the two fine verses of Bhartṛhari's *Vairagyaśataka viz.*, 22 and 24 compare Emerson's poem on "*Earth.*"

मृत्पिण्डो जलरेखया वलयितः सर्वोऽप्ययं नन्वणु-
रङ्गीकृत्य स एव संयुगशतै राज्ञां गणैर्भुज्यते।।
तद्द्युर्ददतेऽथवा न किमपि क्षुद्रा दरिद्रा भृशं धिग्धि-
क्तान्पुरुषाधमान्धनकणं वाञ्छन्ति तेभ्योऽपि ये।। 25।।

यह सारी पृथ्वी जो चारों ओर समुद्र से घिरी हुई है निस्संदेह एक छोटी–सी वस्तु है और जिस पर भी अनेकानेक राजा शतशः संग्राम द्वारा इसको अगणित खण्डों में परस्पर विभक्त करके इसका शासन कर रहे हैं। जिन राजाओं ने कुछ पहले दिया है और न अब देते हैं वह वास्तव में बहुत तुच्छ और दरिद्री हैं, परन्तु जो नराधम इन कृपण राजाओं से भी धन कण की याचना करते हैं उनको तो सर्वथा धिक्कार है।

Surrounded on all sides by water, like a small lump of mud, the entire earth is no doubt a very insignificant object in herself; besides, a number of chiefs have taken possession of her by means of a series of battles, and are thus holding their sway over her in hundreds of paltry states. It is therefore no wonder that these meanly chiefs may or may not give anything to the needy; but, fie on those wretched creatures who can ever degerade themselves by asking a prticle of wealth at even the hands of such contemptible kings.

---

1. *Cf.*—ब्रह्माण्डं कियदस्तु तत्र वसुधापिण्डं किमाचक्ष्महे
तत्राप्येकतरं तु खण्डमभितास्तस्मिन्नृपाः केचन।
तेभ्यो दैन्यशतोपनीतविभवा दृष्यनुकम्पास्तु ते
धिङ्–मूढाः स्पृहयन्ति हन्त किमपि स्वार्थेन तेभ्योपि ये।
(सुभाषितरत्नभांडागारः)

न नटा न विटा न गायका
न परद्रोहनिबद्धबुद्धयः।।
नृपसद्मनि नाम के वयं
कुचभारानमिता न योषितः।। 26।।

राजसभा में केवल नट, विट, गायक, परद्रोही और कुचभार से नम्रीभूत तरुणियों का ही आदर होता है, परंतु हम तो इनमें से कोई भी नहीं हैं इसलिए राज सन्मान की इच्छा करना हमारे लिए सर्वथा वृथा है।

When we are neither professional actors nor fools (buffoons or jesters), nor musicians, nor evil persons bent on ruining others, nor women bending down under the weight of full grown..... there is very little hope of our getting any livelihood in the courts of kings.

---

1. *Cf.*—(*a*) Kings are naturally lovers of low company.
(E. Burke)

(*b*) लघु जन से प्रीती जहां, रसिक नारि से काम।
बुध नर ऐसे देशको, दुरहि से परनाम।।

(रसिक कवि)

2. For further explanations of नटं, विट etc. see our notes.

पुरा विद्वत्ताऽसीदुपशमवतां क्लेशहतये गता
कालेनासौ विषयसुखसिद्ध्यै विषयिणाम्।।
इदानीं तु प्रेक्ष्य क्षितितलभुजः शास्त्रविमुखानहो
कष्टं साऽपि प्रतिदिनमधोऽधः प्रविशति।। 27।।

बड़े ही कष्ट की बात है कि जो विद्या पूर्व काल में शान्तचित्त महात्माओं के क्लेश निवारणार्थ समझी जाती थी, वही विद्या समय पाकर विषयी मनुष्यों के विषयादि की सिद्धि का उपाय हुई, परन्तु आजकल तो राजाओं को शास्त्र से विमुख देखकर इस विद्वत्ता की प्रतिदिन और भी दुर्दशा और अवनति होती चली जाती है।

Learning had formerly been used to remove the mental troubles of clam and tranquil souls; but in course of time gradually came to be employed as an instrument of securing sensual pleasures to the worldlings; however, it is a matter of great regret and shame that seeing the kings (the lords of earth) as quite averse to the spread of its cause learning is daily descending to the lowest level.

---

1. *Cf.*—Learning (young virgin) but few suitors know :
The common prostitute she lately grew,
And with the spurious brood loads now the press ;
Laborious effects of idlenss.

(Cowley)

स जातः कोऽप्यासीन्मदनरिपुणा मूर्ध्नि धवलं
कपालं यस्योच्चैर्विनिहितमलङ्कारविधये।।
नृभिः प्राणत्राणप्रवणमतिभिः कैश्चिदधुना
नमद्भिः कः पुंसामयमतुलदर्पज्वरभरः।। 28।।

संसार में उस ही बड़भागी का जन्म सफल है कि जिसके स्वच्छ कपाल खण्ड को आभूषण बनाकर शिवजी ने अपने मस्तक पर धारण किया है। परन्तु आजकल तो केवल अपनी प्राण रक्षा में तत्पर रहकर दूसरों के आगे मस्तक गमन करने वाले मनुष्य भी न मालूम किस बात का अतिशय अभिमान किया करते हैं?

The birth of that great man is indeed a memorable event in the history of the world whose white skull is ever being borne as an ornament of head by Śiva, the enemy of love; but, now, alas ! we see that the generality of mankind are humbly bowing their heads at the feet of others for the sole satisfaction of securing a few days, living, and the realisation of this boon is looked upon as something really grand. However, we do not know that they can ever justify in the least possible degree the vain pride and conceit which they have the impudence to indulge in this disgraceful step.

---

1. The point of the stanza appears to be this :—Foolish men insteat of being grieved feel a sort of pride in bowing their heads to others.

अर्थानामीशिषे त्वं वयमपि च गिरामीश्महे याव-
दित्थं शूरस्त्वं वादिदर्पज्वरशमनविधावक्षयं पाटवं नः ।।
सेवन्ते त्वां धनान्धा मतिमलहतये मामपि श्रोतुकामा मय्य-
प्यास्था न चेत्तत्त्वयि मम सुतरामेष राजन्गतोऽस्मि ।। 29 ।।

हे राजा! आप यदि धन के स्वामी हैं तो हम भी वाणी के स्वामी हैं, आप यदि शूरवीर हैं तो हम भी प्रतिवादियों का दर्प ज्वर नाश करने में पूर्ण प्रवीण हैं, आपका सेवन यदि धनांध मनुष्य करते हैं तो बुद्धि का अधंकार दूर होने के अर्थ वेदाध्ययन करने वाले श्रोत्रिय जन हमारी भी सेवा किया करते हैं। इसलिए हे राजा! यदि आपको हमारी कुछ भी श्रद्धा नहीं है तो हमारे भी आपकी किंचिन्मात्र भी नहीं है अतएव हम भी जाते हैं।

If thou art the lord of riches, we are the masters of learning (speach); if thou art a great warrior, we are also powerful to suppress the feverish pride of our adversaries in a verbal contest; if thou art served by wealthy persons, we are served by theological scholars who throng to us for the removal of their intellectual darkness; therefore, if thou hast little regard for us we have less for thee, and thus saying we turn our back upon thee.

---

1. Quoted anonymously in the *Subhāṣitāvali* (सुभाषितावलि) at No. 3474.

2. For the idea of the 2nd line, *cf.*—"It is reckoned a great achievement to silence an opponent in disputation."

(Cowper's Letters, No. XXVIII)

अशीमहि वयं भिक्षामाशावासो वसीमहि।।
शयीमहि महीपृष्ठे कुर्वीमहि किमीश्वरैः ।। 30 ।।

जब हम भिक्षा का भोजन, दिशारूप वस्त्र और पृथ्वी का शयन अंगीकार करते हैं तो संपत्तिवानों से हमारा क्या प्रयोजन रहा?

When we live on alms, clothe our bodies with no artifical clothes but only with the ten direction of the (*i.e.*, remain naked), and sleep on the surface of mother earth, we have no concern whatever with the rich.

---

1. Quoted under *Bhartṛhari* (भर्तृहरि) in the *Śārṅga-dharapaddhati* (शार्ङ्गधरपद्धति) at No. 4104.

2. How true is it that the more we go away this world and its pleasures the less is our affection fot it! One who has nothing to do with it cares not a straw for its great worthies and wealthies. Nothing whatever can make a true recluse bow to power and wealth.

माने म्लायिनि खण्डिते च वसुनि व्यर्थं प्रयाते-
ऽर्थिनि क्षीणे बंधुजने गते परिजने नष्टे शनैर्यौवने।।
युक्तं केवलमेतदेव सुधियां यज्जह्नुकन्यापयः
पूतग्रावगिरीन्द्रकन्दरदरीकुंजे निवासः क्वचित्।।31।।

मान के मलिन होने, धन के नष्ट होने, याचकों के निराश होकर जाने, बंध जन के क्षीण होने, परिवार के मरने और यौवन के क्रमशः चले जाने पर मतिमानों को केवल यही उचित है कि जाह्नवी की निर्मल जलधारा से पवित्रित हिमालय की कंदरा के किसी एकान्त लताकुञ्ज में जाकर निवास करें।

At the time when they have lost their self-respect, squandered away their riches, no longer got the power to satfisfy the requests of beggars, suffered the bereavement of their friends and family, and gradually passed away the period of your, the only thing proper for wise men is to seek their abode somewhere in the solitary grave of a mountain cave hallowed by the Gaṅges waters.

---

1. Quoted under भर्तृहरि in the शार्ङ्गधरपद्धति at No. 4178.

Cf.— माने म्लानिमुपागते विगलिते भोगाकुले यौवने
कालेन क्षपितेषु बन्धुषु शनैर्लब्धे विवेकोदये।
विच्छिन्नावसरोपभोगलघुता मुक्तस्पृहाणां परं
सत्यंसत्यमभाव एव हि सुखं जाने धनानामहम्।।

(सुभाषितावलिः । 3325)

परेषां चेतांसि प्रतिदिवसमाराध्य बहुधा प्रसादं
किं नेतुं विशसि हृदयक्लेशकलिलम्।।
प्रसन्ने त्वय्यन्तः स्वयमुदितचिन्तामणिगुणे
विमुक्तः सङ्कल्पः किमभिलषितं पुष्यति न ते।। 32।।

हे मन! रात-दिन दूसरों के चित्त की अनेक भाँति आराधना करता हुआ तू किस पदार्थ की प्राप्ति के हेतु ऐसे-ऐसे कष्ट सहन कर रहा है? क्योंकि तेरे अंतःकरण के प्रसन्न हो जाने पर ही उस चिंतामणि का उदय हो सकता है जिसके प्रगट होने से संकल्प विकल्प से विमुक्त हो जाने पर तेरी कोई अभिलाषा भी अपूर्ण न रहेगी।

Oh my hearts ! for what special reward dost thou try to please the hearts of others, ahd thus to subject thyself to a number of heartrending troubles? If thou succeedest to content thy own innerself, the wondrous virture of contentment will grow of itself into thee, which will, like a *Cintāmaṇi* (चिन्तामणि) or philospher's stone, fulfil all thy desires without a single exception.

---

1. It is quoted anonymously in the *Subhāṣitāvali* (सुभाषितावलि) at No. 3410, and under *Śaṅkuka* (शंकुक) at No. 534.

Cf.—(*a*) The source of true happiness is inherent in the heart; he is a fool who seeks it elsewhere.

(*b*) Happiness depends on the mind, not on any external circumstances. (T. Bartlett)

(*c*) My *conscience* is my crown ;
Contented thoughts my rest ;
My heart is happy in itself,
My *bliss* is in *my heart*. (Robert Southwell)

(*d*) How small, of all that human hearts endure, That part which laws or kings can cause or cure! Still to ourselves in every place consigned, Our own felicity we make or find. (Dr. S. Johnson. Lines added to Goldsmith's Traveller.)

(*e*) Vain, very vain, my weary search to find. That bliss which only centres in the mind.

स्थितिः पुण्यारण्ये सह परिचयो हन्त हरिणैः
फलैर्मेध्या वृत्तिः प्रतिदिवसतल्पानि दृषदः।।
इतीयं सामग्री भावति हरभक्तिं स्पृहयतां वनं
वा गेहं वा सदृशमुशान्तैकमनसाम्।। 33।।

पुण्य भूमि का निवास, हरिणों का सहवास, फल भक्षण से अहिंसापूर्वक भरण-पोषण और प्रतिदिन नवीन पाषाण को शय्या स्वीकार करके शिव भक्ति की लालसा रखने वाले शान्तचित्त मनुष्यों के समक्ष वन और घर सब एक ही से प्रतीत होते हैं।

Those contented persons who having subdued their sensual passions are very anxious to secure the favour of Śiva make no difference between a forest and a house; for, they are earnestly desirous of dwelling in a hallowed desert, keeping company with deer, living, up on the harmless subsistance of fruits, and sleeping every day on new beds of stones.

---

1. *Cf.*—(*a*) सुरमन्दिरतरुमूलनिवासः शय्या भूतलमजिनं वासः।
सर्वपरिग्रहभोगत्यागः कस्य सुखं न करोति विरागः।। 10।।
(शङ्कराचार्यकृतमोहमुद्गरे)

(*b*) कुसुमशयनं पाषाणो वा श्रियं भवनं वनं
प्रतनुमसृणस्पर्शं वासस्त्वगप्यथ तारवी।
सरसमशनं कुल्माषो वा धनानि तृणानि वा
शमसुखसुधापानक्षैव्ये समं हि महात्मनाम्।।
(क्षेमेन्द्रस्य मुनिमतमीमांसा)

अमीषां प्राणानां तुलितबिसिनीपत्रपयसां
कृते किं नास्माभिर्विगलितविवेकैर्व्यवसितम्।।
यदाढ्यानामग्रे द्रविणमदनिःशङ्कमनसां
कृतं वीतव्रीडैर्निजगुणकथापातकमपि।। 34।।

कमलिनी पत्रस्थ जल बिन्दु के समान क्षणभंगु प्राणों के निमित्त अज्ञानवश होकर, द्रव्य के मद से निःशंक चित्त वाले धनाढ्य मनुष्यों के आगे निर्लज्ज होकर निजगुण कथन करने का महापातक करने वाले हम लोगों ने कौन-सा अधम कर्म नहीं किया है?

What efforts have we, that have lost the sense of our own intelligence, left undone of the maintenance of our wretched lives whose condition is exactly resembling that of the drops of water resting on a lotus leaf, when we have shamelessly committed the sin of recounting our own merits before the wealthy whose hearts are hardened and fearless by possessing riches?

---

1. It stands as 19th in the *Śāntiśataka* Part I. (शान्तिशतकम् ।1 परिच्छेदः)

For the idea of the line ; *cf*:—

नलिनीदलगतजलमतितरलम्,
तद्वज्जीवनमतिशयचपलम्।। 5।।

(शङ्कराचार्यकृतमोहमुद्गरे)

अतिक्रान्तः कालो लटभललनाभोगसुभगो
भ्रमन्तः श्रान्ताः स्मः सुचिरमिह संसारसरणौ।।
इदानीं स्वःसिन्धोस्तटभुवि समाक्रन्दनगिरः
सुतारैः फूत्कारैः शिवशिवशिवेति प्रतनुमः।। 35।।

सुंदर स्त्रियों के भोग-विलास में यौवन व्यतीत कर चुके हैं और इस संसारपथ में भ्रमण करते-करते बहुत थक गए हैं, इसलिए अब हम सुरनदी श्रीगंगा जी के तट पर बैठकर पर्वत कंदराओं को प्रतिध्वनित करते हुए उच्चस्वर से केवल शिव नाम का उच्चारण करने ही की अभिलाषा रखते हैं।

We have passed our yout, the proper time for . . . . .charming ladies, and we are quite tired of so long a wandering over the world's thoroughfare; now, we would, therefore, like the rest on the banks of the holy Gaṅges and pass our days in pronouncing the divine name of Śiva with such a distinct voice as to make the surrounding hills quite resound with it.

---

1. *Cf.*—(*a*) यातं यौवनमधुना वनमधुना शरणमेकमस्माकम्।
स्फुरदुरुहारमणीनां हा रमणीनां गतः कालः।।
(शार्ङ्गधरपद्धतिः)

(*b*) रसिक गया सुन्दरि सुरत, यौवन काल विलाय।
अब सुरसरितटपर कहो, हर हर क्यों नहिं जाय?
(रसिक कवि)

भ्रातः कष्टमहो महान्स नृपतिः सामन्तचक्रं च
तत्पार्श्वे तस्य च साऽपि राजपरिषत्ताश्चन्द्रबिम्बाननाः।।
उद्रिक्तः स च राजपुत्रनिवहस्ते बन्दिनस्ताः कथाः सर्वं
यस्य वशादगात्स्मृतिपदं कालाय तस्मै नमः।। 36।।

हे भाई! कैसे कष्ट का विषय है कि हमारे देखते-देखते ही वह प्रतापशाली राजा, उसके आधीन छोटे-छोटे सामंत, उसकी वह राजसभा, वह विधुवदनी सुंदरियें, वह उन्मत्त राजकुमारों का समूह, वह बंदीजन और वह गोष्ठी सबके सब जिस महाबली काल के कराल पेट में समा गए हैं उसे हमारा नमस्कार है।

Oh brother, I cannot but sorrowfully pay my humble obeisance to that Time through whose powerful influence (1) that mighty king, (2) his feudatory chiefs, (3) his magnificent court, (4) the moon-faced charming ladies of his seraglio, (5) the proud assembly of his princes, (6) his heraldic bards, and (7) the instructive tales recited in his court, have all become a matter of history existing only in the memory of survivors.

---

1. Quoted under *Bhartṛhari* in the *Śārngadharapaddhati* 4/64, and under *Kamalāyudha* in the *Subhāṣitāvali* at No. 3328.

Cf.—(*a*) पातयति महापुरुषान्सममेव बहूननादरेणैव।
परिवर्तमान एकः कालः शैलानिवानन्तः।।
(हर्षचरितम् । पंचमोल्लासः)

(*b*) Relentless, Time, destroying power,
Which stone and brass obey,
who giv'st to every flying hour
To work some new decay. (Dryden).

(*c*) The boast of heraldry, the pomp of power,
And all that beauty, all that wealte'er grave,
Await alike the inevitable hour
The paths of glory lead but to the grave.
(Gray's Elegy in a country Churchyard).

वयं येभ्यो जाताश्चिरपरिगता एव खलु ते
समं यैः संवृद्धाः स्मृतिविषयतां तेपि गमिताः।।
इदानीमेते स्मः प्रतिदिवसमासन्नपतनाद्गता-
स्तुल्यावस्थां सिकतिलनदीतीरतरुभिः।। 37 ।।

हमारे जन्मदाता माता-पिता तो बहुत पहले ही इस संसार से विदा हो चुके हैं, जिनके साथ हम बड़े हुए हैं उनकी स्थिति भी अब केवल नाम मात्र ही रह गई है, इसलिए अब हम बालू रेत के टीबों के बहने वाली नदी के तटस्थ वृक्षों के क्षण भंगुर जीवन के समान आसन्न मृत्यु होकर एक-एक दिन काट रहे हैं।

Those of whose we were born are gone long since; the persons with whom we were bred and brought up are only existing in our memory; therefore, we who are daily expecting the end of our existence, are living the precarious lives of those trees which are growing on the sandy banks of a powerful stream so as to be flown down at any moment by its rushing current.

---

1. Quoted under *Bhartṛhari* (भर्तृहरि) in the *Śārṅga-dharapaddhati* (शार्ङ्गधरपद्धति) at No. 4113.

Cf.— गए जन्मदाता गए, सहचर मित्र विलाय।
कितने दिन के पाहुने, अब हम रसिक बताय।।

(रसिक कवि)

यत्रानेके क्वचिदपि गृहे तत्र तिष्ठत्यथैको
यत्राप्येकस्तदनु बहवस्तत्र चान्ते न चैकः।।
इत्थं चेमौ रजनिदिवसौ दोलयन्द्वाविवाक्षौ कालः
काल्या सह बहुकलः क्रीडति प्राणिशारैः।। 38।।

जिस घर में पहले अनेक मनुष्य रहते थे वहाँ अब एक ही रह गया है और जहाँ एक ही मनुष्य था वहाँ बहुत से होकर अंत में एक भी नहीं रहा। इस प्रकार इस बहुत कला-कुशल काल ने अपनी प्राण-प्यारी काली के साथ प्राणीरूप सार और दिन-रातरूपी पाशों से चौसर रच रखी है।

In the house where were formerly seen a great many persons, we can scarcely find, at present, a single soul; but on the contary, where there was only one there grew for a time a lage number leaving out not a single survivor in the end. It is, therefore, evident that artful *Kāla* (काल) or Time and his deadly paramour *Kāli* (काली) or Death are playing a wonderful game of dice in which the pieces are represented by living beings, and the cubes by day and night.

---

1. Quoted under *Candraka* (चन्द्रका) in the *Kavikaṇ-ṭhābharaṇa* (कविकण्ठाभरण), and anonymously in the *Kāvyānuśāsana* (काव्यानुशासन).

Cf.— As flies to wanton boys, are we to the gods,
They kill usfor their sport.
(King Lear, Act IV. Scene. I)

तपस्यन्तः सन्तः किमधिनिवसामः सुरनदीं
गुणोदारान्दारानुत परिचयामः सविनयम्।।
पिबामः शास्त्रौघानुत विविधकाव्यामृतरसान्न
विद्मः किं कुर्मः कतिपयनिमेषायुषि जने।। 39।।

इस बहुत ही थोड़े से जीवन में हम यह नहीं जातने कि तपश्चरण करते हुए श्री गंगा जी के तट का निवास करें, या सकल गुण संपन्न स्त्रियों का नम्रतापूर्वक सेवन करें, अथवा नानाविध काव्या- मृतरस से परिपूर्ण सच्छास्त्रों का ही पान करें!

We do not exactly know, what we are to do in the exceedingly short space of our lives. Whether we are to take our abode on the banks of the holy Gaṅges and then perform the religious rites of our faith, or modestly to pass over days in the lovely society of accomplished ladies, or to drink the poetic ambrosia flowing from the various compositions of the Śāstras, is a point that cannot be solved in a definite manner by man.

1. *Cf.* —Man has two minutes and a half to live—one to smileone to sigh—and a half to love—for in the middle of this he dies."

(J. P. Richter).

अहौ वा हारे वा बलवति रिपौ वा सुहृदि वा
मणौ वा लोष्टे वा कुसुमशयने वा दृषदि वा।।
तृणे वा स्त्रैणे वा मम समदृशो यान्तु दिवसाः
सदा पुण्येऽरण्ये शिवशिवशिवेति प्रजपतः।। 40।।

सर्प और हार, बलवान शत्रु और मित्र, मणि और लौह, पुष्प शय्या और पत्थर, तृण और स्त्री जन में समान भाव से देखते हुए मेरे जीवन के शेष दिवस किसी पवित्र वनस्थल में शिव नाम का निरंतर जप करते हुए व्यतीत हों!

Looking with equal indifference upon a snake or a necklace, a powerful foe or a friend, a jewel or a piece of iron, a flowery bed or a stone, a blade of grass or a bevy of ladies, I now wish to pass the remaining days of my life in a holy forest continually meditating upon the divine name, Śiva !

---

1. Quoted under *Utpalarāja* (उत्पलराज) in the *Aucityavicāracarcā* (औचित्यविचारचर्चा), and anonymously in the *Udāharaṇacandrikā* (उदाहरणचन्द्रिका), the *Kāvyānuśāsana* (काव्यानुशासन), the *śubhāṣitāvali* (सुभाषितावलि), the *Alaṅkāraśekhara* (अलङ्कारशेखर) and the *Kāvypradīpa* (काव्यप्रदीप). It is ascribed to भर्तृहरि in the शार्ङ्गधरपद्धति at No. 4102.

गंगातीरे हिमगिरिशिलाबद्धपद्मासनस्य
ब्रह्मध्यानाभ्यसनविधिना योगनिद्रां गतस्य।।
किं तैर्भाव्यं मम सुदिवसैर्यत्र ते निर्विशङ्काः
संप्राप्स्यन्ते जरठहरिणाः शृङ्गकण्डूविनोदम्।।41।।

श्रीगंगाजी के तीरवर्ती हिमालय की शिला पर पद्मासन लगाए हुए उन उत्तम दिवसों का मुझ को कब दर्शन होगा कि जब विधिपूर्वक ब्रह्म ध्यान के अभ्यास से योगनिद्रा में सोते हुए मेरे शरीर को वृद्ध हरिण अपने शृंगाग्रभाग से निःशंक होकर खुजाने लगेंगे!

I am anxiously waiting for the approach of those happy days when I shall be sitting in a meditative posture somewhere on the Himālayan range and the banks of the sacred Gaṅges, practising the process of *Yōga* or mental abstraction, fully absorbed in the immeditate meditation of the supreme Being, and wholly entranced into ecstatic sleep, quite incognisant of what is passing around me, so that the old antelopes will be gently rubbing their itching horns against my senseless body without the least apprehension of my sentient state.

---

1. The verse stands as 17th in the *Śāntiśataka* Part IV. (शान्तिशतकम् । 4 परिच्छेदः)

Cf.— कदा भिक्षाभक्तैः करकालतगङ्गाम्बुतरलैः
शरीरं मे स्थास्यत्युपरतसमस्तेन्द्रियसुखम्।
कदा ब्रह्माभ्यासस्थिरतनुतयाण्यविहगाः
पतिष्यन्ति स्थाणुभ्रमहतधियः स्कन्धशिरसि।।
(सुभाषितरत्नभाण्डागारः 631 । 59)

स्फुरत्स्फारज्योत्स्नाधवलिततले क्वापि पुलिने
सुखासीनाः शान्तध्वनिषु रजनीषु द्युसरितः।।
भवाभोगोद्विग्नाः शिवशिवशिवेत्यार्तवचसः
कदा स्यामानन्दोद्‌गमबहुलबाष्पाकुलदृशः।। 42।।

निर्मल चंद्रमा की चाँदनी से धवलित श्री गंगा जी के तट पर निःशब्द रात्रि के समय सुखपूर्वक बैठे हुए सांसारिक विषयों के अतिशय भोग विलास से दुःखित होकर "शिव", "शिव" इत्यादि आर्तवचनों का उच्चारण करते हुए आनंद के प्रबल प्रवाह से उत्पन्न हुई अश्रुधारा से हम अपने नेत्रों का कब सिंचन करेंगे?

Reclining at east and comfort in the stillness of night somewhere on a sandy beech of the sacred Gaṅges all whitened with the clear and refulgent light of the moon, when shall we, being hard pressed by worldly misfortunes, be ever able to utter the holy name of Śiva when our eyes will all be closed with the copious flow of joyful tears?

---

1. *Cf.*—गङ्गातीरकृतोटजस्य नियमक्षामस्य शान्तात्मनो
नीवारप्रसृतिंपचस्य दधतो मेध्यां त्वचं तारवीम्।
दर्भप्रस्तरशायिनः शिवशिवेत्याक्रन्दतः प्रत्यहं
भस्मस्नानकृतः कदा मम मनो निवाणमभ्येष्यति।।

(सुभाषितावलिः)

आशा नाम नदी मनोरथजला तृष्णातरङ्गाकुला
रागग्राहवती वितर्कविहगा धैर्यद्रुमध्वंसिनी।।
मोहावर्तसुदुस्तरातिगहना प्रोत्तुङ्गचिन्तातटी तस्याः
पारगता विशुद्धमनसो नन्दन्ति योगीश्वराः।। 43।।

मनोरथरूपी जल से पूर्ण, तृष्णा की तरंगों से व्याकुल, अनुरागरूपी ग्राहादि से भरी हुई, कुतर्कमय पक्षियों से अधिष्ठित, धैर्यरूपी वृक्षों का ध्वंस करने वाली, मोहरूप भवरों के कारण दुस्तर, अत्यंत चिंतारूपी ऊँचे तटवाली, महागंभीर, आशारूपी नदी का तरण करके शुद्धान्तःकरण वाले योगीश्वर ही सच्चे सुख का अनुभव कर सकते हैं।

The River of Hope having Desire for its water, Greed for agitating waves, Passion for its sharks, Sceptic reasonings for birds, Patience for the tottering trees on its sides, and worldly Cares and Anxities for its lofty banks, is very difficult to be crossed on account of its fatal whirlpoor of illusion. Those pure-minded *Yōgis* who have swum over to the opposite bank of this mighty stream are therefore leading a safe and happy life.

---

1. The verse stands as 26th in the *Śāntiśataka* Part IV. (शान्तिशतकम् । ४ परिच्छेदः). It is quoted under भर्तृहरि in the शार्ङ्गधरपद्धति at No. 4103.

Cf.—A contented mind is the greatest blessing a man can enjoy in this world ; and it in the present life his happiness arises from the subduing of his desires, will arise in the next from the gratification of them. (Addison)

आसंसारं त्रिभुवनमिदं चिन्वतां तात तादृङ्-
नैवास्माकं नयनपदवीं श्रोत्रवर्त्मागतो वा।।
योऽयं धत्ते विषयकरिणीगाढरूढाभिमानक्षी-
बस्यान्तः करणकरिणः संयमालानलीलाम्।। 44।।

हे मित्र! सारी त्रिलोकी में ढूँढते-ढूँढते ऐसे महानुभाव का न तो दर्शन किया है और न नाम ही सुना है कि जो सांसारिक विषय रूप हवनी से परिपूर्ण आसक्त हुए अपने मदोन्मत अंतःकरणरूप हाथी को संयम रूप खूंटे से बंधा रख सके।

Oh friend, though I have been searching very carefully throughout the length and breadth of the three worlds I have not yet seen or heard a single person who is able to keep the furious bull-elephant of his own hearts firmly tied to the post of self-control, notwithstanding the maddening intensity of his ardent passion for the beloved cow of sensual objects !

---

1. Quoted under भर्तृहरि in the शार्ङ्गधरपद्धति at No. 4105.

Cf.— यदाऽसौ दुर्वारः प्रसरति मदश्चित्तकरिण-
स्तदा तस्योद्दामप्रसररसरूढेर्व्यवसितैः।
क्व तद्धैर्यालानं क्व च निजकुलाचारनिगडः
क्व सा लज्जारज्जुः क्व विनयकठोरांकुशमपि।। 32।।

(शान्तिशतकम् 1)

महादेवो देवः सरिदपि च सैवामरसरिद्गुहा
एवागारं वसनमपि ता एव हरितः।।
सुहृद्वा कालोऽयं व्रतमिदमदैन्यव्रतमिदं
कियद्वा वक्ष्यामो वटविटप एवास्तु दयिता।। 45 ।।

बहुत कथन से क्या प्रयोजन है विरक्त मनुष्यों के के लिए केवल महादेव ही देवता हैं, सुर नदी गंगा जी ही एकमात्र नदी है, पर्वतकंदरा ही एकमात्र घर है, दशों दिशा ही एकमात्र वस्त्र हैं, काल ही एकमात्र मित्र है, दूसरों के आगे दीनता न करना ही एकमात्र व्रत है और वटवृक्ष ही एकमात्र प्राण प्यारी भार्या है।

What more can we say than to assert that one who wishes the emancipation of his soul must consider (1) Mahādeva, to be his only god, (2) the Gaṅges, as his holy river, (3) a rocky cave, his only home, (4) the ten points of the compass, his only clothing, (5) Time, his only friend, (6) freedom from humiliation, his only vow and (7) a *Vaṭa* tree (banyan), his only wife?

---

1. The canon herein laid down only applies to the case of Yōgis or hermits. Though the poet does not mention that in the text he must, in writing it, have in mind the life of a saintly ascetic. The life of a *Gṛhastha* (गृहस्थ) or householder is guided by rules entirely different from the above.

ये वर्द्धन्ते धनपतिपुरः प्रार्थनादुःखभाजो
ये चाल्पत्वं दधति विषयाक्षेपपर्यस्तबुद्धेः ।।
तेषामन्तःस्फुरितहसितं वासराणां स्मरेयं
ध्यानच्छेदे शिखरिकुहरग्रावशय्यानिषण्णः ।। 46 ।।

जो दिवस धनाढ्य मनुष्यों के आगे याचना के भंग से उत्पन्न हुए दुःख के हेतु बहुत बड़े-बड़े और विषय वासना के विलास में मदान्ध होने के कारण अत्यंत छोटे प्रतीत होते हैं उन सबका पर्वत कंदरा की शिलारूप शय्या पर सोता हुआ मैं ध्यानावस्था से विश्राम पाकर, आंतरिक उपहास के साथ किस अवसर पर स्मरण कर सकूँगा वही चिंतवन कर रहा हूँ।

When shall the days which seem to be lengthened when one is compelled to suffer the pang of asking alms at the hands of wealthy people, or which appear to be much shortened when his intellectual faculty is quite disordered and blunt through incessant enjoyment of sensual pleasures, be recollected with a hearty smile, in the intervals of my mental meditation when I am inclining at ease on the rocky counch of a mountain valley?

---

1. In obedience to the teachings of the Hindu *Śāstras* every man must renounce the world and take himself to forest in his old age. This being the ultimate aim of all good Hindus, the poet here depicts the noble thought of a pious person who though discharging the duties of a householder never never forgests his future end to give up the world and contemplate his Maker in seclusion.

विद्या नाधिगता कलङ्करहिता वित्तं च नोपार्जितं
शुश्रूषापि समाहितेन मनसा पित्रोर्न संपादिता।।
आलोलायतलोचना युतवयः स्वप्नेऽपि नालिङ्गिताः
कालोऽयं परपिण्डलोलुपतया काकैरिव प्रेरितः।।47।।

न तो निष्कलंक विद्या ही का अध्ययन किया और न द्रव्योपार्जन ही किया, तथा न तो एकचित्त होकर माता-पिता की शुश्रूषा की और न चंचल और विशाल नेत्र वाली युवतियों का कभी स्वप्न में आलिंगन किया, किन्तु सच पूछिए तो काक की भाँति परपिण्डदान से अपना पेट पालन करते हुए हमने हमारे बहुमूल्य जीवन को वृथा ही व्यतीत किया है।

We have acquired neither spotless knowledge nor money, nor performed with concentrated attention proper services to our parents, nor have we ever.......(not even in a dream) the handsome person of youthful ladies with large and fickle eyes; but alas ! we have idly passed away our valuable time in the covetous desire of supporting ourselves, like miserable crows, on the alms of others !

---

1. *Cf.*—तेरे यौवन माँहि नारि निजका बिम्बौष्ठे जो ना पिया,
सेवासे गुरु देव तात जननी सन्तुष्ट जो ना किया।
विद्या और पढी न वित्त सुख से खाया कमाया दियो,
ऐसा जन्म वृथा बिता रसिक हे तूने बता क्या किया?
(रसिक कवि)

वितीर्णे सर्वस्वे तरुणकरुणापूर्णहृदयाः
स्मरन्तः संसारे विगुणपरिणामा विधिगतीः।।
वयं पुण्येऽरण्ये परिणतशरच्चन्द्रकिरणैस्त्रिया-
मां नेष्यामो हरचरणचित्तैकशरणाः।। 48।।

सर्वस्व का दान करके तरुण करुणा से परिपूर्ण हृदय होकर संसार की विपरीत गति का स्मरण करते हुए और श्रीशिव जी के चरण-कमलों की शरण लेकर किसी पवित्र वन के बीच में निवास करते हुए शरद् ऋतु के पूर्ण चन्द्रमा की चाँदनी से प्रकाशित रातें हम कब व्यतीत करेंगे?

After charitably giving away with a compassionate heart, the last particle of our possessions, and thinking the worldly objects as productive of no ultimate good, we are anxious to pass the pleasant moonlit nights of autumn in the midst of some holy forest, and abandon ourselves to the concentrated worship of the sacred feet of Śiva, the only shelter from the cares and anxities of the world !

---

1. The footnote appended to stanza 46 may also be appropriately read in connection with this ślōka. We may add that before renouncing the world a man has to give away in charity all his property to the poor and needy so that he may not be any way troubled of its thoughts.

वयमिह परितुष्टा वल्कलैस्त्वं च लक्ष्म्या
सम इह परितोषो निर्विशेषो विशेषः।।
स तु भवति दरिद्रो यस्य तृष्णा विशाला
मनसि च परितुष्टे कोर्थवान्को दरिद्रः।। 49।।

हम तो केवल वल्कल से संतुष्ट हो जाते हैं और तुम धन से होते हो, परन्तु संतुष्ट जो जाने में दोनों ही समान हैं और तब हम दोनों में किसी प्रकार का अंतर नहीं रहता, क्योंकि जिसकी तृष्णा विशाल है वही मनुष्य दरिद्री है, किसलिए कि मन के संतुष्ट हो जाने पर न तो कोई धनाढ्य है और न दरिद्री है।

Oh King! when we are content with barks of trees, and you with riches, there is no difference between us, as regards our mental contentment; for one whose wishes are unlimited is, no doubt, poor; but, when the mind is content in itself no one can be called rich or poor.

---

1. Quoted anonymously in the *Subhāṣitāvali* (सुभाषितावलि । 34375) and the *Rasaratnahāra* (रसरत्नहार:) Ascribed to भर्तृहरि in the शार्ङ्गधरपद्धति (308)।

Cf.—(*a*) को वा दरिद्रो हि विशालतृष्णः
श्रीमांश्च को यस्य समस्ततोषः 5।
(शङ्कराचार्यकृतप्रश्नोत्तरमाला)

(*b*) सर्वाः सम्पत्तयस्तस्य संतुष्ट यस्य मानसम्। (हितोपदेशः 1.109)

(*c*) तृष्णया चेत्परित्यक्तः को दरिद्रः क ईश्वरः। (हितोपदेशः 1.147)

यदेतत्स्वच्छन्दं विहरणमकार्पण्यमशनं
सहार्यैः संवासः श्रुतमुपशमैकव्रतफलम्।।
मनो मन्दस्पन्दं बहिरपि चिरस्यापि विमृशन्न
जाने कस्यैषा परिणतिरुदारस्य तपसः।। 50।।

स्वच्छंदतापूर्वक विहार, दीनतारहित भोजन, सत्पुरुषों का सहवास, चित्त की शांति उत्पन्न करने वाली विद्या और बाहिरी (सांसारिक) विषयों में मंदगति रखने वाला मन कौन से महान् तपश्चरण करने से मनुष्य को प्राप्त होते हैं, सो बहुत विचार करने पर भी हम नहीं कह सकते।

Though pondering over the subject for a long time, I cannot yet understand, for what great religious devotion or hard penance a man is granted the following blessings. —(1) freedom in going from one place to another; (2) sumptuous supply of food without the degradation of asking alms ; (3) company of the good ; and (4) acquirement of that learning which is conducive to the tranquility of mind whose motion is quite tardy as regards its objectve (external) pursuits ?

---

1. *Cf.*—बिन मांगे भोजन बसन, सङ्गति साधु महान।
शान्ति हृदय संतोष मन, रसिक सुकृत फल जान।।

पाणिः पात्रं पवित्रं भ्रमणपरिगतं भैक्ष्यमक्षय्यमन्नं
विस्तीर्णं वस्त्रमाशादशकमपमलं तल्पमस्वल्पमुर्वी।।
येषां निःसङ्गताङ्गीकरणपरिणतिः स्वात्मसंतोषिणस्ते
धन्याः संन्यस्तदैन्यव्यतिकरनिकराः कर्म निर्मूलयन्तिः।। 51।।

जिन महात्माओं के समक्ष अपने हाथ ही पवित्र पात्र, द्वार-द्वार भटकर मांगी हुई भिक्षा ही अटूट अन्न, दशों दिशा ही विस्तृत वस्त्र और यह अखिल पृथ्वी ही निर्मल शय्या का काम देते हैं, तथा वैराग्य को स्वीकार करना ही जिनका मुख्य मनोरथ है, निजात्मा के बीच जिनका संतोष है, और दैन्यरूप व्यसनों का जिन्होंने परित्याग किया है वही महानुभाव शुभाशुभ कर्मों का निर्मूल कर सकते हैं और वही धन्य हैं।

Those persons who have determined to put an end to their actions (*i.e.*, who have entirely effaced from their minds the notion of good or bad) by considering their palms as sacred vessels, eating the plentiful supply of alms obtained by their continued wanderings, taking the ten expansive quarters of the globe as their neat clothing, and lying down upon the bed of extensive earth; those who have secured true mental contentment by thinking the attainment of worldly indifference as the ultimate end of their life; and those who have given up the various ways of degrading themselves before others, are indeed deserving of all praise and honour.

---

1. The verse is same as ślōka 7 in the *Śāntiśataka,* Part IV.

2. For the idea conveyed by "पाणिः पात्रं" Prof. Tawney says that, seeing a little boy drinking water out of hand Diogenes threw away his cup, declaring it superfluous.

दुराराध्यः स्वामी तुरगचलचित्ताः क्षितिभुजो
वयं तु स्थूलेच्छा महति च पदे बद्धमनसः ।।
जरा देहं मृत्युर्हरति सकलं जीवितमिदं
सखे नान्यच्छ्रेयो जगति विदुषोऽन्यत्र तपसः ।। 52 ।।

चक्रवर्ती महाराजाओं को प्रसन्न करना असंभव है, अन्यान्य भूपालों का चित्त घोड़े के समान चञ्चल होता है और हमारा मनोरथ बहुत बड़ा है क्योंकि संसार के सर्वोत्तम पद का लाभ करना ही हमारा हार्दिक उद्देश्य है, और यह वृद्धावस्था हमारी देह का नाश कर देती है, और मृत्यु तो हमारे सर्वस्व जीवन का ही हरण कर लेती है। इसलिए हे मित्र! विद्वान् मनुष्य के लिए इस जगत् में तपश्चरण करने के सिवाय कल्याणकारक कर्म दूसरा कोई नहीं है।

To secure the favour of our lord is a hard and difficult task, and to please the minds of kings which are as unsteady as horses is also impossible ; whereas our ambitions are high, and our minds are bent on attaining to the supreme end (*i.e.*, salvation); the body is old and worn our and death is depriving us of our entire existence; it is, therefore, true that a wise man can look up for no other good in this world except the performance of virtuous actions and penance.

---

1. The word तपस् here means either moral virtue or meditat-ion connected with the practice of personal self-denial or bodily mortification.

भोगा मेघवितानमध्यविलसत्सौदामिनीचञ्चला
आयुर्वायुविघट्टिताभ्रपटलीलीनाम्बुवद्भङ्गुरम्।।
लोला यौवनलालसा तनुभृतामित्याकलय्य द्रुतं योगे
धैर्यसमाधिसिद्धिसुलभे बुद्धिं विदध्वं बुधाः।। 53।।

संसार के विषयभोग सब ही मेघ समूह के मध्यवर्ती प्रकाश करने वाली बिजली के समान चञ्चल हैं, मनुष्य की अवस्था वायु के झखोरे के बिखेरे हुए मेघ पटल की वृष्टि के समान अस्थिर है, और ऐसे ही यौवन सुख की लालसा भी अत्यंत चपल है। इसलिए इन सब बातों का विचार करके हे पण्डितजनो! तुमको उचित है कि धैर्यपूर्वक मन की एकाग्रता की सिद्धि से सुसिद्ध योग के साधन में अपना मन लगावो।

Worldly pleasures are as unsteady as the flash of lightning appearing in the midst of a clouded sky; life is as transient as rain drops falling down from a group of clouds scatterd in various directions by the force of wind; and the aspirations of youth are also extrmely frail and fickle. I would, therefore, implore learned that they must consider all mundane objects as quite transitory and consequently set their minds to the practice of *Yoga* the attainment of which is quite easy through patient concentrarion of mind.

---

1. *Cf.*—भोगास्तुङ्गतरङ्गभङ्गचपलाः प्राणाः क्षणध्वंसिनः
स्तोकान्येव दिनानि यौवनसुखं स्फुर्तिः क्रियासु स्थिता।
तत्संसारमसारमेव निखिलं बुद्धा बुधा बोधका
लोकानुग्रहपेशलेन मनसा योगाः समाधीयताम्।।
(सुभाषितरत्नभाण्डागारः 639 । 188)

पुण्ये ग्रामे वने वा महति सितपटच्छन्नपालीं
कपालीमादाय न्यायगर्भद्विजहुतहुतभुग्धूमधूम्रोपकण्ठम्।
द्वारंद्वारं प्रवृत्तो वरमुदरदरीपूरणाय क्षुधार्तो मानी प्राणी
स धन्यो न पुनरनुदिनं तुल्यकुल्येषु दीनः।। 54।।

प्रतिदिन अपने समान कुल वाले मनुष्यों के सामने दीनतापूर्वक अपने जीवन का निर्वाह करने की अपेक्षा मनस्वीजन के लिए क्षुधातुर होकर किसी पवित्र ग्राम अथवा गहन वन के बीच में स्वच्छ वस्त्र से ढके हुए कपाल खण्ड को हाथ में लिए इस पेट पापी के भरण-पोषण के निमित्त वेदपाठी ब्राह्मणों के लिए हुए हवन से उठी हुई धूम्र से व्याकुल हुए द्वारद्वार पर भिक्षार्थ भ्रमण करना ही सर्वथा श्रेष्ठ है।

Going from door to door to the houses of learned Brahmans which are altogether hidden from his sight on account of the clouds of smoke rising from their sacrificial fires, and begging alms for the satisfaction of his hungry stomach, in the midst of a charitable village or a lonely forest, and holding a broken neck of an earthenpot in his hands, covered with a clean cloth, is justly to tbe preferred to the dragging on of a penurious and humble like among his relatives by one who has the least spark of selfrespect in him.

---

1. Quoted under *Dīpaka* (दीपक) in the *Aucityavicāracarcā* (औचित्यविचारचर्चा), and under भर्तृहरि in the शार्ङ्गधरपद्धति at No. 254.

Cf.—(*a*) वरमसिधारा तरुतलवासो वरमिह भिक्षा वरमुपवासः।
वरमपि घोरे नरके पतनं नच धनगर्वितबान्धवशरणम्।।9।।
(कविभट्टस्य पद्यसंग्रहः)

(*b*) वरं वनं व्याघ्रगजेन्द्रसेवितं द्रुमालयं पत्रफलाम्बुभोजनम्।
तृणानि शय्या वसनं च वल्कलं न बन्धुमध्ये धनहीनजीवितम्।। 14।।
(वररुचेर्नीतिरत्ले)

(*c*) वरं हि मानिनो मृत्युर्न दैन्यं स्वजानाग्रतः ।।22।।
(कथासरित्सागरः। लावाणकलम्बकः 5 तरङ्गः)

चाण्डालः किमयं द्विजातिरथवा शूद्रोऽथ किं तापसः
किं वा तत्त्वविवेकपेशलमतिर्योगीश्वरः कोऽपि किम्।।
इत्युत्पन्नविकल्पजल्पमुखरैः संभाष्यमाणा जनैर्न क्रुद्धाः
पथि नैव तुष्टमनसो यान्ति स्वयं योगिनः।। 55।।

"यह चाण्डाल है अथवा द्विजाति है, या शूद्र है या तपस्वी है, या कोई तत्त्वज्ञानी योगीश्वर है," इत्यादि सर्व साधारण के विकल्प वचनों का श्रवण करते हुए योगिराज ने तो क्रुद्ध होते हैं और न संतुष्ट होते हैं, परन्तु स्वच्छंदतापूर्वक अपने मार्ग में गमन करते चले जाते हैं।

Is he a *Cāṇḍāla* (चाण्डाल or outcast) or a twiceborn, or a Śūdra, or a hermit, or some great Yogī who has renounced the world and sought real Spiritual Truth? Without paying the least heed to the aforesaid remarks of the general public, the Yogīs are quite satisfied with the path they have undertaken, and accordingly they are neither pleased nor offended at the insulting comments of the masses.

---

1. *Cf.*—रथ्यान्तश्चरतस्तथा धृतरजत्कथालवस्याध्वगैः
सत्रासं च सकौतुकं च सदयं दृष्टस्य तैर्नागरैः।
निर्व्याजीकृतचित्सुधारसमुदा निद्रायमाणस्य मे
निःशङ्कं करटः कदा करपुटी भिक्षां विलुण्ठिष्यति।।
(शान्तिशतकम् । 4 परिच्छेदः 19)

**सखे धन्याः केचित्त्रुटितभवबन्धव्यतिकरा
वनान्ते चिन्तान्तर्विषमविषयाशीविषगताः।।
शरच्चन्द्रज्योत्स्नाधवलगगनाभोगसुभगां नयन्ते
ये रात्रिं सुकृतचयचित्तैकशरणाः।। 56।।**

हे मित्र! अंतःकरण के मध्यस्थ विषम विषयादिरूप सर्पों से रहित और संसार के बंधन का संबंध तोड़ने वाले, गहन वन में बैठे हुए सुकृत संचय करने में दत्तचित्त होकर जो मनुष्य शरद् ऋतु के चंद्रमा की चाँदनी से प्रकाशमान रात्रि को व्यतीत करते हैं वह निस्संदेह बड़े बड़भागी हैं।

Oh friend, those persons are indeed very blessed who, having broken as under the worldly ties, have completely rooted out from their minds the venom of poisonous snakes of sensual enjoyments, and are thus enabled to pass the pleasant moonlit nights of autumn in the midst of a lovely forest with the sole intention of performing a series of virtuous deeds !

---

1 *Cf.*—ते धन्याः पुण्यभाजस्ते तैस्तीर्णः क्लेशसागरः।
जगत्संमोहजननी यैराशाशीविषी जिता।।
(सुभाषितरत्नभाण्डागारः 109 । 9)

एतस्माद्विरमेन्द्रियार्थगहनादायासदादाशु च
श्रेयोमार्गमशेषदुःखशमनव्यापारदक्षं क्षणम्।।
शान्ति भावमुपैहि संत्यज निजां कल्लोललोलां
मतिं भूयो मा भज भङ्गुरां भवरतिं चेतः प्रसीदाधुना।। 57।।

हे चित्त! दुःख देने वाले इस विषय भोग रूप गहन वन का शीघ्र परित्याग कर, सारे दुःखों का शमन करने में समर्थ कल्याणकारक शांत भाव का अवलंबन कर, जल के बुद्बुदे के समान चंचल बुद्धि का परित्याग कर और नाशमान संसार में अनुराग मत कर, क्योंकि ऐसा करने ही में तेरा पूर्ण कल्याण है।

Oh my heart, thou must now forsake the troublous and dangerous forest of sensual enjoyments, and soon betake thyself to the path of all good which can instantly chase away the entire host of miseries; be quiet and give up thy billowy and unsteady motion; do not attach thyself to the perishable pleasures of the world; and seek everlasting contentment and bliss within thy ownself.

---

1. *Cf.*—गन्धाढ्यां नवमल्लिकां मधुकरस्त्यक्त्वा गतो यूथिकां
तां दृष्ट्वाशु गतः स चन्दनवनं पश्चात्सरोजं गतः।
बद्धस्तत्र निशाकरेण सहसा रोदत्यसौ मन्दधीः
संतोषेण विना पराभवपदं प्राप्नोति सर्वो जनः।। 19।।
(सुभाषितारत्नभाण्डागारम् ।109)

**पुण्यैर्मूलफलैः प्रिये प्रणयिनि प्रीतिं कुरुष्वाधुना
भूशय्या नववल्कलैरकरणैरुत्तिष्ठ यामो वनम्।।
क्षुद्राणामविवेकमूढमनसां यत्रेश्वराणां सदा चित्त-
व्याध्यविवेकविह्वलगिरां नामापि न श्रूयते।। 58।।**

हे प्रिये! पवित्र कंदमूल, फल, अकृत्रिम भूशय्या और नवीन वल्कलों में अनुराग कर, क्योंकि अब हमको यहां से उठकर उस वन में प्रस्थान करना उचित है कि जहां पर अज्ञानांधचित्तवृत्ति धारण करने वाले, क्षुद्र, धनाढ्य, अविवेकी और मनोविकार के हेतु विह्वल वचन वाले दुष्ट पुरुषों का नाम भी नहीं सुना जाता।

Oh my beloved, you should learn to live upon nice fruits and roots, sleep upon the bed of bare earth, and clothe the body with new barks of trees; get up now and let us go to that forest where the wealthy persons whose minds are stupified by impudence and whose words are always faltering through mental derangement, are never to be heard again, not even in name !

---

1. When one gets accustomed to a simple, inexpensive and easy life of a forest it is but natural that he should look down very contemptuously upon the unjustifiable treatment which poor people generally receive at the hands of their unkind wealthy brethren.

मोहं मार्जयतामुपार्जय रतिं चन्द्रार्धचूडामणौ
चेतः स्वर्गतरङ्गिणीतटभुवामासङ्गमङ्गीकुरु।।
को वा वीचिषु बुद्बुदेषु च तडिल्लेखासु च स्त्रीषु
च ज्वालाग्रेषु च पन्नगेषु च सरिद्वेगेषु च प्रत्ययः।। 59।।

हे चित्त! मोह का मार्जन कर, द्वितीया के चंद्रमा को चूड़ा मणि में धारण करने वाले शिव जी के चरणाविंद में अनुरक्त हो और सुरनदी गंगा के तट का निवास स्वीकार कर। क्योंकि जल की तरंग, बुद्‌बुदे, बिजली, स्त्रीजन, अग्निशिखा, सर्प और नदी प्रवाह में विश्वास करना सर्वथा अनुचित है।

Oh my heart, thou must efface the trace of all affection (or delusion), give thyself to the meditation of Śiva, and soon betake thyself to the heavenly river (*i.e.*, Gaṅges); for, no faith (trust) can justly be put into waves, bubbles, lightning flashes, women, flames, snakes and rushing streams !

---

1. *Cf.*—शम्भूके चरणारविन्द चित से सच्चे खरे शुद्धसे,
ध्याता क्यों न गँवार प्यार करके संसार निःसार है।
माया मोह सुभोग रोग अति ही काया न जाया रहे,
नारी सर्प समान जान घर में भूला भरोसे कहा?

(रसिक कवि)

अग्रे गीतं सरसकवयः पार्श्वतो दाक्षिणात्याः
पृष्ठे लीलावलयरणितं चामरग्राहिणीनाम्।।
यद्यस्त्येवं कुरु भरवसास्वादने लम्पटस्त्वं नो
चेच्चेतः प्रविश सहसा निर्विकल्पे समाधौ।। 60।।

हे चित्त! यदि तुमको अपने अग्र भाग में नाना प्रकार के गान, दोनों पार्श्व में दक्षिण देश के सरस कवीश्वर और पृष्ठदेश में चमर करने वाली लीलावती स्त्रियों के कंकण का कलरव, अनुभव करने का सौभाग्य प्राप्त है, तो भले ही संसार के विषयभोगादि में आसक्त हो, परन्तु यदि तू पूर्वोक्त सुखों से वंचित है तो एकाग्रबुद्धि से समाधि का अवलंबन करने में कुछ भी विलंब मत करे।

In case you can affort to hear sweet and agreeable songs in your front, melodious verses of the Dekkan poets on your sides and the charming tinkling of bracelets worn by graceful ladies fanning your back with beautiful *Chowries,* you are quite justified in devoting yourself to the enjoyment of the world; but when you cannot command the aforesaid pleasures you must not make the least delay in giving yourself to *Samādhi* or absolute meditation of the Supreme Being.

---

1. Quoted anonymously in the *Subhāṣitāvali* (सुभाषितावलि) at No. 3467, and under भर्तृहरि in the शार्ङ्गधरपद्धति at No. 4176.

When in the *Zanānā,* princes are, no doubt, fanned, when necessary, by maidservants.

विरमत बुधा योषित्संगात्सुखात्क्षणभङ्गुरा-
त्कुरुत करुणामैत्रीप्रज्ञावधूनसंगमम्।।
न खलु नरके हाराक्रान्तं घनस्तनमण्डलं
शरणमथवा श्रोणीबिम्बं रणन्मणिमेखलम्।।61।।

हे पंडितजनो! आप सब क्षणभंगुर स्त्री सेवनादि संसार सुख से विरक्त हो, करुणा, मैत्री और प्रज्ञारूपी कान्ता का सेवन करो, क्योंकि चंद्रहारादि से शोभित कुचयुगल और मणिमेखला से शब्दायमान स्त्रियों के कटिभाग नरक यातना से तुम्हारी रक्षा कदापि नहीं कर सकेंगे।

Oh ye sages, you must cease to love the momentary pleasures resulting from your attachment to women, and cultivate the friendship of universal compassion and knowledge as if they were your loving wives; for, the thickest...... adorned with beautiful necklaces, and the rounded .....sounding with the tinkling bells of waistgirdles would be quite powerless to protect you against the hideous punishments of hell.

---

1. Quoted anonymously in the *Subhāṣitāvali* at No. 3385.

Cf.—(*a*) क्वैतद्वक्त्रारविन्दं क्व तदधरमधु क्वायतास्ते कटाक्षाः
क्वालापाः कोमलास्ते क्व च मदनधनुर्भङ्गुरो भ्रूविलासः।
इत्थं खट्वाङ्गकोटौ प्रकटितदर्शनं भंजुगुञ्जत्समीरं
रागान्धानामिवोच्चैरुपहसितमहामोहजालं कपालम्।।27।।
(शान्तिशतकम् । 1 परिच्छेदः)

(*b*) सेवध्वं विबुधास्तमन्धकरिपुं माक्लिष्ट कष्टं श्रुते
यस्मादत्र परत्र च त्रिजगति त्राता स एकः शिवः।
आयाते नियतेर्वशादविरले कालात्करालाद्भये
कुत्र व्याकरणं क्व तर्ककलहः कुत्रापि काव्यश्रमः।।
(सुभाषितावलिः)

मातर्लक्ष्मि भजस्व कंचिदपरं मत्कांक्षिणी मा स्म
भूर्भोगेभ्यः स्पृहयालवो नहि वयं का निस्पृहाणामसि।।
सद्यः स्यूतपलाशपत्रपुटिकापात्रे पवित्रीकृते भिक्षा-
सक्तुभिरेव संप्रति वयं वृत्तिं समीहामहे।। 62।।

हे लक्ष्मी माता! तुम अब किसी दूसरे का आश्रय लो और हमारे भोग विलास की लालसा कदापि मत करो। क्योंकि हमको तो भोगादि की इच्छा नहीं और विरक्त मनुष्यों से तुमको कुछ प्रयोजन नहीं। हम तो आजकल केवल तुरंत तोड़े हुए पवित्र पलाश के पत्रों का पात्र बनाकर भिक्षान्न की याचना से अपने जीवन का निर्वाह करने के अभिलाषी हैं।

Oh mother wealth, you must go to someone else without entertaining the least hope of ever winning my resolute heart; because I have no attachment for mundane pleasures and you are quite worthless in the eyes of those who have renounced the world. The only desire I have now left in me is to lead the life of a religious mendicant begging my simple dole of barley meal into the sanctified vessel of *Palāśa* (पलाश) leaves just plucked from their parent stem, and folded together in a convenient form.

---

1. The stanza is same as ślōka 11 in the *Śāntiśataka* Part IV. (शान्तिशतकम् ४ परिच्छेदः)

For the first line, *Cf.*—

अन्यं कंचिदुपाश्रयन्तु पुरुषं भोगोन्मुखं सम्पदः।

(भर्तृहरिनिर्वेदम्)

यूयं वयं वयं यूयमित्यासीन्मतिरावयोः।।
किं जातमधुना मित्र यूयं यूयं वयं वयम्।। 63।।

हे मित्र! पूर्वकाल में हम आप में और आप हममें किसी प्रकार का भेद भाव नहीं देखते थे, परन्तु वैराग्य भाव के उत्पन्न होने पर अब आप आप ही हो और हम हम ही हैं।

You seemed to me as myself ; as was I to you like yourself. Thus, we used to look upon each other in days gone by. What change, oh friend, has happened since then, that now you are you and I am I (literally, we are we).

PURPORT: Formerly we used to think of no particular distinction existing between us; but some imperceptible change has recently occurred that now we are led to consider ourselves as two distinct entities quite different from one another.

---

1. The stanza would have been much clear had the poet used the singular number for the first and second persons throughout it.

बाले लीलामुकुलितममी मन्थरादृष्टिपाताः
किं क्षिप्यन्ते विरम विरम व्यर्थ एष श्रमस्ते।।
संप्रत्यन्ये वयमुपरते बाल्यमास्था वनान्ते क्षीणा
मोहस्तृणमिव जगज्जालमालोकयामः।। 64।।

हे तरुणी स्त्री! हावभाव से मुकुलित नेत्रों के मंदगति कटाक्ष अब हम पर क्यों चलाती हो? इस वृथा परिश्रम से निवृत्त हो, क्योंकि अब हमारी यौवनावस्था व्यतीत हो गई ओर मोह क्षीण हो गया है। इसलिए अब हम वह नहीं हैं किन्तु और ही हो गए हैं कि, इस सारे जगत् के जंजाल को तृण के समान देखने लगे हैं।

Oh young lady ! why art thou so uselessly wasting away thy languid and graceful glances upon us ? You may better withdraw from your fruitless task ; for, we are not the same fond persons of our youth in as much as having passed the spring of our life we have now taken our residence in a lonely forest and abjured all affections for worldly pleasures on which we consequently look down as mere empty snares as worthless as straw!

---

1. *Cf.*—(*a*) कि लोलाक्षि कटाक्षम्पटतया किं स्तम्भजम्भादिभिः
किं प्रत्यङ्गनिदर्शनोत्सुकतया किं प्रोल्लसच्चाटुभिः।
आत्मानं प्रतिबाधसे त्वमधुना व्यर्थं मदर्थं यतः
शुद्धध्यानमहारसायनरसे लीनं मदीयं मनः।। 23।।
(पद्मानन्दकविकृतवैराग्यशतकम्)

(*b*) विरक्तस्य तृणं भार्या निस्पृहस्य तृणं जगत्।।

(*c*) Pardon me, madam, you mistake the man ;
For I am not the same that I was then :
No flesh is now the same 'was then in me,
And that my mind is changed yourself may see.
(Cowley)

इयं बाला मां प्रत्यनवरतमिन्दीवरदल-
प्रभाचोरं चक्षुः क्षिपति किमभिप्रेतमनया।।
गतो मोहोऽस्माकं स्मरकुसुमबाणव्यतिकरज्वर-
ज्वाला शान्ता तदपि न वराकी विरमति।। 65।।

यह यह तरुण स्त्री जो नीलकमल की शोभा को चुराने वाले अपने कटाक्ष मेरी ओर बारंबार चला रही है इससे इसका क्या प्रयोजन है सो कुछ समझ में नहीं आता। क्योंकि अब हमारा मोहजाल दूर हो गया है और कामदेव के पुष्पमय बाणों से उत्पन्न होने वाली अग्नि भी शांत हो गई है। इसलिए यह मूढ अब भी हमारा पीछा क्यों नहीं छोड़ती है?

What can be the possible intention of this young lady whose condition is indeed very pitiable ; for, she has not yet ceases to direct the constant glances of her beautiful or lotus like (*lit.* the stealer of the splendour of a lotus leaf) eyes towards me who have no longer any affection for the world and its pleasures, and is, therefore, quite free from the burning influences of the fiery arrows of Love ?

---

1. *Cf.*—(*a*) स्मितैश्चित्रे नेत्रे किमिति कुरुषे किं नु परुषे
कृतं स्निग्धालापैः कृतमथ विलापैरपि कृतैः।
मयि त्यक्तास्वादे सभयमवसादेन गुरुणा
व्यतिक्रान्ते कामे विफलमिव वाभे व्यवसितम्।।
(भर्तृहरिनिर्वेदम्)

(*b*) "To me, no pleasure Beauty brings ;
Thine eyes have scarce a charm for me."
Byron's Childe Harold's Pilgrimage. I.84.

रम्यं हर्म्यतलं न किं वसतये श्राव्यं न गेयादिकं
किं वा प्राणसमासमागमसुखं नैवाधिकं प्रीयते।।
किन्तूदभ्रान्तपतत्पतङ्गपवनव्यालोलदीपाङ्कुरच्छाया-
चंचलमाकलय्य सकलं सन्तो वनान्तं गताः।। 66 ।।

निवास करने के लिए सुंदर-सुंदर महल, श्रवण करने के लिए मनोहर संगीत और भोग करने के लिए प्राण-प्यारी समागम का सुख क्या इनके लिए विद्यमान न था? (अर्थात् था)। परन्तु इन साधुजनों ने पूर्वोक्त संसार सुख को भ्रमण करते हुए पढ़ने वाले पतंगों के पक्षों की पवन से अस्थिर दीपक की छाया के समान चञ्चल समझकर गहन वन के एकान्त स्थान में प्रस्थान करना ही उत्तम समझा है।

Notwithstanding the existence of beautiful palatial mansion of their dwelling, sweet music for their hearing and the enjoyment of a beloved wife for their love, the virtuous saints have forsaken them all and retired into forest (for the sake of meditating on God) ; because they have rightly understood the aforesaid objects as frail and momentary as the flickering flame of a lamp which is rendered the more unsteady on account of the flapping of a foolish moth hovering around its small and feeble light.

---

1. The verse which stands as 14th in the *Śāntiśataka* Part II is quoted under *Bhartṛhari* in the *Śārṅgadharapaddhati* at No. 4114, and anonymously in the *Subhāṣitāvali* at No. 3326.

किं कन्दाः कन्देरभ्यः प्रलयमुपगता निर्झरा वा गिरिभ्यः
प्रध्वस्ता वा तरुभ्यः सरसफलभृतो वल्कलिन्यश्च शाखाः।।
वीक्ष्यन्ते यन्मुखानि प्रसभमुपगतप्रश्रयाणां खलानां
दुःखोपात्ताल्पवित्तस्मयवशपवनानर्तितभ्रूलतानि।। 67 ।।

क्या पर्वतों की कंदरा में उत्पन्न होने वाले कंदमूल सब नष्ट हो गए हैं और क्या वृक्षों की सरस फलों के धारण करने वाली और वल्कल युक्त शाखायें सर्वथा विनष्ट हो गई हैं, कि दुःखपूर्वक संचित किए हुए थोड़े से धन के अभिमानरूपी पवन के झकोरों से नाँचते हुए भौंह वाले दुष्टचरित धनाढ्य पुरुषों के मुख की ओर मनुष्य इस प्रकार टकटकी लगाए देख रहे हैं?

It is that edible roots have all disappeared from the caves of mountains, or springs have ceased to flow from rocky slopes, or trees have stopped to grow their fruitful and barky branches, that we are thus forced to look up to the face of those proud and perverse, persons whose brows are ever dancing with the vain conceit of a small quantity of wealth which they have barely succeeded to accumulate after a series of difficulties and troubles ?

---

1. This stanza is same as ślōka 3 in the *Śāntiśataka* Part IV. (शान्तिशतकम् । 4 परिच्छेदः) *Cf.*—(*a*) निष्कदाः किमु कन्दरोदरभुवः क्षीणास्तरुणां त्वचः किं शुष्काः सरितः स्फुदिग्गरिगुरुग्रावस्खलद्वीचयः। प्रत्युत्थानमितस्ततः प्रतिदिनं कुर्वद्भिरुद्धीविभिर्यद्वारार्पिदृष्टिभिः क्षितिभुजां विद्वद्भिरप्यास्यते।। 3।। (शान्तिशतकम् 4 परिच्छेदः) (*b*) किं शाकानि न सन्ति भूधरसरित्कुंजेषु मूलानि वा किं वा जीवनमेतदेव विहितं याच्ञैव नान्यत्क्वचित् । येन श्रीमदमोहमूढमनसां स्थित्वाग्रतो भुभृतां श्वासोत्कम्पकदर्थिताक्षरपदैर्देहीति वागुच्यते।। (सुभाषितावलिः) (*c*) चीराणि क्रिं पथि न सन्ति दिशन्ति भिक्षां नैवांघ्रिपाः परभृतः सरितोऽपशुष्यन् । रुद्धा गुहाः किमजितोऽवति नोपसन्नान्, कस्माद्भजन्ति कवयो धनदुर्मदान्धान्।। (श्रीभागवते द्वितीयस्कन्धे)

गंगातरंगहिमशीकरशीतलानि
विद्याधराध्युषितचारुशिलातलानि।।
स्थानानि किं हिमवतः प्रलयं गतानि
यत्सावमानपरपिण्डरता मनुष्याः।। 68।।

गंगाजी की तरंगों के हिममय जल से शीतल, विद्याधरों के निवास करने के योग्य हिमालय के सुंदर शिलातल क्या इस पृथ्वी पर से लुप्त हो गए हैं कि अपमान सहित दूसरों के दिए हुए टुकड़ों से मनुष्यों को अपना निर्वाह करते हुए हम जहाँ-तहाँ दृष्टि कर रहे हैं।

Is it that the beautiful retreats (lit. slabs) of the Himālayas cooled down by Gangetic waves and inhabited by *Vidyādharās* (विद्याधराः) have altogether disappeared from the face of this earth that people have thus condescended to lead a poor disgraceful life upon the alms of others ?

---

1. The poet indirectly means to say that we should rather leave this world and resort to solitary caves of the Himālayas than submit to the disgrace of begging alms at the hands of our fellow beings. Persons who can give with a good grace are very few. Instead of being pitied beggars are frequently disgraced for their poverty by their wealthy donors.

यदा मेरुः श्रीमान्निपतति युगान्ताग्निदलितः
समुद्राः शुष्यन्ति प्रचुरमकरग्राहनिलयाः।।
धरा गच्छत्यन्तं धरणिधरपादैरपि धृता
शरीरे का वार्ता करिकरभकर्णाग्रचपले।। 69।।

जब हम जानते हैं कि युगान्त करने वाली अग्नि से संतप्त होकर सुमेरु भी अवश्य पड़ जाता है, अनेकानेक मकर ग्राहादिको आश्रय देने वाले समुद्र भी सूख जाते हैं और बड़े-बड़े पर्वतों से दृढ़ हुई पृथ्वी भी अवश्य चल-विचल हो जाती है, तो हाथी के बच्चे के कर्णाग्रभाग के समान अत्यंत चञ्चल इस शरीर के विनाश होने में कौन-सा आश्चर्य है?

When we know that at the end of the four *Yugas* (युगाः) or ages, the splendid *Meru* (मेरु) being attacked by the fire of universal destruction, shall also fall ; when we see that vast seas, the abode of innumerable sharks and crocodiles, shall also dry; and when we are sure that the earth, though sustained by deep-rooted mountains, shall also collapse ; what possible faith can we fairly put into this feeble mortal frame which is as unsteady as the ever flapping ears of a yound elephant ?

Cf.—(*a*) शुष्यत्यम्बुधयस्तरङ्गगहनैरालिंगिताशाङ्गना
गच्छन्त्युद्गततुङ्गशृङ्गमुकुटोदग्रा गिरीन्द्राः क्षयम्।
भ्रश्यत्येव वसुन्धराऽपि सहिता दिग्दन्तिभिर्यद्वशा-
त्सर्वाशी सततं प्रधावति महाकालः स कोऽप्याकुलः।।
(क्षेमेन्द्रविहितदर्पदलनम् । 4 विचारः)

(*b*) पृथिवी दह्यते यत्र मेरुश्चापि विशीर्यते।
शुष्यत्यम्भोनिधिजलं शरीरे तत्र का कथा।। (सुभाषितावलिः)

एकाकी निःस्पृहः शान्तः पाणिपात्रो दिगम्बरः।
कदा शंभो भविष्यामि कर्मनिर्मूलनक्षमः ।। 70 ।।

अकेला, आशारहित, शान्तचित्त, पाणिपात्र (हाथ को ही पात्र समझने वाला) और दिगम्बर (नग्न या दिशा मात्र को ही वस्त्र समझने वाला) होकर, हे महादेव! मैं अपने कर्मों को निर्मूलन करने में कब समर्थ होऊँगा?

Oh God (Śiva), when will the day come when I shall be able to put a stop to all my actions whether good or bad by being (1) alone, (2) devoid of all aspirations, and (3) contented, as well as by thinking my hands as necessary vessels and the different quarters of the globe as a sufficient clothing for my naked self ?

---

1. Quoted anonymously in *Subhāṣitāvali* (सुभाषितावलि) at No. 3404.

The line एकाकी गृहसंत्यक्तः पाणिपात्रो दिगम्बरः also occurs in the Pañcatantra V. 15. (पंचतंत्रम् ५ तन्त्रम् । १५).

The word कर्मनिर्मूलन literally means uprooting actions.

Every action of man is done with some purpose either good or bad. Destruction of actions means doing things without any personal concern. The doctrine is fully explained by Śrīkṛṣṇa to Arjuna in the Bhagavadgītā.

**प्राप्ताः श्रियः सकलकामदुघास्ततः किं
दत्तं पदं शिरसि विद्विषतां ततः किम्।।
संमानिताः प्रणयिनो विभवैस्ततः किं कल्प-
स्थितं तनुभृतां तनुभिस्ततः किम्।। 71।।**

सकल मनोरथ के सिद्ध करने वाली लक्ष्मी को प्राप्त कर लिया तो क्या? शत्रुओं के मस्तक पर पदार्पण कर लिया तो क्या? धनादि से अपने हितैषियों को सत्कार कर दिया तो क्या? तथा देहधारियों ने अपने शरीर को कल्प पर्यन्त धारण कर लिया तो क्या?

भावार्थ–जब तक विधिपूर्वक वैराग्य न लिया तब तक किसी ने भी कुछ न किया।

Although they have acquired riches the unfailing means of fulfilling all desires, although they have succeeded to trample upon the heads of their vanquished enemies, although they have favoured their relations with wealth and prosperity, and although the mortal men somehow prolonged the span of their lives in the end of a *Kalpa* (कल्प), they must all bear it in mind that unless they have secured their future happiness they have done really nothing.

---

1. This verse which stands as 2nd in the *Śāntiśataka,* Part IV is quoted under *Bhartṛhari* in the *Subhāṣitāvali* the *Śārṅgadhara-paddhati* 4112, and the *Udāharaṇacandrikā.* The authors of *Kāvyapradīpa* and *Rasaratnahāra* cite it anonymously.

Cf.— वेदाभ्यासव्यसनरसिकैः स्थीयते तावता किं
सूक्ष्मा बुद्धिः श्रुतमिव विशत्यश्रुतं तावता किम्।
जल्पारम्भे जयति नियतं वादिनस्तावता किं
निर्वेदार्तं यदि न हृदयं शान्तिमभ्येति पुंसः।। 33।।
(नीलकण्ठदीक्षितस्य शान्तिविलासः)

जीर्णा कन्था ततः किं सितममलपटं पट्टसूत्रं ततः किं
एका भार्या ततः किं हयकरिसुगणैरावृतो वा ततः किम्।।
भक्तं भुक्तं ततः किं कदशनमथवा वासरान्ते ततः किं
व्यक्तज्योतिर्न चान्तर्मथितभवभयं वैभवं वा ततः किम्।। 72।।

फटे पुराने वस्त्रखण्डों से शरीर का आच्छादन किया तो क्या और श्वेत निर्मल पटवस्त्र धारण किए तो क्या? एकमात्र भार्या का साथ रहा तो क्या और घोड़े हाथी सेवकादि का भोग किया तो क्या? दाल-भात का भोजन मिला तो क्या और दिनास्त होते-होते बासी भोजन मिला तो क्या? तथा स्वात्मप्रकाश रहित अन्तःकरण को दुःखित करने वाले भयसहित अनेक प्रकार के वैभव का भोग किया तो क्या?

भावार्थ–जब तक भवभय हरण करने वाले परब्रह्म की ज्योति हृदय में प्रकाशमान् न हो तब तक मनुष्य जन्म वृथा ही समझना चाहिये।

Unless we seek real enjoyment of communion with self which is capable of destroying all worldly anxieties and dangers of our hearts, it is of very little importance (1) whether we clothe ourselves in thread bear rags or dress in beautiful and neat silken garments; (2) whether we possess no other companion excepting our only wife or command the services of numerous servants together with horses, elephants and other conveyances for our use ; and (3) whether we feast on delicious tables of rice and other dainties or subsist ourselves on rotten and simple food got towards the close of a day.

---

1. *Cf.*—(*a*) स्वात्मा नारायणोऽन्तः स्फुरति यदि रतिर्दैवतैः कैवतैर्नः। (भर्तृहरिनिर्वेदम्). (*b*) विश्वाः कलाः परिचिता यदि तास्ततः किं तप्तं तपो यदि तदुग्रतरं ततः किम्। कीर्तिः कलंकविकला यदि सा ततः किमन्तर्विवेककलिका यदि नोल्ललास।। 89।। (पद्मानन्दकविकृतवैराग्यशतकम्)

The construction and meaning of this stanza are not quite clear.

भक्तिर्भवे मरणजन्मभयं हृदिस्थं
स्नेहो न बन्धुषु न मन्मथजा विकाराः।।
संसर्गदोषरहिता विजना वनान्ता
वैराग्यमस्ति किमतः परमार्थनीयम्।। 73।।

शिवजी की भक्ति, अंतःकरण में जन्म-मरण का भय, बंधु वर्ग से विरक्ति, कामदेव के विकारों का अभाव और संसर्ग दोष से रहित एकान्त निर्जन वन का वास ऐसे वैराग्य के सिवाय मनुष्य को और क्या वांछनीय है?

When a man is faithfully devoted to Śiva, when his heart is always awake to the pangs of birth and death, when he has not the least attachment to his relatives, when he is dead against passionate excitements of love, when leading a secluded life into the interior of a lonely forest he is quite free from the evil effects of society at large, and when his mind is wholly indifferent to worldly pleasures, there is nothing more to be asked for or desired by him.

---

1. The construction of the ślōka very puzzling and consequently its exposition requires sosme stretching of intellect. The difficulty arises out of the terse and laconie form of diction used by the author.

तस्मादनन्तमजरं परमं विकासि
तद्ब्रह्म चिन्तय किमेभिरसद्विकल्पैः।।
यस्यानुषङ्गिण इमे भुवनाधिपत्यभोगा-
दयः कृपणलोकमता भवन्ति।। 74।।

इसलिए हे मनुष्यो! संसार के मिथ्या विकल्पों को छोड़कर उस अनंत, अजर, परमोत्कृष्ट और प्रकाशरूप ब्रह्म का चिंतवन करो, कि कृपण लोगों के माननीय त्रिलोकी के राज्यादि के भोगादि जिसका स्वयमेव अनुगमन करते हैं।

Leaving aside all sceptic and vain reasonings, you should devote yourself to the contemplation of that endless immortal, supreme, and luminous Brahma in whose imperial train all enjoyments of worldly sovereignty, which are so much coveted by misers, invariably follow.

---

1. This ślōka which is same as stanza 24 in lthe *Śāntiśataka* Part III. (शान्तिशतकम् । 3 परिच्छेदः) is quoted under *Bhartṛhari* (भर्तृहरि) in the *Subhāṣitāvali* (सुभाषितावलि) at No. 3452.

2. Rev. Wortham thus translates the latter half of this stanza in a different way:—"If a man be truly seeking unity with the supreme Being, all earthly pleasures and powers seem worthy only of the notice of low minded men."

3. The point seems to be this:—In the opinion of a truly religious person all earthly powers and enjoyments are worth considering only by the mean.

पातालमाविशसि यासि नभो विलंघ्य
दिङ्मंडलं भ्रमसि मानसचापलेन।।
भ्रान्त्याऽपि जातु विमलं कथमात्मनीनं
तद्ब्रह्म न स्मरसि निर्वृतिमेषि येन।। 75।।

हे मन! तू अपनी स्वाभाविक चंचलता से कभी तो पाताल में प्रवेश कर जाता है, कभी उछल करके आकाश में गमन करने लगता है और कभी दशों दिशाओं में इधर का उधर भ्रमण करता फिरता है; परन्तु कैसे खेद की बात है कि तू भूलकर भी उस आत्मप्रकाश परब्रह्म का कभी स्मरण नहीं करता कि जिसके चिन्तवन करने से तेरी मोक्ष हो सकती है!

By thy natural unsteadiness sometimes thou penetrates into *Pātāla* (पाताल) or the depths of nether regions, sometimes traversest etherial spaces, and sometimes wanderest over different quarters of the globe ; but oh mind ! thou never thinkest, even by mistake, of that Supreme Being who is sitting within thy ownself ; and by whose meditation thou canst easily attain to the highest contentment and happiness !

---

1. The verse is ascribed to *Aragaṭa* (अर्गट) in the *Subhāṣitāvali* (सुभाषितावलि) at No. 3447.

2. The word निर्वृत्ति may also mean tranquility.

रात्रिः सैव पुनः स एव दिवसो मत्वाऽबुधा जन्तवो
धावन्त्युद्यमिनस्तथैव निभृतप्रारब्धतत्तत्क्रियाः।।
व्यापारैः पुनरुक्तभुक्तविषयैरेवंविधेनाऽमुना संसारेण
कदर्थिताः कथमहो मोहान्न लज्जामहे।। 76।।

वही रात और वही दिन समझकर ये मूर्खजन उद्योग करते हुए निज-निज कर्म में प्रवृत्त होकर पूर्वभुक्त विषयादि का बारंबार भोग करते रहते हैं। इस प्रकार इस संसार क्रम से नित्य प्रति विडंम्बित होकर भी मोह जाल में फंसे हुए हम लोग कुछ भी लज्जित नहीं होते यह बड़े आश्चर्य की बात है!

Without entertaining the least idea of the flight of time, the ignorant people who have set themselves to their cherished pursuits are daily led astray to run after their individual undertakings, and earnestly long for the pleasures which they have repeatedly enjoyed a number of times. However though we are thus frequently deceived by the illusionary course of this world we are never ashamed of our own folly. It is indeed a great mystery !

Purport—Day follows night, night follows day, and so it continues uninterruptedly. As there is no end to the repetition of days and nights, so there is no end to man's work. (Every morning man goes without murmur to his work of yesterday, with unabated vigour). Being thus deceived by nature we long to enjoy the same objects over and over without ever being ashamed of our folly.

मही रम्या शय्या विपुलमुपधानं भुजलता
वितानं चाकाशं व्यजनमनुकूलोऽयमनिलः।।
स्फुरद्दीपश्चन्द्रो विरतिवनितासंगमुदितः सुखं
शान्तः शेते मुनिरतनुभूतिर्नृप इव।। 77।।

विरतिरूपी कांता के प्रसंग से प्रमुदित होकर पृथ्वी तल की मनोहर शय्या, भुजलता रूप विपुल उपधान, आकाशरूप मण्डप, अनुकूल पवनरूप व्यजन (पंखा) और चंद्रमारूप प्रकाशमान् दीपक आदि की विविध विभूति से युक्त मुनीश्वर शांतचित्त होकर राजा के समान सुखपूर्वक शयन करता है।

A contened saint who is prone to take this earth for his fine sofa ; his creeper-like arms for ample pillows, the endless sky for his canopy, a favourable breeze for his fan, the refulgent moon for his lamp, and total indifference to world for his loving wife, always sleeps with as much ease and comfort as a great monarch of enormous wealth and power.

---

1. The stanza is same as ślōka 8 in the *Śāntiśataka* Part. IV. (शान्तिशतकम् । 4 परिच्छेदः)

Cf.— भू पर्यंको निजभुजलता कन्दुकं खं वितानं
दीपश्चन्द्रो विरतिवनितलब्धयोगप्रमोदः।
दिक्कन्यानां व्यजनपवनैर्वीज्यमानोऽनुकूलै-
र्भिक्षुः शेते नृप इव सदा वीतरागो जितात्मा।।

(सुभाषितरत्नभाण्डागारः 361 । 61)

त्रैलोक्याधिपतित्वमेव विरसं यस्मिन्महाशासने
तल्लब्धवसनवस्त्रमानघटने भोगे रतिं मा कृथाः।
भोगः कोऽपि स एक एव परमो नित्योदितो जृम्भते
यत्स्वादाद्विरसा भवन्ति विषयास्त्रैलोक्यराज्यादयः।। 78।।

जिस महाराज्य के सामने त्रिलोकी का राज्य विरस प्रतीत होता है, उस परब्रह्म के ध्यान को प्राप्त करके आसन, वस्त्र और मान आदि घटना से युक्त भोग विलास में प्रीति करना सर्वथा अनुचित है क्योंकि भोग भी केवल वही एक है जो परमोत्कृष्ट और सदैव प्रकाशमान् है और जिसका आस्वादन कर लेने पर त्रिलोकी के राज्यादि संबंधी विषय सब ही विरस और फीके हो जाते हैं।

After attaining to that great spiritual knowledge which entirely deprives the sovereignty of the three worlds of all its charms, you must not feel the least affection for rank, dress, and honour for, the only enjoyment worthy of a man's aspiration is that which is supreme and immortal, and which, when once relished by him, renders the pleasures of universal empire as altogether insipid and unpleasant.

---

1. The word शासन literally means rule, government, power. Here it perheps refers to control of passions so absolutely necessary to a Yogī.

Cf.—जिन नरवरने है लिया, रसिक योग का स्वाद।
वे सब जग के राज को, जानत हेतु विषाद।।

(रसिक कवि)

किं वेदैः स्मृतिभिः पुराणपठनैः शास्त्रैर्महाविस्तरैः
स्वर्गग्रामकुटीनिवासफलदैः कर्मक्रियाविभ्रमैः ।।
मुक्त्वैकं भवबंधदुःखरचनाविध्वंसकालानलं
स्वात्मानन्दपदप्रवेशकलनं शेषा वणिग्वृत्तयः ।। 79 ।।

वेद, स्मृति, पुराण और महाविस्तृत शास्त्र के पठन-पाठन से तथा स्वर्गरूपी ग्राम में निवास मात्र का फल देने वाले यज्ञादि कार्यों के करने से क्या प्रयोजन है? क्योंकि संसार के बंधन से उत्पन्न होने वाले दुःख प्रपंच को विध्वंस करने में कालाग्नि के समान स्वात्मानंदु का लाभ करने के बिना पूर्वोक्त निःशेष कर्म वाणिज्य वृत्ति के समान हैं।

What advantage is there in studying *Vedas* (वेद), the *Smṛti* (स्मृति), the *Purāṇas* (पुराण), and the numerous Śāstras; or in performing various sacrificial rites and ceremonies whose only fruit is to secure for man a small residence in the village of heaven ? Excepting the attainment of that spiritual knowledge of self which is the one great source of all contentment and happiness, and the sole deadly fire for the destruction of worldly anxieties and cares, all other pursuits, are nothing more than mercenary crafts.

---

1. *Cf.*—(*a*) किं तर्केण वितर्कितेन शतशो ज्ञानेन किं छन्दसा किं पीतेन सुधारसेन बहुधा स्वाध्यायपाठेन किम्। अभ्यस्तेन च लक्षणेन किमहो ध्यानं न चेत्सर्वथा लोकालोक-विलोकनैककुशलज्ञाने हृदि ब्रह्मणः: । 59 ।। (पद्मानन्दकविकृतवैराग्यशतकम्) (*b*) Know thyself. (Solon.) (*c*) वेदाभ्यासतपोज्ञानमिन्द्रियाणां च संयमः। अहिंसा गुरुसेवा च निःश्रेयसकरं परम् ।।83 ।।सर्वेषामपि चैतेषां शुभानामिह कर्मणाम् ।।किंचिच्छ्रेयस्करतरं कर्मोक्तं पुरुषं प्रति ।। 84 ।। सर्वेषामपि चैतेषामात्मज्ञानं परं स्मृतम्। तव्द्यग्रं सर्वविद्यानां प्राप्यते ह्यमृतं ततः ।।85 ।। (मनुस्मृतिः ।12 अध्याय) (*d*) There is but one key that will unlock the mysteries of Gold and that key is within youself. Science cannot do it, for science deals only with the surface of things. We must leave the surface and go into the depth of our own souls. It is useless to expect to find God any where until you have found Him within yourself ; and having found Him there, you will find Him everywhere. (Great thoughts)

आयुः कल्लोललोलं कतिपयदिवसस्थायिनी यौवन=
श्रीरर्थाः सङ्कल्पकल्पा घनसमयतडिद्विभ्रमा भोगापूराः।।
कण्ठाश्लेषोपगूढं तदपि च न चिरं यत्प्रियाभिः प्रणीतं
ब्रह्मण्यासक्तचित्ता भवत भवभयाम्भोधिपारं तरीतुम्।। 80।।

मनुष्यों की आयुष्य जल के बुद्बुदे के समान चंचल है, यौवन की शोभा थोड़े ही दिन स्थिर रहने वाली है, द्रव्यादि पदार्थ मनोरथ के तुल्य शीघ्र विनाश होने वाले हैं, विषयादि भोग-विलास वर्षा काल में चमकने वाली बिजली के सदृश हैं और प्राण-प्यारी स्त्रियों के आलिंगन का सुख भी बहुत चिरस्थायी नहीं है। इसलिए हे मतिमानो! संसार के भयरूप समुद्र की परली पार जाने के लिए परमात्मा के ध्यान में मग्न होना ही उचित है।

Life is as unsteady as waver of water, beauty of youth is only lasting for a few days, riches are momentary like thought, all enjoyment are as transient as flashes of lightning amidst a raining cloud, and the.....of our sweethearts are likewise extremely fleeting. Consequently, if you be really anxious to cross the ocean or worldly woes you should not fail to concentrate your mind on the absolute devotion of Brahmā.

---

1. The phrase "कतियदिवसस्थायिनि" is also to be found in the *Bhōjaprabandha* (भोजप्रबन्ध) at page 12, Bomay Edition.

Cf.—(*a*) Why should affection cling to the vain world,
Still fleeing, never for a moment fixed?
(Ferdausi's Shāh Nāmeh.)

(*b*) स्थिरापायः कायः प्रणयिषु सुखं सथैर्यविमुखं
महाभोगा रोगाः कुवलयदृशः सर्पसदृशाः।
महावेशः क्लेशः प्रकृतिचपला श्रीरपि खला
यमः स्वैरी वेरी तदपि न हितं कर्म विहितम्।। 11।।
(शान्तिशतकम् । 2 परिच्छेदः)

(*c*) For the second line. *Cf.*—the fine line of Cowley ;
"Riches have wings, and grandeur is a dream."

ब्रह्माण्डमण्डलीमात्रं किं लोभाय मनस्विनः।।
शफरीस्फुरतेनाब्धेः क्षुब्धता जातु जायते।। 81।।

जैसे शफरी जाति को छोटी सी मछली की गति (चाल) से समुद्र में तरंगों का उठना सर्वथा असंभव है, वैसे ही मनस्वी जन के मन में यह ब्रह्माण्ड भी किसी प्रकार का लोभ उत्पन्न नहीं कर सकता।

As the gentle move of a *Śapharī* (शफरी) of a small glittering fish does not cause the least possible undulation into the waters of a deep ocean, so this circumcribed universe is likewise incompetent to tempt the minds of great magnanimous souls.

---

1. Quoted under *Bhartṛhari* (भर्तृहरि) in the *Subhāṣitāvali* (सुभाषितावलि । 495) and the *Śārṅgadharapaddhati* (शार्ङ्गधरपद्धति । 263)

Cf.—अक्षोभ्यं हृदयं बतेह महताम्भोनिधीनामिव।। 137।।

(कथासरित्सागरः । शशाङ्कवतीलंबकः 28 तरंगः)

2. ब्रह्माण्ड or egg of Brahma here stands for this world.

3. The word जातु is an indeclinable and means ever or at all.

4. The mind of a wise man is here compared to an ocean and the world to a small fish.

यदासीदज्ञानं स्मरतिमितरसंस्कारजनितं
तदा दृष्टं नारीमयमिदमशेषं जगदपि।।
इदानीमस्माकं पटुतरविवेकाञ्जनजुषां समी-
भूता दृष्टिस्त्रिभुवनमपि ब्रह्म मनुते।। 82।।

जब मैं कामान्धकार के कारण बिल्कुल ही मूर्ख था तब यह सारा जगत् मुझ को स्त्रीमय दृष्टि आता था परन्तु अब निर्मल विवेकरूप अंजन के आंजने से मेरी समदृष्टि हो गई है कि तीनों भुवन ही ब्रह्ममय प्रतीत होने लगे हैं।

When I was quite ignorant through the dark influence of Love, I saw whole world to be entirely full of women; but, now by applying the collyrium of true knowledge of the eyes, I regain my perfect vision, look on all things as alike, and discern the presence of Brahma throughout the three worlds.

---

1. The Stanza also occurs in the *Śāntiśatakaṃ* Part IV. (शान्ति-शतकम् । 4 परिच्छेद: 14) and the *Śaravatīkaṇṭhābharaṇa.* (सरस्वतीकण्ठा-भरणम् । पंचमपरिच्छेद:)

Cf.—तामसी सा मसीवृष्टिर्यावदावरणं हृदः।
दृग्भङ्गी तावदानङ्गी हरिणी हरिणीदृशः।।4।।
(भर्तृहरिनिर्वेदम् । पंचमोऽङ्कः)

रम्याश्चन्द्रमरीचयस्तृणवती रम्या वनान्तस्थली रम्यः
साधुसमागमः शमसुखं काव्येषु रम्याः कथाः।।
कोपोपाहितबाष्पबिन्दुतरलं रम्यं प्रियाया मुखं सर्वं
रम्यमनित्यतामुपगते चित्ते न किंचित्पुनः।। 83।।

चंद्रमा की किरणें निस्संदेह मनोहर हैं, तृणसहित वनभूमि भी रमणीय प्रतीत होती है, साधुजनों का समागम आनंददायक है, शान्तिजनित सुख और काव्यों की विचित्र कथा भी अत्यंत सुंदर होती हैं और इसी की ही भाँति रति कलह से उत्पन्न हुए वाष्प बिन्दु से चंचल प्राण-प्यारी का मुखारबिंद भी बहुत मनोहर मालूम होता है, परन्तु इस चित्त के संसार की अनित्यता जान लेने पर ये सारे रमणीय पदार्थ कुछ भी सुखदायी नहीं होते।

भावार्थ—चित्त के अस्थिर होने पर सब प्रकार की रम्य वस्तु भी अरम्य ही प्रतीत होती है इसलिए येनकेन उपाय से चित्तवृत्ति का स्थिर करना ही सर्वथा मुख्य है।

Pleasent indeed are the rays of moon, the green and verdent soil of woods, the company of saints, the happiness of contentment, the intreresting stories of the *Kāvyas* (काव्य) or high class literature, and the delightful face of a beloved wife glittering with beads of treas produced by anger; but when the mind is convinced of the mortal state of things, they are all deprived of their several charms.

Purport—As everything pleasent appears unpleasant to one whose mind is unsteady or disturbed, so it is the first and formost duty of man to secure the equanimity of his mind.

भिक्षाशी जनमध्यसंगरहितः स्वायत्तचेष्टः सदा
दानादानविरक्तमार्गनिरतः कश्चित्तपस्वी स्थितः।।
रथ्याक्षीणविशीर्णजीर्णसनैः संप्रोतकंथाधरो
निर्मानो निरहंकृतिः शमसुखाभोगैकबद्धस्पृहः।।84।।

भिक्षा मांगकर खाने वाला, जनसंसर्ग से रहित, स्वच्छंदतापूर्वक विचरने वाला, दान देने और लेने से विरक्त मार्ग में पड़े हुए फटे- पुराने वस्त्र खण्डों की बनी हुई कंथा को धारण करने वाला, मान और अहंकाररहित और शांति सुख के भोग करने की एकमात्र इच्छा रखने वाला कोई विरला ही तपस्वी होता है।

There are but few hermits : (1) who are content with leading a mendicant's life, far away from the crowded throngs of men; (2) who are absolute masters of their senses (actions); (3) who are always indifferent equally to give and take; (4) who clothe themselves with the coarse cloth of torn out pieces of rags found acattered in streets; and (5) who are regardless of every attention and honour paid to them, devoid of vain pride and anxious to enjoy the sole happiness of a contented and tranquil heart.

---

1. The word *tapasvī* (तपस्वी) literally means a person who practices penance. The real meaning of *tapas* तपस् is meditation connected with the practice of personal self-denial or mortification.

मातर्मेदिनि तात मारुत सखे तेजः सुबन्धो जल
भ्रातर्व्योम निबद्ध एष भवतामग्रे प्रणामाञ्जलिः ।।
युष्मत्संगवशोपजातसुकृतोद्रेकस्फुरन्निर्मलज्ञाना-
पास्तसमस्तमोहमहिमा लीये परे ब्रह्मणि ।। 85 ।।

हे पृथ्वी माता! पवन पिता! अग्नि सखा! जल बंधु! आकाश भाई! मैं आपको सविनय प्रणाम करता हूँ, क्योंकि यह आप ही का प्रताप है कि आज मैं परब्रह्म में लयलीन होने को समर्थ हुआ हूँ किस वास्ते कि आपके संसर्ग से किए हुए पुण्य संचय से उत्पन्न होने वाले दिव्य ज्ञान ने मेरे मन से सारी मोहमाया को दूर कर दिया है कि जिसके कारण से आज दिन मेरी आत्मा को परमात्मा में लीन होने का सौभाग्य मिला है।

On mother Earth, father Air, friend Fire, relative Water, and brother Sky, I herewith bow before you all with folded hands; because, it is to you alone that I am really indebted for the final absolution of my soul, in as much as the joint assistance of all of you has enabled me to perform a lot of virtuous actions resulting in the rise of true spiritual knowledge which, in its turn has destroyed the illusionary influences of the world; and having sanctified the soul of all impurities has thus empowered it to merge into *Parabrahma* (परब्रह्म), the Supreme Being.

---

1. The stanza is same as in the *Śāntiśatakaṃ*, Part IV. (शान्तिशतकम् । 4 परिच्छेदः). It is quoted under भर्तृहरि in the शार्ङ्गधरपद्धति at No. 4095.

यावत्स्वस्थमिदं शरीरमरुजं यावज्जरा दूरतो
यावच्चेन्द्रियशक्तिरप्रतिहता यावत्क्षयो नायुषः।।
आत्मश्रेयसि तावदेव विदुषा कार्यः प्रयत्नो
महान्संदीप्ते भवने तु कूपखननं प्रत्युद्यमः कीदृशः।।86।।

जब तक यह शरीर रोगादि से रहित होकर तंदुरुस्त बना रहे, जब तक वृद्धावस्था न आये और जब तक इंद्रियों की शक्ति ज्यों की त्यों बनी रहे और जब तक आयुष्य का क्षय न हो, विद्वान् मनुष्यों को उचित है कि आत्म-कल्याण के निमित्त यथोचित् प्रयत्न कर लें क्योंकि घर में आग लगने पर कूप खोदने का उद्योग सर्वथा निष्फल है।

A learned man should always try for the good of his soul while (1) he is hale and healthy, (2) his body is quite free from attacks of various diseases, (3) he is not set upon by old age, (4) he is in full unimpaired possession of all his senses, and (5) there is no sign of decline of his life. Of what possible use is the effort of sinking down a well when the house is already in flames ?

---

1. The verse is quoted under भर्तृहरि in the शार्ङ्गधरपद्धति at N[illegible] 679.

Cf.—(*a*) यावत्स्वस्थमिदं देहं यावन्मृत्युश्च दूरतः।
तावदात्महितं कुर्यात्प्राणान्ते किं करिष्यति।। (सुभाषितरत्नभाण्डागारः[illegible]

(*b*) न कूपखननं युक्तं प्रदीप्ते वह्निना गृहे।
चिन्तनीया हि विपदामादावेव प्रतिक्रिया।। (समयोचितपद्यमालिका)

(*c*) यावव्द्याधिविबाधया विधुरतामंगं न संसेवते
यावच्चेन्द्रियपाटवं न हरति क्रूरा जरा राक्षसी।
तावनिष्कलनिश्चलामलपदं कर्मक्षयायाधुना
ध्येयं ध्यानविक्षणैः स्फुटतरं हृत्पद्मसद्मोदरे।।
(पद्मानन्दकविकृतवैराग्यशतकम्)

(*d*) Verses 29 to 32 (चन्द्रप्रभचरितम् । ४ सर्गः).

**नाभ्यस्ता भुवि वादिवृंददमनी विद्याविनीतोचिता
खड्गाग्रैः करिकुंभपीठदलनैर्नाकं न नीतं यशः।।
कान्ताकोमलपल्लवाधररसः पीतो न चंद्रोदये तारुण्यं
गतमेव निष्फलमहो शून्यालये दीपवत्।। 87।।**

न तो हमने प्रतिवादियों का दमन करने वाली और विनय सिखलाने वाली विद्या का अध्ययन किया, न खड्गादि के अग्र भाग से गज पुंगव के कुंभस्थल और पीठ को विदीर्ण करके हमारे सुयश को स्वर्ग पर्यंत पहुँचाया और न हमने चंद्रमा की निर्मल चाँदनी में प्राण-प्यारी के कोमल अधरामृत का पान किया। इसलिए हमारी यौवनावस्था शून्य मंदिर में जलते हुए दीपक की भाँति निरर्थक ही व्यतीत हुई है।

Alas ! (1) we have neither studied the philosophy that enables us to lead a moral and modest life, as well as to stop the mouths of our adversaries and disputants; (2) nor have we raised up our fame of heaven by breaking the globular heads of elephants by means of pointed swords; (3) nor have we drunk in moonlit nights the nectar of our sweetheart's tender lips; we have therefore uselessly wasted away our youth like burning out a lamp in a desolate house !

---

1. Quoted anonymously in the *Subhāṣitāvali* (सुभाषितावलि) at No. 3400, and under भर्तृहरि in the शार्ङ्गधरपद्धति at No. 4151.

Cf.—"He lives long who lives well; and time misspent is not lived but lost." (Fuller)

ज्ञानं सतां मानमदादिनाशनं
केषांचिदेतन्मदमानकारणम्।।
स्थान विविक्तं यमिनां विमुक्तये
कामातुराणामतिकामकारणम्।। 88।।

जो ज्ञान सत्पुरुषों के लिए अभिमानादि नाश करने का हेतु होता है वही ज्ञान अन्यान्य जनों के मदमानादि उत्पन्न करने का कारण बन जाता है; वैसे ही जो एकान्त निर्जन स्थान संयमीजनों को विषयादि से विमुक्त करता है वही स्थान कामीजनों के मनों में कामोद्दीपन का कारण हो जाता है।

The same knowledge which is conducive to extirpate the existence of vain conceit from the minds of the good is also productive of vanity and pride into those of others. A lonely place which frees those who have obtained complete control over the senses from attraction to world likewise becomes the cause of lustful excitement in passionate hearts.

---

1. *Cf.*—मदोनशमनं शास्त्रं खलानां कुरुते मदम्।।

(सूक्तावलिः २३)

2. The poet means to say that every thing is either good or bad according to the tendency of our mind towards virtue or vice.

क्वचिद्वीणावादः क्वचिदपि च हाहेति रुदितं
क्वचिन्नारी रम्या क्वचिदपि जराजर्जरवपुः।।
क्वचिद्विद्वद्गोष्ठी क्वचिदपि सुरामत्तकलहो न
जाने संसारः किममृतमयः किं विषमयः।। 89।।

इस संसार में कहीं तो वीणा का मधुर गान और कहीं हृदय विदारक रुदन श्रवण करने में आता है, कहीं मन हरण करने वाली तरुणी स्त्री और कहीं जरावस्था की झुर्रियों से विकलित शरीर वाली वृद्धा स्त्री देखने में आती है, और इस ही तरह कहीं तो विद्वान् मनुष्यों की गोष्ठी और कहीं मदिरा से मतवालों की कलह सुनी जाती है, इसलिए हम यथार्थता से यह बात निश्चयपूर्वक नहीं कह सकते कि यह जगत् अमृतमय है या विषमय है।

Here we hear the music of a flute, and there the weepings and wailings of afflicted souls; here we see a charming lady, and there an old person with worn out and wrinkled body; and here again we find a concourse of learned men, and there a quarreisome lot of drunkards. We are, therefore, quite unable to say whether the worlds is made up a nectar or poison.

---

1. Quoted anonymously in the *Subhāṣitāvali* (सुभाषितावलि) at No. 2941.

2. *Cf.*—God mingles the bitter with the sweet in this life, to set us seeking another life where there shall be sweet alone. (St. Augustina).

जीर्णा एव मनोरथाः स्वहृदये यातं च तद्यौवनं
हन्ताङ्गेषु गुणाश्च वन्ध्यफलतां याता गुणज्ञैर्विना।।
किं युक्तं सहसाऽभ्युपैति बलवान्कालः कृतान्तोऽक्षमी
ह्याज्ञातं स्मरशासनांघ्रियुगलं मुक्त्वाऽस्ति नान्या गतिः।। 90।।

मन के मनोरथ सारे हृदय ही में जीर्ण हो गए, यौवनावस्था भी चली गई, और खेद का विषय है कि गुण ग्राहियों न होने से हमारे गुण भी सब निष्फल ही रहे कि इतने में ही महाबली और क्षमारहित यमस्वरूपी काल झटपट आ पहुँचा। हाय! अब मुझको ज्ञात हुआ कि कामदेव का शासन करने वाले श्री शिवजी के चरणारविंदों को छोड़कर इस संसार से मुक्त होने का दूसरा उपाय कोई नहीं है।

The aspirations have ceased to exist in the mind, and the delightful period of youth is likewise gone; my qualifications have borne no particular fruit with out the appreciator of their real merits; and the powerful and cruel destroyer of all (death) has suddenly come over me. But alas ! I now understand at the eleventh hour that there is no other means of escape from the miseries and cares of the world than the worship of Śiva's feet !

Taking गुणाः for virtues, some render the 2nd line as follows:—

"The very virtues in our own bodies have become barren without being recognised by others." But virtue is virtue whether recognised or not. Virtuous men have nothing to fear from death. The above rendering is therefore objectionable.

तृषा शुष्यत्यास्ये पिबति सलिलं स्वादुसुरभि
क्षुधार्तः सञ्छालीन्कवलयति शाकादिवलितान्।।
प्रदीप्ते रागाग्नौ सुदृढतरमाश्लिष्यति वधूं प्रतीकारो
व्याधेः सुखमिति विपर्यस्यति जनः।। 91।।

तृषार्त्त होने पर स्वादिष्ट और सुगंधित जलपान, क्षुधातुर होने पर शाकादि सहित चावलों का भोजन और कामाग्नि के हृदय में प्रज्वलित होने पर प्राण-प्यारी का आलिंगन करने वाले मनुष्य कैसे मूर्ख हैं कि उक्त तृषादि व्याधियों के उपरोक्त जलपानादि प्रतीकारों को ही सुख मान लेते हैं।

When a man is thirsty he drinks sweet and fragrant water; when he is hungry he eats delicious preparations of rice, vegetables etc. and when his heart is inflamed with passion he embraces his wife very closely to it. But alas ! he is mistaken to imagine the removal of aforesaid pains of thirst, hunger and love to be a real pleasure.

---

1. Quoted anonymously in the *Subhāṣitāvali* (सुभाषितावलि) at No. 3337, and the *Śārṅgadharaddhati* (शार्ङ्गधरपद्धति) at No. 4148.

2. *Cf.*— दुःखमेवास्ति न सुखं यस्मात्तदुपलक्ष्यते।
दुःखार्तस्य प्रतीकारे सुखसंज्ञा विधीयते।।

(हितोपदेशः । 4 । 92)

स्नात्वा गाङ्गैः पयोभिःशुचिकुसुफलैरर्चयित्वा विभो
त्वां ध्येये ध्यानं नियोज्य क्षितिधरकुहरग्रावपर्यङ्कमूले ।।
आत्मारामोऽफलाशी गुरुवचनरतस्त्वत्प्रसादत्स्मरारे
दुःखान्मोक्षये कदाहं तव चरणरतो ध्यानमार्गैकप्रश्नः ।। 92 ।।

हे प्रभो! गंगा जल से स्नान करके सुंदर पुष्प और फलादिक से आपका पूजन करके पर्वत की कंदरा के शिला रूप पर्यंक पर बैठा हुआ ध्यान करने के योग्य आपके चरणारविंदों में मन लगाकर और आत्मानंद में मग्न होकर स्वर्गादिफल प्राप्त करने की अभिलाषा न करके हे महादेव! श्रीगुरुमहाराज के वचनों का पालन करता हुआ आपके चरण-कमलों का एकान्त भक्त होकर संसार के दुःखों में कब निवृत्त होऊँगा?

Oh Śiva (*lit.*, enemy of love), when will it be that after making my ablutions into the sacred waters of the Ganges I shall be able (1) to worship thee with fresh flowers and fruits, (2) to devotee myself to thy meditation while sitting on the stony couch of a mountain cave, (3) to be content in myself, (4) to think of no ultimate end of my actions, and (5) to act up completely to the instructions of my spiritual preceptor, so as to shake off all wordly cares by abandoning myself to the sole contemplation of thy holy feet.

---

1. *Atmārāma* is one who seeks sprititual knowledge. It also means self pleased or contented.

2. Some read फलाशी instead of अफलाशी and translate-eating fruits.

शय्या शैलशिला गृहं गिरिगुहा वस्त्रं तरूणां त्वचः
सारङ्गाः सुहृदो ननु क्षितिरुहां वृत्तिः फलैः कोमलैः।।
येषां नैर्झरमम्बुपानमुचितं रत्यै च विद्याङ्गना मन्ये
ते परमेश्वराः शिरसि यैर्बद्धा न सेवाञ्जलिः।। 93।।

पर्वत शिला को शय्या, गिरिगुहा को घर, वृक्षों के वल्कल को वस्त्र, हरिणों को सुहृद्गण, वृक्षों के कोमल फलों को भोजन, निर्झर के जल को उचित जलपान और विद्यारूपी स्त्री को विलास हेतु समझकर जो महापुरुष दूसरों के सम्मुख सेवक की भाँति हाथ जोड़कर नहीं खड़े होते वह निसंदेह धन्य हैं।

Those who being satisfied with taking a rocky slab for their bed, a mountain cave for their dwelling, the barks of trees for their clothes, the deer for their friends, the tender fruits of plants for the means of their livelihood, spring water for their proper drink, and the study of knowledge for their wife, have never bowed in supplication before others, ought to be revered by us as the supreme lords.

---

1. *Cf.*—वासो वल्कलमास्तरः किसलयान्योकस्तरूणां तलं
मूलानि क्षतये क्षुधां गिरिनदीतोयं तृषाशान्तये।
क्रीडामुग्धमृगैर्वयांसि सुहृदो नक्तं प्रदीपः शशी
स्वाधीने विभवे तथापि कृपणा याचन्त इत्यद्भुतम्।। 19।।
(शान्तिशतकम् । 2 परिच्छेदः)

सत्यामेव त्रिलोकीसरिति हरशिरश्चुम्बिनीविच्छटायां

सद्वृत्तिं कल्पयन्त्यां वटविटपभवैर्वल्कलैः सत्फलैश्च।।

कोऽयं विद्वान्विपत्तिज्वरजनितरुजाऽतीवदुःखासिकानां वक्त्रं

वीक्ष्येत दुःस्थे यदि हि न बिभृयात्स्वे कुटुम्बेऽनुकम्पाम्।। 94।।

यदि विपत्ति रूप ज्वर के संताप से दुःखित अत्यंत दीनावस्था में विद्यमान होने वाले निज कुटुंब की दया हृदय में कुछ भी न हो तो शिवजी के जटाजूट में निवास करने वाली और वट वृक्ष से उत्पन्न हुए वल्कल और फलों से जीवनोपाय की रचना करने वाली श्रीगंगा जी के विद्यमान रहते ऐसा कौन-सा विद्वान् है कि जो अपनी प्राण-प्यारियों की कष्टावस्था को देखना स्वीकार करें?

भावार्थ।

निज कुटुम्ब का पालन-पोषण ही अनेकानेक कष्टों का कारण है।

If there be not the least compassion for the critical condition of his family writhing under the agonies of painful fever of worldly woes and miseries, no learned man will ever condescend to look on the troubled faces of unhappy women; especially when he sees within his easy reach the banks of the holy Gaṅges flowing down from the head of Śiva, and supplying him with the barks and fruits of the banyan trees, in order to enable him to bear a pious and virtuous life.

Purport—Family affection is generally the root of various troubles to man.

उद्यानेषु विचित्रभोजनविधिस्तीव्रातितीव्रं तपः
कौपिनावरणं सुवस्त्रममितं भिक्षाटनं मण्डनम्।।
आसन्नं मरणं च मंगलसमं यस्यां समुत्पद्यते तां
काशीं परिहृत्य हन्त विबुधैरन्यत्र किं स्थीयते।।95।।

जिस काशी के उद्यान में भ्रमण करते हुए अनेक प्रकार के भोजन करना ही अत्यंत तीव्र तपश्चरण, कौपीन धारण करना ही सुंदर वस्त्राभरण, यथेच्छा भिक्षाटन करना ही भूषण और आसन्न मरण ही मंगलावसर गिने जाते हैं, उस सुखराशि काशी का परित्याग करके पण्डित जन अन्यान्य स्थानों में क्यों निवास करते हैं सो कुछ समझ में नहीं आता।

Why is it that the learned are content to live in places other an holy *Kāśi* (Benares) in whose gardens the subsistence on various kinds of fruits will serve as the hardest penance; where the wearing of a small piece of cloth over the privities is considered as a suit of fine garments ; where the act of asking alms from door to door is thought as an honest and respectable calling ; and where the approach of death is heartily awaited like that of a good and auspicious event.

1. According to the Hindus *Kāśi* (Benares) is one of the seven sacred cities that bring final redemption to the man who may happen to die there. The seven sacred cities thus enumerated :—

अयोध्या मथुरा माया काशी काञ्चिरवन्तिका।
पुरी द्वारावती चैव सप्तैता मोक्षदायिका:।।

नायं ते समयो रहस्यमधुना निद्राति नाथो यदि
स्थित्वा द्रक्ष्यति कुप्यति प्रभुरिति द्वारेषु येषां वचः।।
चेतस्तानपहाय याहि भवनं देवस्य विश्वेशितुर्निर्दौवा-
रिकनिर्दयोक्त्यपरुषं निःसीमशर्मप्रदम्।। 96।।

"हे भिक्षुक! तेरे आने का यह समय ठीक नहीं है क्योंकि इस अवसर पर हमारे स्वामी एकान्त में निद्रा ले रहे हैं और यदि वह तुमको यहाँ ठहरा हुआ देखेंगे तो बहुत क्रोध करेंगे।" इस प्रकार के वचन जिन धनाढ्य पुरुषों के द्वार पर सुनने में आते हैं उनका परित्याग करके हे चित्त! तू उस विश्वेश्वर के मंदिर में क्यों नहीं जाता कि, जहाँ पर पूर्वोक्त प्रकार के कटुवचन बोलने वाले द्वारपाल नहीं रहते और जहाँ तुझ को अपार सुख का लाभ करना सर्वथा सुलभ है।

Forsaking the guarded doors of the rich where a mendicant is threatened by the watch, and told, "this is not a proper time for thee ; the master of the house is now asleep ; he will be surely angry if he sees thee here," thou must go straight to the temple of *Viśveśvara* (विश्वेश्वर), the lord of the universe, whose entrance is not guarded by sentries where thou art never to receive a harsh treatment, and which is sure to give thee the highest amount of happiness and shelter !

---

1. It requires no mention that the palace gates of the rich and noble are fast closed upon beggars who are treated very roughly by the guards.

प्रियसखि विपद्दण्डव्रातप्रतापपरम्परातिप-
रिचपले चिन्ताचक्रे निधाय विधिः खलः।।
मृदमिव बलात्पिण्डीकृत्य प्रगल्भकुलालवद्भ्रम-
यति मनो नो जानीमः किमत्र विधास्यति।। 97।।

हे प्यारी सखी! यह दुष्ट विधाता चतुर कुम्हार की भाँति माटी के समान इस मन को बलपूर्वक पिण्डी भूत करके विपत्ति रूप दण्ड समूह के निरंतर परिभ्रमण से चंचल चिंता चक्र को घुमाता हुआ न मालूम अब क्या घटना दिखलायेगा?

Dear friend, we do not really know what is now to be done by cruel fate who, like a clever potter, forcibly pressing the mind of man as if it were a lump of clay, makes it turn round and round on the wheel of anxities by the continued motion of the rod of a series of miseries calamities !

---

1. Quoted under *Vijjakā* (विज्जका) in the *Śārṅga-dharapaddhati* at No. 451 (शार्ङ्गधरपद्धति । 451), and anonymously in the *Subhāṣitāvali* (सुभाषितावलि) at No. 3137.

2. The word खल which is here rendered into cruel literally means wicked.

महेश्वरे वा जगतामधीश्वरे
जनार्दने वा जगदन्तरात्मनि।।
तयोर्न भेदप्रतिपत्तिरस्ति मे
तथाऽपि भक्तिस्तरुणेन्दुशेखरे।। 98।।

जगत् के अधीश्वर श्रीमहेश्वर में और जगद्व्यापक श्रीजनार्दन में किसी प्रकार का भेद मेरी दृष्टि में नहीं आता, तथापि मैं यह नहीं जानता कि, चंद्रशेखर शिवजी की भक्ति में ही मेरा चित्त क्योंकर प्रवृत्त होता है?

Although I am quite unable to make out any difference between Śiva, the lord of the universe, and Viṣṇu, the omnipresent god of the entire creation; yet, my mind is naturally led to the devotion of Śiva whose forehead is adorned with a crescent moon.

---

1. The word *Jagadantarātmā* जगदन्तरात्मा literally means the soul of universe. Bhartṛhari here says that notwithstanding his incompetency to discern any difference between Viṣṇu and Śiva his mind is naturally prone to worship Śiva. Properly speaking Viṣṇu is generally worshipped by worldly men, whereas those who renounce the world adore Śiva. The Author has himself alluded to this fact in a previous stanza.

रे कन्दर्प करं कदर्थयसि किं कोदण्डटङ्कारितै रे रे
कोकिल कोमलैः कलरवैः किं त्वं वृथा जल्पसि।।
मुग्धे स्निग्धविदग्धमुग्धमधुरैर्लोलैः कटाक्षैरलं
चेतश्चुम्बितचन्द्रचूडचरणध्यानामृतं वर्तते।। 99।।

हे कामदेव! बारंबार धनुष्टंकार करके तू अपने हाथ को वृथा परिश्रम क्यों दे रहा है? हे कोकिल! निरंतर सुंदर कलरव से तू वृथा बकवाद क्यों कर रहा है? और हे मुग्धांगना! अनुरागयुक्त, चतुर, सुंदर, मधुर और चंचल कटाक्षों से तू अपने नेत्रों को व्यर्थ खेद क्यों दे रही है? क्योंकि हमारा मन तो अब श्रीचंद्रशेखर शिवजी के चरणारविंदों के ध्यानामृत का पान करने में मगन है।

Why art thou, oh god of love, uselessly tiring thy hand with continued twangs of thy powerful bow? Whey art thou, oh *Kokila* (कोकिल) trying in vain to disturb the peace of my mind with sweet melodious notes of thy voice? Whey dost thou, oh young lady, fruitlessly venture to pierce the heart with thy lovely cleaver, natural, sweet, and flickering glances? You should better cease from your vain endeavours ; for, now I am earnestly engaged in the nectareous meditation of the feet of Śiva whose head is adorned with moon.

1. Quoted under भर्तृहरि in the शार्ङ्गधरपद्धति at No. 4096.

2. *Cf.*—रे कन्दर्थ किमाततत्यमधुना धत्से धनुस्त्वं मुधा
किं भ्रूलास्यकलासु पक्ष्मलदृशः प्रागल्भ्यमभ्यस्यथ।
वैराग्याम्बुजिनीप्रबोधनपटुः प्रध्वस्तदोषाकरः
खेलत्येष विवेकचण्डकिरणः कस्त्वादृशामुत्सवः।।83।।
(पद्मानन्दकविकृतवैराग्यशतकम्)

कौपीन शतखण्डजर्जरतरं कन्था पुनस्तादृशी
निश्चितं सुखसाध्यभैक्ष्यमशनं शय्या श्मशाने वने।।
मित्रामित्रसमानताऽतिविमला चिन्ताऽथ शून्यालये
ध्वस्ताशेषमदप्रमादमुदितो योगी चिरं तिष्ठति।। 100।।

शतशः खण्ड से जर्जरित कौपीन और ऐसी ही कंथा, चिंता- रहित और सुखसाध्य भिक्षा के भोजन, श्मशान अथवा वन का शयन, मित्र और शत्रु में समभाव और निर्जन स्थान में परमात्मा के निर्मल ध्यान के प्रभाव से विनष्ट हुए मद मोहादि के कारण प्रसन्न हुआ योगी निस्संदेह सुखी है।

The hermit or ascetic who wears pieces of threadbare rags over his privities and body, lives a careless life upon the alms of others procured with ease, sleeps in the midst of a cemetery (crematorium) or a forest, looks on his friends and foes with equal regard, abandons himself to the pure meditation of the Deity in a solitary place, and thus cheers himself with the thought of having destroyed all traces of vain conceit and arrogance, undoubtedly leads the happiest life.

---

1. *Cf.*—वेदान्तवाक्येषु सदा रमन्तो भिक्षान्नमात्रेण च तुष्टिमन्तः।
विशोकमन्तःकरणे रमन्तः कौपीनवन्तः खलु भाग्यवन्तः।। 1।।
(यतिपंचकम्)

भोगा भंगुरवृत्तयो बहुविधास्तैरेव चायं भवस्त-
त्कस्यैव कृते परिभ्रमत रे लोकाः कृतं चेष्टितैः।।
आशापाशशतोपशान्तिविशदं चेतः समाधीयतां
कामोच्छित्तिवशे स्वधामनि यदि श्रद्धेयमस्मद्वचः।। 101।।

नाना प्रकार के भोग सब नाशवान् हैं और वही भोगादिक संसार के आदि कारण हैं। इसलिए हे मनुष्यो! तुम किस प्रयोजन से इनके लिए भटक रहे हो सो कुछ समझ में नहीं आता। यदि हमारे कथन पर विश्वास करो तो अनेकानेक आशा पाश की शांति से निर्मल हुए चित्त को काम का नाश करने वाली स्वात्मप्रकाश आत्मा में निश्चल भाव से लगाओ।

The different kinds of sensual enjoyments are all perishable, but it is they that constitute the world *i.e.,* cause our repeated births and deaths on this globe. Why, then, are people trying their utmost to run after them? Therefore, if you believe our words, we would advise you to devote yourself to a concentrated meditation of the self-luminous ego that destroys the manifold snares of desires and aspirations, and entirely extirpates the very existence of passion from your hearts.

---

1. The poet here advises people to give up the pursuit of worldly pleasures and let their souls be free from the bonds of desires and enter into the meditation of self.

धन्यानां गिरिकन्दरे निवसतां ज्योतिः परं ध्यायता-
मानन्दाश्रुजलं पिबन्ति शकुना निःशङ्कमङ्के स्थिताः।।
अस्माकं तु मनोरथोपरचितप्रासादवापीतटक्रीडा-
काननकेलिकौतुकजुषामायुः परं क्षीयते।। 102।।

पर्वतकंदरा में निवास करने वाले और परब्रह्म परमात्मा का ध्यान करने वाले जिन महानुभावों के आनंद के अश्रुओं को उनकी गोद में बैठे हुए पक्षीगण निर्भय होकर पान करते हैं वास्तव में उन ही पुण्यात्माओं का जन्म इस संसार में सफल है, क्योंकि मनमाने भवन, बावड़ी और उपवन में केलि करने की अभिलाषा करने वाले हमारे समान अन्यान्य मनुष्यों की आयुष्य तो वृथा ही क्षीण होती चली जाती है।

Blessed are they whose tears of joy are eagerly drunk by birds, fearlessly lying upon their laps, while living in caves of mountains they are meditating upon the Supreme Light! But, we, on the contrary, are uselessly passing away our days in building airy castles (*lit.* in imaginary enjoyments of whiling away our time in the pleasant abode of luxurious parks either situated in palatial mansions or on the banks of ideal tanks).

---

1. The verse is same as ślōka 5 in the *Śāntisatakaṃ* Part 1. (शान्तिशतकम् । 1 परिच्छेदः). It is ascribed to भर्तृहरि in the शार्ङ्गधरपद्धति at No. 4155.

आघ्रातं मरणेन जन्म जरया विद्युच्चलं यौवनं
सन्तोषो धनलिप्सया शमसुखं प्रौढाङ्गनाविभ्रमैः।।
लोकैर्मत्सरिभिर्गुणा वनभुवो व्यालैर्नृपा दुर्जनै-
रस्थैर्येण विभूतिरप्यपहृता ग्रस्तं न किं केन वा।। 103।।

जिस संसार में जन्म के पीछे मरण, बिजली के समान चंचल यौवन के पीछे वृद्धावस्था, संतोष के पीछे धनेच्छा, शांति सुख के पीछे तरुणी स्त्रियों के विलास, गुणों के पीछे दुष्टजन, वनभूमि के पीछे सर्प, राजाओं के पीछे दुर्जन, ऐश्वर्य के पीछे अस्थिरता जैसे शत्रु लगे हुए हैं वहाँ कोई भी ऐसा पदार्थ दृष्टि में नहीं आता कि, जो किसी प्रकार के शत्रु के आक्रमण से सर्वथा निर्भय हो।

Our existence is threatened by death and fleeting youth (*lit.* as fleeing as lighting) by old age; contentment is destroyed by covetousness after riches ; the happiness of tranquility is disturbed by graceful sports of clever and youthful women ; good merits are subject to the calumnies of the envious ; forests are infested by snakes ; kings are ruined by wicked courtiers ; and prosperity is tarnished by unsteadiness. What is there in this world which is not overpowered by another?

---

1. *Cf.*—(*a*) आक्रान्तं पिशुनैनरिन्द्रभवनं विद्यागृहं मत्सरै-
रायासैर्द्रविणं कुलं कुतनयैर्नानावियोगैः सुखम्।
साधुत्वं खलवञ्चनापरिभवैश्चिन्तासहस्रैर्मन-
स्तन्नास्त्येव न यत्सरोषकलुषं निर्दोषं एकः शमः।।
(चतुर्वर्गसंग्रहः 14 16)

(*b*) For the idea of the first line, compare—
प्रहतं भरणेन जीवितं जरसा यौवनमेव पश्यति।। 69।।
(चन्द्रप्रभचरितम् । सर्गः)

आधिव्याधिशतैर्जनस्य विविधैरारोग्यमुन्मूल्यते
लक्ष्मीर्यत्र पतन्ति तत्र विवृतद्वारा इव व्यापदः।।
जातं जातमवश्यमाशु विवशं मृत्यु करोत्यसात्मसात्त्किं
नाम निरंकुशेन विधिना यन्निर्मितं सुस्थितम्।। 104।।

अनेक प्रकार की मानसिक और शारीरिक आधिव्याधियों से आरोग्य नाश हो जाता है, जहाँ लक्ष्मी का आगमन होता है वहां विपत्ति का द्वार भी खुल जाता है और जन्म लेने वाले मात्र पदार्थों को मृत्यु भी वशीभूत कर लेता है। इसलिए हम निःशंक होकर कह सकते हैं कि निरंकुश विधाता ने ऐसा कोई भी पदार्थ नहीं बनाया जिसकी दशा का परिवर्तन कदापि न होता हो।

We see that health is undermined by several diseases of mind and body, prosperity is attended with a host of calamities, and birth is invariably followed by death. We do not therefore know what is made by the creator to be entirely free from change and decay in this world ?

---

1. *Cf.*—(a) Who is safe,
In this tumultuous sphere of strife and sorrow?
(Ferdausi's Shāh Nāmeh)

(*b*) There'e no calamity in life,
Our being is with changes rife,
What feebler than man's breath?
Our life is ever doubtful here,
One thing alone is plain and clear
And that one thing is—death
(Kovaleuski, Great Thoughts).

(*c*) जन्ममृत्युजराव्याधिवेदनाभिरभिद्रुतम्।
संसारमिदमत्यन्तमसारं त्यजतः सुखम्।। (हितोपदेशः 4।91)

कृच्छ्रेणामेध्यमध्ये नियमिततनुभिः स्थीयते गर्भवासे
कान्ताविश्लेषदुःखव्यतिकरविषमे यौवने विप्रयोगः।।
नारिणामप्यवज्ञाविलसितवदनो वृद्धभावोऽप्यसाधुः संसारे
रे मनुष्या वदत यदि सुखं स्वल्पमप्यस्ति किंचित्।। 105।।

जब गर्भ में निवास करते हैं तो विण्मूत्रादियुक्त अपवित्र स्थान में अपने अंग को संकुचित करके अत्यंत कष्ट के साथ रहना पड़ता है, यौवन समय में कान्ता का वियोगरूपी दुःसह दुःख सहना पड़ता है और वृद्धावस्था में सुंदरियों की अवज्ञा से मन मलीन होना पड़ता है। इसलिए हे मनुष्यो! यदि इस संसार में थोड़ा-सा सुख भी कहीं हो तो बताओ।

While yet unborn man remains imprisoned with contracted limbs in the narrow and impious womb of his mother; in youth, he is subjected to excessive grief resulting from the sad bereavement of his beloved wife; whereas, in old age, he is doomed to wear a sorrowful appearance caused by the dishonourable treatment he meets at the hands of (beautiful young) women. We would, therefore, beg to hear from men where in this world we can find the smallest particle of happiness and pleasures ?

---

1. *Cf.*—I find in life that suffering succeeds to suffering and disappointment to disappointment, as wave to wave." (Lord Lytton's Alice or The Mysteries Bk. V. Ch. I).

2. For the idea of the first line, *Cf.*—

मातृगुरूदरदर्यां कफमूत्रपुरीषपूर्णायाम्।
जठराग्निर्ज्वालाभिर्नवमासं पच्यते जन्तुः।। 9।। (प्रबोधसुधाकरः)

3. For the point of the stanza, *Cf.*—

Never shall the life,
Of mortal man be passed uncharged with ills.
(The Plays of Aeschylus p. 213)

आयुर्वर्षशतं नृणां परिमितं रात्रौ तदर्द्धं गतं
तस्यार्द्धस्य परस्य चार्द्धमपरं बालत्ववृद्धत्वयोः ।।
शेषं व्याधिवियोदुःखसहितं सेवादिभिर्नीयते जीवे
वारितरङ्गचञ्चलतरे सौख्यं कुतः प्राणिनाम् ।। 106 ।।

विधाता ने मनुष्य की आयुष्य 100 वर्ष की नियत की है जिसका आधा भाग तो रात्रि में व्यतीत हो जाता है और शेष आधे के आधे 25 वर्ष बाल्य और वृद्धावस्था के ग्रास बना जाते हैं और बाकी के 25 वर्ष मनुष्यों को अनेक व्याधि और वियोग के दुःख सहित सेवादि में व्यतीत करने पड़ते हैं इसलिए हम कह सकते हैं कि जलतरंग के समान चञ्चल इस जीवन में सुख का लेशमात्र भी कहीं नहीं है।

The term of man's existence is limited to hundred years ; half of it is passed in sleep (*lit.* nights), and half of what remains is taken up by childhood and old age; while the rest is spent by him in disgraceful occupations like that of serving others, not altogether unmixed with the bitter consequences of diseases, separations, and misfortunes. Where, then is the least possible trace of happiness in man's life which is as unsteady as waves of water ?

---

1. *Cf.*—What a world !

   No place of rest for man! Fix not thy heart
   Vain mortal! on this tenement of life,
   On earthly pleasures!

   (Firdausi's Shāh Nāmeh)

ब्रह्मज्ञानविवेकिनोऽमलधियः कुर्वन्त्यहो दुष्करं
यन्मुञ्चन्त्युपभोगकाञ्चकधनान्येकान्ततो निःस्पृहाः।।
न प्राप्तानि पुरा न संप्रति न च प्राप्तौ दृढप्रत्ययो
वाञ्छामात्रपरिग्रहाण्यपि परं त्यक्तुं न शक्ता वयम्।। 107।।

विमल बुद्धि वाले ब्रह्मज्ञानी कैसा दुष्कर कर्म करते हैं कि जो (स्त्री और धनादिक) संसारिक भोग विलास से बिल्कुल निस्पृह हो बैठते हैं, क्योंकि हम तो भूत और वर्तमान काल में अप्राप्त और भविष्यत की प्राप्ति की दृढ निश्चय न होने वाले इच्छा मात्र परिग्रह का त्याग भी कदापि नहीं कर सकते!

The task undertaken by those that have attained to real spiritual knowledge is undoubtedly the most difficult one, as they entirely forsake the actual enjoyments of sensual pleasures and wealth, and become quite indifferent to their attractions ; but we, on the contrary, who have neither enjoyed them in the past, nor possess them at present, nor can say with any certainty of getting them in the coming future, are even unable to give up this nominal possession which exists only in our fond wishes.

---

1. The verse is same as ślōka 4 in the *Śāntiśatakaṃ* Part 1. (शान्तिशतकम् । 1 परिच्छेदः).

2. The idea of the ślōka seems to be this :—To give up actual pleasures may be somewhat difficult ; but to forsake what we have not should not cause the least difficulty to man.

व्याघ्रीव तिष्ठति जरा परितर्जयन्ती
रोगाश्च शत्रव इव प्रहरन्ति देहम्।।
आयुः परिस्रवति भिन्नघटादिवाम्भो
लोकस्तथाऽप्यहितमाचरतीति चित्रम्।। 108।।

वृद्धावस्था व्याघ्री के समान तर्जना करती हुई खड़ी रहती है, रोग शत्रुओं की भाँति देह पर प्रहार करते रहते हैं, और फूटे घड़े से जल के निकलते रहने के सदृश आयुष्य भी प्रतिदिन क्षीण होती चली जाती है, परन्तु तिस पर भी ये मनुष्य दुष्कर्म करने से नहीं डरते यह बड़े ही आश्चर्य की बात है।

Old age is always threatening like a tigress, diseasess are striking the body like its deadly enemies, and life is leaking out like water from a broken jar ; but strange to say that men are still regardless of doing good !

---

1. Quoted under भर्तृहरि in the शार्ङ्गधरपद्धति at No. 4093.

2. *Cf.*—(*a*) चला विभूतिः क्षणभङ्गि यौवनं
कृतान्तदन्तान्तर्वर्ति जीवितम्।
तथाप्यवज्ञा परलोकसाधने
नृणामहो विस्मयकारि चेष्टितम्।।

(सुभाषितावलिः)

(*b*) Why do mankind upon this fleeing world
Place their affections, wickendness alone
Is nourished into freshness ; sounds of death, too,
Are ever on the gate to wear out life.

(Firdausi's Shāh Nāmeh)

सदा योगाभ्यासव्यसनवशयोरात्ममनसोर-
विच्छन्ना मैत्री स्फुरति कृतिनस्तस्य किमुतैः।।
प्रियाणामालापैरधरमधुभिर्वक्त्रकमलैः सनिः-
श्वासामोदैः सकुचकलशाश्लेषसुरतैः।। 109।।

जिन पुण्यवान् पुरुषों की आत्मा और मन योगाभ्यास के व्यसन में लवलीन हो जाते हैं, और योगाभ्यास से जिनकी निरंतर मैत्री हो जाती है, उनको प्राण-प्यारी सुंदरियों के सम्भाषण, अधरामृत, सुगन्धित, निःश्वाससहित वदन कमल, कुचकलश के आलिङ्गनयुक्त मैथुन आदि से कुछ भी प्रयोजन नहीं रहता।

The fortunate being who subjects himself to the practice of mental abstraction, and devotes his soul and mind to everlasing contemplation of God, has nothing to fear from (or to do with) the charming conversations of lovely women, the ambrosial lips, the moonlike faces, the fragrant breaths, and the sensual embraces of their heaving breasts.

---

1. The word अविछिन्ना literally means unbroken.

2. It is not true that an ascetic has nothing to do with women and their sports?

जातः कूर्मः स एकः पृथुभुवनभरायार्पितं येन पृष्ठं
श्लाघ्यं जन्म ध्रुवस्य भ्रमति नियमितं यत्र तेजस्विचक्रम्।।
संजातव्यर्थपक्षाः परहितकरणे नोपरिष्टान्न चाधो ब्रह्मण्डो-
दुम्बरान्तर्मशकवदपरे प्राणिनो जातनष्टाः।। 110।।

इस संसार में एक उस प्रसिद्ध कूर्म (कूर्मावतार) का जन्म ही सफल समझना चाहिए कि जिसने इस विशाल पृथ्वी का भार धारण करने के निमित्त अपनी पीठ को समर्पण किया है, और इस ही भाँति उन ध्रुवजी का जन्म भी अत्यंत प्रशंसनीय है, कि जिनको मध्य में लेकर सप्तर्षियों का ज्योतिमण्डल भ्रमण करता है। परन्तु परोपकार करने में असमर्थ मनुष्यों का जन्म तो इस ब्रह्माण्ड में गूलर के मध्यवर्ती मच्छरों के समान सर्वथा निष्फल है कि वे सपक्ष होकर भी कुछ नहीं कर सकते।

The birth of that great Tortoise *Kūrma* (कूर्म) is indeed to be hailed with loud acclamation ; for, it is He who has voluntarily offered His back for the support of this heavy and extensive Earth ; similarly, the birth of *Dhruva* (ध्रुव or the pole star) is also a matter of memorable record ; for it is he who remains fixed in the midst of the stellar world incessantly revolving around him. All other creatures are daily born and dead within the interior of this universe without the least notice being ever taken of them ; because they pay very little heed in affording the slightest help to their fellow beings, just like the mosquitoes which though possessing wings are unable to fly a great distance either upwards or downwards, and thus and their miserable lives within the Gūlara in which they are born.

1. Quoted anonymously in the *Subhāṣitāvali* at No. 1033, and under *Bhartṛhari* in the *Śārṅgadharapaddhati* at No. 4154.

उन्मीलत्त्रिवलीतरङ्गवलया प्रोत्तुङ्गपीनस्तनद्वंद्वे-
नोद्यतचक्रवाकमिथुना वक्त्राम्बुजोद्भासिनी।।
कान्ताकारधरा नदीयमभितः क्रूराशया नेष्यते
संसारार्णवमज्जनं यदि ततो दूरेण संत्यज्यताम्।। 111।।

हे मनुष्यो! यदि तुम संसार समुद्र में डूबने की अभिलाषा नहीं रखते हो तो इस चारों तरफ से घात करने वाली कान्तारूपी नदी का दूर ही से परित्याग करो, कि जहाँ पर प्रकाशमान उदरवर्ती त्रिवली की तरंग हिलोरे ले रही हैं, बड़े मोटे और ऊँचे कुच युगल रूप चक्रवाक मिथुन विराजमान हैं, और मुखरूपी कमल पूर्णरूप से खिल रहे हैं।

If you do not wish to be drowned into the worldly ocean, you should carefully avoid from a distance the woman-stream that is dreadfully cruel on all sides, having the three curved lines of hair on the . . . . .for its mass of rolling waves, the high and spacious breasts for a pair of *Cakravāka* (चक्रवाक) birds, and the beautiful face for a blooming lotus on its banks.

---

1. *Cf.*—(*a*) तरङ्गभ्रूभंगा क्षुभितविहगश्रेणिरशना
विकर्षन्ती फेनं वसनमिवं संरम्भशिथिलम्।
यथाविद्धं याति स्खलितमभिसन्धाय बहुशो
नदीरूपेणेऽयं ध्रुवमसहनासौ परिणता।।

(ध्वन्यालोके:)

(*b*) रूपजला चलनयना नाभ्यावर्ता कचावलिभुजंगा।
मज्जन्ति यत्र सन्तः सेथं तरुणी तरंगिणी विषमा।।

(रसगंगाधर:)

इह हि मधुरगीतं नृत्यमेतद्रसोऽयं
स्फुरति परिमलोऽयं स्पर्श एष स्तनानाम्।
इति हतपरमार्थैरिन्द्रियैर्भ्राम्यमाणः स्वहित-
करणधूर्तैः पंचभिर्वञ्चितोऽस्मि।। 112।।

"यहाँ पर सुनने को मधुर गान, यहाँ पर देखने को नृत्य, यहाँ पर स्वाद लेने को मिष्ट रस, यहाँ पर सूँघने पर सुगन्ध और यहाँ पर स्पर्श करने को स्तन विद्यमान हैं।" इस प्रकार गोते खाता हुआ मैं निजहित साधन से वंचित करने वाली और परमार्थ नाश करने वाली पंचेन्द्रियों से रात-दिन धोखा खा रहा हूँ।

Here is sweet voice to hear, graceful dance to see, ambrosial juice to taste, fragrant scent to smell, and lovely breasts to touch ; being thus deceived by my fine senses which are very clever to secure their own ends, I am wandering uselessly about the world (without devoting the least attention to my spiritual improvement which is to help me a great deal in obtaining salvation).

---

1. The word इन्द्रिय *Indriya* is here used for those bodily organs which are the medium of our knowledge of the exterior world. These organs of perception are five in number; *viz.*, senses of hearing, sight, taste, smell and feeling.

गात्रं संकुचितं गतिर्विगलिता भ्रष्टा च दन्ताव-
लिर्दृष्टिर्नश्यति वर्धते बधिरता वक्त्रं च लालायते।।
वाक्यं नाद्रियते च बान्धवजनो भार्या न शुश्रूषते हा कष्टं
पुरुषस्य जीर्णवयसः पुत्रोऽप्यमित्रायते।। 113।।

अहो यह बड़े कष्ट की बात है कि, वृद्ध हो जाने पर मनुष्य की कैसी शोचनीय दशा हो जाती है, शरीर में तो झुर्रियाँ पड़ जाती हैं, गमनशक्ति नष्ट हो जाती है, दन्त पंक्ति भ्रष्ट हो जाती है, दृष्टि नष्ट हो जाती है, बधिरता बढ़ने लगती है, मुख से लार बहने लगती है, भाई-बन्धु वचनों का आदर करने से संकोच करते हैं, भार्या सेवा करने से मुँह मोड़ती है और विशेष क्या कहा जाये पुत्र भी शत्रु का-सा आचरण करने को तत्पर हो जाता है।

Alas ! what a distress is old age to man : his body is disfigured with wrinkles, his steps become unsteady, his rows of teeth are broken, his sight is lost, his deafness is increased, his mouth is full of saliva, his words are not respected by his relatives, his wife is disobedient, and his very son is even assuming the part of a foe !

---

1. Quoted anonymously in the *Śārṅgadharapaddhati* (शार्ङ्गधरपद्धति) at No. 4161. It also stands in the *Pañcatantra* IV. 78 (पंचतन्त्रम् । 4 तन्त्रम् । 78).

क्षणं बालो भूत्वा क्षणमपि युवा कामरसिकः
क्षणं वित्तैर्हीनः क्षणमपि च सम्पूर्णविभवः।।
जराजीर्णैरङ्गैर्नट इव वलीमण्डिततनुर्नरः
संसारान्ते विशति यमधानीजवनिकाम्।। 114।।

कभी तो बालक, कभी कामदेव के रस में भीगा हुआ जवान, कभी दरिद्री, कभी पूर्ण सम्पत्तिवान् और कभी बूढ़े नट के समान झुर्री पड़े हुए शरीर से यह मनुष्य नाना प्रकार के दृश्य दिखलाता हुआ अंत में यमपुरी रूप परदे में प्रवेश कर जाता है।

Sometimes playing like a dramatic actor the part of a child, and to others that of a passionate youth; sometimes performing the part of a poor, and at others that of a man of enormous wealth and prosperity ; a human being at last disappears behind the curtain of death, vanishing altogether from the worldly stage, with worn out body all full of wrinkles through the baneful effects of age.

---

1. Quoted under *Bhartṛhari* (भर्तृहरि) in the *Subhāṣitāvali* (सुभाषितावलि) at No 3319, and the *Śārṅgadharapaddhati* (शार्ङ्गधरपद्धति । 4094) *Cf.*—(*a*) In fine, old age may be considered as last scene in the great drama of life. (Cicero.) (*b*) The world itself is an ingenious juggler—very moment playing some novel trick ; exalting one in pomp and splendour ; crushing down another as if in sport,—and death the end of all! (Firdausi's Shāh Nāmeh) (*c*) All the world's a stage. And all the men and women merely players : They have their exits and entrances : And one man in time plays many parts. (Shakespeare's As You Like It. II.). (*d*) Here is the babe in his leading strings, Here is the boy at play; Here is the passsionate youth with wings, Like a bird's on a stormy day . . . . .(Schilelr's The Puppet Show of Life).

प्रशान्तशास्त्रार्थविचारचापलं
निवृत्तनानारसकाव्यकौतुकम्।।
निरस्तनिःशेषविकल्पविप्लवं
प्रपत्तुमन्विच्छति शूलिनं मनः।। 115।।

नानाविध शास्त्रार्थ के विचार की चञ्चलता को छोड़, अनेक सरस काव्य कथाओं से निवृत्त होकर और सब प्रकार के कुतर्क रूप प्रपंच का त्याग करे अब यह मन श्री शिव जी की शरण लेने की अभिलाषा कर रहा है।

The mind that has forsaken its former cleverness in expounding the various *Śāstraic* texts, that has lost all interest in perusing a variety of *Kāvyas* (काव्य; or high class literautre), and that has washed off every perceptible trace of a series of doubtful septical reasonings, is now anxiously seeking its last refuge in the concentrated devotion for Śiva.

1. Quoted anonymously in the *Subhāṣitāvali* (सुभाषितावलि) at No. 3405.

भोगे रोगभयं कुले च्युतिभयं वित्ते नृपालाद्भयं
मौने दैन्यभयं बले रिपुभयं रूपे जराया भयम्।।
शास्त्रे वादभयं गुणे खलभयं काये कृतान्ताद्भयं
सर्वं वस्तु भयान्वितं भुवि नृणां वैराग्यमेवाभयम्।। 116।।

भोग विलास में रोगादि उत्पन्न होने का, सत्कुल में वंश परम्परा के टूटने का, द्रव्य में राजा का, मौन धारण में दीनता का, पराक्रम में शत्रु का, सुंदरता में जरा का, शास्त्र में विवाद का, गुण में दुर्जन का और काया में मृत्यु का भय सर्वदा बना रहता है। इसलिए हम कहते हैं कि इस पृथ्वी तल पर और सब पदार्थ तो भययुक्त हैं परन्तु एक वैराग्य ही ऐसा है कि जो सब प्रकार के भय से सर्वथा निर्भय है।

Enjoyments is subject to diseases, respectable family to degradation, and wealth to the fear of being forcibly taken away by kings ; verbal silence is prone to be misconstrued into penury, and physical valour is always afraid of confronting a powerful foe ; beauty is subject to old age, learning to controversy, body to death, and good qualities to the faultfinding spirit of evil persons. Thus, we see that everythings else in this world is indeed subject to danger and fear, but *Vairāgya* (वैराग्य) or asceticism alone is entirely free from any sort of fear and apprehension.

---

1. This stanza is also found in the Aṣṭaratna. The following verse which differs very slightly from our text stands in the *Caturvargasaṅgaraha* (चतुर्वर्गसग्रह) of Kṣemendra (क्षेमेन्द्रः):—

भोगे रोगभयं सुख क्षयभयं वित्तेऽग्निभूभृद्भयं
दास्ये स्वामिभयं गुणं खलभयं वंशे कुयोषिद्भयम्।
माने म्लानिभयं जये रिपुभयं काये कृतान्ताद्भयम्।
सर्वं नाम भवे भवेद्भयमहो वैराग्यमेवाऽभयम्।।

VARIANTS

2. (b) वि for प्र Sb.; (d) षु for सु N.

3. (b) ष for श Sb.

4. (d) संप्राप्तश्च for प्राप्तः काण N.

5. (a) देशे भ्रान्त for भ्रान्तं देश Sb., में for मे Sb., ल for लं Sb.; (b) मुत्कण्ठापरिखेदितेन मनसा नीतंवृथायौवनम् for (इ) Sb.; (c) त्यक्त्कामानकुलानुरूपमुचितं सेवाकृतानिष्फला for (c) Sb., (d) तृष्णे ब्रूहि किमन्य दिच्छसि परं तत्रापि सज्जावयम् for (d) Sb.

6. (c) भप्रणिहित for भः प्रहसित Sb.

7. (d) मो for मा Ks.

8. (a) र्णांशुका for र्णाम्बरा Sb., (b) द्भिर्विधुरैः क्षुधार्तविघुरां पश्येत्र for द्भिः क्षुधितै र्निरन्नविघुरा दृश्येत Sb., ीम् for नी SB.

9. (c) ष्टयो for ष्ट्यु Sb.

10. (a) यज्ञा for हिंसा Śś.

12. Aucaitya reads तपो न तप्तं वयमेव तप्ता भोगा न भुक्ता वयमेवभुक्ताः। जरा न जीर्णा वयमेव जीर्णा स्तृणा न याता वयमेव याताः।।

13. (d) परानति परै for यदेव्वमुनिभि Nami; रुझितम् for वञ्चितम् Sb.

14. (b) ज्नि for ङ्कि Sb.

20. (b) न for स Sp.

22. (a) र for र्घ Sb.

23. (c) स्त्य for प्या Sb.

29. (a) च्छं for त्थं Sb.; (b) तं for यं Sb.

32. (a) चि for दि Sb.

36. (a) गतः for महान् Sb.; (b) विदग्ध for ऽपिराज Sb. Śp.

37. (c) पतना for पतनाद् Śp.;

38. (a) कः for के Kś.; (c) नेयो for चेगौ Kś., तो for दो Kś.

40. (a) and (b) कुसुमशयने या दृषदिवा for बलवति रिपौ वा सुहृदि वा, and vice versa Sb. Kp. Ud; (c) न्ति for न्तु Sb. T. Kp. Ud. Aucaitya; (d) क for स Sb. क्वचित् for सदा Kp. Ud. Kś. Aucaitya, ल for ज Sb. Aucaitya, जिन जिन जिनेति for शिव शिव शिवेति Kś.

44. (a) तावन् for तादृङ् Sp.

49. (b) षैः for षः Sb.; (c) हि for तु Śp., च for Rasa.

54 (d) स्वदेशे for सधन्यो Śp.

60. (a) मधुरं for कवयः Sb.; योर्गीतिनादाः for तो दाक्षिणात्याः ; Sb. (c); अस्त्येवंचेत् for यद्यस्त्येवं Sb.

61. (c) वधू for धन Sb.

64. (c) नल for ङ्कुर Sb.

70. (c) संसारोन्मू for कर्मनिर्मू Sb.

71. (a) जुष for दुधा Sb.; (c) तापि for मानि Sb., प्रीणि for मानि Kp. Ud.

74. (b) वाञ्छसि सदा यदि चेतनास्ति for चिंतय किमेभि रसद्विकल्पैः Sb.

75. (c) न्त्वा for न्त्या Sb., देश मपरं हि तदा for जातु विमलं कथ मा Sb.; (d) नब्रह्मा संस्पृश for तद्ब्रह्मनस्मर Sb.

81. (c) तैर्ना for तेना Sb.

87. (a) नप्राप्ता for नाभ्यस्ता Sb.; (b) यूथ कुंभ for कुंभ पीठ Sb.; (d) तया for महो Sb.

89. (a) न्नृत्तं गीतं for द्वीणावादः Sb., द्यं for दः T.; Sb. and T. read (c) for (b) with हः for होः (b) द्रम्यानारी for न्नारीभ्या Sb, द्रामारम्याः for न्नारीरम्या T., पु for पुः Sb., गलेत्कुष्ठवपुषो for जराजर्जरवपुः T.; (d) र्न for न Sb.

91. (b) ञ्छा for न्शा Sb., मांसाञ्बकलितान् for शाकादिवलितान् Śp., मांस्पाकं for शाकादि Sb.; (c) घननिविड for सुदृढतर Sb.; (d) रे for रो Sb.

97. (d) करिष्यति for विधास्यति Sp.

102. (b) शयाः for स्थिताः T. G. N.

110. (d) जन्तवो for प्राणिनः Sb. T.

113. (a) दन्ता श्च नाशं गता for भ्रष्टाचदन्तावलिर्; (b) रूपमेव ह्रसते for वर्धते वधिरता; (c) नैवकरोति for नाद्रियते च नः for नो पत्नि for भार्या Śp. P.; (d) जरयाभिभूतं पुरुषं for पुरुषस्य जीर्णवयसः Śp, षः for सः पुत्रैरवज्ञायते for पुत्रोऽप्यमित्रायते P.

114. (d) ङ्क्ते for न्ते Sb.; Śp.

115. (a) सु for प्र Sb.; (d) शंकरं for शूलिनं T. चक्रिणं for शूलिनं Sb.

NOTES

A. As to giving the third or last place to Vairāgyaśataka Kṛiṣṇa Śāstri Mahābala says अथ श्रीमद्राजर्षिप्रवरो भर्तृहरिर्द्वितीयं परिणामे वैराग्यजनकं, शृङ्गारशतकं विधायेदानीं वैराग्यशतकं चिकोर्षुर्वैराग्यफलस्य दाता शिवापेक्षयान्यो नास्तीति तं वर्णयति।

B. *Virāgya* (वैराग्य) literally means absence of affection for the world. *See* also Note to stanza 98(a) in the Śṛṅgāraśataka.

1. *Yogī* (योगी) one well-versed in the practice of Yoga (योग) or union. Mrs. Annie Besant renders the word योग as harmony with the Divine will.

2. There are three classes of men, those who have knowledge and they do not care for other people's learning through envy; those who have no knowledge and they cannot appreciate; and those who have high position in the world and they do not care for learning, being proud of their greateness. So, that there is altogether but a bad lookout for learning and learned men." (K. T. Telang)

3. The Vedānta philosophy teaches us that the acquisition of स्वर्ग itself is of very small importance when compared to मोक्ष or final absolution or emancipation of the soul.

8. "The sense is that if a man of strong mind did not see his wife in the state described, he should not go about to beg. It is the family that constrains him to it." (K. T. Telang)

It will be seen that the translation of the stanza as rendered by me is somewhat different from the above. Prof. Tawney's version is also similar to that of Mr K.T. Telang. Here I have preferred to follow the Sanskrit Commentary of Kṛṣṇa Sāstri Mahābala which gives the purport as विचारवान्जनः पूर्वार्द्धोक्त विशेषणविशिष्टां भार्यां दृष्ट्वाऽपि दुष्टजठरभरणार्थं कस्याप्यंग्रे न याचत इति भावः। The though thus expressed is far nobler than that explained by Prof. Tawney or Mr. Telang. I am, however, glad to observe that Mahārāja Sewāī Pratāpa Singhji's version of this Ślōka is quite to the point. It runs as follows :—

फट्यो पुरानो चीर ताहि खैंचत अरु फारत।
छोटे मोटे बाल भूख ही भूख पुकारत।
घर मांही नहीं अन्न नारि हू निर्दय यातें।
भई महा जड़दरूप कछू मुख कढति न बातें।

यह दशा देखि अर बरत चित्त जीभ थरथर तरुकत सुख।
अपने सुजरे उदरहित 'देहि' कहें को सतपुरुष।

Mr. Durgā Prasāda's translation of this stanza being neither correct nor good deserves no particular mention in this place. The anonymous copy of the Proverbial Philosophy of Bhartṛhari here follows, as usual with it, the Notes of Mr. K. T. Telang.

10. (a) It is a general belief among the people that snakes can live without feeding upon anything but air. The fact is often alluded to by Sanskrit poets. *Cf.* सर्पा पिबन्ति पवनं न च दुर्बलास्ते etc.

(b) "The meaning is that there is no scope for the exercise on one's merits, all the energies being absorbed in the struggle for existence." K. T. Telang.

15. The word अम्बरखण्ड is here used in a double sense of (1) a piece of cloth and (2) cloud.

17. Commentators differ in their interpretation of this stanza.

The difficulty particularly lies in the construction of the third line, which Mr. Telang takes to mean—'wretched by reason of the strong distractions of the enjoyment of greatness old through age.'

Mr. Durgā Prasāda interprets the verse as follows :—

"Avarice rises with selfishness or bad discrimination goes with its extinction and culminates with its excess. When the king of gods falls a victim to it, being tempted under the irresistible prompting of biting destitution and old age, there is no talking of man."

The following versionof the ślōka is found in the Proverbial Philosophy of Bhartṛhari :—

"The desire for worldly pleasures is allayed as restraint full of discrimination develops and when attachment to objects of sense is great that effect takes place on a wider scale. The Lord of Gods Himself becomes subject to desire, wretched by reason fo strong distraction of enjoyment of greatness old through age."

Prof. Tawney's poetical version runs thus:

"As knowledge grows, content expands, and fell desire abates;

But worldly joys, if long embraced, a baneful influence gain;

Thus Indra, like a mortal king, hopes, trembles, loves and hates,

From having and through endless years an undisputed reign."

I have not been able to find out its version in Mahārāja Pratāpa Singhji's Chhappayas. Pandit Rishabhadatta's Hindi translation is usually below the average and hence I have no scruples to omit it here.

The sage commentary of Kṛṣṇa Śāstri Mahābala which seems to give the correct sense of the next by his comments upon the stanza is as follows:—

विवेकस्य व्याकोशो विकसनं यस्मिस्तस्मिन् शमे विदधति कुर्वति सति, तुङ्गे ऽन्नते तृष्णाया: परिष्वङ्ग आश्लेषे शाम्यति सति, सा परिणति: सुखविशेषरूप: परिणाम: प्रसरतितरामतिशयेन विस्तारं प्राप्नोति। सा का। यस्यां परिणतौ विषये जरया जीर्णमैश्वर्यं, ग्रसनं अन्नादि भक्षणं तन्निमित्तो गहनो गम्भीरो य आक्षेपो निन्दा च ताभ्यां कृपण एवंविधो मरुतां देवानामधिपतिरिन्द्रो ऽपि यस्यां परिणतौ तृषापात्रं तृष्णाभाजनं भवतीति। यस्यां परिणतौ विषये साक्षादिन्द्रोऽपि स्पृहां करोतीत्यर्थ:।

18. Commenting on the meaning of the word Prof. Tawney remarks— "More literally retinue, attandants. This expression falls in with the legend that Bhartṛhari was a king and quitted his throne in a fit of disgust."

22. (a) For the unparalleled munificence and magnanimity of Paraśurāma,

Cf. कुलाचला यस्य महीं द्विजभ्य: प्रयच्छत: सीमदृषत्वमापु:।
बभूवुरुत्सर्गजलं समुद्रा: स रैणुकेय: श्रियमातनोतु।।

(b) Bali (बलि)– Name of demon king, grandson of Prahlāda and the most powerful sovereign of his day. He wrested everything from the gods and reigned absolutely supreme over the whole world. To secure the gods from this catastrophe Viṣṇu, in the form of a dwarf, came to him and begged of him three steps of ground. This simple request being granted Viṣṇu assumed an enormous size, covered all of Bali's possessions in two of his steps and putting the third on Bali himself sent him to the Patāla where he is believed to reign still. The story is told in the Bhāgavata.

(c) Of the fourteen spheres, seven are above the Earth and seven below it. They are enumerated as follows :—

(1) भूर्लोक, भुवर्लोक, स्वर्लोक, महर्लोक, जनलोक, तपलोक and सत्यलोक; (2) अतल, वितल, सुतल, रसातल, महातल, तलातल and पाताल।

24. The first two lines of the stanza if translated literally would

stand thus; 'What honour is it to kings to have obtained the earth which has not even for an instant remained unenjoyed by multitudes of kings after acquiring it by means of hundreds of battles'. K.T. Telang.

26. "The following lines of Juvenal may be compared :—

What's Rome to me, what business have I there

I who can neither lie nor falsely swear,

Nor praise my patron's undeserving rhymes.'

(Ancient Classics for English Readers, p. 73)

Prof. Tawney (Indian Antiquary, Vol. V/ p. 3) quots Burke, Vol. II., p. 106 (Bohn's Ed). The implication is that those persons only who can descend to such occupations fine entertainment in the royal household." K. T. Telang.

33. जह्नुकन्या or जाह्नवी is an epithet of the Gaṅges. See Rāmāyaṇa, Ch. XLIII, Book I.

32. *Cintāmaṇi* (चिन्तामणि) is a fabulour gem supposed to yield to its possessor all desires. It is generally known as the philosopher's stone.

35. स्वःसिंधु (literally heavenly river) is another name of the Gaṅges.

38. (a) "The two words काल and काली seem to me here to signify the male and female personifications of the Destructive Principle. Now काल is given by the Medinikāra as a name of Mahākāla or Mahādeva. काली is well known to be a name of Pārvatī. Māhadeva is the Diety of Destruction and is also represented in the Purāṇas as playing with Pārvatī." K.T. Telang.

Śiva and Pārvatī are represented as playing chess with dice in the seven Ślōkas (Nos. 123-129) quoted from Mayūra in the Subhāṣitāvali. See also the learned editors' note at p. 8. Bombay Sanskrit Series No. XXXI. The word काल in Sanskrit is derived from the root कल् to count and hence, it means one who counts. In its secondary sense काल is used both for Time and Śiva. Time is undobtedly the Counter and hence destroyer of all things and Śiva is the diety of destruction. So, there is nothing strange in its being a name both of Time and Śiva. काली is the feminine of काल and consequently represents both Death and Pārvatī.

(b) For similariy of thought, compare the various passages quoted by Prof. Tawney in his Two Centuries of Bhartṛhari, p. 69.

40. (a) केशवमिश्र after quoting the stanza at page 75 of his अलङ्कारशेखर thus remarks : स्त्रैणं स्त्रीसमूहः। अत्र अहिरिव हारो हेयो नतु हारवदहिरप्युपादेय इति बोध्यम्।।

(b) Govinda in his काव्यप्रदीप cites it as an example of शान्तिरस, According to him and the author of उदाहरणचंद्रिका – "वा शब्दाभ्यां द्वयोर्द्वयोस्तुल्यता द्योत्यते"

41. "Yōga is one of the systems of Hindu philosophy. Its chief aim is to teach the means by which the human soul may obtain complete union with me Supreme Being. It is defined by Patañjali, the modifications of though by the practice of self-mortification and by keeping the mind continually unaffected byb all external influence."[1] The final beatitude which is held out as the reward of such devotion, consists in the cessation of all idea of self and of any distinction between matter and spirit." Mr. Growse

See also our Note on stanza *supra*.

(b) Padmāsana (पद्मासन) is thus defined in the Haṭhayōgapradīpikā (हठयोगप्रदीपिका) of Suwātmārāma Yogīndra (स्वात्मारामयोगीऽन्द्र) :–

वामोरूपरि दक्षिणं च चरणं संस्थाप्य वामं तथा दक्षोरूपरि परिश्चमेन विधिना धृत्वा कराभ्यां दृढम्। अंगुष्ठौ हृदये निधाय चिबुकं नासाग्रामालोकमेदेतद्व्याधिविनाशकारि यमिनां पद्मासनं प्रोच्यते।।

Mr. Śrinivās Iyāngāra, B.A. translates the above as follows:—

'Place the right heel at the root of the left thigh and the left heel at the root of the right, cross the hands behind the back and take hold of the toes, the right toe with right hand and the left toe with the left. Place the chin firmly on the breast and look fixedly at the tip of the nose. This is called Padmāsana and destroyes all diseases'.

(c) योगनिद्रा At page 79 of the Bombay Sanskrit series No. III, Dr. G. Büller C. I. E., observes 'योगनिद्रा means originally 'the sleep

1. "योगश्चित्तवृत्तिनिरोधः"। (पातञ्जलियोगशास्त्रम्)

induced by the practice of Yoga,' during which the osul is separated from the body and thereby becomes enabled to see the nature of all things. 'Here it stands for deep meditation'."

44. Dr. J. Taylor in his translation of the Prabō-dhacandrōdaya incredulously remarks in a footnote that when elephants want the female, or are inflamed from any cause, it is *supposed* that a certain liquid is secreted from two protuberances situated on the sides of the heads.

But why *Supposed?* Everyone is fully aware of the fact of which the reader needs not be told or assured that in the rutting season the flows of a strong-scented liquid is generally seen on both sides of the frontal protuberances of bull elephants. The usual place from which the rut begins to come out is just behind the ear, but it is not uncommon to see it appearance in some other parts of the elephant's body. Sanskrit authors are very fond of alluding to elephants in rut, and Bhartṛhari himself has proved no exception to the rule as he has mentioned them several times in these Centuries.

43. How beautiful is the metaphor which speaks of Desire as Rivere, etc.!

45. *Vaṭa* (वट) is a king of tree with large broad leaves. It is one of the long-living, high-growing, and big-dimensioned trees to be found in pretty abundance both in the towns and forests of India. It being considered a favourite abode of Śiva is eagerly sought after by Yogīs.

46. "The idea is this: The supplicant of the rich thinks the days too long, as he has to suffer the trouble the days too long, as he has to suffer the person engaged in the pursuit of worldly objects thinks time too short, as he has never enough of it to all his numerous ends. On the other hand, the philosopher, in the intervals of meditaion he is of course, unconsicious of all these proceedings." K. T. Telang.

49. I would prefer with Mr. Telang the reading दुकूलैः to चलक्ष्म्याः as marking better the contrast with वल्कलैः।

51. The ten directions are the North, North-east Eat, Southeast, South, Southwest, West, Northwest, Zenith (above), and Nādir (below).

53. Samādhi समाधि is thus defined in the 4th Chapter of the

हठयोगप्रदीपिका– 'सलिले सैन्धवं यद्वत्साम्यं भजति योगतः। तथात्ममनसोरैक्यं समाधि रभिधीयते' which is translated by Śrinivāsa Iyāngāra, as follows: "As a grain of salt thrown into the water unites and becomes one with it a like union between the Mind and the Atmā is Samādhi." See also our Note to stanza 40 (b).

55. (a) It needs not to be told that there are four principal castes or Varṇas among the Hindus; which are named ब्राह्मण, क्षत्रिय, वैश्य and शूद्र. The first three are otherwise known as the *Dvijās* (द्विजाः) or twiceborn, on account of their two births of (I) actual generation and (II) investiture with the Sacred thread. But according to some, the epithet *Dvija* (द्विज) is limited only to the Brahmans. Compare

"जन्मना ब्राह्मणो ज्ञेयः संस्कारैर्द्विज उच्यते।"

(b) *Cāṇḍāla* (चाण्डाल)– A general name for the lowest and most despised of the mixed castes originating iron a śudra father and a Brahman mother. In the text the word is used for a man of this degraded caste.

59. "The implication is that nothing except devotion to Śiva is to be depended upon, as, for instance, the things enumerated."

K. T. Telang.

60. (a) The Dekkan poets are held to be great masters of melody of their sweet mellifluous verses See Kāvyādarśa : श्लेषः प्रसादः समता माधुर्यं सुकुमारता। अर्थव्यक्तिरुदारत्वमोजः कान्तिसमाधयः। etc.

(b) *Samādhi* (समाधि) according to Ṇrisimhaṣaraswati, is व्युत्थानिनिरोधसंस्कारयोरभिभवप्रादुर्भावे सति चित्तस्यैकाग्रता परिणामः समाधिः। See Vedāntasāras ṣubōdhini, p. 55. Mr. K. T.Telang thus explains it according to the Vedāntasāra 'an exclusive concentration upon the One Entity without distinct and separate consciousness of the knower, the known, and knowing and without even self consciousness.' Also compare, यत्सर्वं द्वन्द्वयोरैक्यं जीवात्मपरमात्मनोः। समस्तनष्टसंकल्पः समाधिः साऽभिधीयते which occurs in the गोरक्षपद्धतिः at verse 86th.

Strictly speaking Samādhi is the eighth and last stage to Yoga. These eight stages of Rājayōga (राजयोग) are : (1) Yama (यम), (2) Niyama (नियम), (3) Āsana (आसन) (4) Prāṇāyāma (प्राणायाम), (5) Pratyāhāra (प्रत्याहार), (6) Dhāraṇā (धारणा), (7) Dhyāna (ध्यान) and

(8) Samādhi (समाधि). But, here the word Samādhi may be taken to mean perfect and profound absorption of thought into the one object of meditation, i.e. the Supreme. Being. See also our note to stanza 53. *supra.*

(c) Chowry—As to the origin of these luxurious royal fans (चमर) *vide* Chapter 72 śloka 1 of the वाराहसंहिता where it is said:

दवै श्चमर्यः किल वालहेतोः सृष्टा हि लक्ष्माधरकंदरेषु।

आपीतवर्णाश्च भवन्ति तासां कृष्णाश्च लाङ्गूलभवाः सिताश्च।।

Mr. Wilkins in his Fables and Proverbs from Sanskrit observes in his footnote to the word Camara that it is a kind of whisk made of the tail of a particular species of cow, and sometimes of peacock's feathers finely ornamented, used to chase the flies away.

(d) I am inclined to take the stanza as furnishing internal evidence of Bhartṛhari being a king.

(e) In several editions including those of Bombay and Calcutta, this stanza is given a place in more than one Centuries of this poem.

62. *Palāśa* (पलाश) is, according to Mr. Growse, "the Butea frondosa, a tree with scarlet flowers, which precede the new leaves, and when in full blossom make a striking sight, like a fire our the horizon."

63. It will be seen that many persons have been led to translate this stanza in a sense quite contrary to that in which it has here been presented to the reaser. For comparison, we would beg to quote the following:

"Our former opinion was, 'You and We are we and You,' (*i.e.* You are different from we). Oh friend what is become now that we consider you like our selves. (Mr. Durga Prasad).

To my mind the original text as herein given cannot admit of any other interpretation but that which we have sought to convey interpretation but that which we have sought to convey in our Hindi and English translation. For the cessation of worldly ties of kinship, friendship etc. in Vairāgya, we have the authority of the Mahābharāta:

पितामहो ऽस्मि स्थविरः पितापुत्रश्च भारत।

ममैव यूयमात्मस्था न मे यूयं न वो वयम्।।

68. *Vidyādhara* (विद्याधर)– A class of demigods or semidivine

beings. The name Vidyādhara is applied to one of the ten species of divine beings. These are enumerated as follows in the *Amarakōśa* :—

विद्याधराप्सरोयक्षरक्षोगन्धर्वकिन्नराः।

पिशाचो गुह्यकः सिद्धो भूता ऽमी देवयोनयः॥

69. (a) *Meru* (मेरु)– See our Note 80 (a) in the Nītiśataka.

(b) *Yuga* (युग) – See our Note to Stanza 84. in the Nītiśataka.

70. (a) "Actions done is a past life lead to results in the succeeding life, and to obtain freedom from the perpetual round of birth and death thus arising, all कर्म must be destroyed. *Cf.* Śārīrika Bhāṣya, p. 1075." K.T. Telang.

(b) "The bodies and conditions of transmigrating souls are, according to their works, good or evil in antecedent states from time without beginning. The merits and demerits and the embodiments are from eternity. Seed from plant, and plant from see, but who shall assign priority to either? From such fruition of merits as long as soul is implicated with body, there is no escape............ This implication of soul with bodis, animal vegetable, human, ultrahuman, and divine, is the source of all misery. In all its stages the soul tastes little but pain, sickness, death, and severance from all that it would fain cling to. Even in the highest embodiments there is disparity, and a consequent sense of insufficiency, and there is the certainty of their expiring upon the exhaustion of the merits which procured them. Paradise and places of torment are only stages in the endless journey....... This repeated embodiment of souls results from merits, merits from activity, activity from desires and aversions, desires and aversions from identifying the soul with that which is not soul, with the body, the senses, the intellect. (Grough-in Calcutta Review)." Prof. Tawney.

71. *Kalpa* (कल्प)– See Note on Stanza 16. (a) in Nītiśataka.

74. Brahma (ब्रह्म) or Brahman (ब्रह्मन्) is the Supreme Being, regarded as impersonal and divested of all quality and action. Prof. Apte says that according to the Vedāntists Brahman is both the efficient and the material cause of the visible Universe, the all-pervading soul and spirit of the universe, the essence from which are created things produced and into which they are absorbed.

75. *Pātāla* (पाताल) is the lowest sphere as explained in Note (c) to Stanza 22. *supra.*

77. (a) *Śānta* (शान्त) is equal to free from passions.

(b) *Muni* (मुनि) is a saint. In its original meaning the word signifies one who observes the vow of silence.

78. त्रिलोकी–The three worlds are enumerated as the (i) heaven, (ii) earth and (iii) hell.

79. (a) According to Prof. Apte the Vedas or the holy Scriptures of the Hindus were originally three, but a fourth was subsequently added to them, and their number is now generally considered to be four. They are (1) the ऋग्वेद, (2) the यजुर्वेद, ; (3) the सामवेद, ; and (4) the अथर्ववेद. According to the strict orthodox faith of the Hindus the Vedas are अपौरुषेय not human compositions,' being supposes to be directly revealed by the Supreme Being, and are called 'Śruti' *i.e.*, 'what is heard or revealed' as distinguished from 'Smṛti,' *i.e.* what is remembered or is the work of human origin.'

(b) the *Smṛtis* as distinguished from the Vedas are the theological writings from the pen of the Ṛishis, patriarchs and sages.

(c) *Purāṇas* (पुराण) are the well-known sacred works of the Hindus, dealing the theology, history, mythology, etc. They are eighteen in number *viz.* —

(1) ब्रह्मपुराण, (2) पद्मपुराण, (3) विष्णुपुराण, (4) शिवपुराण, (5) भागवत्पुराण, (6) नारदपुराण, (7) मार्कण्डेयपुराण, (8) अग्निपुराण, (9) भविष्यपुराण, (10) ब्रह्मवैवर्तपुराण, (11) लिंगपुाण, (12) वराहपुराण, (13) स्कन्दपुराण, (14) वामनपुराण, (15) कूर्मपुराण, (16) मत्स्यपुराण, (17) गरुडपुराण, and (18) ब्रह्माण्डपुराण. It is generally believed that they have all been written by Vyāsa or Vedavyāsa, the son of Parāśara and Satyavatī. The literal meaning of the word Purāṇa is old. According to Mr. Wilkins the term purāṇa (literally ancient) is given to such Hindu books as treat of Creation in general, with the particular genealogy, and history of thier gods and heroes of antiquity.

81. Professor Tawney translates शफरी as the minnow.

82. *Brahma* (ब्रह्म)– See Note to stanza 74 *supra.*

85. (a) Mr. K.T. Telang notes that 'the force of all my delusion

being diestroyed by the pure knowledge which shines forth in consequence of the great extent of merit resulting from contact with you, I would merge into the Supreme Brahma.

(b) The body is admittedly composed of the Pañcāmahābhūtas or the five elements, *viz.*–earth] water, fire, air and sky or ether.

(c) As a footnote to his poetical version of the stanza, Prof. Tawney quotes the following passage from Green's History of the English People, p. 144 :– "The life of Francis falls like a stream of tender light accross the darkness of the time. He strips himself of all, he flings his very clothes at his father's feet, that he may be one with Nature and God. His passionate verse claims the moon for his sister, the Sun for his brother; he calls on his brother the Wind, and his sister the Water. His last cry was a Welcome, Sister Death."

89. Viṇā वीणा is thus explained by Mr. Wikins in a footnote at p. 120 of Morley's Unviersal Library No. 30–"An instrument of the string kind very much esteemed in India. It is constructed of a long piece of wood upon which a number of steel strings are strained, and which serves also for the finger board it being furnished with frets almost from one extremity to the other, with each and fixed horizontally upon the pole (if the expression be allowed) of a large pumpkin, or an oblate sphere of wood hollowed for the purpose.

91. "People misunderstand the mere cure of pain as itself a pleasure". K. T. Telang.

94. Mr. Telang here differs from all commentators who unanimously explain दुःखासिकानाम् as referring to the family of the कोऽयं विद्वान् spoken of in the text. However, the learned scholar remarks : "I cannot say what they mean. But the idea intended seems to be that or proud wealthy men." However the reader will see for himself the propriety of our following the Sanskrit Commentaries in thus translating the stanza whic as herein rendered gives a very intelligent and powerful idea. Kṛṣṇa Śāstri Māhabala in prefacing the Śloka thus sums up its substance : विपद्रस्ते कुटुम्बे स्पृहां दुःखेनः स्थित्यपेक्षया परमसुखदो गङ्गातीरे निवासः श्रेयान्।

100. शून्य is a technical term of the Yoga philosophy, and refers to absolute non-existence. It is also used as a name of Brahman. In Bhartṛhari-nirveda (III. 18) गोरक्षनाथ thus advises भर्तृहरि–विषयेभ्यः समाहृत्य मनः शून्ये निवेशय। स्वयमानन्दमात्मानं स्वप्रकाशमुपैष्यसि।।

110. (a) Kūrma of Kamatha– See Note to stanza 35. (b) in the Nītiśataka.

(b) *Dhruva* (ध्रुव)– The son of Uttānapāda being slighted by his step-mother left his home with the determination of winning himself a name in the world. By the advice of the seven Ṛṣis he devoted himself to the service of Viṣṇu, and was finally exalted by the God to the heavens where he shines as the polestar.

(c) ब्रह्माण्ड is the egg of Brahman, *i.e.* the universe.

(d) उदम्बर is a kind of large tree known in Hindustāni by the name of Gūlara. The interior of its fruit is the reputed seat of innumerable insects.

111. *Cakravāka* (चक्रवाक)– Name of a bird. Mr. Growse remarks that the male and female Cakvā are doomed for ever to nocturnal separation and are said to pass the night on the opposite banks of a river or pond, vainly calling to each other to cross.

114. I think the reading संसाराङ्के would be far better than that of the text, *i.e.* संसारान्ते.

115. शूली is a name of Śiva on account of his holding a trident in his hand.

116. *Vairāgya See* Note to Stanza 97. (a) in the Śṛṇgaraśataka and also Note B in the Vairagyaśataka.

LIST OF BIBLIOGRAPHY

1. अभिनवगुप्त ध्वन्यालोकटीका।
2. Addison (G. T.).
3. Aeschylus' Plays (Robert Potter).
4. अमरचन्द्रसूरिकृत बालभारतम्।
5. अमरकोषः।
6. अमरुशतकम्।
7. आनन्दवर्धनाचार्यकृत ध्वन्यालोकः।
8. Annie Besant's Lord's Song.
9. अप्पयदीक्षितकृत चित्रमीमांसा।
10. अप्यदीक्षितकृत कुवलयानन्दः।
11. Aristophanes.
12. Asiatic Researches Vol. IX.
13. अष्टरत्नम्।
14. St. Augustina (G. T.)
15. The meditations of Marcus Aurelius. (Jermy Collier).
16. Bailey's Essays on the Formation and Publication of Opinions.
17. बल्लालप्रणीत भोजप्रबन्धः।
18. बाणभट्टकृत हर्षचरितम्।
19. बाणभट्टकृत कादम्बरी।
20. J. Bartlett (G. T.)
21. Beattie (Johnson's Lives of the Poets.)
22. H.W. Beecher (G. T.)
23. भागवतम्।

24. भरतमुनिकृत नाट्यशास्त्रम्।
25. भरतरीचरितम्।
26. भरतरी का ख्याल।
27. भारविप्रणीत किरातार्जुनीयम्।
28. भट्टिकविकृत भट्टिकाव्यम्।
29. Dr. Bhāu Dāji's Paper on Kālidāsa.
30. भवभूतिविरचित गुणरत्नम्।
31. भवभूतिविरचित मालतीमाधवम्।
32. भवभूतिविरचित उत्तररामचरितम्।
33. भर्तृहरिकृत वाक्यप्रदीप।
34. भवभूतिकृत वीरचरितम्।
35. भोजदेवप्रणीत सरस्वतीकण्ठाभरणम्।
36. बिल्हणकृत बिल्हणचरितम्।
37. Dr. Bohlen's Bhartṛhari.
38. Prof. Böthlingk's Indische spruche. St. Petersburg 1863-65.
39. H. S. Brown (G . T.)
40. La Bruyere (G.T.)
41. Dr. G. Büller (B. S. S. Nos. I. III.)
42. Edmund Burke's Works (Bohn's Ed.)
43. Bishop Butler.
44. Robert Burn's The Cotter's Saturday Night.
45. Byron's Childe Harold's Pilgrimage.
46. Byron's The Giaour.
47. Byron's Don Juan.
48. चाणक्य प्रणीतं अर्थशास्त्रम्।
49. चाणक्यशतकम्।
50. Lord Chesterfield's Letters.
51. Cicero (G. T.)
52. S. T. Coleridge (G. T.)
53. Prof. Colebrooke's Essays on Sanskrit and Prakrit Poetry.
54. Cowley (Johnson's Lives of the Poets.)
55. William Cowper's Letters.

56. दक्षिणामूर्तिविरचितलोकोक्तिमुक्तावलिः।
57. दामोदरगुप्तकृतं कुट्टिनीमतम्।
58. दण्डिकृतकाव्यादर्शः।
59. पं० दत्तरामचौबेविरचितं अभिनवनिघंटुः।
60. The Orations of Demosthenes upon the Crown. (H. L. Brougham.)
61. धनञ्जयकृतं दशरूपकम्।
62. John Dryden (G. T.)
63. Alexander Dumas' Margurite de Valois.
64. महामहोपाध्यायपण्डितदुर्गाप्रसाद–काशिनाथपाण्डुरङ्गपरबसम्पादितकाव्य–माला Vol. VIII.
65. Mr. Durgaprasad's Maharajah Bhartrihari's One Hundred Morals.
66. Mr. Durgaprasad's Maharajah Bhartrihari's 100 Couplets on Renunciation.
67. Emerson's Poems.
68. Epictetus. (G. T.)
69. Fenelon (G. T.)
70. Fielding (G. T.)
71. Firdausi's Shāh Nāmeh (Atkinson)
72. Fuller (G. T.)
73. M. Galana's Greek Translation of the Nīti and Vairāgya Śatakas.
74. घटखर्परकृतनीतिसारः.
75. Goldsmith's Traveller.
76. गोपालभट्टकृतरसतरङ्गिणी.
77. पण्डितगोपीनाथदाधीचकृतरामसौभाग्यशतकम्.
78. गोरक्षपद्धतिः.
79. Prof. Gough. (Calcutta Review).
80. गोवर्द्धनाचार्यकृतार्यासप्तशती.
81. गोविन्दकृतकाव्यप्रदीपः.
82. Balthasār Gracian (G. T.)
83. Gray's Elegy in a country Chruchyard.
84. Great Thoughts. Vols. IX. X. XI.

85. Green's History of the English People.
86. Mr. F. S. Growse's Translation of the Ramayan of Tulsidasa Vols. 3.
87. गुणभदाचार्यकृतात्मानुशासनकाव्यम्.
88. Haeberlin's Sanskrit Anthology.
89. हलायुधकृतधर्मविवेक:
90. हरिहरोपाध्यायकृतभर्तृहरिनिर्वेदम्
91. Horace (G. T.)
92. Indian Antiquary Vol. IV.
93. पण्डितराजजगन्नाथप्रणीतभामिनीविलास:
94. पण्डितराजजगन्नाथप्रणीतरसङ्गाधर:
95. जह्लणकृतसूक्तिमुक्तावलि:
96. जनार्दनभट्टकृत शृङ्गारशतकम्
97. जयदेवप्रणीतगीतगोविन्दम्
98. Dr. Samuel Johnson's Lives of the Poets.
99. Dr. Samuel Johnson. Lines Added to Goldsmith's Traveller.
100. Sir William Jones (Asiatic Researches 1876).
101. Juvenal (Ancient Classics for English Readers.)
102. कह्लणकृतराजतरङ्गिणी.
103. कालिदासकृतअभिज्ञानशाकुन्तलम्।
104. कालिदासकृतकुमारसम्भवम्
105. कालिदासकृतमङ्गलाष्टकम्
106. कालिदासकृतररघुवंशम्
107. कालिदासकृतऋतुसंहारम्
108. कालिदासकृतशृंगारतिलकम्
109. कालिदासकृतशृंगारबिन्दु:
110. कालिदासकृतविक्रमोर्वशीयम्
111. कामन्दकोयनीतिसार:
112. कार्तिकप्रसाद रचित महाराज विक्रमादित्यका जीवनचरित
113. काशिनाथदुर्गाप्रसादसंपादितकाव्यमाला Vol. 8.
114. काशिनाथपाण्डुरंगपरबसंकलितसुभाषितरत्नभाण्डागार:

115. Mr. K. T. Telang's Nītiśataka and Vairāgyaśataka.
116. कविभट्टकृतपद्यसंग्रहः
117. काव्यसंग्रहः (Calcutta Ed.)
118. Dr. Kern's Preface to the Vṛhatsaṁhitā.
119. केशवमिश्रकृतालङ्कारशेखरः
120. Dr. Kielhorn. (Bombay S. S. No. IV)
121. कृष्णमिश्रकृतप्रबोधचंद्रोदयः (Dr. J. Taylor).
122. कृष्णशास्त्रिमहाबलकृता भर्तृहरिशतकत्रयटीका.
123. क्षपणककृतानेकार्थध्वनिमंजरी
124. क्षेमेन्द्रकृतौचित्यविचारचर्चा
125. क्षेमेन्द्रकृतचतुर्वर्गसंग्रहः
126. क्षेमेन्द्रविहितदर्पदलनम्
127. क्षेमेन्द्रकृतमुनिमतमीमांसा
128. क्षेमेन्द्रकृतसुवृत्ततिलकम्
129. कुसुमदेवविरचितदृष्टान्तशतकम्
130. Kovalenski (G. T.)
131. Prof. Lassen's Indische Alter thumskundè Vol. II.
132. M. Luther (G. T.)
133. Lord Lytton's Alice or the Mysteries.
134. Lord Lytton's Ernest Maltravers.
135. मधुसूदनकविप्रणीतमन्योपदेशशतकम्
136. माघकृतं शिशुपालवधम्
137. महाभारतम्
138. महेश्वरकृतामरकोषटीका
139. महानाटकम् (Calcutta Ed.)
140. Sir John Malcolm's Sketches of Persia 2 Vols.
141. मम्मटकृतकाव्यप्रकाशः
142. मनुस्मृतिः
143. मथुरादासविरचिता वृषभानुजा नाटिका
144. मत्स्यपुराणम्
145. Maurisius (G. T.)
146. Prof. Max Müller's India: What can it teach us?

147. मयूरकविः (Sb.)
148. Milton's Paradise Lost.
149. Moreshwar R. Kāle's Sāhityasārasaṅgraha.
150. मुरारिकृतमनर्घराघवम्.
151. Muir.
152. नमिसाधुकृता काव्यालङ्कारटीका.
153. नारायणरचितहितोपदेशः
154. नीलकण्ठदीक्षितविरचितशान्तिविलासः
155. नृसिंहसरस्वतीकृतवेदान्सारटीका
156. N. V. Bapat's Beauties of English Literature.
157. पद्मानन्दकविप्रणीतवैरागयशतकम्
158. पञ्चरत्नम्
159. पाणिनीयव्याकरणम्
160. पराशरस्मृतिः
161. पतञ्जलिकृतमहाभाष्यम्
162. पतञ्जलिकृतयोगशास्त्रम्
163. Periander (G. T.)
164. Dr. P. Peterson (B. S. S. Nos. 31, 33, 37.)
165. Alexander Pope's Essay on Criticism.
166. Alexander Pope's Essay on man.
167. Pomponia (G. T.)
168. प्रबोधसुधाकरः। (Kms.)
169. प्राकृतपिंगलसूत्रम्।
170. महाराज सवाई प्रतापसिंहजी रचित नीतिमञ्जरी, शृंगारमञ्जरी और वैरागयमञ्जरी।
171. प्रवरसेनरचित सेतुबन्धम्।
172. The Proverbial Philosophy of Bhartrihari.
173. रामभद्रदीक्षितरचितशृङ्गारतिलकभाणः।
174. Dr. Rajendra Lal Mitra's Notices of Sanskrit Manuscripts. Vol. VI.
175. Mr. R. B. Godbole's भरतखण्डाचा अर्वाचीनकोश.
176. M. Regnaud's Translation of Bhartrihari.
177. Reynold's Loves of the Harem. 2 vols.
178. J. P. Richter (G. T.)

179. पण्डित। श्रीभर्तृहरिकृत नीति, शृंगार, वैराग्यशतक।
180. Roger's A History of the religion of the Brahmans.
181. रुद्रभट्टकृतशृंगारतिलकम्।
182. रुद्रटकृतकाव्यालङ्कारः।
183. रुय्यानकविरचितं अलङ्कारसर्वस्वम्।
184. सदानन्दकृतवेदान्तसारः।
185. Śekha Sāadī.
186. षड्रत्नम्।
187. समयोचितपद्यमालिका।
188. Madame De Sanegue (G. T.)
189. शनिकथा
190. शङ्कराचार्यरचितमोहमुद्गरः।
191. शङ्कराचार्यकृतप्रश्नोत्तरमाला।
192. शङ्कराचार्यकृतशारीरिकभाष्यम्।
193. शङ्कराचार्यकृतश्वेताश्वतरोपनिषद्भाष्यम्।
194. संस्कृतचन्द्रिका Vols. I. II. III.
195. शान्तिशतकम्।
196. सप्तरत्नम्।
197. शार्ङ्गधरपद्धतिः।
198. सातवाहनबृतगाथासप्तशती।
199. Schiller's Poems and Plays (G. Routledge & Sons).
200. Seneca (G. T.)
201. Shakespeare's As Your Like It.
202. Shakespeare's King Lear.
203. Shakespeare's Othello.
204. सिंहदेवमणिकृता वाग्भट्टालङ्कारटीका।
205. पण्डितशिवदत्तकाशिनाथसम्पादिता काव्यमाला 8 Vols.
206. शिवरमप्रणीतरसरत्नहारः।
207. Samuel Smiles (G. T.)
208. Socrates (G. T.)
209. सोमदेवविरचितकथासरित्सागरः।
210. सोमप्रभाचार्यकृतश्रृंगारवैराग्यतरंगिणी।

211. सोमप्रभाचार्यप्रणीतसूक्तिमुक्तावलिः।
212. Robert Southwell. (G. T.)
213. हर्षदेवकृतनागानन्दम्।
214. श्रीकृष्णकविप्रणीतमन्दारमरन्दचम्पू।
215. Śri Niwās Iyāngar's Translation of the Haṭhayōgapradīpikā.
216. सुबन्धुकृतवासवदत्ता।
217. शूद्रककृतं मृच्छकटिकम्।
218. सूक्तावलिः।
219. स्वात्मारामयोगीन्द्रकृतहठयोगप्रदीपिका।
220. Prof. Tawney's Two Centuries of Bhartrihari.
221. Colonel James Tod's Annals and Antiquities of Rajasthan. 2 Vols.
222. उत्तरचातकाष्टम्।
223. वाग्भट्टप्रणीतकाव्यानुशासनम्।
224. वाग्भट्टकृतवाग्भट्टालङ्कारः।
225. वैद्यनाथतत्सत्कृता उदाहरणचन्द्रिका।
226. वेङ्कटनाथरचितसुभाषितनीवी।
227. वल्लभदेवप्रणीतसुभाषितावलिः.
228. वाल्मीकिरामायणम्।
229. वामनकृत काव्यालङ्कारसूत्राणि।
230. Vāman Pandit's Marathi Translation of the Śatakas.
231. Porf. Vāman S. Aptte's Practical Sanskrit English Dictionary.
232. वानर्यष्टकम्।
233. वराहमिहिरविरचितवाराहिसंहिता।
234. वररुचिकृतनीतिरत्नम्।
235. वसिष्ठसारः।
236. वात्स्यान प्रणीत कामसूत्रम्।
237. वायुपुराणम्।
238. वेतालभट्टकृतनीतिप्रदीपः।
239. विदुरनीतिः।

240. विमलाचार्यकृतप्रश्नोत्तररत्नमाला।
241. वीरनन्दिप्रणीतं चन्द्रप्रभचरितम्।
242. विशाखदत्तकृतमुद्राराक्षसम्।
243. विष्णुशर्म्मप्रणीतं पञ्चतंत्रम्।
244. विश्वनाथरचित्तं साहित्यदर्पणम्।
245. Weber's Sanskrit Literature.
246. J. G. Whittier.
247. Charles Wilkins' Fables and Proverbs from Sanskrit (Morley's Universal Library).
248. Prof. Wilson's Viṣṇu Purāṇa.
249. यतिपञ्चकम्।
250. योगवासिष्ठम्।
251. Young's Night Thoughts.

श्लोकानुक्रमणिका

INDEX

S